Donated to
NE/Spruill Oaks Library

by

Jim Cowart

Gifted through the
Friends of Library
June 2002

Race and the Shaping of Twentieth-Century Atlanta

and the Shaping of

RONALD H. BAYOR

The Fred W. Morrison Series in Southern Studies

The University of North Carolina Press | Chapel Hill and London

Race

Twentieth-Century Atlanta

Manufactured in the United
States of America

The paper in this book meets the
guidelines for permanence and
durability of the Committee on
Production Guidelines for Book
Longevity of the Council on Library Resources.

Ronald H. Bayor is professor of
history at Georgia Institute of
Technology.

Some material from this book first
appeared in articles by Ronald
Bayor in the *Journal of Urban
History*, the *Georgia Historical
Quarterly*, and *Atlanta History*.
These publications have kindly
granted the author permission to
reprint this material.

Library of Congress
Cataloging-in-Publication Data
Bayor, Ronald H., 1944–   Race
and the shaping of twentieth-century
Atlanta / by Ronald H. Bayor.
p.   cm. — (The Fred W. Morrison
series in Southern studies) Includes
bibliographical references (p.   )
and index.
ISBN 0-8078-2270-1 (cloth: alk. paper)
ISBN 0-8078-4898-0 (pbk.: alk. paper)
1. Atlanta (Ga.)—Race relations.
2. Urban policy—Georgia—
Atlanta.   I. Title.   II. Series.
F294.A89N424   1996   95-39552
305.8′009758′231—dc20   CIP

04 03 02 01 00   6 5 4 3 2

For Leslie, with love

Contents

Illustrations

Acknowledgments

Because this book has taken a number of years to research and write, involving trips to various cities and their libraries and archives, I must thank a number of people for their assistance. The staff at the Atlanta University Center library and archives—especially Lila Griffin, Minnie Clayton, and Gloria Mims—were especially helpful in the project's early stages. Thanks also to the staffs at the Atlanta History Center; the Atlanta Public School Archives; the Martin Luther King, Jr. Center for Non-Violent Social Change; the Emory University special collections; the Columbia University library; the National Archives; the Library of Congress; the Georgia Tech library; and the Atlanta-Fulton Public Library, and to Esme Bhan, research associate at the Moorland-Spingarn Research Center at Howard University, and Clifton Johnson, executive director of the Amistad Research Center at Tulane University.

Furthermore, the willingness of a number of individuals to graciously give their time for interviews is deeply appreciated. It was a special pleasure and an honor to meet and interview such people as John H. Calhoun, Warren Cochrane, Grace Towns Hamilton, Robert Thompson, and C. A. Scott, who were among Atlanta's civil rights pioneers. My thanks also to Jed Dannenbaum, Kathleen Dowdey, and Cheryl Chisholm of the Center for Contemporary Media for access to their oral history tapes and to Harlon Joye, Clifford Kuhn, and E. Bernard West for use of their Living Atlanta tapes.

I am grateful to Julian Bond, Clifford Kuhn, Robert McMath, and Howard Rabinowitz, as well as to David Goldfield and one other (anonymous) reader for the University of North Carolina Press, for reading the manuscript. Their willingness to take time out of their busy schedules to accommodate yet another task is deeply appreciated.

Special thanks go to Kate Douglas Torrey, my editor and director of the Press, for her always-encouraging words and useful suggestions. She has been the best of editors. Thanks as well to Christi Stanforth, project editor, for her careful attention to the book's preparation for publication. And my appreciation to Lewis Bateman, an editor at the Press, and Iris Tillman Hill, its former editor in chief, for their early encouragement of this work.

LaDonna Bowen typed the original manuscript and subsequent drafts and did her usual good job, which, as always, is appreciated. My thanks as well to Georgia Tech's School of History, Technology, and Society for providing me with a graduate assistant, David Morton, for one quarter. David did very good work in helping me take notes on various articles in the *Atlanta Journal-Constitution*.

My research and writing for this project was aided immeasurably through a summer stipend and a fellowship from the National Endowment for the Humanities; an Albert J. Beveridge Grant from the American Historical Association; a grant-in-aid from the Association for State and Local History; a prepublication grant from the Atlanta Historical Society; and a grant from the Georgia Tech Foundation.

For my wife, Leslie, mere thanks is not enough. She has always been there for me with encouragement, advice and, most importantly, love. This book would not have been written without her, so I dedicate it to her, with love.

Introduction

My first thoughts for this book came from a 1980s newspaper article that cited race as one of the major issues in Atlanta and commented that the question is really one of exactly how race has had an impact on a city. This book seeks to answer that question—to determine the effect of race and race relations on Atlanta's physical development and institutional structure. I do not think racial issues explain everything that has occurred in Atlanta, and this study is not an attempt to reduce all matters to a racial explanation. Yet race was certainly an important part of decision-making—sometimes intertwined with other factors, sometimes as a single element—and, thereby, of what happened in the city.

Race is a complicated matter that is often nuanced by other variables such as class and gender. While class concerns are raised in the study, and gender is part of the discussion in Chapter 4, my intent in this work was to focus on race and policy, to look particularly at race as a factor in city shaping. This intense focus is important to the study, for it enables the detailed tracing of this factor through many periods, movements, and political leaders and events. It is true that in some cases, as in employment, there were gender differences, but the overriding issue was race, not gender or class. Neither black men nor black women, rich or poor, could use most parks in Atlanta; all blacks received poor services in their neighborhoods and had their voting rights, health care, housing choices, and public school use restricted. The desire and fight for services, jobs, political power, desegregation, and other goals cut across gender and class lines. It involved women, men, and upper- and middle-class leaders as well as some activists from poor neighborhoods. Race can also take on different meanings in different periods or with changed circumstances. In Atlanta, white attitudes toward the black community had changed by the late 1960s as blacks assumed a more powerful place within city politics. This was no longer the disfranchised group from earlier decades: they commanded some attention and respect, however begrudgingly whites bestowed it. But race relations still influenced policy. That fact had not changed from the nineteenth century to the twentieth.

The book's main concern, then, is the intersection of racial attitudes or issues with primarily *public* policy and, thereby, the analysis of the ways in which race shaped the city. Encompassing urban, southern, and black history, the book seeks to understand how white and black Atlanta reacted to racial issues and how those issues subsequently molded the city from the nineteenth century until well into the twentieth. As such, this book is not a standard life-and-times history of Atlanta or of the black community. The focus is on the city and its development. Too often cities have been used only as backdrops and framework in studies of racial and ethnic minorities rather than as an interacting element. The intention here is to bring the city's growth and shaping more clearly into the analysis. As a result, some aspects of black community life have been neglected. Attention was fixed on those factors, such as housing and services, that intersected with and were addressed by policy decisions. But the black responses to these policies were also important elements of this study. The development of Atlanta's African American community, its opposition to various city plans and programs, and the forging of its own priorities and policies both before and after the election of black mayors were part of the process by which race shaped the city. This was a vocal and active group; its members pushed, prodded, negotiated, and resisted in order to secure their own goals and have a voice in city affairs. It was also a group that created its own businesses; supported its churches, lodges, colleges, and civil rights organizations; and developed a vibrant life outside of and largely unknown to the white community. Although there were disagreements within the black community—as in the 1960s, over the pace of desegregation—the leadership element generally worked closely together.

By concentrating on the city itself, I was able to explore the genesis of the modern American city and the history and legacy of American race relations for the urban environment. This legacy remains very evident in present-day Atlanta. Politics, the school system, neighborhood development, highways and roads, traffic patterns, public housing placement, city service delivery and amenities, the transportation network, and employment still show signs of its impact. Racial issues, now increasingly combined with class factors, still strongly influence policy. One recent example is the dispute arising out of Olympic site development in neighborhoods that were urban renewal victims decades earlier. The mistrust of city government generated years ago has carried into present discussions of housing removal and resident relocation, even though city officials are now black.

For many reasons, Atlanta appeared to be a good city to study for such an analysis. It had a singular place in the South as a transportation and business center; it is a leading New South and Sunbelt center; it was a headquarters city for a number of civil rights organizations and is a center of black higher education; and it has hailed itself as "a city too busy to hate"—one of progressive race relations. At one time or another such notables as W. E. B. Du Bois, Walter White, Martin Luther King Jr., Whitney Young, John Lewis, Andrew Young, Vernon Jordan, Ralph Abernathy, and Julian Bond lived within its borders. Because Atlanta was a city that had been officially segregated by race, records were available as to how racial factors affected various city elements and services. The issue was frankly discussed in a way that was not as evident in northern cities. Atlanta also holds a certain irony. Although it was the center of the civil rights movement in the 1960s, Atlanta was becoming more segregated in terms of spatial patterns and housing at the same time that lunch counters, public facilities, and schools were being integrated. The white leadership's desire for racial stability in order to enhance economic development resulted in some cosmetic changes but left the city with deep racial divides.

While Atlanta, like any other city, is unique in certain ways, I do not believe Atlanta is unique in regard to the impact of race. Comprehensive and wide-ranging studies on this issue are needed for many cities to understand the long-term and often debilitating effects of racial factors in policy decisions and city shaping, but evidence already suggests that this factor was important. Except in passing reference, I have left a discussion of other cities to the concluding chapter rather than interrupt the flow of the Atlanta material. But readers should be aware that the history of American cities as diverse as Chicago, Richmond, and Miami indicate race as a factor in policy decisions regarding planning, renewal, highways, and zoning. Various cities' physical and institutional development—e.g., neighborhoods, health care services, the school system—were shaped by racial factors. Racially based policies over many decades were part of the city-building process in both the North and the South. Race, then, can be used as an interpretive tool to help in understanding American city development, to understand what aspects of urban life and development were determined by the city's handling of racial issues. Furthermore, analyzing urban growth and structure in a number of cities where one minority group became the focus of attention not only indicates the role of race but by extension may also reveal the role of ethnicity in the shaping of cities.

Except for the first chapter, which is designed to briefly survey late-nineteenth-century Atlanta, and the concluding chapter, this book is arranged topically, and each topical chapter proceeds chronologically. The book could have been organized in other ways, but this approach allowed me to explore each topic through a long-term analysis and carry its examination from the early years to recent times. Given the book's focus on policy history, I wanted to maintain a sense of these topics' continuity as they evolved through several decades. This arrangement for the book allowed for a more precise, analytical, and coherent explanation of particular policies and race.

My initial goal was to end the study after Maynard Jackson's first administration in the 1970s, but at many points I continued further into the 1980s in order to understand the implications of racial, as well as class, concerns into the administrations of other black mayors. Thus, the time frame for this study extends from the end of the Civil War to the mayoral terms of Andrew Young in the 1980s.

I am sure readers will see reflections of their own cities in Atlanta's development.

Beginnings

We realize that every major Southern problem is definitely inter-twined with the race problem.—**Guy B. Johnson**, executive director, Southern Regional Council, 1944

When I first went South I expected to find people talking about the Negro, but I was not at all prepared to find the subject occupying such an overshadowing place in Southern affairs.

—Ray Stannard Baker, *Following the Color Line*, 1908

CHAPTER 1

It was in Atlanta, Georgia, that I was to see the race problem in

greater depth, and observe and experience it in larger dimen-

sions. It was in Atlanta that I was to find that the cruel tentacles

of race prejudice reached out to invade and distort every aspect

of Southern life.—**Benjamin Mays**, *Born to Rebel*, 1971

The Racial Setting

Atlanta, like most urban areas, has been many cities in one. It was a railroad hub, a commercial center, a key part of the Confederacy, a symbol of the New South, a focal point of urban boosterism, and a nerve center for the civil rights movement. Most of all, it was a city made up of blacks and whites, and their relationship has been a major shaping element in the creation of present-day Atlanta.

An Atlanta Urban League statement issued in the late 1940s revealed a basic truth about Atlanta and other cities with large minority populations: "There can be no fundamental improvement in the life and living conditions of the total population without regarding the particular problems facing the Negro segment which constitute one-third of the whole. *Our lives are too completely bound together whether health, housing, education or economic well-being are considered"* (italics mine).[1] And this has been the case since the city's early years, although Atlanta's whites often forgot or did not want to accept this simple fact. Beginning right after the Civil War, the intersection of racial attitudes and public policy decisions began shaping such aspects of the city as its politics, spatial patterns, economy, and city services (e.g., health care, police protection, and education) and setting the tone for the twentieth century. The migration of rural blacks to Atlanta after the Civil War created a substantial black presence, and the treatment, response, and growth of this minority community into the twentieth century was to be one of the most significant factors in the city's development.

As of 1868–69, when Reconstruction was being directed by Congress and the South was under military control, black Atlantans were able to vote and assume office. In the ensuing years, even after a 1908 state disfranchisement law, the city's African Americans would play a substantial role in its politics either as direct players or as an issue around which to rally white voters. Even in the early years, however, impediments were introduced to restrict black voting. The year 1868 represents not only the year when blacks could legally vote in the city but also the beginning of state and city efforts to curtail that vote. Since the Democrats ran the city council, they were able to secure an ordinance imposing a poll tax in 1868. Georgia's Republican-controlled General Assembly struck this ordinance down in 1870, but it reappeared in altered form later. In 1873, an ordinance allowed Atlantans to vote only if their municipal taxes, including those from previous years, were paid in full. These provisions and others were instituted at least partly in response to black voting. Also in 1868, the General Assembly passed a law switching Atlanta from a ward-based to an at-large system for the election of councilmen, which negated the black vote in wards where Atlanta's blacks were a majority. Under an at-large system, all city voters determined the elections for city council. This process served the Democrats well in 1868–69 and kept blacks out of office.[2]

When the Republicans gained control of the state legislature in 1870, they reinstated the ward system, which resulted in the election of two black Republican city councilmen. Through this election, one newspaper claimed, the Republicans were going to impose a black government on Atlanta. White fear of a black-run city and the use of that fear as a campaign tactic reverberated into the 1970s. One of the new black councilmen, William Finch, was influential in securing schools for Atlanta's blacks, repairing some streets in black areas, and preventing the city from cutting through Atlanta University property with a street extension that would have leveled some of the college's buildings. He indicated early on the benefits of political representation, as did changes in other southern cities, where blacks and white Radical Republicans had more political power. Finch also illustrated the ability of black leaders to fight for and at times obtain benefits for black Atlantans, an ability that was evident well into the next century. Although the Democratic-controlled legislature brought back the at-large approach in 1871, and Atlanta would not elect another black to city office until 1953, the black community kept up a steady push for equal treatment. On the local level, the Democrats also instituted a sporadically used white primary in the early 1870s as a way to limit black political power. A restricted primary was used more consistently in the early 1890s, as a white primary was authorized in 1892. Except for a temporary repeal in 1895, the white primary remained in effect into the 1940s. On the state level, this system was instituted in 1900.[3]

The Republican Party declined in the city after at-large voting returned. This decline also meant that blacks would not secure local and state patronage jobs and that what they received—mainly in the post office and the treasury department—came from the national Republican Party when it was in control of the federal government. But even the national Republicans often neglected black patronage desires. While white Republicans were more favorable to blacks than Democrats were, neither party actually offered real redress to black political grievances. The Democrats did make some attempts to secure black voters, but they offered few inducements to the majority of blacks. The tokenism that blacks faced from political allies—who in this era were still mainly the Republicans—was to continue into Atlanta's biracial coalition period of the 1960s. A desire to win black votes did not mean a desire to see blacks taking part in governing the city. The white style of using black voters politically and generally reneging on promises was set early, and blacks had to work within and use that system to their best advantage.[4]

In Atlanta, this meant not simply supporting Republicans in every election but sometimes backing third parties or Democrats or remaining uncommitted as long as possible in order to secure the best deal.[5] The black-owned *Atlanta Weekly Defiance* stated it well in 1882 and foreshadowed the racial political maneuvering of the 1950s and 1960s, noting that "we must follow those who will be found giving us recognition immediately."[6] In some cases, Atlanta blacks even organized tickets of all-black candidates as a way of drawing their community's vote together and offering an alternative to white political dominance, but these attempts failed. In some elections, blacks supported the white business leaders in a coalition against working-class white interests—a scenario repeated in the 1950s and 1960s. And another situation recalling the racial politics of the twentieth century is that blacks could exert influence in both city and state politics if there was a split in the white vote. As key voters in such elections, blacks could bargain for favors. This situation occurred particularly in relation to the battle over Prohibition.[7]

Although white Democrats sometimes won black voters, or used the "danger" of the black vote to scare and prod white voters to come to the polls or to unify their party, they did not like a situation in which blacks could make demands and have some influence and in which whites would actively seek the black vote or try to illegally suppress it. As a result, Democrats used various tactics, including the 1892 white primary and a 1908 disfranchisement law, to eventually end most, but not all, black voting.[8] In both the nineteenth and twentieth centuries, politics and voting were closely connected to improvements in black community life and therefore to how the city developed. As white Republicans and blacks lost power, there was usually little effort to meet black needs except in special situations where the black vote remained important. The period of one-party Democratic control offered politicians much less incentive to improve black life. Although conditions were certainly not good when the Republicans were active, they became worse afterward.[9]

Blacks, of course, did not function only in response to white actions; they actively forged their own institutions, amenities, and place within Atlanta. Black fraternal societies such as the Masons, black churches, the Butler Street YMCA (set up in 1894 at Wheat Street Baptist Church), and various other self-help groups worked to deal with problems ranging from health benefits to education to homes for orphaned children. For example, a black orphanage was opened in 1890. But while white orphans received public funds, the black children did not receive city money, although the city did provide the land for the institution.[10] Nonetheless, the numerous self-help efforts in the black community reveal blacks' desire and effort to develop their own community and plan their own future, regardless of white attitudes and policies.

In spatial terms, right after the Civil War Atlanta's blacks were located in areas around the city's periphery and in alleys, near jobs, and in rear servants' residences. At first blacks were dispersed; but between 1860 and 1890, as their population increased from 20.3 to 42.9 percent of the city's total population (with a peak of 45.5 percent in 1870), concentrations

Table 1. Black Population in Atlanta, 1860–1980

	Total Population	African American Population	Percent African American Population
1860	9,554	1,939	20.3
1870	21,789	9,929	45.5
1880	37,409	16,330	43.6
1890	65,533	28,117	42.9
1900	89,872	35,727	39.7
1910	154,839	51,902	33.5
1920	200,616	62,796	31.2
1930	270,366	90,075	33.3
1940	302,288	104,533	34.6
1950	331,314	121,416	36.6
1960	487,455	186,820	38.3
1970	496,973	255,051	51.3
1980	425,022	283,158	66.6

Sources: Bureau of the Census, *Eighth Census* (1860), 1:74; *Ninth Census* (1870), 1:102; *Tenth Census* (1880), 1:417; *Eleventh Census* (1890), 1:527; *Twelfth Census* (1900), 1:612; *Thirteenth Census* (1910), 2:400; *Fourteenth Census* (1920), 2:77; *Fifteenth Census* (1930), 2:67; *Sixteenth Census* (1940), 2:375; *Seventeenth Census* (1950), vol. 2, part 11, p. 59; *Eighteenth Census* (1960), part 12, p. 51; *Nineteenth Census* (1970), vol. 1, part 12, p. 73; *Twentieth Census* (1980), Housing, 1:337.

evolved—for example, on the east, south, and west—through the establishment of black schools, colleges, and churches (see Table 1). These concentrations eventually became segregated areas. By the 1890s, Atlanta already largely consisted of white or black streets. For the most part, Atlanta's blacks lived on land that whites did not want—near cemeteries, industrial plants, railroad lines, and flood zones and in low-lying sections. But this was not always the case. The westside area surrounding Atlanta University, for example, was on high ground, and some blacks lived in fashionable, well-built homes. The segregated communities that developed in the late nineteenth century, however, set the tone for twentieth-century spatial patterns and the policy decisions that tried to regulate black residential movement into the 1960s. Furthermore, a precursor of 1950s and 1960s urban renewal took place in the 1880s, when black housing on Foster Street was torn down to make way for Edgewood Avenue—a street that allowed for better travel between white suburbs and downtown Atlanta.[11]

The beginnings of twentieth-century Atlanta and the impact of racial policies could also be seen in the city's economy. Restrictions on black employment and occupational advancement appeared early, as did many successful black attempts to overcome white-imposed limitations. Although some whites, and black leaders such as Booker T. Washington, saw that the South would need black economic advancement in order to prosper, little was done to produce this result. Occupational attainment was closely tied to training and schooling, both of which remained severely curtailed for blacks well into the twentieth century. As a result, for example, in 1890, Atlanta's black men were concentrated in unskilled labor (49.4 percent) and its black women in domestic and personal service (92 percent). Of those Atlanta jobs, they filled 90.3 percent and 96.5 percent, respectively. As one historian of Atlanta in these years concluded in regard to the 1880 data, "Race was . . . the only factor that strongly affected occupational rank." Yet there were also a number of black men in skilled work in 1890, and there were small numbers in clerical jobs as well as (for both genders) in professional and proprietary positions—and these workers formed the black middle class. For example, businesses started by blacks in Atlanta included the Georgia Real Estate, Loan and Trust Company, established in 1890, and there were many black-owned barbershops. An 1899 survey by W. E. B. Du Bois's students indicated that black Atlantans were also the proprietors of groceries, wood-yards, meat markets, restaurants, and other businesses. Most professional blacks were teachers or ministers, although there were lawyers, doctors, and dentists as well.[12]

While a niche in some skilled jobs and businesses was evident and would continue, one could also clearly see trends of a negative sort that would appear again in various twentieth-century periods. For example, the call for and occasional replacement of blacks with whites in some occupations in the 1890s paralleled what would happen in later years. Union racial restrictions that either barred blacks or set up separate locals were still a problem in the 1960s. The refusal of some whites to work with blacks and the insistence on blacks above the lowest positions being fired, as occurred in 1897 at the Atlanta Fulton Bag and Cotton Mill, remained an issue. In this case, white women instigated a strike rather than work with black women. The company thereafter used black workers only in certain jobs and in separate departments. And blacks' inability to become public service workers such as policemen or firemen was evident into the twentieth century.[13]

City services would also indicate the shaping impact of race, as well as class, since poor whites were affected in both the nineteenth and twentieth centuries. However, while upper-class white areas received services, *no* black areas did. In the 1870s and 1880s, this situation was somewhat the result of where the classes and races lived. Most wealthy whites lived near the business district and received services as part of the upgrading of the general business section. Individuals residing farther from the business area received much less. Most blacks of all classes, and the majority of working-class whites, lived farther out. But the spatial shaping aspects of race and class had dictated where they were to live. The city's physical improvements continued to occur first in white-collar white areas. Inadequate sanitation arrangements, unpaved streets, poor water supplies, insufficient transportation lines and fire services, deficient public health care and schools, and lack of park space prevailed in black neighborhoods through the late nineteenth century and into the twentieth and became an issue usually only when whites were affected in some way. All white areas received better treatment from the city than black areas. And because they usually inhabited the lowland areas, blacks were in need of more attention with regard to sewers, clean water, and related health issues. Sewer lines, for example, usually went only as far as the end of white areas and thus drained their contaminated water into mainly black Atlantans' low-lying wells, streams, and properties from the businesses and white residences on high ground. When blacks and white Radical Republicans were on the city council, there had been some attempts to improve black neighborhoods (e.g., streets) and even to consider somewhat the hiring of black police. But instead, black police were not to be hired until 1948, and black Atlantans often faced harassment and brutality from the white police—but not without resisting. During the 1880s, for example, crowds of blacks often fought with police in efforts to free arrested members of their race.[14]

Improvements in black life sometimes occurred as segregation replaced total exclusion—as in the case of public hospitals, when Grady Hospital began providing segregated, but far from equal, facilities for black and white indigents when it opened in 1892. Prior to that, there were two city hospitals—one for whites and one for blacks—but they treated only smallpox cases and therefore were not open all the time. Atlanta's private hospitals usually did not accept the black poor, and only two did so after the urging of city officials in the 1880s. But the black patients were segregated, and less money went for their care. Mortality rates among blacks remained much higher than those among whites in the late-nineteenth-century urban South. Public health measures were concerned mainly with whites, and efforts to help blacks were seen in the context of protecting white health.[15]

Segregation, which provided some facilities, rather than exclusion, which provided none, was a system that could be supported by both white Republicans and Democrats, as well as initially by some blacks who at this time hoped for equal along with separate but nonetheless saw segregation as preferable to exclusion.[16] In all cases, blacks received much less than whites, and in all cases, racial considerations were significant in the provision of these services and the establishment of these institutions.

In regard to public schools, for example, it was certainly true that segregated public schools were better than no public schools, but they were set up with the idea of providing as little education as possible. Since whites perceived blacks as fulfilling their educational needs in the missionary-run schools right after the Civil War, they stressed providing free schools to meet the needs of whites. There was dissatisfaction that blacks and not whites were already getting a free education. Concerns were also expressed about race mixing if public schools were approved for whites and blacks. Moreover, the very idea of public schools had been delayed because of Democrats' reluctance to create a system that would spend public funds on blacks as well as whites. Due to the influence of Radical Republicans on the city council, the system that finally opened in 1872, after initially leaving blacks out, soon included two missionary-run schools for blacks that were to be used by the city at no cost. The willingness of missionary organizations to provide the school buildings for black children allowed Atlanta to have a school system without spending money to construct black school buildings, although the city did pay teachers' salaries and other expenses. At first there had been some mention of the need for black public schools in Atlanta; however, white children were considered the first priority, and this attitude was still evident into the 1960s. In 1872, the elementary schools in the city numbered two for blacks and five for whites, and there were just two high schools, both for whites. City officials in 1872 refused to provide a high school for blacks or to fund a plan that would have provided a free high school education at Atlanta University. Black desires for a public high school were rejected again in 1891. Acceptance of those desires would have acknowledged black aspirations for higher levels of education and training and better jobs—none of which white city officials supported. As of 1890, the city elementary schools numbered twelve for whites and four for blacks. With one exception, the new black school buildings were constructed poorly compared to white schools. Black teachers were first hired in 1878, with some reluctance, but in 1887 the decision was made to use only black teachers in the black schools, since they were paid less than whites—a lower pay scale that would continue for many decades.[17]

Early on, white officials proclaimed that black and white children were treated equally in the separate public schools, and they would continue making such statements. Although neither white nor black schools were well-funded, and both were overcrowded, black schools were treated worse. Many black children could not go to school due to lack of space. In the 1880s, only 43 percent of the city's school-age blacks went to school, compared to 74 percent of the whites. Seating space in black schools was restricted in order to keep costs down. Furthermore, in terms of the students-per-teacher ratio, teachers in black schools had excessive numbers of students (by 1896, 89.2 black students per teacher, compared to 61.4 for whites).[18] Curriculum issues also indicated problems for black schools. There were attempts to turn the black schools mainly into places for vocational training, thereby eliminating the upper grades and most academic work. All of these education issues continued to be problems many decades later. The separate schools were unequal from the beginning, and black schools would remain underfunded and inadequate for many years. While some new black schools were built in the late nineteenth century, their construction took place during a time when many black Atlantans could still vote and bargain. Afterward, much less was forthcoming unless there were special circumstances involved. Nonetheless, the black community continued to press for more and better public schools while at the same time setting up their own private schools in order to bypass white resistance to black education.[19]

The Atlanta that emerged by the end of the nineteenth century and the beginning of the twentieth was one in which race played a considerable role in policy decisions and in the shaping of the community. It was also a city that was already receiving some national attention due to race. Booker T. Washington's "Atlanta Compromise" speech at the Cotton States and International Exposition in 1895, in which he called for racial separation in social matters but unity in economic progress and encouraged the black community to emphasize self-help and economic development, was widely reported. Another event that was extensively covered and reflected the racial climate and racial focus in Atlanta during these early years was the September 1906 riot—a devastating attack on black

Atlantans that was directly inspired by an intense gubernatorial campaign that inflamed racial animosities and a number of newspaper accusations against black Atlantans regarding assaults on white women. The *Atlanta Georgian, Atlanta News, Atlanta Constitution,* and *Atlanta Journal* kept up a steady drumbeat of stories designed to provoke fear and anger among whites and, at the same time, to sell many newspapers. Building on many years of white racism and spurred on by the press and rumors, white Atlantans began attacking blacks on Atlanta's streets on 22 September. The mobs that formed, as well as the individuals who were attacked, cut across class lines. Black wealth, education, or position meant little; whites made no distinction in regard to their victims. The riot continued for four days, during which the black community organized to protect their neighborhoods and the state militia was called out. By the time it was over, there had been a number of casualties, the always-tenuous racial peace had been shattered, and a number of downtown stores (black-owned or -patronized) had been wrecked. There were some efforts toward racial harmony (e.g., the work of the Atlanta Civic League), but they were usually short-lived and made no significant long-term changes in prevailing racial attitudes.[20] The race riot brought the community's racial tensions out clearly, and these tensions did not change over the next several decades. The riot also revealed once more the ability of Atlanta's black citizens to fight for their rights and well-being—an ability that would be needed in the subsequent years. Racism and, more generally, the racial factor in relation to policy decisions, retained their prominent role well into the twentieth century and, by the 1970s and 1980s, helped create a city that clearly indicated their impact.

Shaping the City

There are virtually no major decisions that are made in the city of Atlanta that do not have a racial factor built into it. Everything has a racial component.—**Leon Eplan**, commissioner of budget and planning, 1985

Atlanta is regarded as the model of how to handle race relations in the South. A model of progress and enlightenment. . . . That's the image. But Negroes who live in Atlanta, work in Atlanta . . . know that image is false.—**James Forman**, 1963

CHAPTER 2

If you don't have the ballot you aren't anybody. If you can't elect

the officials who govern you, that's tantamount to being a slave.

—Benjamin Mays, 1979

A Voteless People Is a Helpless People: Politics and Race

Race continued to be a shaping element in Atlanta's politics in the twentieth century. Through disfranchisement, bond and recall elections, various political campaigns, coalition building, and finally black political control, the black vote (or the lack of it) helped determine how Atlanta would develop. White politicians who befriended or impeded the black community based their decisions mainly on racial considerations. Friend and foe alike focused on racial factors. Campaigns often concentrated on racial issues, and public policy decisions were often tied to racial voting. Also, the long-term neglect of the black community, its junior partnership role when a racial coalition was formed, and the race-based political turmoil the city faced in the 1960s and early 1970s as blacks pushed for change indicates the lasting role of race in Atlanta's politics and policy.

The establishment of a white primary in 1892 and disfranchisement of most blacks after 1908—over numerous black protests—through a new law stipulating property ownership, literacy, and other requirements for voting neither prevented blacks from taking some part in the political process nor kept whites from fearing black political involvement. Nonetheless, these measures did indicate white concerns about racial stability and control. On the heels of the Populist defeats and the 1906 Atlanta race riot, the reaction from most of the white community, including the progressive element, was to segregate blacks even more than before and to eliminate the black vote. In Georgia, as in the South generally, the establishment of the white primary and other forms of disfranchisement were considered progressive measures. The white-only party vote would, as white Georgians determined, permit reformers to enact social and economic change without concern about black votes being bought and used against them in nonprimary elections. Therefore, the primary and the later 1908 law, which deprived most blacks of their vote in general elections, was regarded as a way of eliminating fraud and corruption in politics and allowing whites to concentrate on economic and social reform.[1] Even before the riot, Hoke Smith and Clark Howell, the gubernatorial candidates in 1906, both supported the elimination of the black vote. Smith desired a state constitutional amendment; Howell was satisfied with the existing poll tax and white primary as a way to deny blacks their voting rights, and he did not want a new law that might also disfranchise poor, illiterate whites. In a contest that dealt largely with the topic of black voting, Smith emerged victorious with his more restrictive plan, which became the 1908 law.[2]

Segregation was also seen as a positive change in the South, for as its supporters noted, it was designed as a social control measure to bring about better race relations and avoid racial violence. Prohibition—although it was more than a racial issue, since both blacks and whites had been among its supporters and opponents—was also viewed by many white progressives as a way to ensure racial harmony and was enacted in Georgia largely on that basis. The 1906 riot figured prominently in this debate. Some whites blamed the riot on liquor sales to blacks, and this perception helped lead to a Prohibition law in the state. As Governor Nathaniel Harris stated in 1916, "Prohibition is self-protection, it is the last hope of the two races—to preserve harmony and maintain peace in their midst."[3]

Even with their limited voting strength, black Atlantans were still able to express their grievances and bargain for some redress through bond, tax, recall, and other special-election voting as well as in general elections. But in the early years of the century, whites often outmaneuvered blacks by promising funds from bonds to win black support and then reneging afterward. However, with the emergence of an NAACP chapter in Atlanta in 1917, efforts were soon made to increase black registration and vote down all bonds unless funds were expressly designated for black use. A bond could pass only if two-thirds of *all* registered voters approved. Black Atlantans could help defeat a bond either by registering and then purposely not voting or by voting no. The former strategy was used most often. Through the use of such tactics, the black community was able to secure some gains, such as the first black public high school, opened in 1924.[4] Atlanta's blacks were clearly not passive in the face of white hostility and resistance to change, and this point is sharply revealed in the city's political history.

The Key Vote

Black leaders recognized early on the need to regain some voting power. As L. C. Crogman, secretary of the NAACP's Atlanta branch, commented in 1919, "The colored people of Atlanta are now realizing that the best weapon with which they have to fight this accursed race prejudice is the proper use of the ballot." In subsequent years, particularly in the 1930s, black registration drives became more frequent, and further efforts were made to increase black involvement in the city's political life. But this course of action was difficult in a city that elected a Klansman as mayor in 1922 (Walter Sims), served as the headquarters of a revived Ku Klux Klan, and often heard racist rhetoric in political campaigns.[5]

In certain situations, however, the black voter became important. For example, in a 1932 recall vote on Mayor James L. Key (mayor from 1919 to 1923 and from 1931 to 1937), brought on by disagreements over Prohibition and the city's response to the Great Depression, black votes played an important role, just as they had in bond voting. Key was seen as relatively sympathetic to blacks. He had been mayor at the time a black public high school had been approved; he had supported more money for black schools, vetoed a plan to reward city contractors who employed whites, graded the grounds of a health center in the black community, and aided in securing a park, swimming pool, library, and some street improvements and other benefits for the black community. Therefore, he was able to win

Table 2. Black Registered Voters in Atlanta, 1918–1977

Year	Number	Percent of Total Registered Voters
1918	715	5.2
1919	1,723	11.0
1926	1,198	8.0
1935	958	6.0
1945	3,000	4.0
1946 (February)	6,876	8.3
1946 (May)	21,244	27.2
1953	17,300	18.0
1956	23,440	27.0
1957	28,604	22.1
1961	41,469	28.6
1965	—	34.7
1966	64,285	35.8
1969	—	40.7
1973	101,091	49.0
1975	—	51.8
1977	—	53.5

Sources: Mary Louise Frick, "Influences on Negro Political Participation in Atlanta, Georgia" (M.A. thesis, Georgia State University, 1967); James Michael Matthews, "Studies in Race Relations in Georgia, 1890–1930" (Ph.D. diss., Duke University, 1970), p. 334; Kesavan Sudheendran, "Community Power Structure in Atlanta: A Study in Decision Making, 1920–1939" (Ph.D. diss., Georgia State University, 1982), pp. 232, 342; Clarence A. Bacote, "The Negro Voter in Georgia Politics Today," 1957, Southern Regional Council Papers, and "Statistical Studies of Elections," Bacote Papers, Atlanta University Center, Robert W. Woodruff Library; Dennis Dresang, "The Political Power Resources of Negroes in Atlanta," unpublished paper, 1966; Sharron L. Hiemstra, "Significance of Elections for Pluralist-Elitist Theory: Atlanta's 1969 Mayoral Election," May 1970, Box 15, Helen Bullard Papers, Emory University, Special Collections Department, Robert W. Woodruff Library; *Atlanta Journal*, 20 October 1975.

needed black support in his effort to ward off recall. The clergy and NAACP led voter registration drives whose aim was to register every eligible black Atlantan. While these drives failed in their difficult goal (in 1935 blacks represented about 33 percent of the city's population but only 6 percent of its registered voters), black political power did undergo some changes in the 1930s and win some recognition from Atlanta's white leaders. For the Key recall vote, 2,500 newly registered blacks were added to the voter lists. When Key won, the black-owned *Atlanta Daily World* was able to claim that "checking the number of Negro votes cast in the Key recall election should make aware to other city, county and state office seekers that our group must be considered in the dealing out of political plums." The *Daily World* stated that, furthermore, "this is one time when it has paid to deal fairly with your fellowmen." While the number of black votes was too small to decide the election, those votes did help Key defeat his detractors. And as one analyst of this contest observed, "The Negro vote . . . in the heavily black fourth ward gave Key the highest percentage of votes of any precinct."[6]

"Get Registered and Get Something"

The successful support of Key did not change most white politicians' views of black political power and needs, but it was part of a process leading to recognition from some whites, such as Mayor Key, and it also spurred the black community to increase its registration efforts. An *Atlanta Daily World* editorial in 1932 reflected the thinking of the black leaders, stating that "with it [the vote] they have something with which to bargain. A people with nothing with which to bargain cannot be surprised reasonably when economic and industrial opportunities pass on by their doors." Some sympathetic whites, such as those in the Commission on Interracial Cooperation, likewise supported black voting rights as a way to improve black life in Atlanta. "If the ballot were in the hands of the Negro he would try to eliminate some of those conditions which affect him directly, but menace the entire community."[7]

Black citizenship classes began in 1932 at Atlanta University in order to increase black registration. In 1933, using the framework of an idea by Lugenia Burns Hope, the NAACP's Atlanta branch set up citizenship schools under the direction of Clarence Bacote, an Atlanta University history professor, to offer blacks six-week courses about registration, voting, government powers, and politics. The classes were eventually located in the black churches. In 1935, Martin Luther King Sr., minister at Ebenezer

Baptist Church, led a large rally and march on city hall as part of a voter registration drive and a demand for voting rights. And in 1936, the Atlanta Civic and Political League was established through the work of such black leaders as John Wesley Dobbs, grand master of Georgia's Prince Hall Masons. Their goal was to register about ten thousand voters in order to push demands for the correction of a number of problems regarding schools, teachers' salaries, hiring of black police and firemen, employment of black doctors at the city hospital, and development of park and playground space in black neighborhoods. Although registration still lagged, the league was very effective in helping to defeat a 1938 bond issue that neglected the black community. However, it could not elect any blacks to office during this period. Other black registration organizations such as the Women's Civic Club and the Georgia League of Negro Women Voters also emerged by the 1940s.[8]

Black registration lagged due to the realities of black voting power. Clarence Bacote, director of the citizenship schools, explained the situation this way: "Now, bear in mind that this [registration and voting] was a hard thing to sell because of the obstacles facing blacks in getting registered. . . . What was the need in getting registered if you did not have a voice in selecting the people who were to be voted on?" And, of course, there was still a cumulative poll tax that kept many blacks (and poor whites) away from registering. To register, applicants had to pay all the poll taxes that had accumulated since they became of voting age. Yet the black leadership persisted because, as Bacote explains, "We always thought that it was time for us to get blacks prepared for the ballot, because we never knew when the Supreme Court might overturn the white primary. When that happened we'd have a representative number on the books." And as the *Atlanta Daily World* emphasized relentlessly in stories and editorials, "Voting is the key which ends police brutality. It is the way to better living standards, to greater justice in the courts, and it is the fountain-head to equality of economic and political opportunity."[9]

The 1940s were to bring various changes. World War II raised the issue of the contradictions inherent in fighting a war against Nazism while maintaining racism in the United States. Considering that this issue was combined with greater black involvement in elections, the end of the poll tax in 1945 and white primary in 1946, and the beginning of recognition from the mayor, some change was evident. While mayoral contests were usually settled in the Democratic primary, in 1942 a special election in which blacks could vote was held when Mayor Roy LeCraw resigned in order to join the army. William Hartsfield, who had been mayor from 1937 to 1941 (after defeating James Key in 1936) and had lost to LeCraw in 1940, was again trying to secure this position. His opponent was Dan Bridges, who had been chairman of the aldermanic police committee at a time when police brutality against blacks was still a major concern. The black leadership decided to support Bridges in a protest vote, because Hartsfield had ignored the black community during his term and because Bridges stated that he would deal with the brutality issue. Hartsfield won after the *Atlanta Journal* reported that blacks were supporting Bridges. He did not change his attitude toward blacks, especially given that they had opposed him. He told Dobbs that "he didn't owe him anything" because of how blacks had voted. However, court decisions and an election in 1946 began to shift his thinking.[10]

In 1944, the Democratic Party's white primary was declared unconstitutional in Texas in the *Smith v. Allwright* case. That decision was a clear indication of where the court was moving on this issue. While Georgia resisted the decision, Hartsfield, a consummate politician, understood what was happening. Discussing the Texas decision with Herbert Jenkins, who later became Atlanta police chief, he said in 1944 that "what the courts have done is give the black man in Atlanta the ballot. And for your information, the ballot is a front ticket for any-damn-wheres he wants to sit, if he knows how to use it. And Atlanta Negroes know how to use it."[11] Although it did not immediately affect black voting in Georgia primaries, the court decision did lead to an increase in black registration, as the black community waited for a decision forcing Georgia to comply.[12]

Before that decision, a special congressional election, which drew black involvement, further inspired a shift in Hartsfield's thinking. In early 1946 an election was held to fill the unexpired term of Representative Robert Ramspeck of the fifth congressional district, which included Atlanta. Of the large number of candidates in the race, only a few were willing to meet with blacks and discuss their candidacy. The leading candidate, Thomas Camp, snubbed the black leaders. As a result, black support went to Helen Douglas Mankin, because, as Bacote comments, "her attitude on the race problem was fair, and she was willing to talk to us. She'd meet us at the YMCA under the cover of darkness. You couldn't afford to come out there in the open. That would be the kiss of death for a candidate to be soliciting black votes in the open." Black leaders announced support for Mankin on the night before the election after the last radio news was finished, and after the morning newspapers had gone to press, so as not to hurt her chances. Mankin won, becoming Georgia's first elected woman representative. She had accomplished this feat with significant black support, and

Register NOW

WHY? In order to help get more and better schools, streets and lights, and police protection. **REGISTRATION DOES NOT COST A PENNY!** It is the duty of every citizen to **REGISTER AND VOTE.**

HOW? You will be asked the following questions: Name? Address? Age? (Anyone 18 years or over may register.) Mother's name before marriage (maiden name)? Type of work (occupation)? How long have you lived in Atlanta?

WHERE? If you live in DeKalb County, go to: The DeKalb County Courthouse in Decatur, Georgia. If you live in Fulton County go to: The Fulton County Courthouse in Atlanta, Georgia.

YOU WILL RECEIVE COURTEOUS TREATMENT FROM THE REGISTRAR.

WHEN? NOW. Monday thru Friday, 9 A.M. to 5:00 P.M. Saturdays, 9 A.M. to 12 Noon.

REGISTER YOURSELF! Take Another To Register!

EVERY CITIZEN A QUALIFIED VOTER

Flyer to encourage black voter registration, c. 1946 (Jacob Henderson Collection, Atlanta-Fulton Public Library)

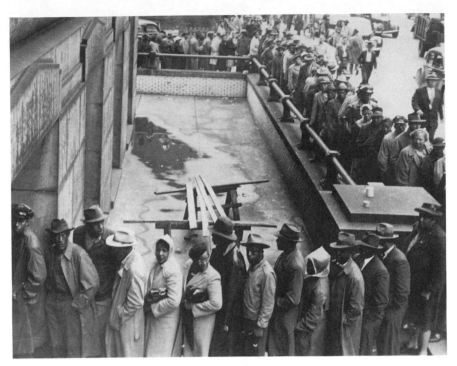

Voter registration line at Fulton County Courthouse, 1946 (Jacob Henderson Collection, Atlanta-Fulton Public Library)

she had needed their vote to win. Bacote notes, "At this time the black vote was recognized." Considering that such publications as *Time* and *Newsweek*, as well as the local press, recognized the black vote's importance in her victory, and that her racial support brought forth angry blasts from the frenetically segregationist governor Eugene Talmadge, it was clear that the black community was coming of political age.[13]

The black vote received another boost soon thereafter with the Primus King decision (*Chapman v. King*) of 1946, in which federal courts eliminated Georgia's white Democratic Party primary. Governor Ellis Arnall, who was considered a racial moderate, refused to call a special legislative session in 1946, as some wanted, to "circumvent the decision."[14] With that important election opened up, black registration drives took on more significance and urgency. In 1946, the bipartisan All Citizens Registration Committee was formed under the leadership of the local NAACP chapter, and was also supported by the Atlanta Urban League; from that point, the work of various voter registration groups, including the Atlanta Civic and Political League, were consolidated under this one organization. Registration in Fulton County soared. The black community's leadership, made

A Voteless People Is a Helpless People   **23**

Segregated entrance at Fulton County Courthouse for blacks registering to vote, 1946 (Jacob Henderson Collection, Atlanta-Fulton Public Library)

up of individuals drawn mainly from churches, businesses, the universities, and national and citywide organizations, and including a number of the city's civil rights pioneers—Dobbs, John H. Calhoun, Grace Towns Hamilton, Robert Thompson, the Reverend William Holmes Borders, Warren Cochrane, A. T. Walden, Jacob Henderson, Bacote (the committee's chairman), and others—forged a highly successful block-by-block effort in Fulton County that increased the number of black registered voters from 6,876 to 21,244 in less than two months. At one registration station, 678 Atlanta blacks registered in just three hours. Backed up by funds from black businesses, particularly Citizens Trust Bank and the Atlanta Life Insurance Company, and help from black churches, colleges, and individuals, the drive was, as Bacote relates, "a community effort." For example, a 1946 letter from the Registration Committee to black ministers noted that two Sundays "have been designated as CITIZENSHIP DAYS" and called on the ministers to urge their congregants to register and vote. The reason, as the committee slogan noted, was that "a voteless people is a helpless people."[15] Atlanta's black community, based on its colleges, churches, and businesses, always had a strong leadership group that was able to provide the expertise and funds to fight for change.

Mayor Hartsfield now paid serious attention to the black vote and began to shift his views accordingly. Earlier, when black leaders came to ask for the hiring of black police or more street lights for their neighborhoods, he had responded, "Come back to see me when you have 10,000 votes." Or, as Bacote paraphrased later, "get registered and get something." It was now time to pay another visit. Hartsfield acknowledged the black vote in 1947 when he agreed to the hiring of black policemen.[16]

Exercising its new strength, the black community organized the Atlanta Negro Voters League in 1949. Made up of black Democrats and Republicans, this nonpartisan organization represented an attempt to prevent the splitting of the black vote in local elections and to offer an united front. The league would interview candidates and, with input from white business leaders, put out a list of endorsements. In 1949, led by Republican John Wesley Dobbs and Democratic lawyer A. T. Walden, the league quickly showed that it would be a factor in local politics.[17]

The Coalition Forms

Hartsfield's 1949 reelection bid was opposed by Charlie Brown, a Fulton County commissioner, and two less important candidates. Both Hartsfield and Brown vigorously sought the black vote in the primary. A "Brown for Mayor" flyer signed by some black Atlantans, for example, touted Brown as the real friend of Atlanta's black community. "It is the opinion of many that the present Mayor has only been friendly to us since we registered to vote," the flyer noted, while Brown "believes we should have decent homes, paved streets, proper lights, improved sanitary conditions and proper fire protection" as well as "equal educational opportunities by the building of modern school buildings in Negro communities" and better treatment from the police.[18] A letter addressed to the "Negro Voters of the City of Atlanta" pointed out Hartsfield's long delay in hiring black police before the end of the white primary and large-scale black registration. Indicating that the mayor did not care about blacks before their voting power increased, the letter argued that he still did not care. It asked, "WILL YOU VOTE FOR MAYOR HARTSFIELD when he spent 500 thousand dollars in building a park which he knows Negroes will not be permitted to use?"[19]

Black leaders such as Bacote were fully aware that Brown's campaign material regarding Hartsfield contained some truth. Bacote commented later that "he [Hartsfield] was not what you would call a racist when he took office as mayor in 1936, but he didn't pay any attention to blacks then." But he was willing to change as black votes increased. "It was the bloc vote that got Hartsfield's attention finally," Bacote observed. And the mayor made the most of his shifting policies. He would make a show of the black policemen in his appearances before black audiences, and he favorably compared the new recognition of black needs in Atlanta to their continued neglect in Fulton County, where Brown served.[20]

This was the first campaign in which mayoral candidates made a direct and at times open bid for black votes through ads in black newspapers and appearances before black groups. It was an ideal time for the Atlanta Negro Voters League to press their demands. When the mayor asked to meet with the league's general committee, they expressly asked to hear his views on hiring more black police; opening a fire station with black firemen in westside Atlanta's black areas; getting more parks, playgrounds, public housing, and land for private homes; and upgrading black city workers. The league endorsed Hartsfield shortly after he agreed to support many of their demands. Although both Hartsfield and Brown were segregationists, the mayor had already shown some flexibility. Brown's bid for white voters who felt that Hartsfield had given too much to blacks and his refusal to continue to appear before Voters League meetings surely influenced this decision also. Finally, a spurious list of league-recommended candidates endorsing Brown was distributed in black neighborhoods on election eve. While Brown denied being party to this trick, it threatened to confuse the situation and benefit him. When the incorrect endorsement was revealed, it became an additional reason, the *Atlanta Daily World* explained, for a large black vote for Hartsfield.[21]

In some ways the election results were not as important as what had already occurred during the campaign. As A. T. Walden wrote to Hartsfield concerning the willingness of candidates to meet with the league, "Regardless of the outcome of the election, it is felt that this gesture of interest and good will has made a distinct contribution toward mutual understanding in the interest of better and more effective government."[22]

However, the voting returns clearly indicated the importance of black votes. In the primary, Hartsfield secured a majority over his three opponents by only 102 votes. He was able to win with 50.1 percent of the vote only through strong and crucial support from black voters. In two predominantly black precincts, Hartsfield received 82.5 percent of the vote. He lost the white vote; his victory was based on a combination of black voters and upper- and upper-middle-class whites in northside Atlanta— racial and class-based voting. The mayor acknowledged his black support when he called the *Atlanta Daily World* the next day and said, "I look forward to another four years of service to the people of Atlanta, and that means all the people, without regards to race, creed, or color." By strongly supporting the annexation of affluent white areas from the 1940s to 1960s, he acknowledged his support from whites and those who he had always thought should run the city.[23]

The 1949 election was a turning point, as blacks and northside whites became part of a biracial political coalition that controlled city politics over the next twenty years. But blacks remained junior partners throughout this era. A paternalism based on race defined this relationship. Whatever Hartsfield's rhetoric, Atlanta's blacks were still treated as second-class citizens. No white leader sought to end segregation. As one stated in the early 1950s, "I'm a true friend of the Negro and will be as long as he keeps his place." Due to their votes there was recognition; there were some rewards, some demands met, and important contacts made between black and white leaders; but basically the main impact of black inclusion in the 1950s and early 1960s was their ability to prevent openly racist whites from winning office, not in securing solutions to many of their community's long-term problems. The contacts that emerged from black voting power also helped limit racial violence in this city, which was certainly no small matter. And compared to such cities as Little Rock or Birmingham, Atlanta seemed racially progressive. However, while these facts explain the general reputation of racial moderation Atlanta had in the 1950s and 1960s, this reputation should not be overstated. Many problems were ignored and allowed to fester over decades. Whites fostered and perhaps believed Atlanta's progressive reputation, but most blacks knew better as they looked at their schools, homes, jobs, city services, and other factors. One indication of this attitude is that civil rights leader and 1980s mayor Andrew Young later commented that neither he nor Martin Luther King Jr. regarded Atlanta as particularly enlightened or moderate prior to the 1960s.[24]

On the state level, a number of racist gubernatorial campaigns and governors through the 1960s indicated the situation when black voting power and influence was more limited. Even Governor Arnall (1943–47), whom many considered a racial moderate because he secured the elimination of the poll tax, accepted the end of the white primary, and opposed the Klan, was only relatively so. He actually did very little for the state's black citizens. To the *Atlanta Daily World* in 1944, the fact that Arnall— unlike the previous governor, Eugene Talmadge—"does not carry on an active campaign of hate toward them [blacks] is a real improvement over his predecessor."[25]

In Atlanta, the 1953 primary election, which again pitted Hartsfield against Brown, brought problems for the mayor in regard to his black support. Dobbs was angry that no black firemen had been hired, so he withdrew his Republicans from the Atlanta Negro Voters League and backed Brown; Walden and his Democrats in the league stayed with Hartsfield. Concerned about his black support, Hartsfield had his campaign manager, Helen Bullard, contact Grace Towns Hamilton, the Atlanta Urban League's executive director, to see what could be done to win back that support. Hamilton advised Bullard to have the mayor call a meeting of league leaders at the Butler Street YMCA, where black leaders often met; provided her with the appropriate names; and recommended that the mayor speak directly to the relevant issues. Hartsfield should note that as mayor of all Atlantans, he had to address black needs in the context "of what was possible for the whole population. He should point out that he had been able to keep city government free of some of the anti-Negro forces so rampant in the state government, but that in this race he strongly believed that his opponent was making a strong effort to turn Atlanta over to those elements in the state." The mayor was advised "to admit that all had not been done that should have been done—and that the Negro did have legitimate gripes. The sore spots should be brought up and discussed—no Negro firemen, more Negro policemen, better schools and parks for the Negroes, appointment of Negroes to planning boards, and the elimination of police brutality." By speaking about these issues openly, Hartsfield could disarm those black community members who were angry at him.[26]

The mayor's eagerness to contact Hamilton and her willingness to give this advice indicated the ties between the black leadership and the mayor —the sense that Hartsfield, even with his faults, was preferable to other white politicians, and the mayor's need to maintain these ties to keep his black support. Yet it also indicates black discontent with the slowness of change that was to characterize the Hartsfield administration.

In 1953 the mayor faced some white dissatisfaction with his overtures to blacks, and he would need black support to win. Brown would be the logical candidate of these whites because he had said earlier, in regard to black housing, that it was fine to do something for black areas "but there are thousands of poor white people who need help and haven't gotten a thing from the city government. Let's help them a little." As early as 1952, Hartsfield, in order to hold his black support, had accused Brown of being the candidate of the race-baiters and of planning to make race a central campaign issue in the 1953 election. The mayor was skillful in using race as an issue and introduced it in this campaign to win black voters. Brown later claimed that Hartsfield tried "to appeal to the fears of black voters." However, it is apparently true that Brown tried to secure white votes with the racial issue. One report from the West End, a white neighborhood, stated that "they are saying in West End that the Mayor being a negro lover will put the white and colored children together and that it is rumors started by C. Brown."[27]

Racial factors again worked in Hartsfield's favor, as they had in 1949. The mayor won with substantial support from blacks, who had a higher turnout than white voters. In six predominantly black precincts, Hartsfield won with 86.9 percent of the vote. Brown acknowledged the meaning of the results. "I was defeated by the Negro bloc four years ago, when I got only about 8 percent of the Negro vote. I had hoped to get about 25 percent of the Negro vote this time, but the percentage this time was about the same as four years ago."[28] Black bloc voting became a source of white fear and concern during the 1950s. But blacks were simply supporting those who promised redress for their grievances. The image of racial bloc voting meant different things to different politicians. As Hartsfield later put it, "Every candidate wants the Negro vote. If he gets it, then it's a civic triumph. If the Negro vote goes to the other fellow, it's diabolical Negro bloc voting."[29]

One notable result of this election was the citywide primary victory of Rufus Clement, Atlanta University's president, over a white opponent for a seat on the school board. An annexation plan that increased the white majority while bringing new black and affluent white areas into the city in 1952 strengthened the racial coalition that resulted in Clement's being the first black to win an elected position in Atlanta since the nineteenth century. Also, A. T. Walden and Miles G. Amos won seats on the City Democratic Executive Committee from the mainly black third ward, but only after the courts ordered the committee, which conducted the primaries and set qualification fees and rules, to allow the black candidates to participate.[30]

We Do Not Want the Hatred of Little Rock

Atlanta's racial coalition worked well in elections and continued to keep Hartsfield in office through 1961. Both on the surface in election campaigns and beneath the surface in discussions and deals between white and black power brokers, race remained a prominent part of the city's political life. Through the 1950s Hartsfield worked out elaborate land agreements between white and black homeowners during periods of racial transition, and he helped to desegregate the golf courses and buses—all with an eye to satisfying his black constituency and avoiding violence from whites. The image of "a city too busy to hate," which the mayor first stated in 1955 in regard to desegregation of the city's golf courses and the idea of Atlanta's avoiding the racial violence that struck and economically hurt other cities, became important aspects of Hartsfield's appeal to both racial communities.

In city politics, this approach was first used in the mayor's 1957 reelection campaign. Because he won the primary against Archie Lindsay with 93.2 percent black support but secured only 36.8 percent of the white vote, in the general election Hartsfield was forced to face a potentially formidable opponent when arch-segregationist Lester Maddox entered the race. In the primary contest, the race issue had remained somewhat subdued, because the United Church Women of Atlanta had asked the candidates to keep it out of the campaign. However, it became the main focus of the general election campaign. Trying to rally whites, Maddox accused the mayor of "being 'a pawn of the NAACP' and with having been kept in office by the Negro bloc vote." He came out squarely against integrated schools.[31] Hartsfield countered with a suggestion from a July campaign strategy meeting that he "boldly develop pride among white citizens in the way Atlanta is solving the problem of separate races living in the same big, thriving community." During the campaign he stated, "I'm proud of the fact that in the face of race trouble all over the South, you have seen none in Atlanta. Do you want boycotting, with the white people always losing?" He further asserted that he was "willing to put Atlanta's racial policy up for public approval or disapproval." Using the threat of racial disorder if politicians such as Maddox won office, Hartsfield defined himself as a protector of the social order ("We do not want the hatred and bitterness of Montgomery or Little Rock") and as a fair administrator who was "just trying to be mayor of every man in this city." Claiming that he was "not playing for any race group and [was] not going to force anything on people who will not tolerate it," Hartsfield apparently was able to satisfy most whites concerned about school integration.[32]

While Hartsfield had defeated Lindsay in a fairly close vote in the primary (by 3,804 votes out of 71,420), he won the general election with 66.3 percent of the vote and by the largest margin in his career (41,300 for Hartsfield, 23,987 for Maddox). As before, he secured his strongest votes in black areas (97.6 percent in thirteen mainly black precincts) and in the city's white north side. However, he also won in many white districts that had gone to Lindsay in the primary. The city's white areas gave Hartsfield

54 percent of their vote. This election was a revealing one in regard to attitudes and trends. First, in comparison to the May primary, there was an increase in voting in black and northside areas and a decrease in white precincts that had supported Lindsay. The fear of a Maddox victory and what that would mean for amicable race relations, particularly during the intense early school desegregation period, appeared to be a strong influence in this election. Second, although more whites were registered to vote, at this time blacks tended to vote at a higher rate than whites. Black voters made up 22 percent of the total vote in the general election, and this percentage would continue to increase into the 1960s. As one newspaper article asked, "Can he [the candidate who runs a racist campaign] attract enough white voters by his extreme stand to overcome the Negro voters he will surely alienate?" Hartsfield did not need the black vote to win against Maddox, although he had needed it in the primary. As an extremist candidate, Maddox apparently pushed many whites into Hartsfield's column. Thus, the mayor's strategy of emphasizing racial calm in Atlanta was successful.[33]

Hartsfield interpreted the election in this way: he said that his victory was evidence that "the people of Atlanta don't want Atlanta growth and prosperity to be stopped by racial controversy." On a later occasion he noted that "our aim in life is to make no business, no industry, no educational or social organization ashamed of the dateline 'Atlanta.'"[34]

Another notable aspect of the 1957 election was the reelection of Rufus Clement to the school board and the narrow loss of T. M. Alexander for the board of aldermen. Both had white opponents. Clement won with 97.3 percent of the black vote and 26.6 percent of the white vote. Alexander, the first black to run for this office since the nineteenth century, received enough votes to throw the election into a runoff after none of the three candidates secured a majority. Segregationist governor Marvin Griffin reacted to Clement's victory and Alexander's good showing by asking whites to bloc-vote against Alexander and support the white candidate. Alexander lost after his white vote dropped by about half. The governor's emphasis on race apparently had an effect on some white voter choices. Nonetheless, the election of Clement and Hartsfield indicates that a segment of the white community was willing to vote for candidates who supported some positive change in the racial status quo.[35]

Hartsfield's terms as mayor represented this type of change, but it was slow and often reluctant. He seemed to regard the black issues and leaders he had to deal with in a demeaning way and as a necessary annoyance. Writing to an individual in Birmingham, the mayor stated in 1961 that "you ought to get some of the power structure in Birmingham to get realistic about the race question. They will never be bothered with more than a small number and they will be fairly well educated, literate, wearing good clothes, etc." Hartsfield was a friend of black votes, not of the black community. As one Atlanta black leader pointed out, "The whole attitude of city government has been affected by the increase in the responsible Negro electorate. Mayor Hartsfield had the good sense to see that the changing times could be used to his advantage." Eliza Paschall, a white civil rights activist, commented in relation to discussing Atlanta's political, government, and state-related issues with Hartsfield, that "I later realized [these issues] were all considered in light of how it would affect the racial balance or the racial business . . . the racial formula, so to speak." Hartsfield's biographer notes that soon after leaving office, the mayor said privately "that he knew how to 'use' the Negro, but was able successfully to avoid letting the Negro 'use' him." In reality, both used each other, deriving benefits from the relationship. It was a trade-off—votes for favors—of the sort seen in many other cities between various groups. However, Atlanta at the end of Hartsfield's last term in 1961 was still a tightly segregated city with little power-sharing and significant race-related problems in regard to schools, city services, housing, and jobs.[36]

Racial Change

The continuing problems were discussed by the Atlanta Committee for Cooperative Action (ACCA) in a pamphlet titled "A Second Look: The Negro Citizen in Atlanta," published in early 1960 with financial help from the Atlanta Life Insurance Company. This report laid out the areas of neglect and the level of discrimination and proposed how the city could respond to black needs. The ACCA, formed in 1958, consisted of "young black businessmen and professionals," such as Carl Holman, Jesse Hill of the Atlanta Life Insurance Company, and Leroy Johnson, and indicated this generation's dissatisfaction with Atlanta's slow pace of racial change.[37]

The discontent is further illustrated by "An Appeal for Human Rights," based on information in the ACCA's report and written by students at Atlanta's black colleges. Published in all city newspapers on 9 March 1960, the "Appeal" noted continued problems for blacks in Atlanta, the neglect of this community, and the need for change. It declared, "We do not intend to wait placidly for those rights which are already legally and morally ours to be meted out to us one at a time." This eloquent statement, penned by this younger generation of black student activists, indicated their displeasure with the results of the gradual approach of the older generation and was the opening shot of a mass direct-action protest. The older black leaders still remained influential. The presidents of the black colleges had met earlier with the students and convinced them to delay direct action until they wrote and published this list of grievances. The presidents hoped that through either an NAACP lawsuit or long-established ties with the white business elite, street protest could be avoided and the dispute settled with discussions and compromises. However, at this point it appeared that the time for gradualism had passed.[38]

Motivated by the sit-ins at lunch counters that began at Greensboro, North Carolina, in February 1960, and cognizant of Atlanta's failings as a "city too busy to hate," these students, led by Lonnie King and Julian Bond, pushed for quicker change through large-scale protests. And the white leadership was not eager to change. The "Appeal" itself received harsh criticism from Georgia governor Ernest Vandiver, who doubted it was written by students or even in this country and attacked it as a "left-wing statement . . . calculated to breed dissatisfaction, discontent, discord and evil." Hartsfield, indicating the different reactions toward black demands by state and city leaders, stated that it was a helpful document in that it made whites aware of black grievances.[39]

In Rufus Clement's office at Atlanta University, the mayor immediately met with the "Appeal" 's authors to try to work toward a solution that would avoid mass protest. Soon afterward, the black college presidents, black student activists, and leading white ministers met for the same reason. The mayor and ministers urged the students to follow a "go slow" policy until the white business leaders could be brought into the discussions. The students were eager to emphasize their concerns and grievances, though, and held their first sit-ins on 15 March. The demonstrations were halted the next day by a newly formed student group, the Committee on Appeal for Human Rights (COAHR), headed by Lonnie King. This group now hoped that serious discussions with the white community would begin. But a few days later, the businessmen rejected the student demands. So in April, Lonnie King, Julian Bond, and other student activists joined with ACCA leaders to plan strategy. By June 1960, in an attempt to present a united black front to white city officials and businessmen, a Student-Adult Liaison Committee had been established, with Reverend William Holmes Borders as chairman. But there were some older black leaders—for example, C. A. Scott of the *Atlanta Daily World*—who strongly opposed the students' protest tactics.[40]

The initial sit-ins, which began on 15 March, targeted restaurants and

A Voteless People Is a Helpless People   **33**

lunch counters in public buildings and at interstate rail and bus stations where the students could provide a good court case for eliminating segregation. After the students' meeting with ACCA leaders, protest activities, including boycotts and picketing, began again, but this time against private businesses such as A&P, where blacks were customers but could not get any but the lowest skilled jobs. During the summer of 1960, demonstrations were extended to white churches, but the major protest took place at Rich's Department Store, the leading retail establishment in downtown Atlanta. Rich's was targeted because, as Julian Bond later commented, "there was a saying . . . in Atlanta that if Rich's went so would everybody else. . . . And we knew that if Rich's changed its racial policy at its lunch counters then every other store in the Atlanta metro area would just have to do the same thing." While there were some discussions with Rich's, nothing was accomplished. In September, Colonial Stores were targeted successfully. Blacks secured new employment and promotions at the store. But the major confrontations came in October, with sit-ins, boycotts, and pickets in the downtown area, again targeting Rich's in particular but also extending to a number of stores. These activities were well planned. The boycott of Rich's was developed over a number of months; the students urged others in the black community to "close out your charge account with segregation, open up your account with freedom."[41]

The demands were simple: the desegregation of lunch counters, restrooms, and restaurants, and more and better jobs. With the sit-ins came massive arrests of students based on a February 1960 state trespass law passed to deal with sit-in situations. The downtown area was in turmoil, businesses were losing money, and the movement was growing stronger. In the fall of 1960, Atlanta captured national headlines when Martin Luther King Jr. was arrested at Rich's for taking part in the protests.[42]

Various attempts to mediate the controversy followed and failed. Hartsfield and others, concerned about Atlanta's reputation, economy, and racial political coalition, tried to end the dispute. A negotiated settlement was finally worked out in March 1961. It delayed lunch counter and restaurant desegregation until school desegregation was begun in the fall of 1961, but it included a deadline of 15 October. Meanwhile, the sit-ins, picketing, and boycotts were to stop, and blacks who had been fired from jobs due to the lunchroom closings were to get their jobs back.[43]

It was an agreement that upset many students and other black activists who wanted to continue demonstrating until full and immediate desegregation was secured; those blacks considered this agreement little more than Rich's had offered earlier. Lonnie King, who was in on the discussions, was dissatisfied with the agreement. He had wanted immediate lunch counter desegregation. However, Martin Luther King Sr. urged him to agree to the compromise. Supported by white businessmen and older black leaders such as King Sr. and Walden, the agreement illustrated the gradualism and reluctance of white Atlanta's earlier racial agreements. According to Lonnie King, King Sr., Borders, and others of the older generation gave in too soon "because they were so afraid that if they walked out of that room they'd never be able to get back in there and get those kind of gains." The older black elite apparently felt that, as in the past, they were not negotiating from a position of strength and would secure little if they did not take what was offered. As a result, any white offer, however meager, was accepted. But although it convinced whites and some blacks that Atlanta was more progressive than the facts indicated, this approach angered the young black leaders and resulted in further protests during the rest of the decade. Meanwhile, many of city's lunch counters were desegregated on 28 September 1961. The demonstrations were essential to even this small shift. Ivan Allen, mayor from 1962 to 1970, said later that Atlanta businesses would not have accepted any desegregation without student protests. The issue "had to be forcefully brought to the attention of the public as a whole." Apparently, he eventually came to feel that Atlanta's usual nonconfrontational and gradual approach to racial reform would not have worked in this case. As he said, "I don't think that we would have ever gotten the action, or it would have been a hundred years in coming, had it not been for the demonstrations." In other words, Atlanta needed the student protest movement. As Benjamin Brown, one of the student leaders, commented later, "I would say that the student movement made Atlanta change the general atmosphere and tone. You see, heretofore, there was a superficial image, superficial image of good race relations. . . . The student movement came along and broke all these falsities down."[44]

48,000 Negroes Voting in Atlanta

It was within this setting that the 1961 mayoral election was held. Black discontent was evident even to the most obtuse whites, and it was obvious that solutions were needed if Atlanta was to progress. The next mayor would immediately find himself within a racial conflict and having to deal with young black leaders who rejected the Hartsfield era gradualism.

Ivan Allen, president of the Atlanta Chamber of Commerce and an active participant in the desegregation agreement, continued the Hartsfield style and rhetoric as he faced Charlie Brown, Lester Maddox, and M. M. "Muggsy" Smith in the 1961 mayoral contest. Race played an important role in this election. As before, the Atlanta Negro Voters League interviewed candidates on various issues, such as support for black appointments to policy-making positions; an end to segregation in public facilities, including parks; more equitable city employment; hiring more black police, upgrading those on the force, and giving them the authority to arrest whites; the placement of a fire station in black neighborhoods on the west side, and the hiring of black firemen; a nondiscrimination clause in school contracts "requiring non-discrimination in all crafts and trades involved in school construction"; and a faster pace for school integration. Black leaders initially felt some reluctance to endorse Allen, since he had made segregationist comments earlier when he considered entering a gubernatorial race. Also, some younger blacks supported Smith, a state legislator who had introduced an anti-Klan bill and who appealed to the black students' dissatisfaction with the 1961 desegregation agreement and with the older black leadership that controlled the Voters League.[45]

Because of Hartsfield's efforts to secure black support for Allen, and the older black leaders' favorable view of him during the desegregation discussions, Allen received the endorsement of the Voters League and NAACP. He also became the first white politician to publicize his meetings with blacks. However, SNCC, the SCLC, and many black students supported Smith. Fearful of a split black vote, which might result in a Maddox victory, the older black leaders drummed into the black community the necessity of voting for Allen. The *Atlanta Daily World*, for example, proclaimed that the black community had to back "the strongest and best qualified candidate who is opposing this race baiter [Maddox] and give that strongest anti-race baiting candidate our support." The paper urged blacks to join whites "who represent progress and fair-play toward our racial group." Allen secured 10,492 votes and Smith 4,435 in black precincts. Citywide, Maddox had a strong showing based on lower-income white voters: he received 23,083 votes, to Allen's 37,853.[46]

The primary gave Allen and Maddox the most total votes, with neither securing a majority, so a runoff was needed. In a battle between Allen and Maddox, black voters had little choice; they went strongly for Allen. He campaigned actively in black neighborhoods, appearing at black schools and churches regularly both before and after the runoff, and he expressed his support for a westside fire station, the hiring of black firemen, the ending of police brutality, the desegregation of city parks, the provision of city jobs for blacks, and allowing black policemen to arrest whites. Maddox refused to attend meetings in black areas.[47]

Essentially, his black support enabled Allen to win. With more blacks voting in the runoff than in the initial primary, Allen secured 99.4 percent (31,224) of Atlanta's black vote and only 47.9 percent of the white vote (but about 81 percent of the upper-income white vote). If blacks had not voted, Maddox would have won 35,919 to Allen's 33,089. Because of the black vote, however, Allen won with 64 percent of the total vote. Given his divisive racial politics, Maddox certainly would have created problems for the city. It is easy to accept Benjamin Mays's later statement that "had the Negro been voteless during the last twenty-five years [the Hartsfield and Allen years], Atlanta would have been a lesser city than it is now."[48]

Allen noted later that in this campaign he recognized the importance of the racial issue: "I could promise all I wanted to about Atlanta's bright, booming economic future, but none of it would come about if Atlanta failed to cope with the racial issue. That[,] I knew, was the *real* issue in this campaign: was Atlanta going to be another Little Rock, or was Atlanta going to set the pace for the New South?" Allen was well aware of the economic damage to Little Rock caused by its resistance to racial change. In a study prepared specifically for him, candidate Allen learned that "anticipated growth" stopped for Little Rock as of 1958, plant expansion came "to a virtual standstill," population decreased, and unemployment increased. And Allen used the threat that Atlanta would become another Little Rock disaster story if Maddox was elected. He surely was also aware, as Walter Crawford, executive vice president of the Atlanta Convention Bureau, stated, that segregation resulted in the loss of convention business to other cities.[49]

During his tenure as mayor, Allen did bring changes for the black community in regard to black police responsibilities, the hiring of black firemen, and the location of a fire station on the west side; more extensive appointments to policy-making boards and committees such as, in 1962, a joint Atlanta–Fulton County bond commission and the traffic and transportation commission; and further desegregation of public facilities such as theaters (in 1962) and city swimming pools (in June 1963). He was also the only southern mayor to testify in Congress on behalf of the desegregation of public accommodations that was to become part of the Civil Rights Act of 1964. Racial issues became a central focus of his administration. "From the time I walked into City Hall in January 1962 until the passage of the Civil Rights Act in 1964, I was deeply involved day after day and hour after hour in trying to solve the racial problems. There was simply no end to it." He also stated, "The civil rights movement would dominate nearly every decision for the next four or five years after that [1961 election]."[50]

Although he made some embarrassing mistakes trying to maintain white neighborhoods, there is no doubt that Allen was more enlightened on racial matters than his predecessors had been. With the behind-the-scenes support of the economically powerful Coca-Cola magnate Robert Woodruff, Allen understood what the city needed if it was to flourish economically and maintained ties to the black community. He also notes that he was pushed to a more liberal position "as a reaction against the totally irrational and irresponsible acts of the white racists around me. . . . I saw what the race-baiters were doing or could do to hold back the orderly growth of Atlanta." Among blacks there were great expectations of significant change under Allen, though these expectations were not always fulfilled.[51]

Further changes came through a federal court ruling that ended the county unit system used in the Democratic Party's primaries and through the 1962 election of Leroy Johnson to the state senate after a court-ordered reapportionment of the senate based on population and mandating district rather than at-large voting. (Johnson thereby became the Georgia senate's first black since the nineteenth century.) As with the senate, court-directed reapportionment of the House in 1965 increased the representation of more populated counties such as Fulton and thereby allowed that body to have more equitable representation. This change initially resulted in the election of eight Atlanta blacks, including Grace Towns Hamilton and Julian Bond, to new districts.[52]

The county unit system had decided state (and in some cases congressional) primary elections, determined the number of state house and senatorial representatives for each county, and allowed politicians to win with less than a majority popular vote and to ignore such counties as Fulton, where blacks were politically active. Each county had a certain unit vote (e.g., Fulton County had six unit votes). Politicians who won the popular vote in that county received all six votes. Less populated rural counties had two or four votes. By campaigning in many rural areas and amassing their unit votes, candidates could win even if everyone in Atlanta voted against them and they received a minority of popular votes. This system worked against Atlanta's voters, decreasing the significance of their vote in these contests and often permitting the election of demagogic, racist governors and other state officials. Another result of this peculiar system was that the Georgia senate and house were controlled by rural legislators. The heavily populated urban counties were underrepresented in these bodies, since representation was not based on population.[53]

Black voter registration climbed in the early 1960s as black votes in both city and state elections now took on more meaning and as sit-ins activated Atlanta's blacks. Between 1960 and 1962, the various black groups—the All Citizens Registration Committee as well as the Committee on Appeal for Human Rights—conducted massive registration drives that added sixteen thousand black voters to the Fulton County rolls in just sixteen months. The repercussions of this registration and reapportionment were felt on the highest state level as well. As John H. Calhoun observed, "A moderate governor, Carl Sanders, was elected; the elected lieutenant governor, Peter Zack Geer, changed from a rank segregationist between the primary and run-off; every larger city sent at least one moderate senator to the state capitol; the race issue was overcome in state politics for the first time since reconstruction; . . . the state House and Senate galleries, as well as the Governor's Inaugural Ball, were desegregated." In 1963, Leroy Johnson and A. T. Walden became the first blacks to be appointed to the State Democratic Executive Committee.[54]

There was also no doubt, as Leroy Johnson stated in 1963 at a voter registration rally in a black church, that "there are 48,000 Negroes voting in Atlanta, and this is why we have a good atmosphere in Atlanta." But how good was that atmosphere? The same flyer that announced this meeting also spoke of the need for better police protection, better schools, and more jobs in Atlanta's city government.[55]

Allen's election and his willingness to respond to some black demands represented change, but in many ways it was too little, too late. After years of gradualism, with sporadic and limited desegregation (for example, the sluggish desegregation of the schools), a new generation of black leaders remained dissatisfied with the pace of change in the city. The Atlanta Committee for Cooperative Action's report and COAHR's "Appeal for Human Rights" in 1960 indicated the discontent that existed before Allen took office. By 1963, however, dissatisfaction with the pace of racial reform under the Allen administration emerged. In March 1963, Gwendolyn Isler, head of COAHR, wrote the mayor about the committee's unhappiness "with the situation regarding desegregation" in Atlanta. "It is our opinion that, despite the many attempts at negotiation with prominent officials of the hotels in the city, the progress is almost negligible. . . . We are confronting you with this problem because we feel that you, as mayor, can exert more influence upon the situation than you have in the past." Asking that Allen remove all racial barriers in every aspect of the city's life, and expressing disappointment that the "Appeal for Human Rights" statement had not brought about the desired change, the letter threatened more demonstrations. "Expect more of the demonstrations which have revealed to the world that Atlanta does not measure up to her 'liberal image.'" Although restaurants were still desegregating, many remained segregated, and some of those that had integrated with the 1961 agreement had now reverted to their racist past.[56]

As a result of this dissatisfaction, a coalition of nine civil rights organizations (including the NAACP, SNCC, and the SCLC) came together in October 1963 in an Atlanta Summit Leadership Conference to coordinate activities and set policy. In a November 1963 document called "Action for Democracy," the Summit Leadership Conference laid out an agenda for dealing with black concerns and the city's continuing ties to segregation. Stating that "Atlanta's race relations image . . . needs considerable improvement," the Summit document asked for an immediate, total desegregation of the city and equality in regard to "housing, employment, education, political participation, law enforcement, voter registration, health and social services, and public accommodations." Specifically, the document called for various policy shifts, such as the passage of a public accommodations law by the board of aldermen; fair employment practices; an open occupancy law; the desegregation of public housing, hospitals, and jails; a plan for total school desegregation; and the appointment of blacks to more policy-making boards, to positions as judges on the municipal and traffic courts, and to more police positions. "We cannot believe that delay is an asset. The time is now! . . . We cannot believe that token desegregation represents a noteworthy achievement. . . . We believe that most of the citizens of Atlanta possess the moral courage to actualize racial equality without delay and without the necessity of overt pressures to effectuate the needed changes."[57]

The earlier sit-ins, the Summit Leadership Conference's statement and new street demonstrations at restaurants and other facilities, and picketing at the mayor's home and office and the city's board of education kept race at the center of Allen's concerns. The Summit Leadership Conference used SNCC and COAHR members as its street soldiers to carry out the nonviolent protests after initial negotiations with city officials failed to produce anything substantial. Summit's first approach was to discuss the problems, to try "to attain these objectives through cooperative action rather than through conflict." But if that attempt did not work, Summit intended to take to the streets. The mayor responded with only limited change. In November 1963, Allen appointed a coordinating committee to work with Summit in dealing with its grievances, and in late January 1964 he organized a biracial meeting at city hall to discuss racial problems because, as he said, the city's reputation and stability were in jeopardy as demonstrations reemerged. Allen tried to secure a cooling-off period on the protests by taking the lead on certain issues. He supported a resolution for voluntary desegregation of public accommodations (which the board of aldermen stalled in committee), appointed A. T. Walden in January 1964 as a judge serving both the municipal and traffic courts, and set up a biracial committee on fair employment. But the end result was that few white public officials initially followed Allen's lead, and relatively little changed in the city. The chamber of commerce did not even agree to allow blacks to become members until late February. A. T. Walden and Clarence Coleman, cochairmen of the Summit Leadership Conference, had already written to their members in early January 1964 to express their disgust: "As you know, several meetings have been held with legislative bodies and responsible committees and boards to rid our city of all segregation and discrimination as outlined in the document 'Action for Democracy'; however, these confrontations have not resulted in the anticipated progress." The sense that little progress was being made was reaffirmed in the following months.[58]

Desegregating swimming pools, theaters, and the fire service was no longer enough. The changes demanded in the 1960s called for an equality of services, rights, and benefits that few whites were willing to acknowledge. The problem, Allen himself explained, was that each racial group had a different definition of racial harmony. The "white community tends to define that as absence of disturbance, [the] Negro Community as establishment of their full rights as American citizens." Or as Julian Bond later commented in regard to the question of which of the 1969 mayoral candidates was best for black Atlantans, "That means, which one is going to see that public housing is dispersed throughout the city? Which one is going to see that black policemen and firemen in the city are no longer *Jim Crowed*? Which one is going to integrate city hall, with all its jobs? Which one is going to keep Hunter Street and Auburn Avenue in the black community as clean as upper Peachtree Street? Which one is going to stop the systematic destruction of black residential neighborhoods by halting the spread of commercial development and jerry-built apartments? Which one is going to revitalize urban renewal so it does not continue to mean 'Negro removal'?"[59] Even for Ivan Allen, who depended on black votes and pledged to work toward both goals of racial harmony, change was too limited and was more cosmetic than substantial. It is one of the

A Voteless People Is a Helpless People **41**

reasons that the election of a black mayor, signifying the possibility of some basic and meaningful change, met with such hostility from the same white leadership that had so strongly supported Hartsfield, Allen, and the racial-political coalition.

Although general black life in the city had not substantially improved, Allen's efforts to support some black demands put him in a good position for reelection in 1965. He won with 31,116 black and 22,117 white votes. His main opponent was Muggsy Smith, who secured 21,907 total votes. And blacks made some notable political advances in 1965. For example, Q. V. Williamson became the first black alderman since the nineteenth century. Smith, who had garnered some black support in 1961, indicated the problem blacks had in regard to which white politicians to trust. After his 1965 defeat, Smith complained that the black community bloc-voted against him to support Allen and that blacks would therefore control Allen. He also expressed concern about Atlanta's future as black Atlantans gained control.[60]

During Allen's second term, racial issues concerning housing, schools, and city services were still prominent, and race riots began to occur, although these disturbances were minor compared to those that took place in other cities in the mid- to late 1960s. Aware of the significant black support he received in the 1965 election and concerned about the city's reputation, Allen worked with black leaders as part of the continuing effort to maintain the biracial coalition. That effort, by itself, was important in maintaining communication between the two racial communities and dealing with some discontent. But blacks were still junior partners in the coalition, and it was never able to deal with basic problems on the long-term, sustained basis needed to solve them. For example, although Allen increased the number of blacks in city service, he did not appoint any blacks as department heads. And in regard to housing, the mayor expressed concern and was involved in corrective efforts, but they neither lasted nor brought about enough of a change.[61] At the time, many black Atlantans thought that a black mayor was essential for understanding and resolving these problems; and they expected to elect one as black electoral power increased.

The Massell Interim

In 1969, the biracial coalition faltered as Allen and northside whites disagreed with black leaders over who to support for mayor. Allen backed Rodney Cook, a white alderman, while black community spokesmen initially supported Leroy Johnson. Johnson decided not to run, recognizing that black registered voters comprised just 41 percent of the total. At first, as the black leadership focused on putting more blacks onto the board of aldermen and the school board, it seemed that the mayoral contest would only have white candidates. However, some surprising events occurred. Horace Tate, an Atlanta school board member and executive secretary of the statewide black Georgia Teachers and Education Association, entered the mayoral contest, and Maynard Jackson, a lawyer and grandson of John Wesley Dobbs, ran for vice mayor, both without prior approval by the established black leaders. The black leadership decided to support Jackson. Tate did not fare as well, although he did have SCLC support. Convinced that a black mayoral candidate could not win, the Summit Leadership Conference's leaders—King Sr., Jesse Hill, Sam Williams, and Leroy Johnson—threw their support to Sam Massell, then vice mayor, who promised to work to redress black grievances and who had helped establish a Community Relations Commission. Massell was not Allen's or the white establishment's choice, though; they stayed with Cook. This was the first election in many years in which the northside white–downtown white business elite and the black leaders did not support the same candidate. It also represents an election where blacks were more assertive, breaking with their junior partnership role and moving toward an era of black political dominance.[62]

In the primary contest that included the main candidacies of Massell, Cook, Tate, and Alderman Everett Millican, Massell captured 44.2 percent of the black vote, and Tate 49 percent. Of the white vote, Cook secured 44.8 percent, Massell 21.6 percent, Tate 2 percent, and Millican 31.1 percent. Northside whites gave Cook 52.2 percent of their vote; just 22.8 percent went to Massell and 23.3 percent to Millican. Massell's black vote was essential for his victory and indicated the effectiveness of his campaign strategy of appealing to black voters. In a runoff between Cook and Massell, the latter received 92.2 percent of the black vote and won on that basis, even though Tate backed Cook. Cook won 73 percent of the white vote (74.2 percent of the northside white vote). Had blacks not voted, Cook would have been elected. Jackson also won (with 97.8 percent of the black vote and 27.7 percent of the white vote). Black representation on the board of aldermen went from one to five (out of eighteen), and on the school board, black representation grew from two to three (out of ten). Although the percentage of blacks among these elected officials was still lower than their percentage of the city's population, this was a turning-point election in regard to the instability of the coalition and the increase in black officeholders.[63]

A Voteless People Is a Helpless People   **43**

As Allen commented later, "For nearly two decades the black community had been a silent partner in the election of city officials in Atlanta, generally going along with whatever moderate candidate the white business and civic fathers endorsed." This changed due to the increase in numbers of black registered voters and to the strength that Thomas Bradley showed in the Los Angeles mayor's race, which indicated that a black politician could do well in a majority white city. By 1971 the white business elite was well aware of what had occurred in the 1960s, culminating with the 1969 election. A report to the executive committee of the Atlanta Chamber of Commerce from its long-range planning committee, chaired by architect Cecil Alexander, contained this statement: "The old marriage wherein City Hall and the Chamber were practically identical in character and goals is dead." The report went on to say that "the 'junior partner' role of the black leadership in the last decade has been rejected by the black leaders. Full partnership or separatism are the two courses now open." Concluding that the chamber, which represented the white businessman, was now in the minority, "a new alliance of equals must be established with City Hall and the black leadership." The report recommended that "the initiative should rest with the Chamber to bring this about." Earlier, Alexander had suggested that an alliance between white and black business leaders be rebuilt and fortified. "This requires acknowledgement of the new political strength of the black community." He called for the involvement of black business leaders in the chamber and its committees to a greater extent than before. But the chamber was still a largely white organization, and unfortunately, neither Alexander's suggestions nor the report's recommendations were immediately supported. When a black mayor was finally elected, this situation produced damaging conflicts.[64] The chamber did not elect its first black president, Jesse Hill, until 1978.

With a black vice mayor and a white mayor indebted to the black community, blacks increased their political power noticeably. Massell fulfilled some of the goals of the black community, and as he commented later, racial considerations were clearly uppermost in his concerns and were always a part of his decision-making. He nominated and secured the appointment of the first black department heads (the first, appointed in 1971, was the director of personnel), appointed black aldermanic committee chairmen, set up the position of affirmative action officer in the personnel department, and pushed for "a goal of 50 percent minority employment in all classifications within 40 months."[65]

Yet in other ways he was a disappointment; for example, he broke a 1970 strike by the city's sanitation workers, who were mainly black. Since it was seen as a racial issue, with black workers opposing a white mayor, black leaders supported the workers. But this decision presented problems. A white mayor who had won with significant black support and received endorsements from many black leaders could not simply be rejected, because such an act would have indicated that the black leadership had made a mistake in supporting him in 1969. Black leaders thus made an effort to back the workers, while not renouncing Massell, and to end the strike. Like his predecessors, Massell also indicated that white politicians could not always be trusted to continue to fulfill the spirit of their rhetoric. While Massell had appointed blacks to all aldermanic committees in 1970 and thereby helped put black aldermen in positions where they could attack racism in various city departments and in the granting of city contracts, he backed away from this strategy in 1971 as he began making a bid to increase his white support, understanding that he would face a black opponent in 1973. Black leaders such as Ralph Abernathy and Joseph Lowery of the SCLC complained about Massell's 1971 aldermanic committee changes, which left four committees (finance, ordinance, legislation planning and development, and zoning) without black members. This change had a clear impact: by the end of his term, it was apparent that blacks were still not on a par with whites in receiving city services and higher-level city jobs. Also, the mayor's nomination and the aldermanic board's appointment of John Inman as police chief in 1972 eventually upset many in the black community, because of the chief's hiring policies and his lack of response to police brutality complaints. Finally, Massell reversed himself on some important issues, foremost of which was annexation to bring more whites into the city. Massell now supported annexation and wanted it to take place before the next mayoral election.[66]

Part of the problem may have been the different priorities black and white government leaders had for the city. A 1971 survey of Atlanta's elected and appointed officials (department heads, state legislators, judges, school board members, aldermen, and so forth) regarding policy "on all 16 program areas" (which included low-cost housing, medical care to the poor, street repair, and housing inspection) "to the extent that leadership preferences coincide with the wishes of followers, it is largely the values of whites which are represented by the city's leaders. There is almost no correlation between what blacks and city leaders would prefer to allocate money for in the program areas." Only in regard to some programs was there consistency between black and white views: street lighting, cleaning up parks, and recreation facilities for teenagers. However, this consistency

A Voteless People Is a Helpless People   **45**

did not extend to the more significant community programs that blacks supported, such as medical aid to the poor, low-cost housing, welfare, street cleaning and repair, garbage collection, and housing inspection.[67]

This survey corresponds to data in Floyd Hunter's 1980 study, which commented on policy preferences for white and black leaders in 1950 and 1970. Hunter concluded that for both years, "the political directions suggested by whites are diametrically opposed by blacks." For example, while white leaders in 1970 stressed business-oriented improvements such as airport enhancement and rapid-rail development, black leaders were primarily concerned about housing shortages, unemployment, employment discrimination, crime, and cross-town rapid transit development. In an earlier work Hunter had correctly predicted the conflict that would arise out of this divergence: "There is so little overt awareness on the part of the top leaders [white] concerning the issues that are of pressing importance to the sub-community [black] that the situation portends increased community conflict, unless structural arrangements can be utilized to communicate these issues to the community policy-makers."[68]

Although white city officials such as Allen and Massell could bring some change and address some black community problems, their priorities were often different from those of black leaders *at this time*. Again, this pushed the black community to seek a black mayoral candidate as a panacea for their problems as black registration increased to 49 percent by 1973. Only later, after the initial racial breakthrough was made for mayor, would it be seen that even black mayors could be limited in their approach and could represent not strictly racial but racial/class interests that did not serve the entire black community.

The increasing black political presence in Atlanta also could be seen in 1972, when Andrew Young was elected as fifth district congressman, with 98.5 percent of the black vote and 25 percent of the white vote. Black registered voters in this election numbered about 16,000 above those in the 1970 congressional campaign, when Young had lost. Also, white registered voters had decreased by approximately 17,000 since the 1970 election. Young's victory was also the result of the reapportionment of Georgia's congressional districts, which had been ordered by the U.S. Court of Appeals following the Supreme Court's one man–one vote decision. The U.S. attorney general considered an initial legislative redrawing of the lines in 1971 to be racially discriminatory. The second redrawing resulted in an increase in black registered voters in the district and Young's victory.[69]

By the 1973 election, Massell's tactic was to draw white voters to his side

Maynard Jackson at the opening of his mayoral campaign headquarters, June 1973
(Boyd Lewis Collection, Courtesy of Atlanta History Center)

by playing on racial fears. With Maynard Jackson as his main black opponent, Massell took as his campaign slogan "Atlanta's Too Young to Die,"
which suggested that a black mayor would destroy the city.[70] Massell
claimed that his slogan was not meant to be a racial statement but simply
one which said that he, not Jackson, was the best man for the job, and that
Jackson would not be able to run the city well. But some white newspapers, such as the *Northside News*, picked up the racial slogan for what it
was and came out in opposition to Jackson, claiming that the same thing

A Voteless People Is a Helpless People　**47**

would happen to Atlanta that had occurred in other cities with black mayors, such as Newark. The black leadership and press, except for the conservative *Atlanta Daily World* and pioneer civil rights leader Warren Cochrane, supported Jackson and were critical of Massell's introduction of an obvious racial issue into the campaign in order to win votes. Cochrane and the *Daily World* maintained that their support of Massell was based on his appointment of blacks to high policy-making positions. Not believing the time was right for a black mayor, Cochrane wanted Jackson to wait one more term—an attitude that reflected the gradualist approach of many of the older black leaders.[71]

It was clear that racial concerns would be an important factor in this election. This highly charged racial campaign—which embarrassed many members of the white power structure, who had never supported Massell anyway—led to Jackson's strong victory in a runoff, with 95 percent of the black vote and 17.5 percent of the white vote. Massell took 5 percent of the black vote and 82.5 percent of the white vote. One study confirmed that in this election, "racial composition of the precinct is by far the most important determinant of Jackson's vote." The new city council now had nine blacks and nine whites, and the school board had five blacks and four whites. The increase in black representation in both bodies was also the result of a new city charter that provided for a number of single-district elections rather than just at-large contests. At-large voting had been used to limit black election to political office, especially after the end of the white primary. With the at-large system, black population concentration did not necessarily translate into black election victories.[72]

A Racial Shift: The Jackson Administration

Jackson began his administration under the new city charter, which gave him more power (over city departments, for example) and replaced the board of aldermen with a city council. As with earlier mayors, racial issues were an important aspect of his administration. Although many of his decisions clearly were not based on racial factors, Jackson later noted that he did not "feel a day went by where we didn't make some decisions that had racial implications." He commented in a 1980s interview that "race was still a major thing, still is a major thing in Atlanta politics." As the first black mayor, he explained, he had to deal with "exaggerated white anxiety and . . . exaggerated black expectations."[73]

The mayor had definite plans to bring blacks into an equal place in the city's power structure. On one level, this strategy initially included delivery of more services to low-income black neighborhoods, appointments of black commissioners, and more minority hiring and promotions. But Jackson also wanted the black community to share in Atlanta's prosperity and economic growth. For this reason, he expanded affirmative action programs that had begun under Massell and minority business set-asides first established by the Metropolitan Atlanta Rapid Transit Authority (MARTA). Jackson developed a Minority Business Enterprise program to increase the percentage of city contracts going to black firms to about 25 percent. This policy was particularly important in relation to the building of Midfield Terminal at the city's airport. He also deposited some city funds in black-owned banks; earlier administrations had made such deposits too, but only in a meager fashion. Jackson pressured white-run banks to bring women and blacks into executive positions. Although the white-controlled banks received deposits of city money, they had no black vice presidents or black members on their board of directors. Jackson even withdrew city money from one bank that did not want to cooperate on affirmative action and equal opportunity demands, even after eighteen months' worth of discussion on the issue. In Jackson's words, "We had to move a half-million-dollar account out of a bank that would not comply with the city policy to a bank that had come in on the twenty-ninth day of a thirty-day last ultimative."[74]

Jackson's victory and first administration represented important symbolic and actual gains for the black community. As Leroy Johnson has observed, it indicated that Atlanta's blacks could achieve this office; furthermore, it provided an articulate spokesman in a powerful position who stood up to whites and thereby fortified the black community, and it opened up the chance for blacks to benefit from a booming city.[75]

Jackson's efforts to move blacks beyond a junior partnership in the city's power structure did not win support from many in the white business establishment. Their reaction, as Dan Sweat, executive director of the powerful downtown business group Central Atlanta Progress (CAP), later recalled, was between serious concern and panic. After years of working with the black community, white business and civic leaders still could not move toward a relationship of equality and therefore resented Jackson's efforts. Race was the stumbling block. The early 1970s thus represented an era of black political ascendancy and demands for power-sharing on an equal basis after decades of white paternalism and neglect and of white reactions that were based on racial concerns. As a black mayor took control, the city's previous race-based policy decisions and an unequal racial coalition led to the political-racial turmoil of the 1970s.[76]

The white business viewpoint was reflected in a September 1974 letter to Jackson from CAP president and Rich's chairman Harold Brockey. Brockey's letter was based on a CAP survey of business perceptions of the new administration. He warned that some Atlanta businesses were leaving or planning to leave the downtown area due to crime, transportation, employment, "downtown image," and racial problems. The sense was that Jackson was mismanaging the city's affairs, "not doing enough to stem the exodus of whites and businesses from the city," and diluting the government-business alliance. He was also accused of being antiwhite. This last accusation was based on Jackson's attempt to bring other groups— blacks, the poor, women—into the previous business–city hall coalition and power structure. For example, he wanted to see more blacks and women on the CAP board before he would deal with the organization. The mayor stated that he was neither antibusiness nor antiwhite.[77]

Former mayor Ivan Allen tried to bring the two sides together soon after the controversy began by bringing to the surface the race issue that was troubling many. At the same time, he revealed some white motivations for the dispute. As he said at a meeting of a large number of business executives and the mayor, "Some of us have gotten too concerned with wanting the city government to fail because it's black." Warning that "black and white racism threatens to kill off Atlanta unless there is more cooperation among local business and government leaders," he called for racial harmony. Most black leaders, according to Jackson, felt that Allen's statement regarding white motives was correct—that "there was a Vietnam-type burn-and-reclaim strategy. Let the city go to hell, blame it on the blacks and they [whites] will come back and rebuild, come back to reclaim it." Furthermore, white business leaders urged the mayor to move toward annexation and metrowide government, claiming that blacks were "selfish in wanting to maintain their dominant political power in the city." This suggestion had been made before, and for the same race-based reasons. An *Atlanta Constitution* editorial also reflected common concerns. "The city that was so proud of preserving harmonious relations between whites and blacks during the bitter civil rights struggles of the past two decades is now in severe danger of dividing along racial lines."[78]

The mayor further responded to this controversy shortly afterward. He declared, "Black people do not want to take over Atlanta. Black people want to participate and to have our influence felt in fair proportions"— something that was obvious from earlier years and should not have surprised whites. He claimed that "Atlanta's white leadership has fallen down on the job of promoting racial harmony" and stated, "'We need some more leadership from the leaders of Atlanta' on the issue of racism, which is 'the most sensitive and often unspoken [issue] in our city." Jackson asked white leaders to stand up against the race-based fears.[79]

The controversy continued throughout the mayor's first administration. An *Atlanta Journal* editorial in December 1974 accused him of demagogic actions for speaking out on behalf of low-income Atlantans. In March 1975, the *Atlanta Constitution* published a number of stories on Atlanta as "a city in crisis," where there has been a "polarization of black and white leadership." Racial divisions were also noted on the city council. Wyche Fowler, city council president, acknowledged that racial tensions and racial politics were not new. What *was* new, as he saw it, was that "we have a situation where we have a minority race, for the first time in this city being the majority, who are still trying to play minority politics, by voting together and establishing black issues and black caucuses." He also claimed that "the mayor in the past has tended to cast any opposition to his policies in racial terms." In a number of cases the council witnessed race-based voting—a legacy of earlier racial politics, when whites controlled and blacks had difficulty getting their demands met.[80]

What had occurred was a racial shift of political power that brought blacks to a position of equality. White business and political leaders resisted and complained about this shift and saw it as antiwhite. It was not antiwhite, however. In fact, Jackson made efforts to calm the white business community and understood, as he said in 1974, that "Atlanta can't prosper without city hall and business 'in bed' together." What was happening, Jackson explained, was that "blacks are merely seeking their legal rights to inclusion in Atlanta's politics and economy. We are simply taking our rightful place with whites as citizens of the city." He continued, "We wish the city to acknowledge our existence as more than an amorphous 'problem' to be patronized." Whites, however, saw their privileges threatened, their contacts with city hall jeopardized, and their economic power challenged. As Julian Bond later commented, Jackson "just upset the applecart."[81]

White coolness and occasional hostility toward Jackson, the symbol of this racial succession, did not fade easily. When the mayor ran for reelection in 1977, according to Dan Sweat, "there was an attempt to find a great white hope on the part of a lot of the business community who were up to here with Jackson at that point. There was a significant attempt to do that." Major white prospects, such as former governor Carl Sanders, decided not to run, presumably because Jackson looked too strong. However, the mayor did face opposition from Milton Farris, a white Fulton County commissioner, and Emma Darnell, a black women who had formerly been in charge of joint venture programs as Jackson's commissioner of administrative services. Jackson won reelection with 19.5 percent of the white vote and 93.2 percent of the black vote. In 1981, after a campaign in which racial issues were raised, a white hope, state representative Sidney Marcus, secured the large majority of white votes but lost to Andrew Young in race-based voting.[82]

Jackson was important as the initial black mayor who forged a new relationship with the white business and political establishment. Yet the benefits of black empowerment did not reach all black community members equally. Efforts waned in relation to low-income black needs; interest was not sustained over the years of black political control. In 1956, John Wesley Dobbs had stated that "eventually, and ultimately, most of our problems will be solved and settled at the ballot box."[83] But the vote was not enough. Problems were too entrenched after decades of neglect; federal support was inadequate; programs such as joint venture tended to favor blacks in the middle class (which also represented the background of the black mayors); and Jackson, who wanted and needed to win business support and, because of class splits in the black community, did not always support low-income black interests. A 1977 sanitation workers' strike found the mayor opposed to the workers even though he had aided them in their strike during Massell's administration. And many Atlanta black leaders, including the clergy, backed Jackson's antiunion stand. Race (support for a black mayor) and class issues were the salient ones in this case.[84] Jackson's successor, Andrew Young, worked closely and well with Atlanta's white business leaders, reestablishing an alliance between white and black elites. Young's administration was marked by support for business-oriented goals rather than support for the black poor.[85] While racial factors were significant in Atlanta's political history, and continued to be so, racial political empowerment highlighted the class-based differences in the black community and brought the class factor sharply to the surface.

CHAPTER 3

Restricting any growing population to limited land areas increases the population density, and high density is a main cause
of slums.—**Robert A. Thompson**, 1959

City Building and
Racial Patterns

Racially segregated cities exist throughout
America. In Chicago and New York as well as in Richmond and Atlanta,
blacks and whites usually live in different neighborhoods or sections of the
city. The creation of these separate racial enclaves is the result of various
perennial factors, including decades-old migration patterns, occupational
choices, and federal government and local banking appraisal and mortgage policies. Discriminatory mortgage policies, for example, were evident in Atlanta into the 1990s. By the 1980s, according to a Federal Reserve
Board study, "Atlanta ranked among the 20 worst American cities in inequality in home loans to white and minority neighborhoods."[1] Viewed

53

from a historical perspective, the racial residential pattern in Atlanta was also part of the city's long-term segregation process, designed to manipulate black residential mobility, open up only certain sections of the city for black housing, and hold on to the white population. Like lending procedures, the pattern occurred less by chance than by design and involved various tactics that reveal the role of race-based policies in the physical shaping of the city. Through zoning, urban renewal and relocation, the building and placement of public housing, annexation efforts, racial agreements on which land would be used for housing, and the use of highways and roads as dividing tools, white city leaders planned to guide and segregate the black population and maintain a majority white city. For example, the urban renewal, relocation, and public housing site selections of the 1950s and 1960s used the basic framework of a 1922 racial zoning law, with some variations.

In the period after the Civil War, black neighborhoods formed both throughout the city and beyond its limits, in the eastern, southern, and western areas bordering downtown; near railroad tracks; in industrial sections; on cheap land in the valleys and bottoms; as servants' quarters on the primarily white north side; and near the black colleges on the south and west sides.[2] As the black population grew in size (see Table 1), efforts were made to regulate the mobility and control the areas in which this increasing black population could live.

Zoning for Race

Atlanta enacted its first segregation ordinance in 1913, and subsequent ordinances or racial zoning legislation were passed in 1916, 1922, 1929, and 1931; these measures used various tactics to curtail black movement into white areas. The first laws designated city blocks by race. Then, in 1917, the United States Supreme Court declared segregation ordinances unconstitutional; as a result, in 1922 the city moved to the tactic of citywide comprehensive zoning, which included separation of the races. Racial designations for city areas were discussed not in terms of a segregation ordinance but rather in terms of land uses, building types, and tenant categories that Atlanta's white leaders felt could legally bypass the court ruling. A racial zoning designation was regarded as a property usage classification for parts of the city and therefore within the city's authority. Atlanta was divided into white and black single- and two-family dwelling sections, apartment-house areas, and racially undetermined commercial and industrial districts (see Map 1). Some dwelling and apartment-house sections were not put into either racial district. Invariably, blacks were given less land than whites for residential dwellings, and a number of their neighborhoods were classified as industrial. The racial zoning represented an effort to oversee the migration of the black community and to create buffers between white and black residential neighborhoods. Black residential sections were placed near the central business district (CBD), near industry, and in parts of the west side. The north side was classified as a white area. A white section would be rezoned for black use only if the rezoning fit in with the general plan to regulate black residential growth. Although the racial aspects of the 1922 zoning law were declared unconstitutional in 1924, racial zoning still prevailed in other efforts to pass ordinances that would maneuver around the court's ruling. For example, in 1929, a law denied any individual the right to move into a building on a street in which "the majority of the residences . . . are occupied by those with whom said person is forbidden to intermarry." A 1931 law made it illegal for "any person of either the white or colored races to move into a . . . building last occupied by persons of a different race . . . if such . . . building is situated within fifteen blocks from a public school" of the other race. Although the courts struck down all these laws, city officials nonetheless remained cognizant of what sections had been designated as appropriate for black use and continued to think of these areas as the only ones suitable for Atlanta's black citizens.[3] Zoning also continued to be used to create commercial or industrial buffers between white and black neighborhoods.

Planned Barriers and Boundaries

Zoning and racial ordinances represented only one approach to planning Atlanta along racial lines. To separate black and white areas, highways and roads were used as barriers and boundaries to hold the black community in certain areas. The first plan to use highways in this manner in Atlanta occurred in 1917, when city officials suggested a 150-foot-wide parkway that would officially divide the races along predetermined routes and curtail further black migration in certain directions. A fire that had destroyed a good deal of the fourth ward on Atlanta's east side, a district where many blacks lived, led to an attempt to replan the area with a racial dividing line in mind. The parkway, called the Grand Boulevard, would run along Hilliard Street, bounded by North Avenue on the north and Houston Street on the south. Land south of Houston and east of the parkway was designated for blacks, and the area north of Houston and west of the parkway was set aside for whites.[4] The white community would therefore

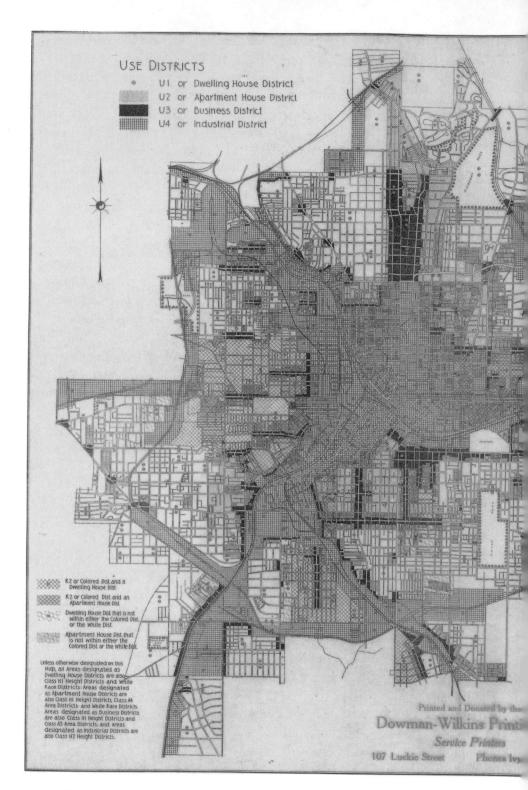

USE DISTRICTS

- U1 or Dwelling House District
- U2 or Apartment House District
- U3 or Business District
- U4 or Industrial District

R2 or Colored Dist. and a Dwelling House Dist.

R2 or Colored Dist. and an Apartment House Dist.

Dwelling House Dist. that is not within either the Colored Dist. or the White Dist.

Apartment House Dist. that is not within either the Colored Dist. or the White Dist.

Unless otherwise designated on this Map, all Areas designated as Dwelling House Districts are also Class H1 Height Districts and White Race Districts; Areas designated as Apartment House Districts are also Class H1 Height Districts, Class A4 Area Districts, and White Race Districts. Areas designated as Business Districts are also Class H1 Height Districts and Class A3 Area Districts; and Areas designated as Industrial Districts are also Class H2 Height Districts.

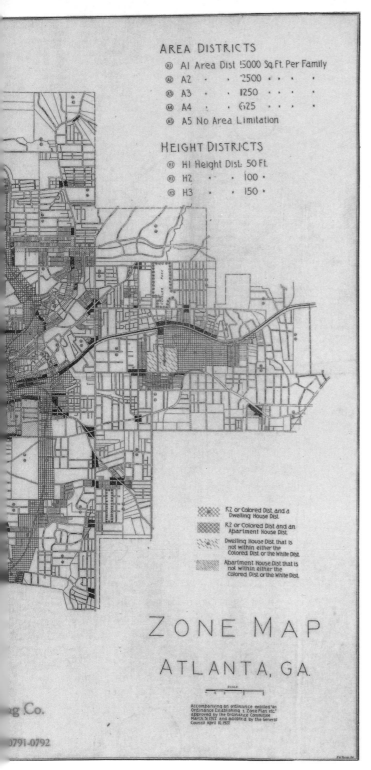

AREA DISTRICTS

Ⓐ¹ A1 Area Dist. 15000 Sq.Ft. Per Family
Ⓐ² A2 · · 2500 · · · ·
Ⓐ³ A3 · · 1250 · · · ·
Ⓐ⁴ A4 · · 625 · · · ·
Ⓐ⁵ A5 No Area Limitation

HEIGHT DISTRICTS

Ⓗ¹ H1 Height Dist. 50 Ft.
Ⓗ² H2 · · 100 ·
Ⓗ³ H3 · · 150 ·

R2 or Colored Dist. and a
Dwelling House Dist.

R2 or Colored Dist. and an
Apartment House Dist.

Dwelling House Dist. that is
not within either the
Colored Dist. or the White Dist.

Apartment House Dist. that is
not within either the
Colored Dist. or the White Dist.

ZONE MAP

ATLANTA, GA.

Accompanying an ordinance entitled "An
Ordinance Establishing a Zone Plan etc."
approved by the Ordinance Committee
March 31, 1922 and adopted by the General
Council April 10, 1922

g Co.

0791-0792

City Building and Racial Patterns **57**

control the territory closer to the business district, and the black area would be contained. Although this highway was never built, probably because the racial zoning and segregation ordinances proved more effective at the time (even after they were declared unconstitutional), the parkway proposal set a planning precedent in the city in the use of roads for segregation purposes.

Attention shifted to the west side of the city during the 1920s. Already an area of black growth, the west side eventually became migrating blacks' main destination and a major racial battleground. The push toward the west was largely the work of Heman Perry, a black realtor and developer. As one contemporary noted, "Perry wanted to get hold of the West Side before Negroes were fenced in by whites."[5] Although parts of this area were already designated for blacks under the 1922 racial zoning plan, the purchase of more land and its development into housing, plus continued black movement farther west, led to a reaction from whites.

By the 1940s, approximately 40 percent of the city's black population resided in this section, and once again highways were proposed as possible barriers. In 1941 and again in 1947, another highway (the West View Parkway) was suggested as a way of stemming black mobility. Raymond W. Torras, an engineer and the secretary of the Planning Commission, who had helped develop earlier racial zoning proposals, planned and supported the building of a parkway that would contain blacks on the west side. The design called for two parallel highways enclosing a park, which was to serve as a racial forbidden zone between black and white neighborhoods. The Planning Commission also recommended that a fence be constructed on the park sides of the roads to prevent any integrated use of the parkland. The parkway was to run "South of Mozley Drive and extending in an 'L' shaped manner east to connect with the Louisville and Nashville Railroad belt line." Whites were to have the land west of the road and blacks the territory to the east, thereby preventing further black encroachment into the westside area claimed by whites.[6] This ambitious, racially inspired roadway plan was at first delayed until after World War II; it was never constructed, but like the Grand Boulevard plan, it set the tone for what was to come.

Another predecessor to city policy from the 1950s on was Fulton County's 1947 slum clearance, which removed all black housing in the Bagley Park section of the county and used the property for a whites-only park. No plans were made for housing the displaced blacks; they were simply evicted and forced to move into Atlanta's already overcrowded black neighborhoods.[7]

Expansion Areas

The need for new residential areas for blacks became critical after World War II, as many soldiers returned home and began looking for housing. The lack of building during the war, the dearth of construction for black housing afterward, federal government mortgage insurance policies that kept blacks out of suburbia, the 1950s and 1960s highway development and urban renewal efforts that destroyed black housing, and continued black migration into Atlanta all made it obvious that black incursions into white neighborhoods were going to occur and result in violence. Sporadic bombings of black homes and other violent episodes—mostly the work of a group called the Columbians—were already taking place along fringe areas. In an attempt to avoid racial bloodshed and decide their own land needs, a group of black community leaders and real estate developers, under the auspices of the Atlanta Urban League, in 1946 established the Temporary Coordinating Committee on Housing. Out of this group's Land or Expansion Area Committee emerged, in 1947, the Atlanta Housing Council, which was to determine areas for peaceful black development. The council desired to locate housing for blacks in safe areas, for as Robert Thompson, the Atlanta Urban League's housing expert at that time, commented years later, "the town was about to explode." Six expansion areas were designated on developed land largely owned by blacks to the west, south, and north of the city near sections where blacks already resided (e.g., the Atlanta University neighborhood). Information on the choice and location of these six areas was sent to various white and black organizations, including the Atlanta Chamber of Commerce, for their endorsement. Mayor Hartsfield was also aware of the effort to find development property for blacks and worked with the initial housing committee. City officials privately agreed to these six areas when they were chosen in 1947. The city and Metropolitan Planning Commission (MPC) eventually endorsed the concept of the expansion areas publicly (in 1952, when the city expanded and absorbed most of these areas) and added additional ones (some outside the city) as safe for black migration, in its "Up Ahead" planning report. The commission's action basically acknowledged what the black community was already doing. Urban League–sponsored housing was being built in one of the westside expansion areas as of 1948 and continued into the 1950s with a number of privately funded developments in various sections—developments that were financed by both white- and black-owned banks or insurance companies and approved by city and county officials. Since the land was mostly black-owned and did not initially threaten any white neighborhoods, there was no serious opposition.[8] However, in one case "white objectors as far as two miles away had to be placated." These events and agreements were not unusual. Other cities, such as Miami, followed similar expansion scenarios.[9]

The willingness of white city officials to accept some black expansion and the black community's push for more land was also the result of the growing black political presence of the mid- to late 1940s. The mayor and other city officials now had to accommodate black housing needs somewhat.[10] However, city officials also increased their efforts to control the black population's movement. Therefore, as black voting power increased over the next few decades, the racial factor in policy decisions included both racism based on segregating the black population and racially based attempts to acknowledge and appease black discontent. For the black community, the following years became a time of forging agreements with the city on racial boundaries, trying to avoid racial violence, attempting to secure more housing, and secretly buying more westside land beyond the racial barriers and boundaries. Atlanta's blacks were never easily confined, and the black leadership was determined that whites would not decide the future of the black community. In the late 1940s, the Urban League conducted an analysis of all land on the west side and had a map noting every landowner in the area. They then convinced black professionals and real estate brokers, as well as some sympathetic whites, such as attorney Morris Abram, to quietly buy land throughout the area, enabling blacks later to leapfrog over white neighborhoods and barriers.[11]

During the 1950s and 1960s, city officials tried to avoid racial violence related to neighborhood transition from white to black. The biracial West Side Mutual Development Committee (WSMDC), established in 1952 by Mayor Hartsfield to work out racial land agreements and peaceful residential change, was active in a number of ways.[12] For example, homeowners in neighborhoods that faced possible racial transition received questionnaires designed to determine their willingness to stay or sell. In one case in 1957, residents of an east Atlanta street responded to a mail survey and were then asked to attend a meeting at the office of the Metropolitan Planning Commission "in order to determine upon a course of action that will establish your block as either a white or a Negro real estate market." Block-by-block assessments of white intentions were ascertained.[13]

In some cases, arrangements were made to buy back homes already sold to blacks. Very often, these efforts to keep some neighborhoods white were part of larger agreements that also involved highway and road development.

Highways and Roads to Racial Segregation

The black community's demands for more residential areas coincided with Atlanta's extensive highway and road building in the 1950s and 1960s. The framework for the postwar plans was set forth in 1946 in the Lochner Report, which was paid for by the Georgia State Highway Department and the Federal Public Roads Administration and requested by the City of Atlanta and by Fulton County. Completed by outside consultants, this report analyzed traffic patterns and expressway locations. After it became public, city officials became actively engaged in laying out Atlanta's highway system. The Lochner Report had been commissioned in 1944 and indicated an effort to prepare for postwar growth by planning the highway/road network. The highways and roads were to be built for the purposes of easing traffic flow around the city and subsequently furthering commercial activity and neighborhood development.[14] However, wherever the highway/road system could possibly serve a racial function, it was developed with that in mind also. During the postwar decades, some new highways became a factor in the creation of buffers and barriers to try to confine blacks to certain parts of mainly westside Atlanta. The 1950s and 1960s were periods in which the various racial uses of roads became evident, as the city attempted to maintain segregation while acknowledging the need for additional black housing.

In a 1960 report on the transitional westside neighborhood of Adamsville (see Map 2), the Atlanta Bureau of Planning noted that "approximately two to three years ago, there was an 'understanding' that the proposed route of the West Expressway [I-20 West] would be the boundary between the White and Negro communities." Before the highway was built, therefore, the city envisaged the road on Adamsville's northern perimeter as a dividing line that would stabilize this neighborhood, and marked out its route in the Adamsville area, where it intersected major streets. When black developers wanted the city's permission to build low- to moderate-income housing south of the planned highway route, they were refused because, as the planning bureau stated, the city had "obligations to the Adamsville citizens to adhere to the expressway route boundary."[15]

Racial factors were not the only consideration in planning this highway and other roads; economic concerns also played an important role and would continue to do so as new highways were planned in the 1970s and 1980s. Yet race was a significant factor in the highway layout in this neighborhood and others. In various areas, this highway was used to form a racial wall between black neighborhoods to the north and white ones to

Map 2. Atlanta's Black Population, 1950–1970

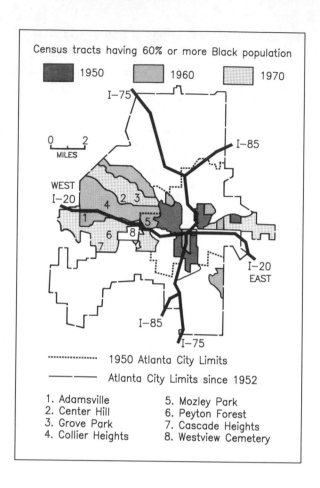

Census tracts having 60% or more Black population

■ 1950   ▨ 1960   ▫ 1970

I–75

0   2
MILES

I–85

WEST
I–20

4   2 3
1
5
6   8
7

I–20
EAST

I–85

I–75

•••••••••••••••••• 1950 Atlanta City Limits

———————— Atlanta City Limits since 1952

1. Adamsville
2. Center Hill
3. Grove Park
4. Collier Heights

5. Mozley Park
6. Peyton Forest
7. Cascade Heights
8. Westview Cemetery

the south.[16] Also, it was not unusual for white Atlantans to request from the mayor or other city officials that highways be planned and built as racial barriers. And these requests were encouraged when the city's white leaders acknowledged the use of roads, as well as urban renewal, housing projects, and industrial developments, in this way.[17]

As another part of the racial arrangements in Adamsville, houses that had been sold to blacks were bought by Southwest Inc. and the Adamsville Civic Club. Southwest Inc. was a corporation set up to prevent racial transition in southwest Atlanta. According to the WSMDC, the entry of black homeowners into part of Adamsville made it harder for white community members to secure loans. "With the previous doubt in regard to race of residents, we understand the leading institutions were not approving loans," the WSMDC stated in a letter to real estate and home mortgage brokers. "[But] the purchasing of houses by the Adamsville Civic Club and Southwest, Inc., in our opinion, assures the future of this area as part of Adamsville. The Committee has studied this matter thoroughly in consultation with real estate and finance brokers, city officials, and community leaders. We believe the area now is stable for white occupancy and hope that you will extend full home financing to persons purchasing homes in this area."[18]

In various neighborhoods, a white neighborhood association or corporation would raise money and buy back black-owned homes to establish a street as a racial boundary line. Once such a line had been established, blacks trying to buy in a white area faced significant difficulty, while "mortgage brokers have cooperated with the Mayor and Board of Aldermen by extending full financing to white buyers," according to Robert C. Stuart, MPC director for most of the 1950s.[19]

In another case a few years earlier, Mayor Hartsfield had stressed the need for the extension of an access road to be built immediately as a racial dividing line in the northwestern neighborhoods of Center Hill and Grove Park (see Map 2). "As you probably know," he said to his construction chief, "the bi-racial committee is trying to assure residents of Center Hill and Grove Park that the proposed access road will be a boundary which will protect them as Negro citizens move farther out." He urged that "something rather definite be done immediately about establishing a right-of-way for an access road" before whites in the area began to panic and sell their homes, "which would . . . make the extension of the access road rather useless as any voluntary racial boundary." Also, an effort was made to buy back homes sold to blacks. Robert Stuart noted that "the Mayor's bi-racial committee feels that with prompt action on the Access Road location and $50,000 to be used to purchase black homes, the community boundary can be permanently stabilized at the highway." He added that "if the line can be stabilized, a potentially explosive situation will have been prevented, and both racial and political attitudes will be saved strain." After stabilization, he further stated, everyone must be made aware of which parts of the area were for white or black housing, so that "a market for white homes in Center Hill and Grove Park" could be maintained.[20]

By 1960, attempts were still being made to hold the racial line. For example, the president of the Grove Park Civic League wrote to an area builder who was renting apartments to blacks, arguing, "We have had the cooperation of the city administration and the planning commission in our efforts to preserve our white community and as you know it is their desire to maintain our close-in white community." Hartsfield received a copy of this letter and replied, "We certainly wish to preserve the Grove Park neighborhood in every way possible."[21]

In both of these situations, blacks had been involved in the discussions of boundary lines. The Empire Real Estate Board, a coalition of black-owned real estate firms, met with the Adamsville Civic Club and city officials in regard to the boundary in that neighborhood, and the biracial West Side Mutual Development Committee was active in the Center Hill–Grove Park negotiations. Black involvement in any discussions of this type represented an attempt to avoid the violence that they faced from whites while securing needed land.[22] But although white leaders saw these boundary lines as final statements on the black land and housing issue, blacks viewed them as temporary and expedient; they expected to eventually cross the boundaries and barriers. Sometimes elaborate agreements were worked out to assuage whites while providing blacks with more living space. Roads were often laid out only as part of more complex racial boundary accords.

An agreement of this type was made in 1954, when the WSMDC, the Metropolitan Planning Commission, a number of white neighborhood associations, and a black firm called the National Development Company reached an accord regarding some westside white neighborhoods—for example, Collier Heights (see Map 2). The National Development Company supported a boundary agreement so as to avoid opposition from the city government in developing their desired area. The area east of a proposed access road extension was to remain white; the west was to be developed as a black community. According to the WSMDC, the road, which would be built for traffic and commercial reasons as well, would "serve as a 'Gentlemen's Agreement Line' in various locations." It would "provide an artificial line at least 200 feet wide between white Collier Heights and the future Negro development to the west." The agreement called for "no limit . . . to continued negro expansion to the west." The National Development Company agreed to sell all the lands it held east of the access road and to instead build in the west. The white community groups would help the National Development Company secure the western lots for a new black residential area. In regard to black real estate firms operating in the area, the Empire Real Estate Board stated "that it DOES NOT NOW NOR WILL ANY TIME IN THE FUTURE want to disrupt Collier Heights" and commented that both black and white real estate agents had indicated "that they will respect the integrity of white communities." Black real estate agents stopped working in the white eastern section. Furthermore, a land corporation was established to buy back any homes sold to blacks in the area designated for whites. The corporation would also buy the homes of whites who wanted to sell in an effort to prevent sales to blacks. "These homes," explained the WSMDC, would "be rented or sold to white only." Finally, the agreed-upon western site was to be approved by the Zoning Board, the Planning Commission, and the Board of Zoning Appeals, and the city promised to provide paved streets, sewers, water lines, and other amenities, which would all be "put in place," the agreement read, "before the sales [of east and west properties] . . . shall begin. . . . [Also,] Collier Drive shall be paved, free of cost to National Development Company . . . to the western limits of its property."[23]

The paving of Collier Drive illustrates another racial use of road development. In the above case, as the WSMDC noted, the paving of Collier Drive westward "will allow paved road access to the 'Crestwood Forest' Negro development without having to use Baker Ridge Drive through the Collier Heights [white] community."[24] The problem of black areas that could only be reached through white communities sometimes resulted in land being left vacant for racial purposes. For example, a report on Atlanta housing in 1961 suggested that a bridge be constructed over Proctor Creek south of Perry Homes, a black low-income housing project. The bridge "would make the land now lying vacant south of the creek politically available for Negroes by providing access to it through areas now occupied by Negroes. The land is now only approachable through the all-white Grove Park Community."[25]

Establishing already-built roads as boundaries, rather than planning them as racial dividing lines, occurred in many cities. In Atlanta, however, as new areas were developed, the paving of new roads in conjunction with old road boundaries became another use of streets for racial purposes. In the west side's Mozley Park neighborhood in the late 1940s and early 1950s, white residents attempted to establish the north side of Westview Drive as a southern boundary for black expansion (see Maps 2 and 3). In 1952, that boundary line was unofficially set when the Empire Real Estate Board agreed to accept it in return for residential concessions. But the city's role had already been determined earlier, when it allowed black developers to offer housing only up to one hundred yards of Westview Drive. Streets going from the new black housing to Westview Drive were paved only up to one hundred yards of the road. Thus, by the early 1950s, the unpaved area as well as Westview Drive itself had become the unofficial dividing line; in 1957, the strategically placed Joel Chandler Harris Homes, a low-income project for whites only, continued this barrier.[26]

Another tactic with long-term consequences for the city was simply to close off roads. That there are few continuous north-south streets in Atlanta is the result of efforts to block black expansion, particularly on the

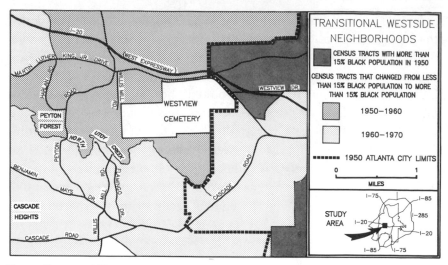

Map 3. Transitional Westside Neighborhoods, 1950–1970

west side. One example of this segregation technique was the dead-ending of Willis Mill Road (see Map 3). In the late 1950s the city and county agreed to cut Willis Mill Road five blocks south of Martin Luther King Jr. Drive (formerly Gordon Road) so that it would be impossible to drive from that street to Cascade Road. Willis Mill begins again north of Cascade. Previously, Willis Mill could be used as a north-south entrance to Cascade Heights, a white neighborhood. To prevent the southward migration of blacks into the white area, part of the road was abandoned, and over one hundred acres of land were left undeveloped between the dead-ended parts of the road. Willis Mill Road's two parts remain unconnected to the present.[27]

The best-known example of a closed-off north-south road was the short-lived Peyton Road "Wall," which attracted nationwide attention. By the early 1960s, as blacks crossed barriers and buffers and moved farther into white areas on the west side, whites reacted by overplaying their hand. When a black doctor attempted to purchase a house in the Peyton Forest subdivision in 1962, residents of this white development secured the aldermanic board's approval for the closing and barricading of sections of Peyton and Harlan Roads (see Maps 2 and 3). Both roads were used for north-south travel, and their closing was designed to maintain the white neighborhoods south of the barriers. Mayor Ivan Allen understood and approved of this undertaking and actually asked the public works committee of the aldermanic board to set up the concrete and steel barricades as racial roadblocks.[28] This action was unprecedented, as SNCC commented in a 1962 news release: "In past years, city officials have attempted to block Negro expansion by using parks, cemeteries and expressways as artificial buffer zones between whites and Negroes. The metal barricades represent the first instance of blocking roads to stop Negro housing advances." The mayor's explanation for these barricades, which newspapers dubbed the "Atlanta Wall," was to justify the wall as beneficial to both races: "I promptly decided to close off the subdivision—entrenched whites on one side, encroaching blacks on the other—with a barrier on Peyton Road. I saw it as a way of accomplishing two things: calming the white people in the neighborhood and focusing attention on the unused eight hundred acres so we could get it rezoned and put to use for low- or middle-priced housing."[29] The "eight hundred acres" refers to the undeveloped land north of Peyton Forest that had been zoned commercial to keep blacks from building homes there and to serve as a buffer. If the whites felt protected and secure, Allen argued, the eight hundred acres could be provided for blacks without opposition.[30]

Black resistance to the unilaterally decreed wall was intense. Besides strong objections from the Atlanta Negro Voters League and the Committee on Appeal for Human Rights, an All-Citizens Committee for Better City Planning (a coalition of a number of black organizations) was formed to protest the barricades and stated that "this move to wall-in Negroes will not be tolerated at election and purchasing time." The All-Citizens Committee organized a selective buying campaign to punish the white merchants who had supported the construction of the barriers. They asked Atlanta's black community not to patronize these merchants "until the City of Atlanta realizes that this is everyone's city and that we have the right to live where we choose." Some whites also opposed the barricades, since they would now be forced to drive miles out of their way to travel north. The Fulton County Superior Court ended the controversy soon after it began by ordering the barricades' removal.[31]

The embarrassing nationwide publicity of Atlanta's "Wall," which occurred at a time when the city boosters were still hailing Atlanta as "a city too busy to hate," and the strong reaction from blacks led to a greater willingness by city officials to acknowledge and respect black needs for housing on the west side. Concerned about the negative publicity, Mayor Allen called for a biracial group to come together to solve this problem. He commented, "Recommendations satisfactory to all of you [blacks and whites] would be of great help in maintaining Atlanta's very fine reputation." After this incident, there were no more blatant attempts to restrict black mobility. As the Southern Regional Council noted, "The city's planning and zoning policies once were bent toward the maintenance of racial boundaries and the confinement of the Negro population through the use of barriers and buffers. Since the Peyton Road conflict was resolved, there has been a substantial easing of such applications of public policy."[32] The black population soon moved farther out, into areas such as Cascade Heights. The WSMDC had already ceased functioning, because the agreements of earlier days were no longer needed by blacks or seen as workable by whites. Also, white and black realtors agreed that physical barriers would no longer be used to maintain segregation and that efforts would be made to ease tensions in neighborhoods undergoing racial change.[33]

The Willis Mill Road and Peyton Road attempts to block the north-south migration of blacks of all economic classes were not unique. In 1967, Samuel Adams, former director of research for the Southern Regional Council, commented, "Drive from downtown Atlanta six miles southwest through Atlanta's bulging westside Negro community on out into the unincorporated areas of Fulton County, and you will find exactly three streets that provide fairly direct access between the Negro area to the northwest and the white areas to the southwest. In a city the size of Atlanta which always is struggling to relieve traffic congestion problems, this is a situation difficult to fathom on any sound or logical basis." According to Adams, this road plan and other barriers were set up "to complicate the process of going from Negro neighborhoods to white."[34] Leon Eplan, long active as an Atlanta city planner, and commissioner of the city's Department of Budget and Planning from 1974 to 1978, commented that "streets were terminated as they passed from black neighborhoods to white ones. A map of Atlanta will show how few continuous streets traverse the urban community."[35] These racial tactics have produced long-term problems. The 1980 Atlanta Comprehensive Plan lists as major concerns for the city the traffic congestion on the west side because of the "limited street network" and "lack of adequate north-south arterial capacity."[36]

Another segregation tactic is worth mentioning, although it did not have the same dramatic effects. It was common in Atlanta for streets to change names as they passed from one racial community to the other. "Whenever streets were long and continuous," according to Leon Eplan, "sometimes these streets took on new names as the racial composition changed."[37] For example, as black migration on the east side moved in a certain direction, Boulevard north of Ponce de Leon was changed to Monroe Drive. On the west side, Hunter Street was renamed Mozley Drive as it went from black to white beyond Chappell Road. Whites who wanted these changes had to make a request to the Atlanta–Fulton County Planning Board, and apparently they had little trouble getting the board's approval. As late as 1960, the fact that blacks were moving onto a street was enough to make the board support a name change.[38]

None of the highway/road barriers lasted as racial barriers. Blacks, particularly middle-class blacks, jumped over all obstacles to their mobility— roads, railroad spurs, commercial strips, industry, or even cemeteries. For example, the elaborate agreement involving the Collier Heights area lasted only a short time. With white Collier Heights eventually bounded on both sides by black developments or black-owned property, racial transition was fast. The black community's ability to migrate relatively quickly across the west side surprised many whites in that area, according to Collier Gladin, Atlanta's chief planner from 1959 to 1965 and director of city planning from 1965 to 1979. Whites were not aware of the economic power blacks had through such black-owned institutions as the Atlanta Life Insurance Company, the Citizens Trust Bank, and Mutual Federal Savings and Loan Association of Atlanta, which provided loans for mortgages, and therefore they had expected black mobility to be much slower.[39]

Roads were more successful as instruments of displacement rather than confinement, because of the class level of the black population affected by each tactic. Displacement had its main impact on poor inner-city blacks, who had few resources to fight urban renewal and highway construction and were forced to move. Confinement was directed equally at all blacks, and many blacks on the west side had substantial economic and political resources with which to resist and thwart the process. At no time were blacks totally at the mercy of white planners and city officials. The initial movement into the west side before 1945, the effort to secure expansion land and develop housing in the area in the late 1940s and early 1950s, the negotiated land agreements, the resistance to the Peyton Road "Wall," and the usually successful attempts to leap over racial barriers and buffers in order to expand their residential area indicate that black leaders were neither powerless nor passive.

Renewal and Removal

While the black community was eventually able to deal with the barriers and buffers, it could not prevent the destruction of large parts of its eastern and southern neighborhoods for commercial and civic redevelopment and the subsequent relocation of many displaced citizens. This failure indicates that policy decisions often served the politically powerful white business elite and fit in with a long history of residential control. Economic motives were certainly evident in the revitalization of Atlanta's downtown in an attempt to enhance business activity; but from a historical perspective, renewal's other components—the large-scale relocation of a poor black population and the building and placement of public housing—reveal the continuation of a long-term effort to guide and segregate the black population. These goals were not simply incidental by-products of the economic redevelopment process. Renewal did not occur in a historical vacuum. Actually, the renewal decades of the 1950s and 1960s fit in with the long-standing uses of public power to shift and confine the black community to certain parts of the city. Urban renewal, as critics in the 1950s were inclined to say, was actually "Negro removal." Postwar redevelopment simply added to the segregative process that was already evident. The clearance of low-income housing from neighborhoods adjacent to the central business district (CBD), the building of a stadium and civic center, and the relocation and public housing problems all illustrate the racial, and to some extent class-related, functions of redevelopment, and in this way they connect postwar renewal to previous efforts to control black residential patterns.

The first phase of urban renewal, which took place in the 1950s, consisted of tearing down the slums for commercial rebuilding; in the second stage, in the 1960s, slum clearance was used for the needs of the city—a stadium, a civic center, an expressway; the third phase, in the 1970s, finally centered on the rehabilitation of the slums. In all of these stages, including the last, more housing was destroyed than was built or repaired, even though the federal government had ordered by 1968 "that a city could no longer destroy more housing than it created."[40] The large-scale elimination of housing, the relocation strategies, the setting up of racial buffers, the city's policy until 1962 to maintain segregated public housing, and the policy until 1963 not to use renewal land for public housing resulted in both a major displacement of blacks who lived near the CBD and a shortage of housing. As a result of the renewal process, by 1968, 95 percent of those displaced were black, and the majority of Atlanta's newly built or soon-to-be-constructed public housing units were located on the city's west side, with most of the rest on the southeast. No public housing was built in the affluent white northeastern part of the city. Initially, in the 1950s period of urban renewal, the Atlanta Housing Authority concluded, over black objections, that two new outlying housing projects, plus the empty units in both existing public and private housing, would be enough to handle the displaced black population.[41] They totally miscalculated the problem, or perhaps never gave it serious analysis in the first place.

It was clear from the earliest stages of the postwar renewal planning that white officials' segregative efforts would continue. Using the National Housing Act of 1949 on slum clearance and redevelopment as its justification, the all-white Metropolitan Planning Commission laid out its design for future planning in its 1952 "Up Ahead" report. This plan proposed not only the provision of land for needed black housing in particular (expansion) areas, as already noted, but also the destruction of black housing in the central city through slum clearance and the relocation (in some cases, outside the city limits) of those who were displaced. Furthermore, it was suggested that the black business enclave on Auburn Avenue be eliminated and that the business district be relocated to the western areas, indicating that more was involved than an effort to remove *low-income* blacks. T. M. Alexander, a black realtor and business leader and president of the Empire Real Estate Board, said at an MPC meeting that the Auburn Avenue suggestion "was considered especially insulting and insensitive. Comparable White business interests would not have been treated so cavalierly." Business spokesmen in the black community also complained that in addition to the fact that blacks were not consulted about "Up Ahead," the design would also leave blacks "out of the expansion of the downtown business area."[42]

Black leaders had wanted and needed the expansion areas that the Atlanta Housing Council had designated earlier but did not desire or agree to the loss of close-in housing, because both were essential for a growing black community faced with land and housing shortages. "At no time" during Atlanta Housing Council meetings on the expansion areas, the black Atlanta Business League complained, "was there any discussion of slum clearance nor any reference to relocating Negroes out of present business and housing areas." The expansion areas were planned to meet a housing emergency, deal with overcrowding, and avoid confrontations in fringe white/black neighborhoods. The Metropolitan Planning Commission took the earlier emergency plans and used them in laying out new ghettos, or, as the *Atlanta Daily World* wrote, "blueprinting segregation for the future." Atlanta University history professor L. D. Reddick prophetically warned that with this plan, "the Atlanta of the future would be more of a Jim Crow city than it is today." Furthermore, black leaders such as John H. Calhoun also saw the plan as an attempt to weaken black political power by dispersing the black voters to the outskirts of the city. Calhoun urged that black residents be allowed to return to cleared areas, which would then be protected from further blight through zoning and green-belts. Calhoun argued, "It is indeed unfortunate that we were forced to live in central areas, but since we are here, is it democratic to attempt replacement with other citizens?" While decentralization of the population was important, he continued, it should not be accomplished "at the expense of the well-being of one-fourth of the population." C. A. Scott, publisher of the *Atlanta Daily World*, also wanted black residential areas near Auburn Avenue to be maintained, and he called for the construction of improved housing for blacks in that area. Although complaints from the black community drew support from Mayor Hartsfield and secured changes in the planning report that resulted in the rejection (although only temporarily) of plans to demolish or weaken the black hold on Auburn Avenue, renewal, relocation, and public housing development eventually followed the intent of the 1952 plan (and its unconstitutional predecessors): to control black residential mobility and maintain the segregation of the black population.[43]

Initial efforts to relocate the downtown black population in surrounding neighborhoods met with strong opposition, as seen in the 1959–60 dispute over the Egleston Hospital site. Because of the need for black housing and the increasing political presence of Atlanta blacks by the late 1950s, white political leaders had to address the issue of a black housing shortage. Many white leaders also felt that it was important to shore up moderate black support through housing concessions during a time of sit-ins and protests. The black leadership remained opposed to the displacement, renewal, and relocation policies that moved blacks out of the downtown area. They still wanted public housing built in or near the CBD renewal areas. Black businessmen, in particular, were concerned that they would lose their customers as renewal destroyed black housing. The inclusion of the Butler Street area to the east of the CBD as one of the first renewal projects continued the earlier worry that the Auburn Avenue business district would be affected. In 1960, after much discussion with white and black leaders, Mayor Hartsfield agreed to support the building of a small 350-unit black public housing project east of the CBD and Butler Street renewal area, on the site where Egleston Hospital, which by 1960 had been abandoned, was located. A second site was chosen in a far-off west-side section and met little opposition. The Egleston site selection, however, caused strains in Atlanta's race relations and raised the issue of where to relocate displaced blacks. The main opposition came from Georgia Baptist Hospital, a white facility located nearby; from white churches in the area; and from white neighborhood residents. The concern was that the public housing would result in further and faster racial transition in this section of the city. Thus, both whites who supported rezoning Egleston for public housing and those who did not had as their aim the control of black residential mobility. Hartsfield commented that if the Egleston rezoning were not approved, it could result in "uncontrolled infiltration [of blacks] all over the city and very largely to the detriment of the people who are fighting this site."[44] The white business and political leadership's support was based on the desire to manipulate black migration and at the same time maintain their contacts with the black leadership.

When the board of aldermen voted against the rezoning in 1960, due to neighborhood pressure, the first director of the Department of Urban Renewal, Malcolm Jones, told Hartsfield, "I am convinced that the pressure on East Atlanta has been aggravated by the failure of the city to permit housing for Negroes on the Egleston site. This is, of course, exactly what we have been predicting would happen if adequate living space for Negroes is not provided in an orderly manner." He suggested that land be offered to blacks "even though some White people may be hurt, but where the least amount of damage be done existing White Communities." Another official who agreed with the idea that black residential mobility must be carefully guided was Thomas Parham, the MPC's housing relocation coordinator. Parham warned Hartsfield that if outlying land was not offered to blacks, white neighborhoods would face transition and the central city would become solidly black, with the "political, social, and economic consequences of which you are well aware."[45] As a result, city officials and the business elite did not abandon their efforts to direct black relocation; rather, in the 1960s they simply turned to the easier solution of putting most blacks displaced from CBD renewal into the confines of the black neighborhoods on the west side and, to a lesser extent, to the southeast of the CBD. The continuing goal was to try to hold them to certain locations in those sections with minimal infiltration into white neighborhoods, or, in the cases of the black neighborhoods still on the fringe of the CBD, to develop racial buffers. When black migration did push into white sections and racial transition was under way, these neighborhoods then became suitable for rezoning for low-income projects.[46]

While discussions went on regarding the rehousing of displaced blacks, highway development and renewal in the CBD area had continued unabated. Highways not only had the intended effect of regulating and confining black residential mobility in the western areas; they also displaced blacks in the downtown section. The east/west and north/south expressways (I-20 and I-75/85, respectively) were completed by the mid- to late 1960s and resulted in the removal of many low-income blacks in or near the CBD. While blacks had little or no input into the early planning decisions affecting highway placement, black leaders were able to sway some opinion later on. The highways did tear through black neighborhoods and displace many people, despite the black leadership's efforts. However, black leaders were influential in getting the north/south expressway moved a few blocks east when it threatened to cut through the black-owned Atlanta Life Insurance Company on Auburn Avenue and virtually destroy that street—a major close-in retail section for Atlanta's blacks. But black influence was limited in regard to the highways: the highway still cut Auburn Avenue, although in a less damaging place. Nonetheless, this retail area, clearly hurt by being cut off from many of those who patronized its stores, never recovered.[47] Again, the destruction of black neighborhoods and the negative impact on Auburn Avenue was in line with longstanding city policy.

The destroyed black housing was replaced by the expressways, the stadium (on the south), and the civic center (on the east). The initial plan for the already-cleared land that was to become the stadium site had been to build some middle-class housing there, but developers viewed that venture as risky. Pressure from the federal government's Urban Renewal Administration in 1963 made city and business leaders increasingly concerned about the rehousing problem connected with both the stadium and the civic center areas. After years of neglecting public housing in favor of slum clearance and nonresidential development, as indicated in the Housing Act of 1954, in 1963 the federal government stated that support for continued renewal in Atlanta would be granted only if applications were accompanied by consideration of and an appeal for more public housing. In response, Mayor Ivan Allen had plans for a white public housing project at the future stadium site that would serve as a racial buffer between the CBD and black communities to the south. However, black leaders protested against this plan because black housing was desperately needed in the city, and they urged the development of a black housing project. According to the planner who worked with him, Allen was caught between the white business elite, who did not want a black project on renewal land on the edge of the CBD, and the black leadership, who had helped elect him; therefore, he opted for a stadium—the building of which he had supported anyway—and asked for an economic feasibility study that would show that the stadium had to be built on that renewal property. As a result of Atlanta's constant racial tug-of-war, black housing demands were not

Urban renewal in Buttermilk Bottom. The sign says "Forrest Avenue Shoe Shop," and the photographer noted that this shop "was one of many black-owned businesses in Buttermilk Bottom which were forced out of business by urban renewal." (Boyd Lewis Collection, Courtesy of Atlanta History Center)

met in this case at a time of extreme housing shortages for black families. Instead, the stadium was put in place as a racial buffer on cleared land that had removed many blacks from near the CBD.[48]

In relation to the civic center complex, which was also one of Mayor Allen's suggestions and also served as a racial buffer, a dispute emerged in 1963 between white and black leaders. The two groups disagreed regarding the extent of black displacement, the destruction of a black school, and the need for a relocation plan before work began on the center. The area where the center was to be built was the Buttermilk Bottom section, which lay east of the downtown business district and within the Auburn Avenue business district orbit. Although the stadium and civic center were built in their respective renewal areas, the pressure from the federal government and the black community did bring some changes. To secure federal and black city and neighborhood support for his renewal and CBD strategy, Allen proposed the development of new public housing to the west (on renewal land); soon after that, he agreed to only a partial redevelopment of the Bedford-Pine renewal section, a black area that was contiguous to Buttermilk Bottom, thereby limiting the number of displaced persons in the entire area. Also, city officials made concessions on school integration and on the school that had been razed. The earlier agreement, which

City Building and Racial Patterns   **75**

called for no public housing in renewal areas, was terminated in 1963, while Allen remained under considerable pressure to provide housing.[49]

Maintaining Segregated Housing Patterns

The Egleston controversy and its aftermath; the expressway, stadium, and civic center issues; and the relocation problems in general were part of Atlanta's long-term attempt to control black residential patterns. In a statement before the Advisory Committee of the United States Civil Rights Commission, which met in Atlanta in 1967, the NAACP warned of the danger that the "'relocation program' may be used to rebuild the ghettos as *ghettos*." The organization also noted that "the pattern was established and continues through the past 25 years or more where all available housing for Negroes, publicly aided or not, has been done either in the ghetto or adjacent to it." According to interviews in 1967 with black community members who were knowledgeable about housing patterns in the city, the "interviewees repeatedly cited Expressway route location and urban renewal project location selections as being dictated by a desire to create and maintain segregated patterns of residences in the city in the past." Public housing, they maintained, "has been and is being used to force segregated housing patterns," particularly through the use of segregated housing application offices. In this way whites and blacks could be pushed in certain directions. Furthermore, some interviewees claimed that housing code enforcement "was deliberately not carried out in some areas in order to speed deterioration so that Negro families could be removed through urban renewal."[50]

The NAACP became so disturbed by the attempt to control black spatial mobility and solidify and perpetuate the ghetto that in April 1967 they asked Robert Weaver, secretary of HUD, "to withhold all funds to public housing and Urban Renewal Programs until all discriminatory practices are eliminated and a balanced dispersion of public housing units are accomplished . . . [and] to withhold funds of the Model Cities Program until Atlanta officially adopts an 'open occupancy' ordinance." The NAACP complaint to HUD also accused the city and the Atlanta Housing Authority of initially preventing blacks from being involved in Model Cities Program planning, discrimination in public housing tenant selection, and lack of service planning for public housing projects.[51] As Robert Flanagan, executive secretary of the NAACP's Atlanta branch, noted in 1967 in regard to plans for placing another public housing project on the west side, any more rezoning for public housing in western black neighborhoods "would lend confirmation to the obvious attempt by the power structure to systematically relocate Atlanta's Negro citizens to the southwest and northwest sections of the city."[52] And as part of a 1968 report to the U.S. Commission on Civil Rights, Amos Holmes of the Atlanta NAACP commented that "we must insist that the Federal and State governments have a responsibility to insure that local housing authorities and urban renewal agencies stop using public funds to entrench and extend segregation." By 1967, 88 percent of the land approved for high-density zoning was in the western and southern parts of Atlanta. While HUD did not agree with all of the NAACP's complaint, it did state in April 1967 that any further effort to put public housing just in majority black areas would be rejected unless some effort had been made to build the housing in other areas.[53]

Although land on the west side was cheaper—and Atlanta officials often cited this as the rationale for putting public housing there—the economic factor in Atlanta's racial patterns has only limited application, since public housing placement fit in with the general efforts to restrict the black population to certain parts of the city. During the Civil Rights Commission hearings that took place in Atlanta in 1967, Kenneth Wexler of the commission's Research Division stated that "segregated housing patterns in Atlanta have increased since 1940, although the economic justification for them has diminished." By 1960, more than two-thirds of the residential segregation could not be explained by differences in economic status between the races. As Atlanta's Community Relations Commission noted in 1967 regarding housing, "Race is an important factor still, no matter what the income."[54]

The appeals to HUD to halt the further construction of segregated public housing presented a dilemma for the black community. Its situation recalled that of the plaintiffs in the Dorothy Gautreaux suit—a 1966 case heard in a federal court in Chicago, in which the judge's ruling to place public housing in white areas resulted in a long-term halt in its construction. Like blacks in Chicago, blacks in Atlanta faced the question of whether to acquiesce to needed public housing no matter where it was put or to insist that this housing be dispersed into white areas. Also, there was a similar dilemma over Model Cities that sought to rehabilitate the slums. The Atlanta NAACP commented that these "programs are aimed at refurbishing the ghetto," creating "sophisticated ghettos" rather than dispersing the housing and supporting desegregation.[55] But there were benefits to be derived from accepting the racial design for Atlanta. From the early stages of renewal, the white business elite had offered the black community enticements in order to win their approval. These included promises to rehabilitate some black neighborhoods, to support the construction of 221 housing (low-cost private housing for displaced persons with incomes above the maximum for public housing), to provide the black colleges on the west side with land for expansion, and to offer construction loans. And black real estate firms could and did benefit from the business created by renewal, although in 1967 there were also some complaints about black exclusion from urban renewal's financial rewards.[56]

Dispersing Public Housing

Regardless of the consequences, Atlanta's black leaders, like Chicago's, pursued their effort to force a change in the city's housing policy. This strategy was evident in black objections to the "Up Ahead" plan, in A. T. Walden's asking the board of aldermen's Urban Renewal Committee in 1958 to build housing either "close in or easily accessible to transportation," and in later complaints. By the late 1960s, black leaders wanted the dispersal of public housing, with particular attention to fringe neighborhoods, where the housing would attract both white and black tenants.[57] The black leadership and residents of black neighborhoods were concerned that the westside areas could no longer sustain more population; the schools were already overcrowded and city services strained.[58] The black community therefore made an effort to force city officials to scatter or disperse the public housing and, in particular, to move it into the northeast, the elite white enclave. Black leaders' demands were supported by interracial groups, such as the Council on Human Relations of Greater Atlanta, and by some neighborhood organizations on the west side, such as the West End Business Men's Association. Some of the same groups supported a simultaneous movement to secure open housing and fair housing laws in order to ensure a dispersal of the black population.[59]

Thus, the mayor was faced with either adhering to the new federal guidelines and also giving in to primarily black pressure or losing all further renewal money or federal support for much-needed low-income housing. As expected, the regional administrator of HUD refused to approve further northwest sites for public housing that the mayor had suggested. Mayor Allen began looking for a solution to the problem. In the fall of 1967, the regional office of HUD relented on its ruling regarding the development of future public housing in racially identifiable areas. But Allen's housing plans still faced difficulty. For example, efforts to place public housing in the middle-class southwest area that a biracial neighborhood group worked to maintain failed in late 1967 due to neighborhood opposition and its impact on the board of aldermen. The board gave some initial consideration to service needs or racial stability problems in some westside areas slated for low- or moderate-income multifamily housing, and it rejected plans to rezone and build in late 1967 to 1969, but this concern dwindled as the area became majority black. The southwest area reaction indicates, as well, the class splits in the black community: middle-class blacks were working to keep low-income housing out of this section.[60] Their failure to do so reveals again the predominance of race over class in city policy.

In 1968, as a way out of the impasse, the Housing Resources Committee (set up by the mayor in 1966 to study housing needs and accelerate construction of low-income housing) proposed a "package deal" for the rezoning of a number of sites at once and the dispersal of low-income housing in all parts of the city.[61] The mayor was faced with a split in the white political-business leadership. The chamber of commerce supported the plan, but the board of aldermen and the Atlanta Housing Authority did not. However, while the chamber favored the general plan, it never expressed support for the specific sites where the housing was to go, and the business and political leadership never fought strongly for the "package" plan. Eventually, business support waned because of fear over the future of white neighborhoods, as well as concern that building more public housing would just bring more blacks into the city. Mayor Allen rejected the "package" plan and opted instead for a plan by which the city would consider only individual sites rather than a number of sites at any given time.[62] The only low-income housing developed from that point on was either in outlying areas or in sections earlier determined as areas for black expansion; for example, two public housing projects were placed in white areas on the east and south. Both areas were considered expendable: one was already experiencing increasing black in-migration, and both were in parts of the city that were regarded as black expansion sections. All efforts to put public housing in the affluent white northeast failed. On one occasion in 1972, a northside site that a federal-court-appointed housing committee recommended for public housing was quickly rezoned by the board of aldermen for commercial development, even though the board had turned down two earlier requests for this rezoning. The neighborhood civic association that had earlier opposed commercial zoning for this property now supported this action.[63]

Surrounding counties also remained opposed to public housing. As metro Atlanta counties saw a population surge in the 1960s, partly due to white flight from the city, their public housing agencies resisted any construction that would provide residences for Atlanta's poor. Therefore, low-income housing was built only in areas in Atlanta that were already black or were expected to be black soon.[64] The housing difficulties thus remained, further concentrating blacks in their designated ghetto areas.

White Housing Projects and the Black Community

It was not only black housing projects that were used for racial purposes; white projects also were part of the segregation design. In general, low-income projects were placed in areas in which either one or the other race predominated. As a result, according to a report by the Greater Atlanta Council on Human Relations in 1959, "racial segregation is much more complete in new housing developments than in established neighborhoods. Public housing developments have extended and strengthened patterns of segregation in some localities."[65] This effect was evident from public housing's earliest stages.

Techwood, the first federal housing project in the United States, was built in an area where the majority of inhabitants were white (72.4 percent in 1930) but where a number of blacks also lived (27.6 percent). The project was intended for use only by whites, and none of the 224 black families on the Techwood site was living in the project after its opening. As part of the effort to remove blacks from the Techwood area, the Atlanta delegation to Colonel H. B. Hackett, general manager of the Public Works Emergency Housing Corporation, recommended that the boundaries of the project be amended "in order to remove all of the colored population from the area." In terms of controlling what residential sections were available to blacks, the Atlanta representatives' intentions were clear. Techwood's building and opening in 1936 thus displaced many blacks in that neighborhood and led to a more segregated area than before (only 15.8 percent of the neighborhood population remained black by 1938), and there was an expectation that businesses and further white occupancy would soon force out the remaining blacks.[66]

In 1957, the white-only Joel Chandler Harris Homes was strategically placed on the border of a black/white fringe area, with blacks to the north and whites to the south. Before the Harris project was built, the white section was beginning to see an influx of blacks. As early as 1949, white residents had asked the mayor and council to take some action against this black incursion. Mayor Hartsfield first gave public support to the idea for a white housing project as a racial buffer in this area in 1952. The building of the project, along with a cyclone fence on its northern boundary and, as we have already seen, the city's refusal to pave one hundred yards of road connecting the black and white areas served as a barrier to protect the white West End neighborhood from black incursion. At least until 1965, long-standing vacancies at the Harris Homes were not filled with anyone from the long waiting lists of black prospective tenants, in an effort to maintain the project's role as a racial buffer.[67]

Politically Unavailable for Negro Use

The 1950s–1960s residential manipulation was made easier as a result of earlier segregation practices, which further connected renewal and relocation to their historical past. One of the problems with developing public housing sites was the earlier racially oriented zoning in Atlanta, which provided too little land for multifamily structures and too much for commercial or industrial building. A Housing Resources Committee report noted that the amount of land zoned industrial was excessive, especially in relation to the problem of finding land for low-income housing.[68] It was clear, as Mayor Allen and others acknowledged, that an artificial shortage of land for blacks had occurred because the city used zoning to develop racial buffers between black and white areas. "The result was," Allen explained, that "Atlanta city maps were dotted with scores of these unused plots of land. And this at a time when we needed all the good land we could find for housing."[69] Malcolm Jones, the director of the urban renewal department, recognized the problem as early as 1959 and commented that finding land for black housing was a major concern. "Unless solved quickly," he stressed, "this will greatly hamper the progress of the Urban Renewal program throughout the city." He called for a reanalysis of the zoning ordinances in order to meet the need for black housing.[70]

Nonetheless, there was little attempt to rezone or use land in areas of Atlanta where city officials had determined that black housing would not be built. This was true both of multifamily low-income housing and of 221 housing. Race again appeared to be the prime motivation, as indicated by a number of situations. A 1961 report on housing prepared for Atlanta's business leaders stated, "It is clear most of the additional vacant acreage within the city which is zoned for residential use is 'politically unavailable for Negro use.' " The report continued that there was an "artificial scarcity of land available for black housing in a community in which there are no natural barriers to geographic expansion and in which the white community has effective possession of considerable residential acreage which is vacant or very thinly occupied."[71] As the Atlanta Bureau of Planning stated in 1965, "it should be remembered that there would be more than enough land for construction of Negro housing as well as all that needed for whites if it were not for the restrictions inherent in our community customs." Land that was politically suitable for blacks followed the racial land patterns of earlier decades. During the 1965–67 period, applications for rezoning for high density secured the approval of the board of aldermen mainly in black areas. And this policy continued. The aldermanic zoning committee had refused to rezone a white area for apartments in 1967; in 1970, when the area had become black, it was so rezoned. As one analyst of Atlanta's zoning concluded, "It is inescapable that zoning within the City of Atlanta is utilized to preserve the status quo and to segregate the white and nonwhite populations."[72]

In regard to a controversy concerning the placement of two apartment projects in an area just north of the city limits in Fulton County, a federal judge stated in 1971, "This court is constrained to find that the only objections the county authorities have to Boatrock and Red Oak [the two projects] is that the apartments would be occupied by low-income black tenants." The Fulton County commissioners had refused to issue building permits until ordered to by the judge. Other tactics used to limit low-income black expansion were to zone for large lot sizes and square-footage floor space and for low density, which would make the zoned area too expensive for moderate- and low-income housing.[73]

Ironically, Atlanta was becoming more segregated in terms of housing and neighborhoods at the very time that lunch counters, public accommodations, and schools were being integrated. The contrast between image ("a city too busy to hate") and reality, between a city that was the headquarters of some national civil rights organizations but was becoming more and more residentially segregated, is not difficult to explain. As blacks increased their pressure on city officials to intensify the desegregation of schools and public facilities—issues that were very prominent in the newspapers of the nation—Atlanta's white leaders acquiesced, although reluctantly and slowly, rather than ruin the city's image and damage economic growth. The lessons of Little Rock and Birmingham were clear to Atlanta's white elite. However, Atlanta's racial residential patterns were not a front-page issue; this topic rarely attracted the attention of the nation's newspapers in the same way that lunch-counter desegregation did. As a result, the conscious attempt to resegregate and control black spatial mobility could be achieved more quietly, and with black demands for dispersed public housing more easily ignored.

Although there was some temporary interest in conserving rather than displacing low-income black neighborhoods and in bringing local residents into planning decisions (mainly because of the race riots during the Allen mayoralty) and federal program requirements, long-standing racial residential goals were not affected during either the Allen or Massell administrations. Nor were they seriously affected after the election of Maynard Jackson in 1973. While there was some shift in the policy of displacement and renewal under Jackson, it was again temporary. The goal for central Atlanta (an area larger than the CBD) now was to increase housing for the middle and upper classes "without relying on displacement of low and moderate income households." Any renewal that resulted in displacement should entail "no net reduction in city-wide stock accessible to the type of households displaced." For those who did not wish to move elsewhere, housing in the site area should be provided. Also, neighborhood residents were brought more clearly into the planning and development process through the creation of Neighborhood Planning Units throughout the city. But this priority shift did not last into the 1980s: the next mayor, Andrew Young, tied himself more closely to the business community (white and black), and the federal government lost interest in protecting neighborhoods undergoing redevelopment and reduced housing subsidies to cities. While class-related policies were apparent, race still remained an important part of decisions. As Leon Eplan, Jackson's commissioner of budget and planning, said in regard to policy determinations, "There are virtually no major decisions that are made in the city of Atlanta that do not have a racial factor built into it. Everything has a racial component." However, as black politicians assumed control, class divisions over policy became sharply evident in the black community. Class determined which Atlanta blacks would benefit the most. Although both Andrew Young and Maynard Jackson (after his election to a third term in 1989) promised to provide more housing for the poor and to improve their housing stock, very little was done. In the 1980s, when a domed stadium was built in Vine City, the black poor were again displaced, as they would be in the 1990s because of the development needed for the 1996 Olympics.[74]

But the damage had already been done. By 1959 the black community, which represented 35.7 percent of Atlanta's population, was confined to 16.4 percent of the land; and by 1965, blacks accounted for 43.5 percent of the city's population but occupied only 22 percent of the land, although the city contained much vacant land that was incorrectly zoned commercial or industrial. The segregation index in Atlanta increased from 87.4 in 1940 to 91.5 in 1950 to 93.6 in 1960 (the third highest in the nation) to 91.5

in 1970 as attempts were made to confine the black community through renewal displacement, public housing, and highway/road barriers. Between 1950 and 1970, census tracts that were mainly inhabited by blacks (90 percent or more) increased from 13 to 21 to 37. By 1980, just four cities, all outside the South—Chicago, Philadelphia, Cleveland, and St. Louis—"were more segregated than Atlanta."[75] Also, the 1960s policy of placing public housing mainly in one section of the city increased the number of students at already-overcrowded schools and further strained city services. Black areas became severely overcrowded by the 1960s: overcrowding in black households "was four times more frequent . . . than among white households," with 40 percent of blacks occupying rental units characterized as overcrowded.[76]

Also, those black projects placed in outlying areas, such as Perry Homes in the city's northwest section, were not near any public transportation or jobs. For years these projects were isolated and their residents' employment opportunities restricted. According to a report on Atlanta's housing completed in 1966–67, "Many Negroes have found it necessary to live in areas which are inconvenient to their place of employment. This has resulted in both higher transportation costs for low-income Negro families and in some cases has prevented Negroes from taking jobs of their choice." The report recommended that in the future officials pay more attention to the location of jobs before selecting public housing sites. As a 1975 report on public housing stated, in Atlanta there was a "tendency to construct housing units in isolated areas of the city with poor public transportation and limited access to shopping and other community facilities." The failure to locate public housing in northeastern Atlanta, in particular, resulted in removing blacks from proximity to jobs in that area. According to the Council on Human Relations of Greater Atlanta in 1966, the refusal to disperse public housing had increased the problems of those living in public housing elsewhere in the city to get to the jobs on the city's white north side. The divergence of jobs from job-seekers was just one of the consequences of Atlanta's efforts to control black spatial patterns. But generally, even in low-income black areas that were not in isolated far-off locations, according to a city report in 1967, "public facilities serving many neighborhoods where Negroes inhabit low-income housing are typically below city-wide standards. Public transportation in many of these areas is sometimes remote or unavailable."[77]

The postwar removal of black housing from some sections near the central business district and the expansion of the CBD also created an area largely devoid of neighborhoods and street life, an area that is deserted after the commuters return to the suburbs. This area reflects the truth of the Atlanta Negro Voters League's 1959 warning: "To deny Negro citizens of Atlanta the opportunity to live and spend their money in the downtown area threatens the life-blood of the Central Business District; a luxury that Atlanta cannot afford."[78]

Furthermore, the predominantly black south side of metro Atlanta, unlike the largely white north side, has experienced relatively little development into the 1990s. Northern regions have become overdeveloped and choked with traffic, while the south has been neglected and even has difficulty attracting retail investments. As Joseph Martin, director of the Atlanta Economic Development Corporation, said in 1981, "Atlanta is certainly characterized by a northward drift in new development certainly in the office sector. . . . One cannot separate that drift from housing patterns in the city. Obviously, there's a racial dimension to all of that."[79] The racial residential manipulations of earlier years has warped the economic development of the Atlanta metro area, creating in essence two separate cities—a situation that is not conducive to balanced economic growth.

On the west side, although the highway and road barriers never proved to be a long-term impediment to black expansion, they do represent costly and enduring relics of the segregation system. The laying out of certain roads as racial boundaries, the abandonment of others so that traffic would be cut between white and black neighborhoods, the use of paving to control black migration, and the effort to change street names affected the city in numerous ways, including traffic flow, the creation of distinct neighborhoods, linkages between various parts of the city, and city expansion in certain directions, as well as the endurance of racial divisions.

Annexation and a White City

While trying to regulate black movement in the city, white officials also worked to keep Atlanta a majority white city by annexing the burgeoning, predominantly white suburbs. Although Atlanta had successfully annexed surrounding areas a number of times in the nineteenth and twentieth centuries, the major absorption came in 1952 with the Plan of Improvement, which increased Atlanta's size from 37 to 118 square miles. Discussion over this plan began in the 1940s and was related to a growing black political presence, white migration to the suburbs, the need for new areas for black expansion away from white neighborhoods, and the inefficiency of parallel services in the city and county. (As early as 1912, and particularly during the late 1930s, this last factor had led to discussions on city-county consolidation rather than annexation.) While race was certainly not the only factor involved in this issue, it did play a prominent role.[80]

Mayor Hartsfield became an early and enthusiastic supporter of an annexation plan. An astute politician who worked closely with and often spoke for the white business elite, he recognized that racial changes were taking place and began considering black needs in the late 1940s. But at the same time he worked to keep Atlanta majority white, populated by the white upper middle class and upper class who supported him. During World War II, Hartsfield began to urge the annexation of Buckhead and Druid Hills, two affluent white communities to the north and east of the city, respectively. In 1943 he wrote to some influential residents in these sections that both areas would benefit in terms of taxes and water rates as well as services if they became part of Atlanta. But his argument for annexation was not based on such mundane considerations. He wrote that "the most important thing to remember, cannot be publicized in the press or made the subject of public speeches. Our negro population is growing by leaps and bounds. They stay right in the city limits and grow by taking more white territory inside Atlanta. Out-migration is good white, home owning citizens." He continued, "With the Federal government insisting on political recognition of negroes in local affairs, the time is not far distant when they will become a potent political force in Atlanta if our white citizens are just going to move out and give it to them." Claiming that his comments were "not intended to stir race prejudice because all of us want to deal fairly with them," he added, "but do you want to hand them political control of Atlanta, either as a majority or a powerful minority vote?" He urged civic leaders in the two areas to convince other residents to support annexation. "The question involves the future of our City. Shall it continue to grow and keep pace with other cities, or shall we sink into the doldrums of civic indifference and selfishness."[81] Hartsfield's thinking was based on both racial and class concerns; as the governing force in the city, he preferred affluent whites to blacks of any income level.

Annexation plans failed in the 1940s in the legislature and in a 1947 referendum that mainly concerned Buckhead, where some residents worried that they would have to pay higher taxes if they joined the city, and some supported consolidation rather than annexation. However, the issue continued to stir debate. The eventual outcome, based on a legislative study commission set up in 1949, a voter referendum in 1950, and legislative revision and support in 1951, was the Plan of Improvement, which took effect on 1 January 1952. This plan brought various unincorporated county territory (both black and white) and thirty-nine county schools within the city limits and developed a sharing of services between city and county governments. Atlanta was responsible for police, fire, parks, and sanitation services, the county for public health, and a joint Atlanta–Fulton County Planning Board was created.[82]

Although there was some opposition from whites fearful that all county schools would merge with Atlanta's system just as segregation was being challenged in the courts, whites supported the plan, because the schools remaining on county land were left out of any services consolidation.[83]

Racial issues surfaced in the Plan of Improvement discussion and vote, but these issues worked to draw white and black support to the plan. Whites, for example, were able to insure a white majority in the city as the black percentage of the city population decreased from 41 to 33 percent, and blacks saw their earlier approved western expansion areas brought within the city limits along with the corresponding black population (over 20 percent of the population in the annexed area was black). Black leaders quickly made plans to organize the western area politically.[84] But this was to be the last time these groups converged in favor of annexation. The 1960s, which brought the next major round of annexation plans, indicated markedly the racial splits in the metro community.

In the mid-1960s, white city leaders were once again concerned about the growing black population, and once again, Hartsfield (though he was no longer mayor) led the charge for annexation, hoping to bring various white suburbs—particularly Sandy Springs, to the north of the city—into Atlanta. Claiming that Atlanta might not emerge as a major city if "the proper white balance" was not maintained, he stated that "we saved Atlanta with the Plan of Improvement in 1952. We must do it again." Urging immediate action, he said that "we have only 5 or 6 more years until the racial balance is 50–50 and then on its way to further racial imbalance at an accelerated pace."[85]

The public campaign to annex Sandy Springs, backed by Hartsfield as well as Mayor Allen and the Atlanta Chamber of Commerce, was fought on the basis of taxes, fair representation in city decisions, and services, but the underlying issue was clearly racial. The *Atlanta Journal* noted that "civic leaders have registered concern that the non-white population inside city limits is increasing so rapidly that Negroes may constitute a majority within perhaps six years. To civic leaders the prospect of a Negro majority in the city holds serious sociological and political implications." A "Save Sandy Springs" booklet opposing annexation commented that "they have not stated it publicly as of yet, but another reason they say they wish us to come into the City is to help them prevent the City of Atlanta being taken over by a majority of Negro voters. . . . Spokesmen for the City of Atlanta have stated this in private meetings, and at least one head of a City department has stated this reason over the telephone." The booklet rejected annexation for a number of reasons, including the fact that there were not enough white voters in Sandy Springs to offset black voting power in Atlanta. "Past records of elections will show conclusively that the city power structure bases its ability to stay in office on being able to satisfy a Negro voting bloc. We do not have the voting power to change this power structure base. We would be drawn into the quagmire and swallowed up without even making a ripple." Opponents to annexation complained that Sandy Springs would be under black political control and that parks in the area would be ruined by those who ruined Atlanta parks for its white citizens.[86]

Hartsfield realized just before the vote that Sandy Springs would not support the annexation plan. Admitting to the actual scenario in a letter, he wrote that "the white power structure originated and wanted the annexation of this large white suburb, but in my opinion the quest for more white votes will simply result in the addition of more Negro votes." Sandy Springs voted against annexation in 1966 by a more than two-to-one ratio. As part of an agreement between white and black state legislators to have a referendum on annexation in this area, a mainly black southwest section of unincorporated Fulton County (Boulder Park) also voted on annexation of their community to Atlanta. Boulder Park voted to join Atlanta. The *Atlanta Journal* noted the irony of what had occurred: a new black area had become part of the city at a time when "Atlanta was candidly seeking to bolster the in-city white population."[87]

Hartsfield understood the implications of this vote for maintaining a white city. "This is going to be a body blow to Atlanta, because in my opinion, the Negro members of the reapportioned local delegation [to the state legislature] will not approve another Bill annexing any more white suburbs." White leaders were outsmarted in 1966 by black legislators such as state senator Leroy Johnson, who, as Hartsfield said, "demanded and got a referendum on the annexation of a large Negro section . . . as the price for the local Bill authorizing this [Sandy Springs] referendum"; nevertheless, the frantic activity to bring more white voters into Atlanta continued.[88]

By 1968–69, with the city's black population at about 47 percent and growing, and with increased black political power evident, Hartsfield and Mayor Ivan Allen feared for the future of Atlanta. Although both men—

particularly Allen—had been elected with considerable black support and owed their positions to black voters, they did not like what was happening. In a letter to Atlanta's planning director, Collier Gladin, Hartsfield spoke of a state legislative committee that was "highly interested in the idea of extending the Atlanta city limits where the white people have gone. . . . They wish us, without publicity, to get up new city lines . . . showing how the new wards would contribute to restoring the proper racial balance" by bringing in northern white communities. In 1969, Hartsfield was working on this project with state legislators as well as with some city department heads in the Allen administration. "All the problems of school re-adjustments, water mains, street maintenance, etc., Atlanta has done before and the department heads involved tell me they could easily take over and administer this territory which would restore the badly needed racial balance." Allen put it in different terms that carried the same meaning. He claimed that he did not see the problem in racial terms, then went on to state that "the established leadership of several generations is moving to the suburbs. New people are moving in without the skills of leadership and taking over responsibilities of the central city." In 1968 and 1969, some state legislators' efforts to secure bills to merge Atlanta with Fulton County and other areas into one government or to support annexation failed. Blacks saw these plans and others as attempts to offset black political strength. Even if annexation would result in a stronger tax base for the city, blacks opposed it. Many saw experiencing economic problems as preferable to losing political power and returning to the past.[89]

The most bizarre annexation scheme to keep Atlanta white involved Mayor Sam Massell, who understood that in 1973 he would face a significant challenge from a black candidate and a majority black city. Although Massell had opposed annexation or consolidation in 1969, when he won with black support, in speeches in late 1971 he raised the prospect of annexation. He spoke of both his fears of losing whites to the suburbs and his plans to rectify the situation. Before a black audience, he stressed the danger to the city's economy of losing affluent whites while more poor blacks moved to Atlanta. Putting his rhetoric in economic terms, he urged blacks to "think white" in order to keep tax-paying whites in the city. He meant that blacks should try to understand white concerns, allow whites to maintain political control in the city, and encourage measures to bring white suburbanites within Atlanta city limits and thereby insure white control. According to Massell, only a white-controlled and white majority city would be an economically viable one. Massell understood, of course, that annexation was a racial issue in terms of what could be accomplished or not and who it would hurt or not. He opted for a plan that he felt could be politically and racially acceptable and economically sound.[90]

The plan he developed to bring Atlanta back to a majority white population involved the creation of two major cities in Fulton County. Atlanta would annex areas mainly in north Fulton that would allow it to become 53 percent white (up from 49 percent) and 47 percent black (down from 51 percent) and would increase its white public school population to 35 percent. While Atlanta's white population would increase by 50,000, the black population would be enhanced by only 500. A second city would be formed to the south, with the small city of College Park as its center. While Atlanta would annex primarily unincorporated northern areas, College Park, which would remain majority white, would focus on the unincorporated sections of Fulton County to the west and south. "This North Fulton open land," according to Massell, "permits what will be predominantly white growth to maintain a competitive pace with the inner-city growth which is mostly black." White suburbanites would be within Atlanta city limits. As Massell surely knew, a two-city plan probably was the only way for white politicians to keep the city majority white. A simple merger between Atlanta and Fulton County, as a 1969 Model Cities Program study noted, would only postpone, not forestall, an eventual black majority.[91]

The black community was strongly opposed to Massell's plan. Nonetheless, the mayor tried to get it passed by the state legislature. Annexation bills failed to pass in 1972 but almost did so in 1973. The 1973 measure won support in the Georgia house and was on its way to probable victory in the senate but, ironically, was stopped in committee by segregationist lieutenant governor Lester Maddox, who was at odds with the bill's supporters over other issues.[92] Even if the bill had passed, however, it still had to secure approval from the U.S. Justice Department, a requirement of the 1965 Voting Rights Act.

Even after the 1973 election of a black mayor, annexation or consolidation plans to bring more whites into Atlanta still surfaced. None secured the necessary support, but the motives behind them remained the same. One 1975 proposal discussed in the legislature called for "all unincorporated territory in Fulton to be annexed into an existing city or formed into a new city." The "second phase of that proposal," according to an article in the *Atlanta Journal*, would "set up a commission to devise ways of 'dividing' services between the cities and the county. . . . [and] it . . . could be used as a vehicle to transfer the major municipal functions to the county." This would occur at a time when blacks had gained political control of the city. In discussing a number of these annexation/consolidation proposals, the *Atlanta Journal* article also noted that "there are other reasons for the talk about changing Atlanta's boundaries. But it seems to be the presence of blacks at the helm in—and their policies and performance[in]—City Hall that is causing much of the behind-the-scenes discussion of the issue. . . . Race—and the fact that blacks are in political control of Georgia's capital city—are clearly major reasons that the expand Atlanta movement is heating up again this year." The article continued by stating that all the proposals "would immediately dilute black voting strength to some degree." Only one, a proposal by Maynard Jackson to annex a lightly inhabited industrial area for needed tax revenues, would have retained a black voting majority in the city. Black leaders were convinced that race was a main factor behind a number of the proposals. Many white leaders said publicly that race was not the issue, or was only a minor concern. Privately, however, they admitted that race was a major issue, although not the only one, and that their motive was to regain some political control of the city government.[93]

One black legislator, Ben Brown of Atlanta, backed a county consolidation plan that would have initially reduced black voting percentages. But in this case the expectation was that the county would be majority black soon and that black voting percentages would increase, enabling blacks to control a larger area than Atlanta. As Brown stated, "We could control a larger piece of a larger pie." However, most black leaders did not want any dilution of the black vote, no matter how temporary, even if annexation would increase the city's tax revenues. As John Cox, a black community leader, put it, the annexation-consolidation controversy ultimately indicated that "blacks don't want to lose their newly gained political power and whites don't want to be ruled by blacks."[94]

As a result, the territorial growth of the city was finished, and the great white hope of land and population acquisition to offset black majorities eventually sputtered out, although annexation-consolidation plans continue to surface at times. Annexation-consolidation, Maynard Jackson commented later, was an issue in which race played an important role, an issue that is "generally analyzed with a careful eye to the racial implications." This situation never changed. The *Atlanta Journal-Constitution* reported in 1983 that "race now so dominates the issue that neither black nor white elected officials really can afford to pursue it."[95]

With its downtown, which is deserted at night; its concentrated public housing; its uneven economic development; the distance between jobs and housing for the low-income, segregated city neighborhoods; and the annexation battles that prevented city expansion and thereby the absorption of the more prosperous suburbs, Atlanta stands today as the product of decisions substantially based on long-term racial considerations that culminated in the postwar period of black population growth and mobility, neighborhood transition, urban renewal, and black political empowerment. That *some* of these city building decisions were designed to benefit the black community by controlling white violence, easing racial transition, and providing land and housing for the city's blacks does not alter their racial aspect and the effect they had on the shaping of Atlanta.

CHAPTER 4

The Atlanta Urban League believes that many of the ills which plague Atlanta's growth and prosperity stem from the lack of educational and economic opportunities of the Negro third of the population.—**Atlanta Urban League**, 1948

Race, Jobs, and Atlanta's Economy

One of the common themes that ran through Atlanta's economic history in the nineteenth and twentieth centuries was the attempt to subordinate the black community. Both public and private policy decisions left a large segment of the city's population in the lowest economic positions, although the black community, particularly through the Urban League, resisted these policies and worked to change them. For a city so concerned with economic growth, its white leaders were amazingly shortsighted to allow the city's significant black population to endure low wages, inadequate training, and persistent discrimination. Race-based policies through the decades also set the stage for the controversy over affirmative action and joint ventures, a conflict that began in the 1960s and has continued. During the period of the black mayors, race remained a shaping element in the city's economy as efforts were made to secure an equal place for Atlanta's blacks.

Pluses and Minuses

The black position in the city's economy in the early years of the century was a mixed one. There were some significant success stories. For example, Alonzo F. Herndon, who was born a slave and later became a successful barber, organized the Atlanta Mutual Insurance Association in 1905 out of a Mutual Aid Association started by two black ministers a year earlier. The Atlanta Life Insurance Company, as it came to be called, grew into one of the leading black-owned companies in the country and made Herndon a millionaire. Heman Perry, beginning in 1911, began to create a number of businesses, starting with the Standard Life Insurance Company and eventually including the Service Realty Company, Citizens Trust Bank (1921), and the Service Pharmacies. Although his businesses ultimately failed, Perry served as the inspiration and training ground for many others who took his place. Furthermore, there continued to be many black artisans and black-owned stores in the city, some of which, like barbershops, catered to a white clientele. The first black-owned bank in twentieth-century Atlanta, the Atlanta State Savings Bank, was started in 1909. Atlanta's black colleges (Morris Brown, Atlanta University, Spelman, Clark, Morehouse, and the Interdenominational Theological Center) provided the city with an educated middle class that was essential to the fight for equality in every facet of the city's life. These colleges trained many of the educators, clergy, entrepreneurs, and others who led the black community. The black colleges and the black business community worked closely together, providing each other with training and counsel.[1] Although there were class divisions within the black community, race remained the overriding issue into the 1960s. As Martin Luther King Sr. commented, "Negroes who considered themselves well off in terms of social station or economic security had only to go into downtown Atlanta to discover again just how little those things meant in a racist environment."[2]

The bulk of the black community, however, was relegated to unskilled and semiskilled manual labor or domestic and personal services. And after the 1906 race riot, in which many stores were destroyed, downtown black businesses began to abandon the downtown section and relocate to other areas, especially Auburn Avenue, which became the center of black com-

Atlanta Life Insurance building on Auburn Avenue, original structure (Courtesy of Atlanta History Center)

merce. Black business now began to serve primarily the black community and found an economic niche there. Unions added to the difficulty African Americans faced in getting hired: some Atlanta trade unions made a decided effort to deny black workers any jobs and investigated cases where blacks were said to be securing positions. Although there were some integrated black-controlled locals (e.g., the International Association of Plasterers and Cement Finishers), they were far outnumbered by white-only unions or white-run locals that discriminated against blacks by offering fewer benefits with higher initiation payments or less desirable jobs. Most black artisans did not join unions, however, either because of segregated locals or out of a sense that the unions were interested only in white workers' needs. And some secret black societies functioned as unions, as in the case of domestic workers.[3]

Replacing Black Workers

In both skilled and unskilled work, whites made a continued effort to replace blacks in the early years of the century, which culminated in the 1930s depression era. And between union policies that denied blacks apprenticeships and representation and general employer policies of hiring whites for the higher-paying jobs or not employing blacks at all, the skilled and unskilled black workers found it difficult to secure anything but the lowest-paid work with the longest hours. This situation was to endure throughout most of the twentieth century, often with the government's blessing. Ironically, though white workers may have been satisfied in their sense of race superiority, they also suffered from these policies. Low wages for blacks meant decreased wages for whites, and union hostility to blacks sometimes led to blacks' being used as strikebreakers. The end result was the impoverishment of many members of both races; and this situation, too, would persist for many decades.[4]

By 1920, blacks made up 88.8 percent of the unskilled and 32.1 percent of the semiskilled workers in the city, but only 13.3 percent of the skilled workers, 4.4 percent of the white-collar workers, 13.9 percent of the professionals, and 5.1 percent of the proprietors, bankers, managers, and officials (see Table 3). The unskilled represented 70.3 percent of the black workforce. This community profile remained fairly consistent into the 1960s, although there were a number of individual cases of upward mobility. There was also a slight decrease in the number of black women in housework between 1900 and 1920 as they moved into related fields, such as commercial laundries.[5]

Even after the large and, to many whites, disturbing migration of black workers from the state and city around World War I, there were few serious attempts to open opportunity and training to blacks. Black movement north in search of better jobs and away from repressive conditions in the South led to various efforts, forcibly and otherwise, to convince black workers to stay in Georgia. In some cases, feeble attempts were even made to improve conditions in the black communities, but little changed.[6]

Although the chamber of commerce's "Forward Atlanta" program of the mid-1920s excelled in its urban boosterism in regard to publicizing the

Table 3. Occupations by Race in Atlanta, 1920

| | Proprietors, Bankers, Managers, and Officials | | Professionals | | White-Collar Workers | |
	n	%	n	%	n	%
Blacks	405	5.1	914	13.9	987	4.4
Whites	7,575	94.9	5,658	86.1	21,245	95.6

| | Skilled Workers | | Semiskilled Workers | | Unskilled Workers | |
	n	%	n	%	n	%
Blacks	1,051	13.3	6,421	32.1	26,640	88.8
Whites	6,860	86.7	13,569	67.9	3,327	11.1

Source: Kesavan Sudheendran, "Community Power Structure in Atlanta: A Study in Decision Making, 1920–1939" (Ph.D. diss., Georgia State University, 1982), p. 51.

benefits of the city and attracting many new businesses, the economic growth did little for Atlanta's black citizens. For example, an increase in clerical jobs during this period did not result in the hiring of black women in this occupation. The Atlanta Urban League tried to open up jobs and provide training for the black community through their Free Employment Bureau and Opportunity Training School in 1924, but the 1920s did not represent a less restrictive period. Instead, this decade saw the continuation of a trend that became more pronounced soon thereafter, in the 1930s depression—the replacement of black workers with whites and an effort to limit black business contact with the white community. Whites replaced trained black truck drivers in the sanitation department, and at higher wages. This racial transfer of truck drivers occurred in private firms as well as city divisions. The Georgia Baptist Hospital fired its black workers and brought in whites at a higher wage. However, the blacks had done a much better job, and after protests from white patients, the black workers were rehired, but at their previous wage. Race took precedence over economics as experienced black workers were replaced, either permanently or temporarily, by higher-paid, untrained white workers. In regard to limiting black businesses, in February 1926 the city council passed legislation that would have denied black barbers the right to serve white customers. The small white barbers union, resentful of black success in this trade, pushed for this law. After some public outcry from whites who went to black barbers and from white community leaders who saw this legislation as excessive, another ordinance passed that only denied blacks the right to cut the hair of "white women, girls and children under 14 years of age." The city council's attention to even such minor economic restrictions illustrates the degree to which some whites wanted to control and limit black economic opportunity, and the degree to which, at least initially, the city government listened. During difficult economic times the white efforts to restrict the black business sector increased.[7]

In June 1930 an organization officially called the American Fascist Association but known as the Black Shirts appeared in the city. Their aim was to supplant blacks with whites in as many jobs as possible. The organization was at times effective in using intimidation against employers and workers to secure race replacement. At times violent, the group quickly became a concern to blacks. Reginald A. Johnson, executive secretary of the Atlanta Urban League, indicated his worries about the Black Shirts' efforts when he wrote in 1932 that "the Black Shirts and other groups have done some very intensive work in attempting to displace Negroes from their jobs here and a number of white employers and employees believe that the Negro is employed out of his just proportions and is not being affected to as great extent as whites in employment. There are continuing instances of intimidation of Negroes on jobs." Combining the depression's economic insecurities with long-term racial animosities, the organization drew thousands of whites to their parades, rallies, and meetings but actually had less than twelve hundred official members. Those who signed up with the Black Shirts' employment service were given preference in getting jobs as black workers were fired.[8]

The group was initially successful in securing supporters and some jobs because its goals were similar to existing attitudes and policies. As a result, city officials and the police did not seriously respond to the group until after the murder of Dennis Hubert, a black teenager. The organization dissipated for a number of reasons, including internal conflicts, the negative reaction to Hubert's murder, lack of backing from competing hate groups, and resistance from some employers who either refused to be intimidated or did not want to give up their low-paid black help (white workers would be paid more). The success or failure of this particular group, however, is less important than its place in the city's ongoing economic structure. While it lasted only a short time, its goals were evident in racial hiring policies before, during, and after the 1930s. There were numerous instances of whites replacing blacks in various jobs in the 1920s and after, during a period when more rural blacks were moving to Atlanta in search of jobs. As Forrester B. Washington, director of the Atlanta School of Social Work, commented, race replacement in jobs began be-

fore the economic collapse of 1929; the Great Depression merely quickened a trend that was already clear.[9]

In a report prepared for it in 1933 by the Atlanta School of Social Work,
the Atlanta Urban League cited the cases of thirteen black workers displaced in 1929, 1931, and 1932. Most had been in their jobs for years and
served as bakers, bellboys, store porters, night watchmen, waiters, shipping
clerks, janitors, cooks, busboys, and a boilermaker's helper. Five were
simply fired, and whites immediately took their jobs. The others were
pressured to quit through the lowering of their wages or were told (even in
the case of a thirty-seven-year-old) that they were too old. Some were given
a vacation and replaced by whites during their absence, and some were
driven from the job by the Black Shirts. Of the thirteen who lost their jobs,
seven did not find new jobs by 1933, and for those who did secure work,
their new wages were lower than their old. A 1936 United States Employment Service report stated that "in Atlanta practically all the hotels have
replaced Negro bell boys with white help." However, "Negro maids in the
hotels and other public places appear to be holding their own."[10]

Generally, as the depression made any job worthwhile, white workers
were willing to take positions that earlier they had seen as only suitable for
blacks and to work at lower wages than before. As one 1937 government
report related, "Economic necessity has forced the white workers into
lower occupational levels, and the tendency is to push the Negro still
further down in the scale."[11] Even federal government policies sometimes
resulted in racial replacement. For example, the minimum wages set by
the National Recovery Administration (NRA) resulted in many blacks'
losing positions to whites. As one union official commented, "If they
[employers] had to pay so much an hour, they would give the job to a
white person," or the employer might keep the black workers but institute
his own racial wage differentials. Blacks would be forced to buy their own
uniforms or food, whereas whites were provided these goods at no charge.
Blacks would thus get a lower net salary than whites, regardless of the NRA
minimum wage. Furthermore, a 1934 Atlanta Urban League report stated
that "the economic necessity, under the recovery program of the government, to discontinue many marginal jobs by combining duties, has apparently worked a greater hardship on the Atlanta Negro than any other
factor."[12] NRA policies also led to blacks' being laid off temporarily. The
Atlanta Urban League tried to correct these cases of race-based wage
differentials and job displacement, even setting up an intelligence unit to
investigate NRA-related problems. The league also became part of an

Atlanta unit of the National Emergency Advisory Council, organized in 1933 and made up of such groups as the Atlanta Negro Chamber of Commerce and the Atlanta branch of the NAACP. The council's purpose was to make blacks aware of the laws governing all the new government programs and agencies, to serve as a clearinghouse for complaints of violations and contact the federal government about these inequities, to function as a coordinating agency, and to secure black support for following NRA regulations.[13]

African Americans could lose their jobs to whites even within government agencies. The Georgia State Employment Service planned to fire its black workers in Atlanta in 1938 and replace them with whites, even in the office that served only blacks. There were also reports that the same fate was in line for other blacks staffing federal agencies such as the WPA, the Social Security Board, and so on. Lawrence A. Oxley, special representative for Negroes in the U.S. Employment Service of the Department of Labor, worked with others to prevent the firings.[14]

Unemployment and Relief

The replacement and firing policies caused great difficulties for a group already in a precarious economic situation. In 1930, blacks accounted for 90.9 percent of Atlanta's unskilled workers (see Table 4), and among all black workers, the unskilled made up 69.7 percent. Therefore, they were in jobs most readily affected by the economic collapse. Blacks in industrial jobs were the first fired, and in all jobs they generally lost their positions or had their wages reduced to a greater extent than whites. In 1932, Atlanta's black unemployed made up 50 percent of the city's total unemployed, although blacks represented only 33.3 percent of the population. In the 1931–32 period, the number of unemployed blacks rose by over 95 percent, compared to 25 percent for whites. An Atlanta School of Social Work survey of black families in need in 1933 revealed that of the 277 families interviewed, most heads of households, both male and female, were unemployed. Among the men, their previous work had been in manufacturing (e.g., carpenters), transportation (e.g., chauffeurs), domestic and personnel service (e.g., janitors), and miscellaneous (e.g., laborers). Women's occupations had been primarily as cooks, as laundresses, and in housework. The reasons for leaving their jobs for both men and women were mainly due to layoffs, sickness or accident, or employers' going out of business. And for both men and women, the largest number of unemployed workers took one to two years or more to secure employment. The

Table 4. Occupations by Race in Atlanta, 1930

	Proprietors, Bankers, Managers, and Officials		Professionals		White-Collar Workers	
	n	%	n	%	n	%
Blacks	696	7.71	1,559	16.1	797	2.65
Whites	8,329	92.3	8,184	83.9	29,184	97.3
	Skilled Workers		Semiskilled Workers		Unskilled Workers	
	n	%	n	%	n	%
Blacks	1,204	13.8	7,223	32.7	35,293	90.9
Whites	7,530	86.2	14,858	67.3	3,529	9.1

Source: Kesavan Sudheendran, "Community Power Structure in Atlanta: A Study in Decision Making, 1920–1939" (Ph.D. diss., Georgia State University, 1982), p. 51.

survey results indicated long-term unemployment based on the depression and on sickness/accidents—a comment on blacks' precarious economic situation, the level of medical care available to them, and the danger in the workplace. For those heads of households who found jobs during this period, the report stated that "the jobs these men and women held were, on the whole, less desirable, because poorer paying, than those formerly held by the unemployed wage-earner."[15]

Atlanta's black women, most of whom, in contrast to white women, had jobs as of 1930, faced a higher unemployment rate than white women. Various jobs were closed to them. For example, clerical jobs were still not available in white firms. Domestic work, which made up the bulk of black women's jobs, were also differentiated by race, with whites getting the better positions. Black professional women—for example, teachers—had fewer jobs to choose from than white women, and those jobs offered lower pay. Generally, black women's jobs decreased in number during the depression, while white women's jobs increased. As one historian of Atlanta's women during the 1930s concluded, "Throughout the Depression decade race was the primary determinant of a woman's place in the work force and of her access to public and private relief. . . . The effects of the Depression on Atlanta women differed most according to race."[16]

Relief measures also indicated a high unemployment rate for all blacks (see Table 5). And there were also some differences in the factors that led whites and blacks to apply for relief. According to an Atlanta School of Social Work report covering the years 1931–33, whites sought relief due to the economic emergency, while blacks "were the victims of long existing

Table 5. Total and Black Relief Percentages, Atlanta and Georgia, October 1933

	Percent of Total Population on Relief	Percent of Total Black Population on Relief
Atlanta	13.6	22.7
Georgia	9.5	10.9

Source: "Georgia, December 16, 1936—A Report on the Availability of the Services of the U.S. Employment Service to Negro Applicants in Georgia," Box 1385, Oxley Files, RG 183, NA.

economic evils, which were only intensified by the depression." While aiding the city's blacks, government relief efforts in Atlanta, as elsewhere in the South, favored whites in every way. At the simplest level, as a 1933 CIC report notes, blacks were "disproportionately numerous" on the bread lines because of their being last hired and lowest paid, their inability to secure positions in certain occupations, and their displacement by whites. Yet blacks had to stand in segregated lines and usually received "smaller food allowances than the whites." The Central Relief Committee of Atlanta provided black families with up to seventy-five cents weekly for food, but whites received up to $2.50. Furthermore, although more black than white women were unemployed, "white women received the majority of female emergency jobs." And when 102 families were removed from the relief rolls in 1935 due to funding problems, eighty-nine were black, and the majority of those were female-headed. In some cases, black women were more poorly treated than black men; in other situations, black men received worse treatment. Also, black men consistently had higher unemployment rates than black women. Nonetheless, in all situations during the decade, blacks were more poorly treated than whites. The Atlanta Urban League commented in 1933 in relation to the federal recovery program that "we have found ourselves faced with exclusion from some benefits, misapplication as well as mal-application of other emergency measures by many concerns and groups." The league pushed for "fairer relief practices and a greater recognition of our needs."[17]

Augusta Dunbar, a white social worker for the Federal Emergency Relief Administration (FERA) and a supervisor for the Works Progress Administration (WPA), commented later that blacks not only had to go to a different office than whites for relief aid but also had to go through separate entrances to the building that housed both offices. She revealed as well that white social workers may have "treated [blacks] more harshly"

Table 6. Fulton County WPA Employment, by Race, September 1938

	Professional, Technical, and Supervisory	Skilled	Semiskilled	Unskilled
Blacks	17	196	59	8,373
Whites	565	1,589	1,186	4,573

Source: "Study of the Unemployment Situation in Georgia, Particular Consideration Given to Fulton and DeKalb Counties by Committee on Unemployment and Racial Attitudes for Fulton-DeKalb Committee on Interracial Cooperation, 1939," Box 154, Commission on Interracial Cooperation Papers, Atlanta University Center, Robert W. Woodruff Library.

than white applicants for FERA aid. "It is quite possible that some of the white workers were harder on them [blacks] than they were on the whites." Atlanta whites had more FERA case workers than blacks, although fewer whites than blacks were on relief. As for the WPA, Dunbar stated that "on the job I feel pretty sure that they [blacks] were given different types of work. More manual labor and the whites in charge of the projects" (see Table 6). There were complaints, for example, of black women given jobs as common laborers, while white women were spared hard physical labor. Also, in one case in 1938, the city council passed a resolution stating that a sewer project using WPA funds would be reserved only for white workers. Mayor Hartsfield rejected the resolution, because he was concerned about the impact of more unemployed blacks on the city. But he stated, "Surely if there is any place for the negro on our city payroll it would be at the place where sewerage is treated." WPA work was highly desired. Blacks' average wages in WPA work were less than whites', but the gap was narrower than in private industry. Whites received less than they would have earned in private labor, but blacks' average wages were higher.[18]

The problems with the WPA are also noted in a 1939 Fulton-DeKalb Committee on Interracial Cooperation report that stated, "It is interesting to notice that less than a thousand Negroes on WPA in the entire state were classified above the unskilled level. Of the 8,645 Negroes on WPA in Fulton County only 272 were classified above the unskilled level" (see Table 6). In an early advocacy of quotas, the report suggested that "in view of an apparent tendency to generally regard Negro workers as manual or unskilled workers whenever possible, community leaders should work for a non-discrimination clause in contracts guaranteeing to Negro craftsmen a percentage of the total pay-roll for craftsmen based on occupational census ratio." This suggestion was directly based on an earlier Public

Works Administration requirement of "an employment quota for blacks of one-half of the percentage of blacks in the city work force, based on occupational statistics in the 1930 census." This requirement was first used on the Techwood and University Homes federal housing projects. Based on a percentage of black skilled laborers in relation to total skilled laborers in the city's 1930 census, black workers were provided with a specified percent of the skilled work and weekly wages on these projects. In 1939, because of the success of this plan, black painters and bricklayers asked for a nondiscriminatory clause in contracts for building new housing projects and requested that a percent of the payroll be set aside for black craftsmen. The Atlanta Urban League also supported these goals.[19]

But in many cases, given the inequality that pervaded various government programs, the black community, as usual, had to depend on itself. It did so by, for example, organizing its own relief agencies and coordinating the use of the city funds it did receive. On the neighborhood level, in 1931–32 the West Side Unemployment Relief Committee provided clothing, fuel and food to over 1,684 families, kept children in school, and offered some health care services. The Atlanta Colored Committee on Unemployment Relief, a coordinating agency formed in 1931, was made up of various local black committees. The Neighborhood Union helped with various programs dealing with unemployment, food, clothing, housing, and health care. Furthermore, under Atlanta Urban League sponsorship, a workers' council was started to aid black efforts to open up unions. Black Atlantans were also involved in campaigns to urge patronage at businesses that employed blacks and to convince other businesses to hire minorities. This goal was pursued by the Georgia Urban League and various black women's organizations in Atlanta.[20]

The work of securing a job, even with help from the available state agencies, followed the usual discriminatory pattern and did not alleviate significant long-term employment placement problems. According to a Fulton-DeKalb Committee on Interracial Cooperation study, in 1938, for example, the Georgia State Employment Service had the following private employment placements for blacks and whites (see Table 7): blacks secured very few positions as sales or clerical workers and were placed in lower-paying jobs, usually as unskilled domestic and industrial workers. Furthermore, according to this study, "The large numbers of white workers placed in domestic occupations and in industry by the Georgia State Employment Service and the Community Employment Service suggest displacement of Negro workers in these fields." The majority of the unemployed in 1938 came from semiskilled male laborers and female domestic

Table 7. Georgia State Employment Service Placements in Private Employment, by Race and Gender, Fulton County, 1938

	Domestic Workers			Clerical Workers			Salespersons			Industrial Workers		
	M	F	Total	M	F	Total	M	F	Total	M	F	Total
Blacks	380	562	942	4	0	4	6	6	12	537	60	597
Whites	295	165	460	520	137	657	196	150	346	360	77	437

Source: "Study of the Unemployment Situation in Georgia, Particular Consideration Given to Fulton and DeKalb Counties by Committee on Unemployment and Racial Attitudes for Fulton-DeKalb Committee on Interracial Cooperation, 1939," Box 154, Commission on Interracial Cooperation Papers, Atlanta University Center, Robert W. Woodruff Library.

workers, and both of these categories had heavy black representation. One of the difficulties was that many industries in Georgia either did not hire blacks or did not employ them for any but unskilled jobs. In 1938, the unemployment figures indicated the continued bias in hiring: Atlanta's blacks had a 22 percent unemployment rate, while the rate for whites was at 12 percent.[21]

Because of its numerous black colleges and black businesses, Atlanta also had many black white-collar workers. Their problem is illustrated by James Boston, an unemployed black white-collar worker who wrote to President Roosevelt in 1938 complaining that he had been waiting a year "to be placed on a project; but I was told that no preparation has been made for the Negro White Collar Workers as yet." At the relief offices, he was informed that there was no program for black white-collar workers.[22]

Discrimination clearly did not vanish during the New Deal; but in providing aid to all unemployed, including blacks, and in some cases offering training, as well as particularly helping black construction workers, New Deal agencies also had some positive impact on the black employment profile. In 1937, federal government agencies, along with support from the Julius Rosenwald Fund, were influential in the start of the depression-era Negro Occupational and Trade School. The school, however, trained blacks in the usual low-skill occupations; but during the depression the Atlanta Urban League set up courses to train skilled workers such as brickmasons and painters. Clubs of craftsmen were established as part of these courses. One such club, a group of brickmasons, was able to secure a union charter and become part of the International Brickmasons Union. And as the 1930s progressed, young black men and women

Table 8. Occupations by Race in Atlanta, 1940

	Proprietors, Bankers, Managers, and Officials		Professionals		White-Collar Workers	
	n	%	n	%	n	%
Blacks	593	5.6	1,447	15.7	1,243	3.7
Whites	10,042	94.4	7,784	84.3	32,079	96.3

	Skilled Workers		Semiskilled Workers		Unskilled Workers	
	n	%	n	%	n	%
Blacks	2,074	16.3	7,488	35.7	31,799	80.3
Whites	10,641	83.7	13,484	64.3	7,781	19.7

Source: Kesavan Sudheendran, "Community Power Structure in Atlanta: A Study in Decision Making, 1920–1939" (Ph.D. diss., Georgia State University, 1982), p. 53.

exhibited a trend toward white-collar work. The Urban League and the Atlanta School of Social Work were influential in this regard: they conducted campaigns to interest black youth in careers such as law, social work, and engineering. By the end of the depression, as the economy improved, while black percentages of Atlanta's proprietors, bankers, managers, and officials had decreased, as had black percentages of professionals and the unskilled (although at 70.8 percent, the latter still contained the large majority of all black workers), there had been a slight increase in percentages for white-collar, skilled, and semiskilled workers since 1930 (see Table 8). One illustration of the decline of proprietors was the decrease in black-owned grocery stores from 139 in 1929 to 70 in 1940.[23]

The War Years

Yet finding jobs still continued to be a problem into the World War II years. Many employers simply refused to offer jobs to blacks. According to B. F. Ashe, regional director of the Information Service, War Manpower Commission, in 1943, some employers were willing to hire blacks due to severe labor shortages in the defense industry but were stopped by the prevailing attitudes of white workers and the segregation laws: "In nearly every case where Negroes are to be employed in the same plant with whites, the employing of Negroes would necessitate the duplication of locker rooms, toilets, and many other employee facilities, the cost of which double installation is prohibitive, or too serious a consideration to make the hiring of Negroes an attractive solution for labor shortage." White workers, he continued, resented seeing blacks in any but domestic or "heavy unskilled labor jobs." Given the creation in 1941 of the President's Committee on Fair Employment Practices, which prohibited racial discrimination in hiring for government agencies and companies engaged in defense work, the above reasons might have been more an excuse to evade fair employment than anything else. A wartime job on an equal basis with whites could readily translate into a similar position in the postwar period, thereby threatening the racial status quo.[24]

The question of employing blacks in defense plants was raised particularly in relation to the Bell Aircraft factory outside the city. Blacks were barred from the training courses that led to work in the plant, although the Atlanta Urban League argued that denying blacks, a large segment of Atlanta's workforce, entry into the training program would have a negative impact on the city. Jacob Henderson, head of the league's Industrial Committee, and William Bell Jr. and A. T. Walden, the league's executive director and board chairman, respectively, tried to influence Atlanta and Georgia school board officials and the Atlanta Labor Advisory Committee to change the policy. It finally took complaints to the President's Committee on Fair Employment Practices to rectify the situation. An investigation resulted in the opening of an aircraft training school for blacks at Washington High School.[25]

Due to the delays, however, the training school did not open until October 1942, after whites had already begun their training. Blacks therefore lagged behind whites in the instructional program and in securing jobs as they became available at the plant. Nonetheless, the Atlanta Urban League was able to establish "a cooperative working relationship" with the aircraft factory managers and, on that basis, were able to obtain a number of jobs for skilled and semiskilled black workers.[26]

The Atlanta Urban League was in the forefront of the effort to open up jobs for blacks during the war years and in employment planning for the postwar period. The same people were active in a number of groups to bring about fair employment. Jacob Henderson, of the league's Industrial Committee, also was head of the Negro Citizens Committee, which in 1943 urged the Atlanta Board of Education to build a Negro Vocational School in order to diminish overcrowding at Washington High School. After the war, a training school eventually was opened where black veterans could learn various skills (e.g., auto mechanics). However, the improvements for blacks were done reluctantly and with much effort from black organizations. The resistance to opening up better training facilities and the full economic life of the city to blacks continued into the postwar years, as did black efforts to change the situation.[27]

"No Jobs Were Available"

Although the southern economy expanded during the postwar period, as some northern companies relocated, commercial aviation boomed, and industrialization quickened, there was continued resistance to black inclusion. Some Atlanta companies that needed skilled help in the mid- to late 1940s did not consider black applicants. Western Electric, which had a stated policy of hiring without concern for race or religion, refused to hire black veterans as linemen or for other skilled jobs. Blacks who had been trained in the army signal corps were turned down. Southern Bell refused to hire black men as installers or repairmen or black women as switchboard operators. AT&T ran ads in Atlanta's newspapers stating that experienced linemen "were badly needed," but the company would not hire black workers except for specific, short-term, unskilled jobs. These workers would then be fired when their particular job was completed. Robert Thompson, industrial secretary of the Atlanta Urban League, even suggested that a segregated all-black clerical staff for the black west side would be acceptable—anything to secure needed jobs. The response from the Southern Bell president, Hal Dumas, was that he liked the idea and would consider it, adding that "it is our sincere hope that we can continue to increase Negro employment in our business within the framework of the customs of the communities in which we operate." But he continued that no jobs were available at that time, even though the company was running employment ads in the local newspaper. As of 1949, little had changed for black job-seekers. A Labor Market report stated that over "a third of the total [job] openings for white workers were in clerical and sales occupations" while for blacks over half were in service positions, especially domestic work, and the rest in semiskilled and unskilled employment. Because most black job-seekers were still relegated to service, semiskilled, or unskilled occupations, they faced significant unemployment. The report concluded that "this occupational analysis in a large measure accounts for the greater percentage increase of unemployment among the non-whites than among white workers." The percentage of blacks among the total unemployed in 1949 Atlanta was higher than their percentage among the city's total population.[28]

In various jobs blacks were not considered, were put in the least skilled

Black laborers repairing Forsyth Street, 1949. This work is representative of the type of city jobs open to African Americans. (Courtesy of Atlanta History Center)

position, were denied training, or, in some cases—as with city employment—were hired but paid less than whites for equal work. The impact of the lost talent of blacks who could have fully participated in and contributed to the city's economy will never be known, but what is evident, as one white columnist for the *Atlanta Constitution* commented in 1946, is that among blacks in the mid-1940s there was a growing sense of anger and frustration regarding the absence of opportunity. This journalist correctly predicted that the city would face a period of racial upheaval unless the public began to support equal rights.[29]

Yet some change, however reluctant and inadequate, was observable. In part this change came from the success of major black institutions, such as Citizens Trust Bank, Mutual Federal Savings and Loan Association, and Atlanta Life Insurance Company. Each had illustrated the business skills evident in the black community, had furnished home mortgage and other loans to black applicants, and, along with the Atlanta University Center colleges, had provided the basis for a growing black middle class. As L. D. Milton, president of Citizens Trust, noted in 1956, the success of these black institutions had also proved to the white financial community that blacks were good mortgage, bank, and insurance risks. Milton was aware of the potential power of black money to change Atlanta. He said, "And in downtown Atlanta—as white bank presidents have abandoned segregated lines before their cashiers' windows, as department-store clerks have generally come to address Negroes politely and even allow them to try on clothes—the decisive factor has not been the citizenry's quickened sense of charity or prosperity. As the men along Auburn Avenue often murmur wryly, 'Dollars, you see, are not segregated.'" Also, good jobs were available in some areas. Federal government offices hired black clerical workers. Scripto employed black skilled workers, as did Lockheed, although complaints about discrimination in hiring, wages, promotions, and training continued for Lockheed into the 1970s.[30]

Although the black community had a vibrant economy centered on Auburn Avenue and had penetrated somewhat into the white-controlled economic life of the city, most avenues to either an integrated or an equal workforce were still blocked in the 1950s. Even when some whites considered hiring black workers it indicated the white resistance that was still evident as the city moved toward the 1960s showdown on these and other related issues. The *Atlanta Constitution* columnist and editor Ralph McGill, answering a question in 1956 in regard to a firm's possible hiring of black workers, stated that while it would be easier to do this in Atlanta than elsewhere in Georgia, "I would assume that he [the employer] would have in his plant enough extra management organization to prepare the way for an addition of Negro help. Certainly whatever he does, he should do slowly but steadily. Also, he should not over-do it." In regard to black office help, he suggested that the office manager hold a meeting of his employees "and gently break the word that he knows they will understand but he is going to have to hire one or two Negro girls to serve as file clerks."[31]

By the end of the 1950s there were still numerous jobs closed to blacks— for example, certain city jobs, including positions as firemen or building inspectors, were still closed, although black leaders had often complained to Hartsfield and other city officials, such as aldermen and the city personnel director, about the need for more city jobs for minorities. In the private sector, blacks could not get positions as truck drivers on bread, milk, beer, and candy delivery routes; office workers and clerks in department stores and pharmacies; auto mechanics; workers at Southern Bell and Western Union; and skilled workers at Atlantic Steel Company.[32] Even in federally sponsored work, black craftsmen lost out. One such case involved black painters, all union members, who were denied jobs in the construction of Atlanta's housing projects in the 1950s. Complaints to the Public Housing Authority at first brought inadequate responses. H. A. Sayles, the black secretary of Local 102 of the Brotherhood of Painters, Decorators, and Paperhangers of America, stated that he had complained for years about this discrimination. "Each time there is so much delay that the job is completed and Negro painters are not hired." In relation to Perry Homes, he reported, "after much negotiating and protests to Washington, we got one or two men on at the very end of the painting contract and now it looks like this is the same approach that is being used on the construction of another housing [project]." Out of twelve painters used for the second public housing project job, two black painters were eventually hired, but black painters still faced discrimination in relation to other government building projects, including those at Dobbins Air Force Base near the city. Local 102 found persistent neglect of black workers; white employers showed little inclination, regardless of nondiscrimination clauses in government contracts, to give blacks a fair share of the jobs.[33]

While some union locals were black, Atlanta unions generally worked against black entry into employment fields and were part of the restrictive job environment. As one report on unions noted, "Over 40 affidavits filed with the NAACP and with the President's Committee on Equal Employment Opportunity by Negro employees here in Atlanta have clearly indicated that, in many instances, on-the-job segregation and definite discrimination have persisted through a tacit understanding between union and management for which collusion would hardly be too strong a word." Some unions (e.g., those in the building trades) did not allow black members; others created segregated locals. For example, in 1961 blacks were still being kept out of the sheet metal workers' and plumbers' unions. In the electricians' union, blacks could only belong to the industrial section, not to the craft section. In one contract with management, a union demoted blacks from permanent workers to nonpermanent helpers as a way of pushing them out of the union. As nonpermanent helpers, blacks were "not covered by the terms of the contract as they related to wages, job classifications, upgrading, seniority, lay-off and termination, etc." Other cases also indicate the denial of seniority and promotions to black employees as a result of union agreements; thus, such agreements became "an effective instrument for denying equal job opportunities."[34]

Blacks often could not even find positions on the office staffs of the Atlanta locals to which they belonged and paid dues. Training as apprentices was limited as well. Also, unions worked with students at the white vocational school, but except for black Local 102, none did so at the black vocational school. The end result of such marginalization, as one survey by civil rights groups noted in 1962, was "a feeling of estrangement on the part of Negro members of the unions. The unions' frequent lack of interest in their jobs is countered by a failure on the part of Negroes to support union objectives, as has been evidenced several times in strike votes."[35] Racist policies clearly weakened the union movement in the city.

The Civil Rights Movement and Jobs

All of these many work-related grievances and frustrations were part of the civil rights protests of the 1960s. Though they initially focused on lunchroom and school desegregation, the protests also had an important component concentrating on equal employment. Both the 1960 report "A Second Look," issued by the Atlanta Committee for Cooperative Action (ACCA), and "An Appeal for Human Rights" made reference to the lack of equal employment in government positions. The ACCA report commented on the discrimination of private employers, unions, and government, which produced ratios of two hundred white to one black among bookkeepers and twenty white to one black among electricians. The "Appeal" also stated that the employment of blacks was only "in the most menial capacities." Courses for whites that were not available to blacks were noted in "A Second Look." For example, blacks could not get advanced courses preparing them for positions in law, medicine, or many engineering fields.[36]

The 1960s student protests showed forcefully the black community's role in the city's economy. Black purchasing power had increased as incomes had gone up after the war, and blacks began to use this power to try to open the city to black employment in all occupations. Whites were already worried about losing investments and industries relocating from other parts of the country; their concerns were raised further by the controversy over school desegregation and the boycotts and picketing that hit downtown stores, since these actions resulted in decreased sales. In February 1961, for example, department store sales had dropped 12 percent from sales for the same week in 1960.[37]

Regardless of the opening of the political process in Atlanta, new jobs for blacks, with few exceptions (e.g., as firemen), continued to remain closed in the early 1960s. One result was that in 1961, blacks made up about 34 percent of the total urban workforce but accounted for 41 percent of the city's unemployed. Even when inroads were made, the progress itself indicated the barriers that remained. The black firefighters, for example, were segregated in a specially built firehouse. Also, after discussions with Urban League representatives and other black leaders, such as

Q. V. Williamson, Southern Bell decided in 1961 to promote two black workers to mechanic level as part of a program to upgrade black workers, and the company was urged to bring blacks into white-collar positions as well. However, an Urban League memorandum stated that "it was made clear by the Company's officials that this program had not been projected beyond the two promotions which were referred to."[38]

The Georgia State Employment Service sent requests for skilled, technical, or professional jobs only to its white division. Requests for semi-skilled workers were also sent to the white division, and then the leftover requests were sent to its Negro division. And as a spokesman for the service stated in 1961, "If job requests are not specified as white or Negro, they usually decide according to the present custom or the pay. If it is $1.15 an hour, they send a Negro; $1.75 an hour, a white man." Discriminatory policies continued at the Employment Service at least into the mid-1960s. By that time Arthur Chapin, the U.S. Labor Department's special assistant on equal opportunity and manpower programs, had the service under "close surveillance" in order to take "corrective action" to eliminate discrimination.[39]

Public employment in city and state positions remained a particularly upsetting situation for blacks, given that Atlanta University Center college graduates needed jobs and that black political clout was on the rise. An illustration of the remaining roadblocks to black employment is the case of a black Morehouse graduate who took a housing code inspector's exam in the early 1960s. Black applicants were allowed to take this exam only after black leaders had strongly urged the city to open up the job. Although this individual scored third highest among those taking this exam, he never got the job. When he was asked to take a blood test, he did so, waited for a reply from the city office, and after a month was told that his blood test had been lost. Then the office cut off contact with the applicant. After complaints to the city's personnel director and some aldermen, the office eventually hired a black applicant (although not the original applicant, who was now told that he did not have enough experience); but obviously, it took a good amount of effort for a black to get this job. This was not the only case in which various tactics were used to deny or delay positions for qualified blacks in city, county, and state jobs. Qualifications were changed abruptly in one case in which an applicant who scored well on an exam was told that the exam was not as important as prior service (for the state); in other cases, jobs were abolished or the hiring agency simply did not respond to the black job-seeker. The result was a loss to Atlanta, as black college graduates left the city to seek employment elsewhere. In an early 1960s interview, Frankie Adams, acting head of the Atlanta University School of Social Work, noted that her school's graduates were leaving the South because of "racial barriers, salary differentials . . . [and] scarcity of job openings and very limited opportunity for promotion." She continued that "out of 124 graduates over a period of 4 years, 7 graduates have remained to work in Atlanta. Only 3 are employed by the State or Fulton County." Most went north to find employment, and this was true of jobs in other fields as well. One 1962 employment survey concluded that most graduates of the Atlanta University Center schools had to "leave Atlanta to find positions on a par with their qualifications."[40] Atlanta was clearly a community whose economy suffered due to discrimination. As the President's Council of Economic Advisors stated in 1962 in relation to racial bias and the economy, "Losses to the economy through racial discrimination result from two factors: (1) inefficiencies in the use of the labor force resulting in failure to utilize fully the existing skills of our population; and (2) failure to develop potential skills fully." Atlanta was guilty of both, as was the state. For example, black public colleges did not offer most of the technical degrees found at white public colleges.[41]

Although blacks' chances of securing a job in Atlanta was better in the public sector than in private industry, within public work it remained more difficult to get state government positions for many years. As late as 1966, the black-owned *Atlanta Inquirer* saw little movement by state government in opening jobs to blacks. The paper reported, for example, that "in August the State of Georgia advertised that 20,000 state jobs go begging. A local Negro College placement officer inquired about the positions. 'I got nothing but the run around. Our students would get worse.'" Metro Atlanta blacks had fewer workers in state government than in federal or city government. By 1973, only 3.9 percent of appointees to state boards and commissions were blacks, indicating a cause as well as an illustration of the difficulties blacks had in securing state positions. In 1968, the jobs where blacks were concentrated within city government were still mainly "the lower-paying blue-collar positions—laborers and services." Early in the 1960s, this situation was somewhat the result of a dual employment register. Mayor Allen later explained, "If you wanted a white employee you took him off the white register. If you wanted a Negro employee for a menial job, you took him off the Negro register."[42]

Within this context of increasing protests to secure jobs, Mayor Allen was under pressure from the black community to respond to the low overall level of city jobs and the general lack of these jobs for black Atlantans. In 1962 he set up a Temporary Committee for the Elimination of

Discrimination in Employment to deal with city positions. During the 1961 mayoral campaign, the Atlanta Negro Voters League had requested, particularly, "the upgrading of Negro policemen, installation of Negroes in the Fire Department and removal of the dual register for Negro and white job applicants," as well as the employment of blacks in all city departments. While the mayor complied with the first three requests, the movement of blacks into all city departments, as into the white-dominated private sector, was slow and uneven and brought about further frustrations. The problem was that it was not only an issue of firefighter and police hiring and separate job registers but also involved different qualifications for the same city job, depending on race.[43]

One indication of black disgust with Atlanta's employment situation came in 1962, when Operation Breadbasket, a group made up of Atlanta's black ministers, was organized by the SCLC under the direction of the Reverend Ralph Abernathy. According to a 1962 SCLC report, the clergy associated with this attempt to open up jobs "were moved by the terrible injustice in the area of employment which exists here in Atlanta, where it is often necessary for Negro girls with one or more years of college training to work as maids. Negro men must take their college diplomas to the Post Office to work sorting mail. Hundreds of Negro youth drop out of school in disgust each year because they know that even if they are trained, there are no jobs open to them beyond the level of menial servitude, because they are Negroes." Attempts to secure "equalization of employment" through negotiations that had gone on for two years had failed to produce any changes. Black leaders' tactics thus shifted to include boycotts of selected companies—particularly those that had significant black patronage but in most cases hired blacks only for manual or menial positions. Local food and department stores were targeted, as were larger operations, such as Coca-Cola Bottling Company. Some success was evident by 1963. For example, Southern Bakery Company stated they would promote blacks into positions then only filled by whites. Other companies followed suit over the next few years, usually only after threats, marches, boycotts, and lengthy negotiations. Nonetheless, employment problems remained. Operation Breadbasket at times worked with COAHR and SNCC, thereby increasing its persuasive powers. For example, in 1963 the three organizations came together in a large demonstration and buying boycott aimed at Rich's. Like many other Atlanta enterprises, this department store had promised to upgrade black employees but had done so only superficially. Rich's downtown store had 740 salespeople in 1963, but only six of them were black. As Ralph Abernathy, chair of Operation Breadbasket, pointed out, "Atlanta's image as a progressive city did not measure up to the facts."[44]

This realization still held true for city government jobs as well. In March 1963, the General Citizens Committee on Employment and Economic Opportunity contacted Mayor Allen and suggested changes in Atlanta's hiring process. Clarence Coleman of the Urban League had written the statement presented to the mayor. Specifically, the committee wanted "new employment opportunities for Negro workers" and the establishment of a permanent committee to end employment discrimination in city government. Months passed, and the mayor took "virtually no significant action" to redress the group's grievances. However, the black community did respond, first through an August 1963 protest report issued by a number of southside black civic leagues working with SNCC, and soon thereafter through a meeting between the mayor and an Urban League committee. Allen felt that he was dealing with discrimination at city hall; job applications already were being sent to the Urban League offices. But the league did not hear about *all* jobs. After the league did a thorough study of city hiring, Allen became convinced of the discrimination. The report looked at job classifications and turnover rates in city departments. In the sanitation department, for example, garbage truck drivers were considered the supervisors of the five-man teams assigned to each truck. In a five-year period, there was a 60 percent turnover rate for drivers, but not one black was hired for this job; for garbage collectors, the turnover rate was 30 percent, but not one white was hired. The same relationship between higher- and lower-status positions and race could also be seen in other departments. Allen agreed that change was necessary—that discrimination was evident in regard to what were considered "white jobs" and "black jobs"—and promised to correct the situation. In October 1963, at the time of the initial Atlanta Summit Leadership Conference meeting, Allen appointed a City Job Opportunities Committee and had two blacks hired as truck drivers in the sanitation department.[45]

In November 1963, as the city faced obvious problems that included hesitation and outright discrimination in city hiring and promotion, the Atlanta Summit Leadership Conference issued its "Action for Democracy" statement, which asked, among other things, for a new and quick response to a persistent and damaging employment discrimination. "The absence of equal employment opportunities is one of the key problems facing Negroes in Atlanta," the statement argued. "Discrimination in employment finds expression through making Negroes the last hired and the first fired, through assigning them to sub-standard jobs, through applying differential wage scales when Negroes and whites engage in the same type of work, through preferential employment of white workers, and through limiting the training and the up-grading of Negro workers. Even Federal Civil Service, and State, County, and City Merit Employment utilize various types of subterfuges to prevent Negroes from obtaining many jobs for which they are qualified." The document then called on public and private employers and union leaders to provide "equality of opportunity in employment, up-grading, and apprenticeship training. . . . Establish machinery in government and private places of employment for the implementation of fair employment practices [and] give serious consideration to offsetting the Negro's lack of opportunities for education and training." In a meeting the same month between Summit leaders and the administrators of Atlanta's Family and Children's Services, black leader Warren Cochrane pointedly stated that unless the employment issue is addressed, "and this goes back 100 years and . . . this includes not only housing but schools also," more blacks would be forced to go on welfare.[46]

While there was some improvement in hiring and promotions, change was slow. By the end of 1964, with considerable prodding from Summit, the Urban League, SNCC, and others, Allen already had set up a biracial committee on fair employment, and the number of blacks in city jobs had increased and, more important, had risen from thirty-six to fifty-two in classes of employment (types of jobs). For example, in the Water Works Department, there were four black mechanics in 1964; previously, there had been none. The majority of job classifications opened to blacks by 1965 had no blacks before 1963.[47] But this opening of doors was to be a long-term and frustrating process.

As parts of the South experienced an economic boom during the 1960s and Atlanta emerged as an example of Sunbelt prosperity, and as northern cities simultaneously declined, there were new economic opportunities and an increased migration of northern whites into the region and Atlanta metro area. However, as one analyst of the southern economy noted, "The sunbelt boom proceeded largely without black participation in the new prosperity." This was due not only to insufficient educational and training programs but also to persistent discrimination. Although various public and private sector jobs continued to be opened up to Atlanta blacks through the 1960s, strong levels of discrimination remained. Donald Hollowell, regional director of the Equal Employment Opportunity Commission (EEOC), stated later that while blacks in Atlanta did not have to suffer the sort of physical abuse that blacks in other places did, there was "considerable resistance to the idea of equal opportunity." The EEOC was set up to eliminate racial discrimination in hiring among firms doing business with the federal government. But due to enforcement problems, its impact in the South was small, and it "rarely forced southern employees into more than token compliance with the anti-discrimination laws."[48] Within unions, some definite progress was made, as apprenticeship programs were made available to blacks in various trades—for example, in sheet metal, electrical work, and carpentry—but discrimination continued in certain unions, such as the plumbers' union.[49]

In city government, blacks were finding positions above the lowest categories, but there was resistance from various department heads. In 1967, Summit complained to Mayor Allen about discrimination in the construction department, the need for an equal opportunity clause in the enforcement provisions of city purchasing contracts, and the need for a black to be appointed to a staff position and as a recruiter in the city's Personnel Department. Blacks also were not yet city department heads or assistant heads, and few were on a supervisory level by 1969, at the end of Allen's two terms. In response to Summit's demands, a city ordinance was approved in 1967 that stated that companies engaged in work for the city had to agree to a nondiscriminatory hiring policy.[50] Nonetheless, in many private businesses, race remained an important employment criteria. A survey of forty-eight Atlanta firms in 1968 still indicated a lack of desire to hire blacks, a negative view of the graduates of the city's black colleges ("employees . . . look to these schools to turn out clerical and selling rather than professional expertise"), and a racially restrictive promotion policy. Not only did the firms pursue recruiting techniques that bypassed blacks; they also promoted very few to positions higher than the selling or clerical categories. Of those few, "most were put into jobs that involved only contact with the black community." A survey of metro Atlanta's fifteen leading industries in 1966–67 found that white-collar jobs mainly went to whites and that blacks were overly concentrated in blue-collar jobs. Among blacks in white-collar positions, most were in lower-paying sales or clerical jobs.[51]

Federal Action

Like other programs, the federal government's efforts during the 1960s to increase job opportunities through training for the unemployed and underemployed, including many black Atlantans, did not achieve the hoped-for results. The Manpower Development and Training Act of 1962 and the Vocational Education Act of 1963 did provide needed training programs for the unemployed. But the programs' vocational courses were held either at white DeKalb Technical and Vocational School or at black Carver Vocational School; and the state employment agency, which decided what courses would be taught in each school, decidedly favored the white institution. At DeKalb, students could train to be auto mechanics; at Carver, they could only train to be auto mechanics' helpers. There were seventeen courses in Georgia's white vocational schools that were unavailable in the black ones (e.g., aviation mechanics), but there were no courses at the black vocational schools that whites did not already have at their school. Complaints about Carver's lack of a "full curriculum" predated federal programs. As a Southern Regional Council report stated regarding white school boards in the South, the thinking of whites toward vocational training for blacks was that restrictions were "justified . . . on the grounds that jobs in the crafts and technical areas as well as in sales, clerical, and other white-collar positions are not generally open to Negroes; therefore training would be costly and useless." But this logic was of course circular: because blacks were not trained for these jobs, they could never take advantage of any openings that might occur. After a suit was brought against the Atlanta Board of Education, new courses and machinery were added at Carver, and a black was allowed to take courses at the white school. The Smith-Hughes Vocational School in Atlanta was desegregated in 1963, but few blacks were initially accepted for the school.[52]

Another federal government effort was the Economic Opportunity Act of 1964. Atlanta was one of the first cities to receive funding under this act, and the city established Economic Opportunity Atlanta Inc. Part of this program was designed to set up neighborhood service centers in a targeted area to help with employment, education, and other social services. But it was not until 1968, when a new executive administrator was selected, that black families received significant attention from the agency. At first there were perceptions of racial discrimination and a sense among black leaders that a white-controlled program would do little for blacks. Basically, these programs tended to help those who were already motivated or already in a position to be employed, rather than those who were chronically unemployable due to inadequate training or other factors. Efforts to specifically target these long-term unemployed through, for example, the Atlanta Concentrated Employment Program (begun in 1967) did not succeed; reasons for its failure included ineffective counseling and the inability to secure jobs for those whom it trained. Ultimately, though, the program failed because it could not change the long-term problems in the school system or job market that had created Atlanta's unemployment and poverty. The Model Cities Program provided yet another avenue for the solution of problems. This program was set up to deal with the multifaceted issues—social, economic, and physical—that kept a targeted neighborhood poor. The program was to provide a general improvement of the conditions of life for the people of that area by coordinating the activities and planning of the various agencies that served it. Model Cities could also provide funding to supplement other agencies operating in the targeted neighborhood.[53]

All the government programs faced a seemingly intractable problem in regard to training and employment. A 1968 Community Relations Commission report cited the following as reasons for a higher black unemployment rate: racial discrimination in hiring, inadequate schools that did not provide the education necessary for the job market, lack of vocational training, "lack of job producing industry and business in some areas of the City," and recruiting channels that unintentionally excluded blacks. Unions could be added to this list: some, such as the Atlanta Plumbers and Pipefitters, still refused to admit blacks even in the late 1960s. The hiring situation, the school and vocational training inadequacies, the union policies, and even the lack of business investment in black areas were, again, the result of decades of race-based, and to a lesser extent class-based, policy decisions. Little occurred by chance; much was the result of conscious decisions in which race was a major factor.[54]

There was a sense in the city, even among whites, that black employment problems were related to earlier policy. In 1967, Eugene Paterson, editor of the *Atlanta Constitution*, wrote in regard to the unemployment in one black neighborhood that its residents were "products of inferior schooling, inflicted upon them by segregation; yet they hear whites who segregated them demanding to know why they aren't as 'qualified' for jobs now as whites are." When the board of aldermen passed its "nondiscrimination in hiring" ordinance in 1967, it also stated that the lack of public transportation hindered access to jobs in the Atlanta area and that housing segregation kept people out of neighborhoods where jobs could possibly be found. For example, blacks, who made up the majority of riders on the bus lines, found these lines inadequate in connecting them with suburban jobs, and in 1970 more than 40 percent of inner-city black workers had to travel to the suburbs for their jobs. Inadequate schools and training; black spatial patterns, along with suburban location of factories and new businesses; and transportation deficiencies all were recognized factors in the lack of jobs for Atlanta's black residents, and these problems were evident into the 1980s. Added to these factors was the decline in manufacturing jobs in the metro area since the 1950s and the increase in service and government positions.[55]

A First Step

In the Massell mayoral years, as black political power grew and awareness of the ramifications of earlier racial policy decisions increased, there were new attempts at some redress, although such attempts were primarily confined to city government employment. The situation by May 1970, five months after Massell's inauguration, still reflected the inadequate hiring policies of earlier years. Although blacks accounted for 38 percent of total Atlanta city workers, a mere 9 percent of Atlanta's minority employees had white-collar jobs; 70 percent held low-income, low-status positions—for example, as garbage collectors, janitors, and maids. While Massell had appointed blacks to some high-level positions, there was, according to a 1970 Community Relations Commission report on city hiring practices, "a large gap to be bridged in the employment of minorities in middle management, professional and technical categories." Twenty-three city departments had no minorities as officials or managers, and two had no minorities in any job. Eighteen departments did not even have a program to spur black recruitment. Most departments worked through the personnel department to recruit new workers. However, that department had only one individual for the job of securing black applicants. "He operates without any organized program," the CRC report stated, and it also noted that *"it is unreasonable to expect that one person could effectively handle minority recruitment for all of Atlanta."* However, Massell's personnel department, which had a black director as of 1971, did initiate an advertising campaign in black newspapers to encourage black job applicants. After the CRC report and based on its recommendation, the mayor began an affirmative action program, urged his department heads to hire blacks, and set a hiring goal. For government positions, the large black vote and the pressure of powerful black politicians such as vice mayor Maynard Jackson significantly changed how the city conducted itself. The city's water department, for example, still had segregated facilities in 1971. Racial segregation was eliminated only after complaints by Jackson and by aldermen Marvin Arrington and Henry Dobson.[56]

Although the majority of black city workers in 1972 were still poorly paid laborers and service workers, the percentage of professional positions filled by blacks increased from 15.2 to 19.2 in the 1970–72 period; managerial jobs grew from 7.1 to 13.5 percent. Massell's efforts represented a good first step, but after years of neglect, it was too little. And resistance from some departments continued. The mayor was unable to fulfill his goal of 50 percent minority employment in city positions. For the private sector, the federal government's efforts in 1971 to impose hiring guidelines on those bidding for federally funded projects helped blacks break some racial barriers in the building trades. Public hearings in Atlanta had revealed the extent to which blacks were kept out of the skilled trades. Black political power also had some effect on this local job situation. For example, in 1971 black aldermen were able to secure the employment of black apprentices in some of the city's craft union jobs.[57]

Black Political Control and Jobs

Maynard Jackson's election was expected to be the turning point for full black participation in Atlanta's economy, and to a certain extent it was. He played a key role in pushing through a number of long-needed programs to bring Atlanta's blacks into the city's economic mainstream. However, given the city's past racist hiring policies, the reaction was somewhat predictable. With a black mayor leading the city, the effort to redress past employment inequities caused an uproar in the white business community.

The mayor's affirmative action efforts increased the percentage of blacks in city government jobs in the 1973–78 period (the beginning of Jackson's second term) from 41.5 to 55.6 percent; to some extent, this increase reflects the result of his hiring the city's first affirmative action officer. (This position had been established under Massell but was left unfilled until Jackson's first term.) Of those in professional positions in public employment, black percentages increased from 19.2 to 42.2 percent from 1973 to 1978; the number of black managers increased from 13.5 to 32.6 percent between 1972 and 1978, and during the Jackson years their numbers included a black woman who worked as personnel director.[58] A number of elements came together at this point to increase the percentage of blacks in government jobs. For example, the prohibition against employment discrimination in the private sector that was part of the 1964 Civil Rights Act was expanded by the 1972 Equal Employment Opportunities Act to encompass jobs in state and local government as well. Through annual reports to the Equal Employment Opportunity Commission, cities had to show that they were not discriminating in hiring. Furthermore, under Jackson a greater effort at recruiting blacks was made; standardized tests, although still used, had less significance in hiring; and a residency requirement for appointed city workers was enacted.[59]

The mayor's desire to increase the number of city contracts going to black-owned firms also had some impact on black employment. In the 1973–78 period, the percentage of city funds paid to black firms increased from 2 to 33 percent. Companies interested in doing business with the city had to agree to minority hiring goals as a result of the Finley Ordinance, which was passed by the city council after Jackson became mayor. The position of city contract compliance officer was created to establish the goals and insure agreement. Out of these hiring goals and companies' initial difficulty in meeting them came the joint venture program that allowed a white-owned company and a minority-owned company to jointly bid on and fulfill a contract. As in other southern cities with black mayors who supported such initiatives, this approach did help black firms and thereby their employees to secure city work, but in Atlanta—and perhaps elsewhere—it was primarily black business owners and the black middle class that benefited. Under a Minority Business Enterprise (MBE) program, approximately 25 percent and then eventually 35 percent of city government business was required to be contracted to minority firms outright (through contracts or subcontracts) or through joint ventures. The contract compliance office oversaw the procedure, and this task—not employment opportunities—became its main concern.[60]

The number of black-owned firms in metro Atlanta showed significant increases by the early 1980s due to government contracts, although there were problems related to prior racial policies and relationships. A 1986 report on minority business development listed the following problems as a legacy of discrimination: "persistence of inaccurate preconceptions underestimating MBE capabilities among white leaders and businesses; insufficient capital, stemming from inordinate difficulty obtaining loans and from the comparative poverty generated by lack of equal educational, employment, and business opportunities; exclusion of minorities from informal business networks; restricted MBE access to non-minority markets; disproportionately weak technical and management skills, traceable to educational inequality and shortage of business role models." Many minority businesses still faced barriers into the 1990s based on previous and current racial discrimination. Also, aiding low-income blacks by increasing job opportunities became of secondary interest: this goal was unenforced by the city, which only asked that businesses make a good-faith effort to pursue it.[61] These approaches, while clearly important, were perhaps like the federal government programs in that they came too late and provided too little, particularly to low-income blacks.

On the upper levels, although blacks moved into decision-making positions in city government and the number of blacks in white-collar jobs and in the upper-income brackets increased, the private sector still showed significant resistance. Jackson had great difficulty in getting banks to agree to promote blacks and women to executive jobs or to put them on their boards of directors. A Community Relations Commission report issued in 1979 stated that blacks held only three of the 458 total positions on the governing boards of fifty-three white-owned Atlanta firms. However, for some black entrepreneurs, there was better news. By the 1980s, Atlanta had four out of twenty of the country's biggest black-owned firms, including Atlanta Life Insurance Company and H. J. Russell Construction Company.[62]

In the lower income levels, employment conditions remained dismal. Jackson's affirmative action, MBE, and other economic uplift efforts did not benefit all. This was partly the result of the focus of the mayor's programs, which stressed economic development for the city as a way to help the poor. This approach was based on the concept that as the city's economy expanded, all Atlantans would benefit. But it did not happen this way. In 1980, blue-collar jobs still accounted for "seven out of every ten Atlanta black workers." The unemployment rate for the city's whites was 4.1 percent in 1980; for blacks, it was 10.5 percent—up from 7.3 percent in 1969.[63] A 1983 report stated that Atlanta's high unemployment rate was due to a "mismatch between existing jobs and skills of the city's labor force." Office, managerial, and technological positions were increasing, while unskilled and semiskilled jobs were decreasing, partly because they were moving to the suburbs. City efforts to bring more lower-skilled jobs into the city failed. Atlanta experienced a net loss of over eight thousand manufacturing jobs between 1970 and 1978, while during the same period these jobs increased in the suburbs by more than twelve thousand. Another problem was the inability of poor blacks to secure housing in nearby counties where factory jobs were locating. This mismatch had been evident at least since the late 1960s, when 30 percent of all metro Atlanta jobs could be found in the inner city, but those jobs (largely white-collar) did not fit the blue-collar and service employment needs of that area's population. Of blacks employed in the Atlanta metro area in 1969, more than 70 percent worked in the blue-collar or service area, partly because of long-inadequate schools, lack of job training, and employment discrimination. There were jobs in the city, but they were the wrong jobs for the skill and educational levels of the inner-city population. As a result, even when the city's economy was good—for example, in 1969—many inner-city blacks could not find jobs. Particularly for black women, discrimination and the lack of skills and education were more the problem than an inability to get to suburban jobs: a number of white-collar office jobs would have been available to them in the downtown area if they had had the skills. Also, Atlanta had a decreasing percentage of the metro area's private-sector jobs from 1970 to 1985.[64]

Although there was some improvement over the years, it was more geared to the middle class, which had the skills and education needed. By 1980, 31 percent of Atlanta's black families, as opposed to 7 percent of whites, were classified as below the poverty line. The large majority of the city's poor were black, and almost half "were concentrated in areas of high poverty"—a legacy of earlier housing and urban renewal policies. Newark was the only major U.S. city that had a higher percentage of its poor in concentrated poverty sections. Another notable occurrence was the movement out of the city of many middle-class blacks into south Fulton and south DeKalb Counties during the 1970s and 1980s; their departure increased the percentage of poor black families among total black families in the city.[65]

Black political empowerment did open up jobs, particularly in government service and through affirmative action and minority set-asides. Atlanta's economic climate for blacks improved under a black mayor in ways that it did not, and perhaps could not, under whites. That serious problems remained for the black poor indicates numerous variables—for example, city policies that favored the black middle class, long-term lack of training and education, the loss of low-skilled jobs to the suburbs, the lack of transportation to and housing in the suburbs for poor blacks, the inadequacies of federal and city job training programs, and persistent racial discrimination.[66] Specific race-based policies were used in the attempt to move blacks into economic equality, just as they had been used earlier to deny blacks their place. Through both white and black administrations, race remained a prime factor in the shaping of the city's economy, but class too played a role, particularly as blacks came into political control. If race- and, subsequently, class-based policies helped to create the economic problems of Atlanta by the 1980s, race- and class-based policies must be used more extensively to solve them and to deal with the legacy of misguided past policies.

City Services and City Institutions

A community is going to pay the price for decent housing and the good life whether or not it obtains these blessings. The price may be in terms of high welfare costs, high hospital charges, high police costs. . . . The community has the choice, however, of paying an equivalent amount of money and obtaining good housing and a decent community as preventive measures.

—Citizens Crime Committee of Atlanta, 1959

CHAPTER 5

We know Atlanta to be a city where restrictions because of race
in all areas are the rule and the practice rather than the exceptions. *We can no longer tolerate these restrictions.* This is not a
matter which can be solved piecemeal or gradually, for a man
cannot become a whole man "in pieces" or gradually.

—**Atlanta Summit Leadership Conference**, 1963

Where the Sidewalk Ends:
Urban Services and Race

A. Overview

The case of Atlanta's African American pop-
ulation illustrates that disfranchised and segregated groups can easily be
neglected in regard to city services. Because their political power was
limited into the 1960s and they were pushed into distinct geographical
areas, blacks could expect little help from city government. Funds and
attention were concentrated on white neighborhoods, particularly middle-
class ones. Although some poor white areas experienced inadequate services, indicating a class factor in service delivery, it appeared that the main
issue was race, not class. To some extent, blacks of *all* classes found themselves in areas that received the least attention and money from city gov-

ernment throughout most of the twentieth century. As a result, street paving, streetlights, sanitation services, parks and other recreational spaces, health care, police and fire protection, and mass transit in black communities periodically suffered. The long-term neglect of basic services in black neighborhoods, the unequal disbursement of recreational areas and health care, the effectiveness of the police and fire departments, and the efficiency and development of mass transit systems were all tied to racial factors and helped shape the city and its neighborhoods in certain ways. The Atlanta of the 1970s and 1980s, still struggling with the problems created by earlier, often race-based policy decisions, was very much a product of a past that had emphasized race.

Black Neighborhoods, City Services, and Urban Reform

White city officials' lack of interest in the black community and their needs continued into a period of urban reform connected with the Progressive movement. Urban reformers during the Progressive Era sought to change the environment of slum-dwellers in an effort to enhance stability in the city as well as improve the lives of those living in dilapidated areas. The parks, playgrounds, improved housing, and city services for slum sections were designed to aid the poor and to protect the rest of the city from the disease and crime that emanated from these neighborhoods. The urban Progressives thought that by ameliorating the physical environment they could also eliminate social problems, ensure a stable and orderly society, limit social and economic turmoil, and improve the behavior and morals of slum residents. The city's very existence, not to mention its future growth and prosperity, depended on a stable, efficient, orderly society. Historian Paul Boyer notes the social control and moral improvement aspects of Progressive urban reform. For example, in Pittsburgh, playground advocates claimed "that money spent on playgrounds would pay high dividends in cultivating the 'moral nature' of children, promoting 'civic unity' and supplying the 'social training and discipline' urgently needed." Spurred by a concern about social disorder and class violence during the 1890s depression, the movement to reshape the environment grew quickly in the years just after that economic collapse.[1]

While urban reform during the Progressive Era was a national movement, in the South it took some different forms. Although white southern Progressives were also interested in social control, moral behavior, and bettering the environment, most, including those in Atlanta, did not consider it necessary to work toward improving the well-being of blacks. Although some white reformers were motivated by humanitarian concerns for blacks and supported an enhancement of the environment, the notion of black inferiority was widely accepted, and paternalism dominated the approach of these white Progressives. For example, after the 1906 riot, some whites showed a greater awareness about conditions in black neighborhoods. City officials were more willing to listen to black complaints, and the Atlanta Civic League was set up and showed an interest in improving conditions in black neighborhoods. But these reactions to the riot were short-lived, and familiar attitudes persisted. The one possible exception to the usual thinking of most whites was the Commission on Interracial Cooperation (CIC), which was founded in 1919, with headquarters in Atlanta. This biracial organization and its local affiliates made some effort to avoid the paternalism evident in white attempts to help blacks and to have blacks and whites in the group collaborate as equals. Among whites in the group there was a sense that the poor treatment of blacks negatively affected whites as well. For this reason, they addressed such issues as inadequate schools, housing, and recreational facilities for blacks. The organization accepted segregation, however, and was interracial more in theory than in practice. Nonetheless, for most white Progressives the CIC was too liberal on the race issue. But even the CIC defined its *main* concern not as improving the environment of black neighborhoods but as preventing social disorder in the form of white mob lynchings.[2]

Among other southern Progressives, the desire for social control, social efficiency, and racial harmony was clearly directed at blacks and usually took a restrictive turn, as, for example, in the disfranchisement and segregation measures. Disfranchisement and segregation ameliorated city budgetary problems by making it easier to neglect black neighborhoods and schools and thereby to concentrate funds and city services on white areas. Humanitarian-minded Progressive legislators concentrated on the white poor, often disregarding the state's blacks. Urban Progressivism in the South thus had the effect of denying blacks their rights, segregating them geographically, and leaving them out of improvements (including better schools) going to white parts of the city. As John Dittmer states in his analysis of Georgia in the Progressive period, "Blacks in Augusta and other Georgia cities viewed those marching under the banner of reform with cynicism and dismay, for they knew from experience that most 'progressive' urban reforms either excluded blacks or were directed against them."[3] Atlanta's response to Progressivism mirrored that of other southern cities.

In the 1960s, the urban reform demands of the civil rights movement joined other factors, including a renewed concern among white city officials about social control, urban cohesion, and growing disorder, to bring

Atlanta's black neighborhoods some of the beneficial changes that had come to most white ones fifty years earlier. Improved housing, the development of parks and playgrounds, and enhanced services—all designed to uplift the black community and ensure the city's orderly development— suddenly became major issues during this decade, after years of white neglect and black demands for improvement. The civil rights movement's urban reform component became a catalyst for local, neighborhood-based change at a time when the larger issues of segregation and integration occupied the country's attention.

During the Progressive period and continuing into the 1960s, black needs were largely disregarded. Their neighborhoods in Atlanta lacked parks, decent schools and housing, recreational facilities, libraries, and city services such as paved streets and regular garbage collection. As Mayor Hartsfield stated in a 1961 interview, "When I became mayor, you could always tell where the Negro sections started. Lights stopped, streets, sidewalks stopped." The factor in the black community that most interested whites was health. A high black disease rate would invariably affect the white parts of town. Thus, health (and subsequently sanitation and clean water) in black neighborhoods was of some concern. City leaders therefore offered certain services, but at times reluctantly, since high disease and death rates were often blamed on the blacks themselves—on their "immoral and unclean" lifestyle and their biological propensity to contract various diseases. Improved sanitation and water supply facilities were provided to black areas, but due to the unwillingness of many landlords to connect their rental housing in black neighborhoods to the city's lines, and the city's failure to maintain or improve these services, they remained inadequate. As late as 1931, black areas, unlike comparable white sections, still suffered in the very basic service of water supply. A study in that year found only 19.1 percent of black homes with running water, compared to 69.8 percent of white homes in similar low-income neighborhoods. While bathtubs were evident in only 6.8 percent of the black residences, for whites the percentage was 36.4. And the city remained culpable in other ways as well. For example, garbage collection in black neighborhoods continued to be deficient: service was sometimes unavailable for months.[4]

Self-Help

The main response to black problems came, as it would later, from the black community and black Progressives. The city's blacks worked to upgrade their environment and improve their lives first through the black churches, fraternal orders, and colleges; then through the Neighborhood

Union, a Progressive black social service organization founded in 1908 by community activist Lugenia Burns Hope (wife of John Hope, president of Morehouse College); through the local branch of the NAACP, established in 1917; through an Atlanta Urban League chapter, established in 1920; and later through such organizations as the Atlanta Civic and Political League. Using funds secured from donations as well as bake sales, athletic tournaments, and other planned events in black areas, the Neighborhood Union was involved in health clinics, neighborhood cleanup campaigns, sanitation improvements, unemployment relief, playground development, settlement houses, and improvements in housing and schools. The Neighborhood Union and all of the other black organizations, as well as the CIC, were also active in urging the city government to enhance conditions in black neighborhoods, and at times they were successful in securing "better sewerage, lights, and water facilities," as noted in the Neighborhood Union's 1933 report. Basically, however, the Neighborhood Union's success was through self-improvement—getting black community members to uplift themselves without dependence on the white city officials, who did the least they could.[5] White Atlanta's concern with the black community remained minimal, although a sense of a shared destiny was evident. The *Atlanta Constitution*, in a 1911 editorial in support of the chartering of the Neighborhood Union, stated that "co-operation from the superior race is called for in the degree that the white man is inevitably affected by the progress or retrogression of the negro."[6] While some whites continued to recognize the danger to the city in neglecting a large portion of its population and urged that improvements be made in black areas, relatively little was done until the civil rights movement forced a rethinking of urban reform efforts in Atlanta.[7]

There were even attempts to shame the white community into a response. In 1938, in answer to the racially inequitable bond issue of that year, the Atlanta Civic and Political League issued a pamphlet titled "DOES ATLANTA Know and Approve These Conditions?" The pamphlet reported on the dire needs of the black community in regard to schools, parks, playgrounds, and health services, and spelled out the consequences of the city's policy of neglect.[8]

Inadequate and Unequal

In the mid- to late 1940s, the black community exercised its emerging political power to push for change in the city's attitude. The All Citizens Registration Committee's flyers urged Atlanta's blacks to register to vote in order to secure parks, playgrounds, new and better schools, paved streets, lights, police protection, and other urban necessities that now seemed within reach. The connection between votes and services was illustrated in 1949, when Mayor Hartsfield picked John Wesley Dobbs, cochair of the Atlanta Negro Voters League, to give the signal that turned on the newly installed streetlights on parts of Auburn Avenue, the center of black business in the city.[9] But this voting power only went so far. While white officials provided some parks, built some schools, opened some libraries, offered some street lighting, and paved some streets, black neighborhoods continued to show evidence of gross neglect. In the mid-1950s, there were still complaints of inadequate and unequal services and facilities for blacks in both low- and middle-income neighborhoods (garbage collection, parks, recreational facilities, street lighting, street paving and maintenance, water supply, transit services). And city officials were well aware of these problems. A 1954 Atlanta Urban League report stated that there were 128 parks in the city for whites and four for blacks; ninety-six tennis courts for whites and eight for blacks; seven community centers for whites and one for blacks; eighteen playgrounds for whites and three for blacks. Money had been appropriated in a 1949 bond issue for developing and improving park space for the black community, but it either was not spent or was spent very slowly. Although Hartsfield commented in 1956 that the city had to provide blacks with a fair share of funds in order to upgrade their living conditions, city spending and bond issues both before and after the 1950s neglected black areas. In the case of a 1957 bond referendum, blacks were able to secure funds for widening streets in their neighborhoods only by impressing the bond committee with their voting power. However, as demonstrated in the initial draft of this bond proposal, whites continued to easily forget or purposely ignore black community needs and tended to plan funding with only white areas in mind. This type of neglect occurred many times. Black neighborhood demands still pointed out the lack of street lighting, paved streets, parks, adequate garbage collection, and other services in various sections of the city. The inadequate delivery of services to black neighborhoods also had an effect on neighborhood racial transition. Q. V. Williamson, a black real estate businessman who in the 1960s became a city alderman, commented that "one reason why Negroes buy from whites is because city services (sewers, etc.) are in areas built for whites, easier than getting them for Negroes."[10]

As court cases were decided, black voting increased, and the civil rights movement was organized in the city, Atlanta's officials slowly and reluctantly began to desegregate lunch counters, parks, schools, libraries, golf courses, and other public facilities. Blacks were put on the police force as early as 1948 in response to the surge in black registration and voting, and beginning in 1963 they were allowed to serve as firemen. The effort to desegregate peacefully was inspired by the disruption caused by the sit-ins, plus a concern about the decrease in downtown business activity and the loss of a good race relations reputation.[11] But an attention to basic services in black neighborhoods, to the urban reform that had benefited most white areas of the city decades earlier, was initially left out of this response. Although the white city leaders' response to the sit-ins was evidence of a desire to ensure an orderly, stable society and curtail social disorder, their actions did not touch the neighborhood issues—the efforts to improve slum life and eliminate social problems—that had been evident in the Progressive period.

While Atlanta's civil rights organizations were primarily interested in expanding voting rights, ending segregation in schools and public accommodations, and securing equal representation in city government and in employment, the movement also had an important urban reform aspect, and this component also brought changes to the city. In its "A Second Look" statement in 1960, the Atlanta Committee for Cooperative Action discussed the city's inadequate health facilities, housing, schools, and other services for blacks. Also, the Urban League, the NAACP, the Atlanta Negro Voters League, and other civil rights organizations had consistently pushed for improvements in black areas of the city over the decades. For example, in the 1950s the Atlanta Urban League's community services department helped organize and work with neighborhood councils (e.g., in South Atlanta) to deal with problems in water supply, sewerage, paved streets, traffic lights, public transportation, health, housing, and schools. Although the league's organizational work was generally focused on low-income areas, other areas also received attention. An *Atlanta Daily World* article complained of the decreased garbage collection and maintenance as westside sections made the transition from white to black, and area school superintendents noted that service declined after blacks became a majority in various areas. Service reductions of this sort were common features of racially transitional areas in 1960s cities. Displaced blacks pushed to the west side also created service problems in black middle-income areas, because the increased population did not lead to increased city services (e.g., in an area where the biracial Southwest Atlantans for Progress was active in trying to maintain an integrated neighborhood). And there was always concern that good black residential neighborhoods would decline as city officials permitted commercial or industrial development near homes.[12]

Although neighborhood vitality was a concern addressed by various black organizations, it was SNCC that became the immediate and primary catalyst for a slow awakening of Atlanta's white officials in the 1960s to the problems of poor black neighborhoods. SNCC forcefully urged white city leaders to respond to black area needs or face continuing and escalating social unrest.

SNCC's work in South Atlanta in the summer of 1963 signaled the beginning of its South Atlanta Project—a project "aimed at bringing about radical change and improvement in what came to be called the 'forgotten side of Atlanta.'" Southeast Atlanta was described as one of the city's most neglected areas. Essential city services such as garbage collection, street cleaning, traffic controls, housing inspection, sewage, health facilities, libraries, and recreational facilities such as playgrounds were inadequate. At times garbage was not picked up for a month; bus service was poor; many streets were not paved; schools were still segregated and overcrowded; discrimination was evident in city employment; houses did not have sufficient plumbing; there were "few parks in the entire south Atlanta area, and these [were] either incomplete or inadequately equipped." In short, this section of Atlanta was in need of attention. The area had a number of established civic associations that had been petitioning and complaining to city officials about the deficient city services, but to no avail. A SNCC report on the project related one telling example: the Georgia Avenue–Pryor Street Civic League had been trying to secure "a stop light at an intersection where 14 children had been hurt and two killed within a year's time; the stop light still had not been obtained, the argument of the City officials being that the money was not available at that time. (Yet, strangely enough, the City had been able to finance a stop light at an intersection in a white section of Atlanta within one half-hour after a child in that community had been struck by a car.)" Deciding that it was a lack of community political organization and consciousness that allowed the city to neglect this area, SNCC became determined to mobilize the community politically, work with the community civic associations, organize youth councils, engage in voter registration drives, and subsequently use political power to force the city leaders to respond to the area's needs. They were also critical of "wealthy Negroes from the West Side" who did not pay attention to southside issues and problems. During the summer of 1963, SNCC and neighborhood civic leagues worked together in a voter registration drive that culminated with an early August march on City Hall to present a grievance statement to the mayor and demand immediate action. The grievance report ("The City Must Provide"), which SNCC helped prepare, stated that it represented the demands of "Atlanta's Forgotten Communities: more than 60,000 Negro citizens living on the south side of the city." Noting that requests for services had been made for years but had received little response, the report continued, "Our communities still lack many of the essential services which it is the duty of *every* city to provide to *all* its citizens." The document called for a change in the attitude of city officials to the needs of the southside black communities and demanded "that *all* the grievances of our communities be met—and met at once." But change was to come slowly.[13]

While city officials did make some response in regard to services, this response was initially minimal. The South Atlanta Civic Council, a coalition of local civic associations that was working with SNCC, warned that protest would continue unless demands were met and stated its determination to get the city to "live up to its responsibilities of supplying our areas with *continuous* and *adequate* services." Replies from the heads of various city departments were not satisfactory: city officials either said that they could not provide the services requested or claimed that adequate services already existed. Within a few months, after voter registration drives and continued pressure on public officials, some reforms were enacted. The development of park projects was speeded up; sewage facilities were improved in one area; and more crossing guards were hired at schools that needed them. However, problems remained, including "discrimination in city employment, insufficient recreational facilities, inadequate traffic control, poor street lighting, inadequate and segregated health facilities, and continued school segregation."[14]

As a result of these persistent problems, and spurred by the Georgia legislature's unwillingness to seat Julian Bond because of his anti–Vietnam War position, in 1965 SNCC's South Atlanta Project was expanded to involve other neighborhoods and thus became simply the Atlanta Project. Their goal was to deal with community neglect by organizing these areas politically, and they expressed a willingness to use sit-ins, picketing, rent strikes, and boycotts to secure their demands. They still urged that services such as adequate medical care and schools be provided, but they also spoke about segregated and run-down housing, low wages, and employment discrimination. SNCC operated independently but also worked within the larger Atlanta Summit Leadership Conference coalition. In its "Action for Democracy" document and other statements, Summit expressed its concern with a broad array of issues, including school desegregation, segregated housing and residential patterns, and equal employment opportunities, as well as access to all public facilities and medical care.[15]

Summit also addressed various neighborhood services, such as school overcrowding, health services, parks, urban renewal, and inadequate housing. For example, in a 1966 report Summit stated that the slum housing in various black areas created an environment that was conducive to disease. A 1967 letter to Mayor Allen called for, among other things, "a Crash Program to correct the many years of discrimination in the location of park facilities and the quality of park facilities and golf courses in our city." Faced with SNCC's activity on Atlanta's south side and Summit's desire for change, Mayor Allen at first tended to respond—slowly—to some of the larger desegregation issues affecting the city as a whole. The city's desegregation efforts quickened as Summit authorized sit-ins, but many neighborhood service problems remained largely neglected.[16]

Strikes and Riots

Because the problems had not been solved, the issue of neighborhood neglect emerged again in 1965. By this time national events slowly began to affect the handling of the slum question. In particular, the Watts riot, which took place in early August 1965, sparked some concern among the city's leaders about the possibility that a similar riot could occur in Atlanta. Also, the California disorder had followed on the heels of a number of *Atlanta Constitution* articles on slum housing; the neglect of particularly run-down neighborhoods, such as Vine City, on the west side; and the way in which urban renewal depleted the city's low-income housing stock. The mayor had responded to the newspaper articles with a weak effort to enforce the housing code in some slum areas, but that move did little to improve housing.[17]

In October 1965 a number of southside (and one westside) neighborhood associations, some of which had worked with SNCC earlier, expressed their complaints in a statement to the city's Citizens' Advisory Committee for Urban Renewal. They spoke of the need for housing code enforcement, long-promised public housing, clean streets, more traffic lights, playgrounds, and other city services. "Our children have no place to play but the street," the neighborhood groups noted. These neighborhoods were already actively involved in self-help efforts. Through its Improvement Association, for example, Vine City established recreational programs, built playgrounds, and tried to secure park space, improved street cleaning, and housing from the city. The city needed to help; the neighborhood residents could not do it all with limited resources. But although a rent strike was threatened, the city offered little to appease the neighborhood activists except an agreement to build the already-promised public housing. The threat of another rent strike—in the westside Vine City and Lightning areas in February 1966 due to housing conditions— and Martin Luther King Jr.'s entrance into the dispute prompted the mayor to make an immediate but stopgap response that comprised increased building code compliance and some effort to clean up the area. The rent strike soon materialized, but other than publicizing conditions in the area, it accomplished little. The Vine City Council, which along with SNCC was active in the rent strike, had also urged the city to provide street paving and playgrounds, but it received little response.[18]

The southside neighborhoods once again received attention when the city's Community Council issued a report in March 1966 on the neighborhoods near Atlanta–Fulton County Stadium. The report described these communities' problems and the residents' growing disaffection toward the city. The report also commented that the Summerhill area was ripe for a violent incident because of the neglect of neighborhood problems. The city had no immediate reaction, but changes were taking place that would soon be evident. In addition to presenting their grievances, the southside residents had also been urging the city to apply for federal Model Cities funds in order to upgrade their areas as soon as the program was put into effect. The mayor was interested in this suggestion and began to develop a proposal. In May 1966 he also asked city departments to pay particular attention to the lack of services in slum areas. A new concern with upgrading slum areas was clearly emerging, but neighborhood issues became a main focus of city policy only after local disruption and disorder occurred.[19]

The westside rent strike in February was followed by a blockage of traffic on the south side in July and, most important, a riot in the southside Summerhill neighborhood in September 1966 and, shortly thereafter, a disturbance in Bedford-Pine, on the east side. These events vividly illustrated both the urban reform component of the civil rights struggle and the neglect of urban services that SNCC and others had been emphasizing for years.[20] The initial reaction of city officials was to accuse SNCC and "outside agitators," such as Stokely Carmichael, of fomenting the violence. SNCC's earlier activity in the southside and Vine City protests, its militancy, and its emerging racial separatist philosophy, which was evident during the Atlanta Project period of the mid-1960s, made this organization the focal point for white anxieties. A fear of SNCC and its confrontational policies could be seen in the mayor's reaction and was probably a factor in his eventual willingness to address neighborhood issues. SNCC's response to the mayor was that poor living conditions were the source of the riot and that the mayor had been warned that neighborhood discontent might erupt into violence. A particular source of resentment in the area was the construction of Atlanta–Fulton County Stadium, which led to the destruction of needed housing.[21]

Mayor Allen was subsequently deluged with complaints and warnings about the neglect of black neighborhoods. For example, a letter sent to the mayor by a variety of intergroup relations organizations (the NAACP, the Anti-Defamation League, and the Southern Regional Council) noted that "if Atlanta is to spare itself from future disorders, the leadership of the city . . . must focus on the real problems which face too many of its people: inadequate housing, overcrowded schools, under-employment; a lack of adequate recreational facilities; a dearth of public services to these disadvantaged areas; minimal enforcement of the city's building code."[22] The Council on Human Relations of Greater Atlanta commented that "the incident was another in a long series of warnings, that poverty and segregation breed conditions" that will take more than the police to solve; the organization called on the city to "alleviate the social and physical blight which inevitably results in such unfortunate incidents." The council also tried to convince city leaders that the problem was the conditions in the area, not SNCC. Its news release pointed out, "SNCC members are not responsible for parking space for 4,000 cars [the stadium parking lot] in the middle of an area which has no parks for children to play in." Nor was SNCC responsible for overcrowded schools, lack of housing, employment discrimination, or other factors precipitating the riot. City officials were lambasted for doing too little in response to earlier expressions of discontent in the neighborhood.[23] These neighborhood disturbances were clearly the result of a long history of neglect of black areas.

But now that the social order had been disturbed, civic cohesion had been disrupted, and the fear of more riots had started to grow, the mayor and other politicians began to take serious notice of the grievances of the black neighborhoods as the city services and urban reform issue was brought dramatically to their attention. It was quite natural for attention to be drawn to an issue after discontent and violence were demonstrated, and this occurred in a number of cities. Yet the particular reforms made in Atlanta and the reasons offered for them fit very well into the earlier Progressive Era efforts. A desire for stability, a concern about social disorder, and a willingness to uplift the poor, protect the rest of the city, eliminate social problems, and improve the morals and behavior of slum-dwellers were all elements of the city's response. Just as it had earlier, the desire for social control and racial harmony played a significant role in white officials' response to blacks. But this time, rather than restrictive legislation or rationalizations based on blacks' supposed biological and lifestyle inferiority, some black areas finally began to receive the consideration that during the Progressive Era had been reserved for white sections of the city. And this was one of the first times a southern city had moved actively and aggressively to respond to black grievances with Progressive-type social reforms. Certainly traditional civil rights issues and urban reform issues were merging at this point.

Because of the growing discontent and tension in Atlanta's black slums, the organizing activities of SNCC and the Summit Leadership Conference, and the 1966 summer riots that occurred in a number of cities, the mayor had already quickened his efforts during that summer to avoid a violent outbreak in Atlanta. He started the Atlanta Community Improvement Program to deal with street cleaning, installation of street lights, enforcement of housing codes, and development of recreational projects in specific slum neighborhoods. The program made a comprehensive survey of facilities in all black areas and determined that these sections suffered from all or some of the following conditions: overcrowded schools, below-standard housing, lack of public transportation services, congested and poorly paved roads, deficient park and recreational space, inadequate street lighting, and insufficient fire protection services. The report also noted what specific actions were planned toward the development of more recreational areas, the construction of new schools, and the improvement of street lighting. Furthermore, studies regarding sanitation services were in the process of being completed. A subsequent report stated that "the people living in slums and poverty areas, especially those living in Negro slums, have never received an equal share of services in the city. Their streets are unpaved; the schools are much more crowded; the enforcement of sanitation, housing, and other standards is much less stringent; in many neighborhoods, street lights are virtually nonexistent. Coupled with the absence of service have been many unfulfilled promises to improve conditions. Bond issues have been sold on the pledge of improved schools or streets or parks, but these services have not materialized."[24]

The board of aldermen also took notice of events in other cities, and in early August 1966 it passed a resolution expressing a willingness to provide services to Atlanta areas "lacking certain essential facilities." The board also stated a desire to set up a committee of aldermen to cooperate with a committee of Summit members in visiting these slum areas (including one white one) and recommending improvements to the mayor in order to "standardize the services" throughout the city. The aldermen further urged the creation of a Human Relations Commission. The riot seemed to speed up the process of change that had already begun. Within a few days after the riot, Mayor Allen brought the aldermanic and Summit committees together to tour the areas that lacked appropriate services and to make recommendations for improvement.[25]

Furthermore, there was a noticeable, although temporary, shift in the urban renewal program. In 1966 Allen became interested in conserving and improving low-income areas and in providing more low- and moderate-income housing to replace destroyed and deteriorated units. There was also more interest in securing input from neighborhood residents during the planning process. In part, such changes also resulted from federal programs such as Model Cities.[26]

The riot also led to the development of a permanent biracial Community Relations Commission (CRC), organized in November 1966 to deal with neighborhood grievances and other issues. The commission held public hearings in a number of communities in an effort to enhance racial harmony and prevent future disorders. A riot in Dixie Hills, a northwest Atlanta neighborhood, in June 1967 spurred even more fervent activity. Once again, the riot area was described as lacking housing and recreational facilities. Immediately after the riot, the city responded by building playgrounds, repairing streets, and improving health inspections. As a result of the riot and the city's response, the Atlanta Committee for Cooperative Action urged the mayor to pay more attention to the city's moderate black leadership or deal with more violent and irresponsible groups. Albert Johnson, president of the NAACP's Atlanta branch, pointed out that "responsible Negro Leaders had worked for months to get the city to construct recreational facilities in the Dixie Hills area, but were ignored." However, when outsiders appeared in the neighborhood and a riot developed, "the city reacted immediately." He warned, "If you lived in Dixie Hills would you not assume that Stokely Carmichael had a better program than we have?"[27]

This complaint, as well as the need for more neighborhood improvement, was also voiced by the CRC. As CRC reports noted in 1967, the requests presented at CRC hearings dealt mainly with fundamental urban services rather than with "civil rights or discrimination." Adequate housing, "safe streets and sidewalks," streetlights, recreation, improved public transportation, sufficient sewers and sanitary services, an end to police brutality, and increased police patrolling were the usual needs and concerns expressed. One CRC report commented that "the lack of streets and sidewalks, much less public transportation, in many cases accounts for apparent lack of neighborhood spirit." After the Dixie Hills riot, the CRC urged the mayor and the board of aldermen to take action on these complaints rather than continue to fortify poor residents' impression that they are neglected until "they start 'making things happen.'" The commission commented on the city's persistent slowness in upgrading services in a number of neighborhoods and on the "apparent unwillingness of the city to move in areas until, as it is phrased, 'The City has to.'" As a way to avoid further riots in the summer of 1968, the mayor and others developed a plan in March that provided for better communications between city hall and six poverty-stricken neighborhoods and between the mayor's office, federal program workers, and the targeted areas; and for improved sanitation services, street and streetlight repair, housing, water delivery, summer recreational facilities, library service, police protection, and employment opportunities. Apparently some attention was being paid to ongoing complaints about city inaction, particularly at a time when other low-income black areas, such as Vine City, were described as ready to explode. City officials also expressed some fleeting concern about controlling public housing construction in areas where service facilities were already inadequate.[28]

The work of SNCC, other civil rights organizations, and the Summit group, and concern over riots in Atlanta and elsewhere brought some change in white city leaders' attitudes toward the problems of blacks and what could be done to improve their communities and help the city. Other elements of this change included the growing black vote, the emergence of blacks into positions of political power, and Atlanta officials' efforts since the late 1940s to maintain an alliance between the city's white business elite and black middle class. The passage of the 1965 Voting Rights Act, plus federal court actions that mandated reapportionment of the state legislature and district rather than at-large voting, also played a role. This shift can be clearly seen not only in the reaction to the riots but also in a willingness to deal with certain issues such as black crime and its causes. The white community as a whole had generally neglected the roots of black crime during earlier decades, but again, the 1960s was somewhat of a turning point. During the summer of 1965, as other cities rioted, Atlanta's mayor had set up a biracial Atlanta Commission on Crime and Juvenile Delinquency to study the causes of crime in the city. Black areas were the main topic of discussion; one white neighborhood was mentioned as well. In its February 1966 report, the commission had noted that the lack of recreational facilities in densely populated areas affected the city's crime rate. With statements that seemed to be lifted out of the literature of the playground advocates of the early twentieth century, the report argued, "Children need places to play other than the streets. In addition, supervised play and recreation are valuable means of teaching children self-discipline and self-control." The report urged that parks "be built in congested high crime areas of the city. . . . It is inescapable that juvenile delinquency is directly related to conditions bred by poverty." A desire to enhance the environment in black slums as a way to decrease crime had been voiced before. Earlier reports and Crime Commission studies had noted the link between poverty, lack of recreational facilities, slums, and crime, and had called for changes. However, little action to rectify these problems was taken until the 1960s. Now city leaders began to recognize the need to improve black neighborhoods and turned away from earlier excuses based on blacks' supposed propensity for crime. Environmental determinism held sway. The causes for the shift in the thinking of white city officials is clear. Mayor Allen commented later that the city tried "to help our poor onto their own feet, and consequently, avoid the outbreaks of violence many of the other cities were going through."[29]

The Atlanta Commission study also called for a full schoolday for children in poverty areas where overcrowded schools were then on double sessions. It stated that "there is a significant relationship between delinquency and educational achievement. In addition, there is a significant relationship between educational achievement and the conditions bred by poverty." High poverty rates, poor educational skills, and high crime rates were clearly related, the report maintained.[30]

Of course, the city's new attitude was helped along by a presidential administration that was oriented toward urban social reform, by federal programs that supported community activism, and by poor citizens' involvement in the development of these programs. For example, Economic Opportunity Atlanta (EOA) aimed to eliminate local poverty through neighborhood employment, job training, housing, and recreational and social service programs. EOA elected citizens' advisory councils that to some degree brought the poor into the decision-making process for their neighborhoods. Furthermore, in March 1967 the city's leaders actually acknowledged their shift when they applied to the Department of Housing and Urban Development for Model Cities funds. The application for Summerhill and other southside neighborhoods (including two white

Model Cities program in Summerhill. This sign promises new housing. (Boyd Lewis Collection, Courtesy of Atlanta History Center)

ones) noted their lack of city services, recreational facilities, and decent housing. The area had declined, the application continued, due to the "poor condition of streets," inadequate sewer system, the "low level of municipal services," poor housing, lax enforcement of the housing code, and "lack of educational opportunities for adequate employment." The area and its people were to be uplifted through street repair, better housing, development and improvement of park space, a higher level of city services, better police protection, improved health care, less crowded schools, and a transportation network that would provide easier access to jobs. The connection between environment and social uplift was a basic element of the Model Cities Program, and in their application for federally supported community improvement, Atlanta city officials eagerly expressed their changed view about black Atlanta's poor neighborhoods.[31]

The goal of the CRC, Economic Opportunity Atlanta, and other such programs was to uplift the black poor, promote racial understanding and, most of all, to ensure stability and order in the city. The CRC, which listened to neighborhood grievances in public hearings and then returned a month later to report to the community about action taken on their complaints, received recognition from the *Atlanta Journal* in 1970 for allowing Atlanta to have a quiet summer. However, the paper stated further, "There is no assurance that such will continue unless city leaders accelerate corrective action."[32] Such editorials illustrate that it was now widely accepted that poor services, neglect, and general deterioration in various neighborhoods encouraged social disorder, that black life could be improved, and that black communities were overdue for attention. The Southern Regional Council warned that both housing and employment conditions had to be improved to "reduce the potential for social explosion that would frustrate Atlanta's economic growth." In a statement reminiscent of the Progressive period, the SRC noted that "social tranquility is necessary for the orderly economic development of the city."[33] The business leadership of the city surely took notice. As in the earlier reform years, business leaders wanted stability and order. Economic and racial policies often intertwined and fortified each other.

Enthusiasm for neighborhood improvement, however, declined quickly after the disorders of the 1960s had passed, as intraneighborhood conflicts over renewal goals and area leadership, particularly in Vine City, frustrated City Hall, and as federal funds decreased; but for the time being some black neighborhoods received close attention, and there were some improvements.[34] When Jackson became mayor he reallocated city funds and used some federal money to provide the black south side with park space, sanitation, paved streets, and other needs. There was also a change in federal policy. The Housing and Community Development Act of 1974 expressed a stronger interest in "upgrading existing communities." However, conditions in low-income black areas had been so bad for so long that uplift proved difficult and costly, not only in Atlanta but in other southern cities as well. The 1960s federal and local spending in neighborhoods such as Summerhill did not significantly improve the area: complaints continued over substandard housing, lack of recreational facilities, and insufficient city services. Neighborhoods that had been neglected for decades could not be brought up to the level of better-off sections in just a few years. And as federal funds decreased in the 1970s and 1980s and local government interest in this issue waned, problems continued.[35] Atlanta's neighborhood blight had a solid foundation in the city's past and continued to function as an active reminder of earlier policies based on race and, to a lesser extent, class.

The class factor also surfaced sharply in some housing-related cases as blacks assumed political control. Although Jackson aided low-income black sections, he was removed from their world and plight. In October 1974, Jackson spent two days at the Bankhead Courts public housing project in order to get a personal look at conditions there and to prove that it was a safe place to live. His lack of prior knowledge of life in the projects is indicated by his realization during his stay that it was a terrible place to live. After his stay, improvements were made but not maintained.[36]

A close working relationship between a black mayor, the white business elite, and the black middle class was especially evident in Andrew Young's mayoralty in the 1980s. This coalition benefited business interests of both races, not low-income black neighborhoods. For example, Young strongly supported the construction of the shopping-recreational mall Underground Atlanta as part of an effort to revitalize the downtown area. The *Atlanta Journal and Constitution* reported in 1987 that during Young's mayoralty the city government "diverted $6 million in federal funds earmarked for the poor to the $130 million entertainment complex." These funds, the newspaper continued, came "from the federal Housing and Community Development Act. The law directs that most of the money must benefit poor people. City leaders say Underground will provide jobs for the poor. Others are skeptical." Also, with less federal funds for low-income housing in the 1980s, housing and services for the poor (most of whom were black) deteriorated. In 1987, one-third of rental housing in Atlanta was classified as below "the minimum standards for safe and sanitary housing." In other words, the housing code was still not being enforced.[37]

The long-term neglect of black neighborhoods, which had pernicious effects on the city, involved more than the basic services. The city was also shaped by other aspects of this issue that I have touched on only briefly so far. Park and recreational space, health care, police and fire services, mass transit, and the biracial school system were all significant factors in developing the city in certain ways.

B. "Our Children Have No Place to Play"

The black community's recreational needs had never been a major concern to white city officials. The dearth of parks and play areas, the many black leaders' complaints over the years, and the city's slow and reluctant response characterize the history of this service in Atlanta. Decisions influenced by racial considerations have affected park and recreational development regarding placement and use and even design and foliage: as early as the 1880s, blacks' use of Grant Park prompted the park commission to support the partial removal of dense forest areas in order to facilitate police work and allow residents to see into the park to prevent crime. In the 1880s, blacks were at times excluded from some Atlanta parks but allowed to enter others, sometimes based on the parks' segregated events and facilities. And in the 1890s, Atlanta's largest park, Piedmont Park, hosted various segregated activities. In general, however, black utilization of Atlanta's parks was discouraged in the late nineteenth century, and this attitude was evident by the 1890s, when some of the city's park space was officially segregated, although there was no separate or equal parkland for blacks. Grant Park saw its black use decline sharply as segregation became the norm in the city in the 1890s.[38]

Once segregation and disfranchisement were in place, white Atlantans put city park funds to work almost exclusively for their community. Neighborhood parks, which had been advocated in earlier years, emerged in the period after 1910 only in white, mainly middle-class sections of the city. However, while lower-class white areas saw little parkland developed, and the city neglected the two parks that it had provided, indicating that the city's funding had a class aspect, whites of all classes, unlike blacks of any class, could use any of the city's parks. Playgrounds, too, increased in numbers and primarily were located in white neighborhoods.[39] Although the "separate but equal" concept was still voiced, there was no equality. Blacks of all classes faced decades of neglect and exclusion that was ameliorated only slightly by city action but was altered more substantially by neighborhood racial transition in the 1950s and 1960s.

There were some whites, such as park department general manager Dan Carey, who beginning in 1911 supported parks for blacks as a way to improve their health and morals and thus benefit white Atlantans as well. Seeing that blacks in service jobs, such as cooks, nurses, and porters, had frequent contact with whites, Carey couched his argument in terms of whites' being protected from disease and crime if blacks were treated fairly in regard to parks and other recreational space.[40]

As they did with other service needs, black Atlantans provided their own help. Black businessmen set up recreational areas such as Luna Park, established in 1910. The Neighborhood Union was active in providing playgrounds and establishing boys' and girls' clubs. Meanwhile, groups such as the Urban League, the NAACP, the Negro Anti-Tuberculosis Association, and the Neighborhood Union pressured city officials to open parks, playgrounds, tennis courts, and swimming pools in black neighborhoods. Finally, in 1920, the city started to develop Booker T. Washington Park on the west side. In keeping with black migration to that area and with the racial zoning of the time, the park was a sure magnet for further black movement to the west. Although Washington Park was much needed and welcomed, its physical condition from the beginning left much to be desired, and city maintenance was not adequate. There were complaints about the pool, lights, seats, grounds, and police protection.[41]

Playgrounds also remained inadequate both in numbers and facilities. By 1914, white children were provided with nine playgrounds, while blacks had two. Programs and personnel at the white playgrounds were not duplicated for the black children. By 1926, whites had twenty-one playgrounds and blacks three. The Progressive impetus to uplift through recreational facilities at times extended to black children also, but just barely, compared to reformers' attention to white needs. This inequality related to all aspects of recreation. By 1932, whites could play at sixty-two tennis courts, five golf courses, twelve baseball fields, seven football fields, and one indoor basketball court; blacks had none of these amenities. Acreage for white parks and playgrounds numbered 1,100; for black parks and playgrounds, 16. The expenditure for operation of the white recreational facilities was $2.33 million; of the black facilities, $6,000. The New Deal programs provided some temporary help in the form of recreational activities under WPA control (eight of twenty-six supervised WPA playgrounds were for blacks), but these efforts had no lasting effect.[42]

Although black community leaders continued to work to secure more recreational space, as they did with other needs such as schools, there was little change. By 1940, blacks still only had about 16 acres of parks and playgrounds, while whites had approximately 1,324 acres. In some cases, the situation worsened. A 1940 city ordinance forbade blacks and whites from entering the parks of the other race. This ordinance was enforced so strongly that black domestics who walked through Grant Park to get to their jobs faced police harassment.[43]

The problem was not only in the use of parkland but also in its development. City officials could plan parks quickly, if they wanted, in black or white areas; however, they hesitated to do the same in mixed areas, where the park could conceivably be used by both groups. As a Municipal Housing Authority report stated in 1941, "Planning in the mixed [areas] is a very vexing and delicate problem." Given the battles that erupted at various times over which race would use a park, areas that were racially mixed or transitional probably received little consideration for new recreational space even if they needed it—and this situation grew worse as black migration into white neighborhoods increased in the 1950s and 1960s.[44]

Blacks and some whites did see problems in denying such a large percentage of Atlanta's residents adequate recreational and other amenities. Echoing Progressive Era rhetoric, a 1945 article in the *Atlanta Journal* argued, "We white people must remember this: No section of society is secure if another section of society suffers. Negro people are entitled to schools, churches, parks, playgrounds, and other facilities which will enable them to be mentally, physically, and spiritually better citizens." Also, the Atlanta Civic and Political League's 1938 pamphlet "DOES ATLANTA Know and Approve These Conditions?" urged the development of more parks and playgrounds in black areas as a way to reduce crime. "It is a known fact," the league report maintained, "that there is a close relationship between juvenile delinquency and the absence of play facilities." One of the four goals of the league was to have the city provide better parks and playgrounds for the black community—an objective that was later supported by other black political organizations, such as the All Citizens Registration Committee.[45]

Regardless, until the 1950s black Atlantans still had only three parks: Washington and Anderson on the west side and Pittman on the south. By 1954, Atlanta provided one acre of parkland for every 155 whites and one acre for every 1,020 blacks, including the addition of a park for blacks that year through neighborhood racial transition. A park on the east side had been suggested by the Urban League, by five Fulton County grand juries in the early 1950s, and, going back to 1911, by the park commissioner. A planned eastside park for blacks had been part of the 1946 bond program but had not been built, initially because of funding problems and uncertainty about the expressway route going through that area. After those problems were eliminated, the board of aldermen approved a land purchase in 1954, but the park had still not been developed by 1956, twelve years after the favorable bond vote. Other inadequacies also remained by that year: only two of eight community centers, one of seven indoor gyms, three of eight pools, and four of twenty-one equipped playgrounds were available to blacks. And it was not only the lack of recreational facilities but also their location that was troublesome. The Carver Homes (1953) area on the south side and Perry Homes (1955) on the west side lacked community centers and recreational space. The east side lacked any park for blacks. Blacks from various parts of the city often had to travel long distances to get to parks, playgrounds, or pools. As the parks and recreation committee of the NAACP's Atlanta branch stated in 1956, it was clear that "delay in providing a 'downtown' [eastside] park and in improving present facilities adequately indicates that the city administration has been derelict in making use of available funds." The committee suggested that local NAACP leaders meet with city officials to urge the city to develop an eastside park by 1958, provide parks in the Carver Homes and Perry Homes areas by 1959, open all tennis courts and pools to all Atlantans, and improve recreational facilities for blacks. Although a U.S. Supreme Court decision in 1956 had eliminated white-only city golf courses, compliance was slow, as it was with other rulings affecting segregation. Problems with the desegregation of golf facilities were still occurring in 1959.[46]

Conditions as of 1960 had not changed: whites had 20 football fields, blacks none; whites 16 recreation centers, blacks 3; whites 12 swimming pools, blacks 3; whites 22 baseball fields, blacks 3; and whites 119 tennis courts, blacks 8. Parks in the city were overwhelmingly in whites' hands (42 for whites, 3 for blacks).[47]

Although few parks were provided for blacks, their migration into white areas such as Mozley Park and the elaborate boundary agreements that followed left them with more park space. In March 1954 the Westside Mutual Development Committee approved the transfer of Mozley Park to black use and agreed "that the Empire Real Estate Board [would] be officially represented [at the ceremonies transferring the park] and receive the park on behalf of the Negro people." For whites, the WSMDC decided that to make up for the loss of Mozley Park, a swimming pool would be constructed in John A. White Park by June 1954. The mayor was aware of these agreements.[48]

Efforts to eliminate segregation and provide decent facilities for blacks sped up, of course, in the 1960s. Through a lawsuit filed by the leaders of the Committee on Appeal for Human Rights and black organizational pressure placed on Hartsfield and then Allen, the parks, pools, tennis courts, recreational centers, city auditorium, and other public facilities were desegregated by court order in 1962 and 1963. But desegregation of these facilities solved only part of the problem. The lack of park and recreational space in black neighborhoods remained an issue of racial contention. Complaints to city officials about inadequate recreational facilities brought some reluctant response. Black neighborhoods from the Perry Homes area, on the northwest, to the southern section that SNCC was organizing, voiced dissatisfaction with the city's neglect. In "The City Must Provide," their grievance statement about South Atlanta, civic leaders not only called for more parks but also spelled out where the new parks should be developed and how existing parks should be completed. In response to this statement, a march, and other pressure on city hall, Atlanta's officials eventually agreed to complete the long-delayed work on Joyland and Poole Creek Parks in the area.[49]

But even though city interest was increasing due to black pressure, past policies made the problem difficult to solve. For example, the planning department recognized the need for a park in the Perry Homes–Browntown area in the northwest, "where the city has allowed wholesale population increases without provision for park space." As a result, there was little suitable land left for development of a park. There was a park nearby—Gun Club Park—but as the planning department commented, "The proximity of Gun Club Park to Perry Homes is deceiving as a park resource because the city hasn't been able to agree on a bridge to cross Proctor Creek; consequently residents of Perry Homes are denied access to Gun Club Park." The location and building of this bridge was part of a larger discussion involving what housing and land was politically available for black use. Until these various issues were settled, this park remained unusable in an area desperate for park space. The bridge in question was first suggested in 1961; it was still being discussed in the mid-1960s.[50]

Past policies based on race and class had determined where parks would be located. Blacks could now use all the parks, but they had to travel considerable distances to get to them. Few parks were in black areas, and those that were remained run-down. Even white parks such as Mozley, which the city had once maintained well, were allowed to deteriorate after their transition to black use. "At Mozley Park," stated a 1964 article in the *Atlanta Inquirer*, "the general run-down conditions make it hard for a person to believe that this is the same recreational facility that existed when it was tabbed 'For White Only.'"[51]

In other cases, parks promised in 1950s and 1960s bond issues and never built, or ones started when areas were white but abandoned when blacks moved in, left the city with uneven park development and, again, left black neighborhoods with inadequate recreational space. Until the 1960s riots, which woke the white leadership up somewhat, blacks had received excuse after excuse as to why park space could not be developed in their areas. The *Atlanta Inquirer* complained in 1964 that "as far back as the Hartsfield Administration Negroes have been given the following stalls: We will study the situation, land not available, funds not available and when appraised of available land, turned to excuse that parks have to be 18 acres." Later this paper's editors complained that the city goes "too far when [it] can maintain 159 parks and parkways with only three conveniently located for Negroes." At times, however, black leaders had the leverage to secure parkland, and they used it. In July 1965, the city agreed to develop a park in the eastside Bedford-Pine area as part of a school–civic center agreement that provided for speeded-up school desegregation, the completion of the civic center complex, the razing of the C. W. Hill School, and the rebuilding of the school with an adjoining park.[52]

One problem for blacks was their lack of representation on influential committees that directed park maintenance and placement: the aldermanic board's Parks Committee, the Citizens' Parks Advisory Committee, and the Atlanta–Fulton County Recreation Authority. Ultimately, this was a political issue and required the political solution of electing and appointing blacks to offices that controlled policy-making. The *Atlanta Inquirer* urged an increase in voter registration in 1964 in order to elect individuals who would care about "little children . . . no matter what the color."[53]

Parks and race relations played another role in Atlanta's development, as illustrated in the following case. A bond issue in 1962 offered a plan to build a cultural center, including a new concert hall, in Piedmont Park as part of a project to improve the park. The bond was rejected as a result of the racial issue. Mayor Allen described the situation in this way: "The plan for the beautification of Piedmont Park suddenly blew up in my face and became a raging racial issue." Many whites apparently feared that the center would result in more blacks using the park and coming into the white northside section.[54]

Although Mayor Allen, with federal help, made a belated attempt to correct the recreational imbalance, as did Massell and Jackson, it was too little, too late. As Jackson's Parks Department director, Jack Delius, said in 1974, "There was a period when there was rank discrimination, but we've tried to equalize." The city had to do "some catching up" in black areas; by 1970, though, one-half of the city's park funds were being used to amortize the bonds issued for stadium construction. Although the Model Cities Program aimed to equalize recreational expenditures around the city and improve facilities and services in the Model Cities neighborhoods, it was not effective over the long run, as funds dried up. Park space in the city remained insufficient and inadequate because of a legacy of race- and class-based policies.[55]

C. "Against the Public Interest": Race and Black Health Care

The health of the black community did concern many whites due to both humanitarian and self-interest factors. Worried about diseases spreading from blacks to whites and about maintaining the city's reputation as a healthful place to live, city leaders did think about black health needs. But like other urban services, health care was largely neglected until black votes and organizational pressure brought some redress. The burden for providing and improving heath care again fell to the black community.

Health itself is a product of many factors, some of which the city has no control over, but health care and prevention were within the local government's purview in regard to such factors as sanitation, public hospitals, and doctors' rights to attend the sick. Atlanta's health care system was based on neglect, on substandard segregated facilities, and on some continuing exclusion of its black population through a good part of the twentieth century.

Early in the twentieth century, racism was seen as a factor in high black disease and death rates. The *Atlanta Independent* in 1908 blamed racism for the neglect of sanitation services in black neighborhoods and its consequences: "Just as long as Atlanta seeks to confine all city improvements to white settlements, just so long will our death rate lead every other city of our size."[56] The Neighborhood Union engaged in heroic efforts to improve the health of the black community through health campaigns, infant care and nursing courses, home visitations, a health center, portable medical clinics (in cooperation with the Anti-Tuberculosis Association), and sanitation drives. The group began to stress health concerns in its activity in black neighborhoods. During a short time in the 1920s, it received some meager funding from the city's Community Chest for its health program for infants and children; generally, though, neither the Community Chest nor the city provided much help in the 1920s or after. The Neighborhood Union's work ultimately failed due to the poverty and neglect of the neighborhoods in which they operated.[57]

The official city response to black health needs was uneven, reflecting concern and indifference at the same time. For example, beginning in 1901 the city's schools employed one black doctor and one nurse to conduct physical examinations. Two white doctors and four nurses were hired for the white schools. However, by 1912, the program for the black children (but not the white) was terminated due to funding problems. A black doctor was rehired in 1914, and in 1920 the Atlanta Urban League was able to secure two black nurses for the black schools. But there was never equality between the races. By 1929, there were still two black nurses aiding one black physician in the black schools; for white children, thirteen white nurses assisted three white doctors. As Jesse Thomas, the National Urban League's southern field director, pointed out in 1929, "This gives the Negro nurses about four times as many children to handle as the white nurses and yet they receive about 60 percent of the salary paid the white nurses."[58]

Given the inadequacy of a public health program for black schoolchildren and others, plus the poverty and dearth of services for black neighborhoods, it is easy to understand some of the factors that contributed to the high disease and mortality rates of Atlanta's black population. Health problems would be expected just from the fact that in 1910 a number of the city's sewer lines emptied into or close to black communities.[59]

Crossing Racial Lines

Although many whites recognized that disease crossed racial lines and that blacks did not have adequate medical care, the city's response was generally meager. Concerned about the city's growing reputation as an unhealthy place to live, city leaders did push a 1910 bond issue that expanded sewer and water lines into poorer areas (both black and white) and a black middle-class section. Only after the *Atlanta Constitution* argued for the establishment of a hospital for blacks with infectious diseases, where these patients could be quarantined from the general population, was a temporary hospital set up in 1914; a city hospital for whites with such diseases already existed. The tendency of many whites was to blame the black victim for the disease, rather than the environmental factors that caused it, and to be only concerned with blacks infecting whites, not whites infecting blacks.[60]

The Atlanta Anti-Tuberculosis Association was one organization that stressed the impact of black health on the white population. Rosa Lowe, the group's executive secretary, stated in 1914 that "any program of work which ignores them [the Negroes] is an incomplete one." The association began allowing blacks to attend its clinic in 1909 and established a Negro branch of the organization in 1914, and it also pushed for wider reforms: "playgrounds which will keep the young people in the open air[;] . . . better sanitary conditions in their sections of the city[;] . . . better lighting as a check to vicious conduct[;] . . . better housing as a means of physical protection and mental order. Better educational facilities and hospital care. All these things enter into a program of health." The association wished not only to cure but to prevent the disease through "better living conditions, better sanitation, education and recreation."[61]

"I Couldn't Put Anybody in Grady Hospital"

Hospital care became the black community's main health-related issue, for this was one area in which Atlanta was dismally inadequate. Hospital space for the black population, which had a higher disease rate than the white population, was woefully lacking. Although black institutions provided some facilities—Fair Haven Infirmary of Morris Brown College and MacVicar Hospital of Spelman Seminary—and some small private hospitals also existed, there were not enough beds for the nonindigent black population and not enough teaching facilities for black doctors. Indigent patients went to Grady Hospital, the city's segregated facility, which contained buildings for blacks and whites and for which the Emory University

Medical School was contracted to provide medical services. Grady served as the teaching hospital for the medical school at first only in relation to black patients and by 1931 for whites as well. Specialized health care facilities such as Battle Hill sanitorium for TB cases had racially separated and very unequal wards. Ruby Baker, who worked at Battle Hill, explained that the "white ward was in front with the beautiful lawn. The black ward was down by the boiler room in the back." On the state level, Georgia had set up a facility for white TB victims in 1911. Blacks did not get a sanitorium until 1927, when they received the 1911 structure as whites moved into a new building.[62]

Racist policies put Atlanta's black doctors at a decided disadvantage. Some, such as Louis T. Wright, began their practice in Atlanta (Wright started practicing in 1917) but could not work in such a demeaning atmosphere and left for the North. Others stayed, putting up with intolerable conditions. Homer Nash, a black physician who started his practice in Atlanta in 1910, stated, "I couldn't put anybody in Grady Hospital . . . because of segregation. I couldn't even visit there as a doctor. . . . You lost your patient at the front door." Nash remembered that as early as 1910, black doctors were trying to get access to Grady but were denied. And throughout the twentieth century, black organizations worked to secure that goal. This exclusionary policy had serious repercussions for the black community. It meant that white doctors had to be called in when black patients were sent to Grady—a humiliation for black physicians and a not-so-subtle indication that black doctors were considered less valid. This suggestion had an impact even within the black community; as Dr. Nash recalled, "It took a long time to make the black person feel that the black doctor knew what he was talking about." Because of prejudice and segregation, blacks came to feel that "white was right, although there was some lessening of this attitude by the World War I years." Relationships between white and black physicians were worked out on the following basis, Dr. Nash explained: "You'd contact him [the white doctor]. He'd come over, look him [the patient] over and agree with your diagnosis. Then he'd put him into Grady Hospital. And operate on him. . . . You couldn't do it. Your face is black." The black physician received a small payment from the patient, but the white doctor got the larger fee, since he had done the operation.[63]

This arrangement may also have affected black patients' health. In an open letter to city officials in 1919, the NAACP's Atlanta branch complained about the exclusion of black physicians from Grady, which left their patients "to secure attention from a physician certainly less interested and sometimes less skilled." And as Asa Yancey, who many years later became the first black doctor on Grady's staff, suggested in a 1987 interview, blacks may have felt unwelcome at a segregated hospital and perhaps waited longer to go there, until their symptoms were worse. Dr. Yancey also felt that black patients' care was affected in a segregated hospital. He commented, "You can't take a human being and teach him that another human being is a second-rate human being and expect him to respond as rapidly as he's going to respond to a first-rate human being. I'm calling it time factor." What this meant, he said, was that "the staff responded a few minutes later [with a black patient], and that response probably would continue with the entire treatment." For these reasons, he argued, blacks had higher mortality rates than whites at segregated hospitals or than other blacks at black teaching hospitals. He thought that black physicians making the rounds at Grady might have created a different situation or atmosphere in regard to responding to the needs of black patients. He stated that some white doctors did, of course, treat black patients equally, but there were others, he maintained, who dealt with them as less than human beings.[64]

Segregated care was also difficult for black patients. Not only would their black doctors be denied entry into Grady (except as a nonmedical visitor), but going to the offices of white physicians was also a demeaning event. Although white doctors did usually treat black patients, they did so in segregated offices with segregated reception rooms. Whites were taken first, and only when the examinations of whites were over did white doctors look at their black patients. Ruby Baker related her experiences at a white doctor's office: "We had to wait in examining rooms, and they would usher you down the halls to the back room and you wait for the doctor. . . . But you never saw the white patients. They would usher you around the back room and out through the hall, as if to . . . make sure you avoided contact with the white patients."[65]

Grady's segregated emergency rooms, wards, and ambulances were also part of the racially based services for black Atlantans. When a health emergency occurred and Grady was called for an ambulance, the first question was about the race of the injured. If a black ambulance was not available (they numbered few), one designated for whites would not be sent. Thus, crucial care could be delayed. Given the segregated hospital care for indigent blacks, the inadequate hospital space for paying black patients, and the race-based emergency room and ambulance service, it is easy to understand the precarious position of the black community's health.[66]

Other aggravating factors included the poor training facilities for black doctors and nurses. A school for black nurses opened in 1914; its classes were initially held on the Spelman College campus, but in 1917 it became a separate, accredited training school affiliated with Grady Hospital (Grady Municipal Nurse Training School). Black interns and established doctors, however, could not use Atlanta's major public hospital for training and improving their skills, and that issue was a sore point for decades. Also, schools for X-ray technology and other medical technology did not admit blacks.[67]

Mortality Rates

By the 1930s it was evident that the combination of racist health care policies, inadequate city services, and high poverty levels was a damaging one for the black community. In 1930, the infant mortality rate was 147.3 per 1,000 live births for blacks and 55.6 for whites. The death rate for blacks was 22.7 per 1,000; for whites, 9.48. (The black mortality rate was up from 19.5 in 1900, while the white rate was down from 11.6.) In 1930, TB deaths accounted for 268.75 per 100,000 blacks but only 51.05 per 100,000 whites. By 1939, conditions had improved, but blacks still were overrepresented in the mortality figures. For example, the black death rate from TB was now 226.75 per 100,000; for whites it was now 30.07. Atlanta's black population in 1938 was 97,200, and just forty-one black doctors served that community. For whites, whose population numbered 194,800, there were 571 white doctors. Although white physicians did treat blacks, black doctors lived in black neighborhoods, so they were the first line of defense and the source of information against disease.[68]

The deficiency of health care for blacks is also revealed in a 1938 conference on health held by the Fulton-DeKalb Committee on Interracial Cooperation. The major problem they cited was the shortage of hospital beds for both indigent and nonindigent blacks. Grady had only 200 beds for the black poor, but based on the population it should have had 450. For those who could pay, private hospitals needed 100 beds but only had 45 (available at two small hospitals). In 1939, Grady admitted 10,372 whites and 10,902 blacks, but given the small amount of space assigned for black use, according to the hospital's annual report, "the waiting list for operations on colored women extends from five to six months ahead." This shortage had been evident for some time and remained a consistent problem. The 1937 annual report stated that "with its present bed capacity, the white wards function very well, although at times we experience extreme congestion. In the colored wards, however, there is a continual shortage of bed space, thus we are compelled to reject patients who should be admitted, and we frequently send home, too soon, patients who ought to remain longer in the hospital." In 1937, the average stay for maternity and obstetrical patients was 3.8 days for blacks, 7.5 days for whites. For surgical patients in 1938, it was 8.5 days for blacks, 9.1 for whites. This scenario may help explain why Atlanta's death rate for whites in 1940 was below the national average, while for blacks its mortality rate was much higher than the national average.[69]

By the 1930s, various organizations were working to improve black health care. The Atlanta Committee on Women's Interracial Activities, the Atlanta Civic and Political League, the Georgia Committee on Interracial Cooperation (and its Fulton-DeKalb Committee), the Atlanta Urban League, and others discussed such issues as overcrowding in Grady's black wards, black physicians' rights to treat their patients at hospitals like Grady, placing black interns in public hospitals, building a hospital for blacks of all incomes, and the general neglect of black health needs. Most important, in the 1930s the federal government became more involved in health issues.[70]

Federal Initiatives

The 1930s depression initially affected health care in the city in numerous ways: for example, it put more strain on black self-help groups such as the Neighborhood Union. During the 1931–32 period, the union aided 1,100 families and operated a medical clinic for preschoolers. In a petition to the mayor and city council, the organization asked for a $500 appropriation to help pay for its services. Appealing to long-term white fears about the consequences of black health problems, the petition stated, "We must improve the health of these thousands of undernourished children, for should an epidemic break out among them, no child in the city of Atlanta would be safe." This argument still hit a resonant chord among whites. When the University Homes project was opened in 1937, replacing the slums that had been on that site, the *Atlanta Constitution* wrote an editorial that hailed the new housing. The editors commented, "No matter how comfortable the living circumstances of one group of the population may be, they never know complete safety while, within easy range of their door, there is another population group living, under conditions conducive to ill health, infectious disease and undesirable moral life."[71]

The influence of New Deal programs was one aspect of the depression years that improved black health care. Federal funds through the Federal Emergency Relief Administration and, later, the Works Progress Administration were used in the state for such problems as TB cases, medical examination of schoolchildren, and nutrition. Nursery schools run by the WPA provided children with medical examinations as well as immunizations. Also, the Civilian Conservation Corps and National Youth Administration attended to health issues among their workers. The Social Security Act provided funds for Georgia to further develop its county health departments, prenatal clinics, and overall public health work.[72]

A New Hospital

By the 1940s, concern again centered on hospital space. The idea of a new hospital for nonindigent blacks where black doctors could practice—an idea that had been discussed for a number of years—began to take shape during the 1940s, as did the establishment of a black health center on the west side. The Atlanta Urban League was the main organization pushing for these goals. The health center, which was to provide basic health care and educate the area's population on health matters, opened its doors in September 1944 and represented the first of its kind for Georgia's blacks.[73] The longer fight involved securing more hospital facilities, especially for nonindigent blacks, who had few places to go.

Tentative plans for such a hospital were discussed in 1941, before America entered World War II, and the plans' architects had hopes of securing federal funds. The Fulton-DeKalb Hospital Authority was set up in 1941 with the right to borrow from the federal government. This agency took over control of Grady in 1946, when the city relinquished its jurisdiction (the city had control over Grady from 1892 to 1945). There was some question in 1941 of whether the new hospital would simply be an extension of Grady, specifically for black patients, with the same provisions barring black physicians. However, an effort was made to convince the federal government to provide the funds only if black doctors could treat their patients in the facility. While this action was taken in regard to the planned hospital, federal funds did not always breach the racial divide. The subsequent Hill-Burton Act (Hospital Survey and Construction Act) of 1946 allowed federal funds to be used for the construction of local hospitals even if there were separate facilities based on race (under the "separate but equal" concept).[74]

Atlanta's lack of hospital space for nonindigent blacks, the inadequate health care afforded to all Atlanta's blacks, and the high black death rate remained an issue of concern to blacks and some whites during the 1940s, but the catalyst that brought this issue to a head was the Atlanta Urban League's December 1947 report on the hospital care of the city's black community. The report revealed an improving but still depressing picture of health care for the city's African American population. For example, blacks had access to only 21.7 percent (391) of the general hospital beds in the Atlanta area (Fulton and DeKalb Counties) in 1946, although they made up about 35 percent of Atlanta's population. Furthermore, there were only eighty-seven general hospital beds available in the three black-owned hospitals for the nonindigent. Only thirteen beds were available in Fulton and DeKalb Counties for nonindigent maternity patients. According to a Commission on Hospital Care formula for what constituted an adequate number of hospital beds, blacks (of all income levels) should have had 251 more beds in 1947. Meanwhile, based on the same formula, whites had an excess of 435 beds for their needs and population size. The hospital bed space was available in the city, making a new black hospital unnecessary, but the excess white beds were racially restricted. There was also only one black doctor for every 3,074 blacks in Atlanta, although "it is generally accepted," according to the report, "that one physician cannot adequately serve more than 2,000 persons for medical care, and one physician for each 1,000 to 1,500 persons is considered a more desirable standard." The 1946 figure was worse than in 1938 when there had been one black doctor for every 2,371 blacks in the city. And these doctors lacked diagnostic facilities to treat their paying hospital patients.[75]

Atlanta could not attract black physicians because of their inability to secure accredited postgraduate training in the city's hospitals, to serve as interns or residents in the public hospital, to work in Grady's clinics, to treat their own patients who were admitted to Grady, or to join county or state medical societies. As the Urban League report stated, "The fact that Negroes do not share in the internships, residencies and fellowships of the municipal hospital restricts seriously the growth of the medical profession in the city. No recruits to the Negro medical group are possible through local training." For black nurses, conditions were only slightly better. Black nurses could serve in Grady's segregated unit, but there were no nursing schools in the city that could provide them with "advanced or specialized training." There was one accredited nursing school for blacks, but it was small and did not have space for the many applicants.[76] Although health is a complex matter, it is clear that the long-term restrictions on black medical professionals and the inadequate facilities had a persistently negative effect on the health of the black community.

Health conditions continued to improve considerably for both racial groups into the mid-1940s, but disease and death rates were still significantly higher for blacks than for whites. For example, in 1946 the infant death rate was 53.36 per 1,000 live births for blacks, 26.46 for whites. Although the black infant mortality rate was double that of whites, the city provided only four infant health centers for blacks, compared to twenty-one for whites. The death rate for all blacks was 13.02 per 1,000 population in 1946, while for all whites it was 7.48. Another revealing fact, reported by the Urban League, was that the black death rate in Atlanta in 1940 was higher than the same group's rate in thirty other leading cities across the country (including southern cities such as Memphis, Birmingham, Jacksonville, New Orleans, and Richmond). Emphasizing also the impact of black health on white health, the Atlanta Urban League study stated that "the health of the whole population of Atlanta is affected by the health and well being of the Negro portion of the population."[77]

Whether for humanitarian or self-interest-based reasons, the league's report affected leading whites. Hughes Spalding, chairman of the Hospital Authority's board of trustees, was the most influential white to work toward the goals suggested in the report. Echoing that document, he agreed that "probably the most desperate need of this community is a private hospital for Negroes. It is estimated that there are some 90,000 Negroes in our community who are ineligible to receive treatment at Grady. They have nowhere to go." Spalding's intention was to establish such a hospital and to begin a training program for black doctors and surgeons. After the 1947 report, the Urban League also invited leading blacks and whites to meet and discuss the black community's health needs. Out of these meetings came the Advisory Committee on Hospital Care for Negroes. The league's efforts thus sparked the concern of others and began the process of correcting a decades-old problem.[78]

By 1948, Emory University Medical School and Grady Hospital had agreed to open some of their postgraduate education programs to black physicians. Weekly postgraduate clinics were started for black doctors. The plans for a Negro hospital for the nonindigent proceeded quickly. Emory acknowledged that the new hospital would serve to train black interns and residents. As of 1949, land had been acquired next to Grady, and funds from the federal government (through the Hill-Burton Act), the state, and the Hospital Authority were available. The goals of the hospital were both to provide needed nonindigent care and to train black doctors. As part of the process, the Hospital Authority appointed a biracial advisory board of trustees to help direct the new facility. Blacks thus took some part in the planning and governing of this hospital, although the usual practice in Atlanta was to completely omit blacks from decision-making. The advisory group could only make recommendations, however.[79]

The Pavilion

The Hughes Spalding Pavilion of Grady Hospital (134 beds) opened in June 1952 as a segregated facility for the nonindigent black population. It was to be a self-supporting hospital, receiving county funds only if it went into debt. The construction of this building was much easier than the next step: a graduate training program under the auspices of Emory University Medical School. Although Emory and the Hospital Authority had approved an initial teaching plan in 1952, it had not been implemented. Emory was also to supervise professional services at the Hughes Spalding Pavilion. The medical school moved very slowly on these points, using various reasons, including financial problems, to explain its failure to begin a graduate program. The Urban League, under Grace Hamilton, pushed hard for such a program. She stressed, "The most important, if not the most publicized, purpose of the hospital was to provide a means to increase the number and quality of Negro physicians in this area and thus to improve the medical care of the Negro population." Spalding was to be a teaching hospital. However, during its first few years it functioned "with neither supervision of professional services nor teaching program."[80]

As the years passed and numerous meetings were held and plans made to begin the teaching program, Emory and Grady continued their delaying tactics. By 1955, according to Asa Yancey, who was going to direct Spalding's surgical training program within a few years, the facility still was lacking in patient care, graduate and postgraduate training, and research. As a result, Atlanta still had difficulty getting black physicians to move to and practice in the city.[81]

Black nurses also continued to experience problems such as lower salaries than those of white nurses, disrespect from white doctors and hospital officials, inadequate promotions, and barriers against membership in local or state nursing associations. The Grady Nursing School still limited its black admissions. After some black student nurses at Grady were fired in 1955, a citizens' committee made up of leading blacks—Martin Luther King Sr., A. T. Walden, L. D. Milton, C. A. Scott, and Benjamin E. Mays—complained to the Hospital Authority that this was just part of a series of racist occurrences at the hospital. "It is alleged that if Negro nurses do well on an examination they are accused of cheating—once at least it is reported that they had to take another examination because of this accusation. It is the feeling in the Negro community that the medical and surgical work at Grady is good but the Negro nurses and patients are not given the same respect as that given to white patients and white nurses."[82]

In 1955, disgust with the treatment of nurses and the training program delay led to meetings with the hospital administrators and a more determined effort to secure a teaching plan. Hamilton and other black leaders set up the Foundation for the Advancement of Medical and Nursing Education to push for the teaching that had been promised. The organization was able to work out a plan that was accepted by both the Hospital Authority and Emory. Its provisions called for Emory Medical School to supervise the program and for Spalding's interns and residents to be allowed to treat all of Grady's black surgical patients and to utilize various Grady facilities, such as the radiological laboratories and the medical library. But at first nothing changed.[83]

Finally, with funds provided partly through grants in 1956, Asa Yancey was hired in 1958 as Spalding's chief of surgery. His job was to begin a training program in surgery for black interns and residents at Spalding and secure accreditation for the program. Yancey had been promised that such a program would be established. Although a small graduate program in surgery was started for one fourth-year resident, the implementation of an expanded program (one for interns or one- to three-year residents) was delayed. Yancey found white resistance still strong, although a number of whites had supported the creation of such a program. Although seemingly agreed to, the issue that stalled the training for years was the right of Spalding's black interns and residents to study and treat black surgical patients in the segregated wing of Grady. According to Ira A. Ferguson, chief of surgical services at Grady, a teaching plan was being fulfilled: ten beds for Grady's black indigent surgery patients had been placed in Spalding to provide access for Spalding interns and residents. Also, Dr. Yancey and residents at Spalding could treat black outpatients at Grady's clinic. However, they had no staff privileges, and the small number of black beds in Spalding made their access to surgical patients quite limited, so this situation did not provide the Spalding teaching program with enough patients to secure accreditation. All it did, as the *Atlanta Inquirer* stated, was further delay the black doctors' entry into Grady's wards.[84]

Racial concerns prevented black doctors at Spalding from using an already-established graduate program at Grady. Since Spalding Pavilion was associated with Grady (a tax-supported institution), treating the Spalding and Grady doctors separately in regard to training meant that programs were being duplicated. Moreover, efforts to expand the teaching of black physicians to include fields other than surgery failed, as did attempts to further develop the surgical program for Spalding interns and residents in 1959 by finally allowing them access to Grady's black surgical inpatients. Emory University bluntly rejected this effort for the reason "that it would not be practical at this time to modify the existing teaching and service programs in Grady Hospital as requested." A separate, full training program at Spalding could not be effectively established due to lack of funds, but Emory Medical School still opposed allowing black doctors to train in Grady's black wards.[85]

Furthermore, as Grace Towns Hamilton stated in late 1959 at a meeting of the Spalding Advisory Board of Trustees, seven years after the opening of the pavilion, "a fully accredited four-year training program" did not yet exist. One could not be developed, she noted, "unless the size of the Pavilion is substantially increased." However, "increasing the size of the Pavilion for the sole purpose of providing accredited graduate training cannot be justified in view of Grady Hospital's unmet needs for medical staffing." Another approach would have been to designate a sufficient number of Grady patients for "exclusive" treatment by black residents. But this approach would be "extremely cumbersome administratively." The logical scenario would be simply to allow blacks to train at Grady within the existing program.[86]

The effort to open up Grady's intern and residency program to blacks persisted into the 1960s. Concerns were also raised about inadequate funding for Spalding and the continued shortage of black doctors in the state, partly due to lack of training facilities and staff privileges at Grady. Georgia actually had one of the nation's worst ratios of doctors per 100,000 residents. As a result, there were growing demands that the remaining barriers to full black participation in the medical field be removed. By 1960, even the white press was arguing that restrictions should be abolished due to the shortages of black doctors in Atlanta. Spalding's advisory board of trustees firmly stated that the "discrimination which prevents participation in the learning opportunities of the publicly supported teaching hospital is against the public interest."[87]

Medical Care and the 1960s Civil Rights Movement

The civil rights organizations in Atlanta during the 1960s cited black health care as one of the main areas needing change. In its January 1960 publication "A Second Look: The Negro Citizen in Atlanta," the Atlanta Committee for Cooperative Action complained about the lack of hospital facilities for blacks and the higher black mortality rate; and in its March 1960 "Appeal for Human Rights," COAHR attacked the inequality of Atlanta's hospital facilities. Groups such as COAHR, SNCC, and the NAACP protested against Grady's segregated facilities and its policy toward black doctors. One of the complaints was that blacks had to wait many hours for treatment in the Negro clinic, "although the white clinic is often almost empty." The NAACP's Atlanta branch agreed that "limiting the use of emergency clinics . . . strictly and solely on the basis of race, regardless of the volume of patient traffic" was "dangerous and medically unethical." By this time, blacks had more available beds at Grady than whites, but blacks made up 70 percent of Grady's patients and should have had even more bed space than they had. The NAACP's Atlanta branch criticized segregation policies that led to duplication of medical services "at a time when the cost of public health services is already painfully high." The organization also condemned the practices of restricting black interns, denying black doctors visiting staff rights at Grady, and keeping blacks out of Grady's medical technology training programs. SNCC, working with its South Atlanta Project, wanted more health clinics in that section of the city. "The City Must Provide," the document that SNCC helped draft in 1963, declared,

> Atlanta city officials have striven to create an Image of Atlanta as a rapidly growing, modern, progressive city where all citizens can live in decent, healthful surroundings. This image is a blatant lie so long as the city provides NO health clinics for its citizens, but relies entirely upon inadequate county facilities. It is a lie so long as these health clinics are segregated and the city takes no action to end this segregation. Because of segregation, only one of the four health clinics in the southside area is available to over 60,000 Negroes. This clinic . . . is small, its equipment inadequate and outdated, and its service dangerously slow due to general overcrowding.

Among other demands, the report called on the city to provide more clinics. The city, however, made no immediate response.[88]

In 1961, a black dentist named Roy C. Bell and various civil rights groups filed a suit in federal court to end segregation at Grady and to integrate the local white medical associations. (Membership in these medical groups was required for staff privileges at Grady.) The separate but unequal medical care was still very evident as the court case continued into 1962. Of the 4,000 hospital beds available in Atlanta, blacks could use only 680 (most of which were at Grady or Spalding); this number represented only 17 percent of the city's hospital beds, although in 1960 the city's blacks comprised 38.2 percent of the total population. Also, blacks made up nearly 50 percent of the deaths from the major illnesses (e.g., heart disease) and were more likely than whites to need hospital services. Yet

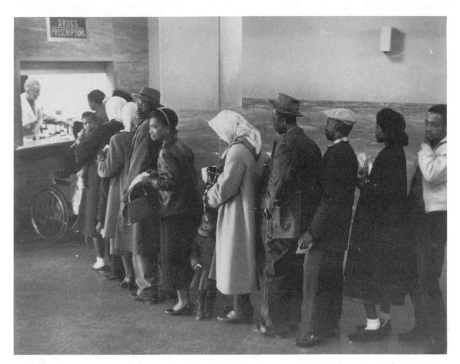

Segregated waiting lines at Grady Hospital pharmacy, c. 1950s (Boyd Lewis Collection, Courtesy of Atlanta History Center)

while there was one white doctor for every 469 white patients in the city, there was one black physician for every 4,500 blacks—a worse ratio than in 1946. In 1962, the black mortality rate stood at 11.7 per 1,000 persons; the white rate was 8.3.[89]

There are many other ways, as well, to note the inadequacy of black health care in Atlanta. For example, whites who could afford to pay had over fourteen hospitals from which to select, while blacks had five. Whites could secure treatment at Grady's psychiatric clinic, while blacks had to leave the city for inpatient psychiatric care. For whites who desired a career in nursing, there were five schools available in Fulton and DeKalb Counties; for blacks there was only one. For training as a doctor, whites could go to Emory University Medical School and choose from among five hospitals for their internship; blacks had to leave the city for medical school, and they could intern only at Spalding, which did not have a complete graduate training program. For established white physicians, there were many facilities and positions, as well as various medical associations; for blacks, further training was difficult and staff privileges scarce.[90]

COAHR's picketing of Grady, which had begun in November 1961, continued into 1962 as SNCC, SCLC, COAHR, and others pushed for change. The demands were simple and designed to provide integrated and adequate health care: blacks should be allowed into Grady's internship program; black doctors should get full staff privileges; the ambulance services, emergency clinics, wards, nursing schools, medical schools, and programs for technical training (e.g., in X-ray technology) should be integrated; black nurses should be accepted into postgraduate programs; and a black should be appointed to the Hospital Authority.[91]

In February 1962, the Hospital Authority approved a plan that changed Spalding from a private facility tied to Grady to an actual unit of Grady— a paying ward—under the supervision of Grady's superintendent. Plans were then made to put a black intern at Grady for the 1963–64 period. In March 1962, Asa Yancey was given visiting staff rights at Grady and became the first black doctor on the hospital's staff. He also retained his position as Spalding's director of surgery. Many in the black community were angered by the long delay in accomplishing even this meager act and by the inadequacy of this step in dealing with health care problems. For example, the Reverend John Middleton, president of the SCLC's Atlanta chapter, and Roy C. Bell, its special projects committee chairman, issued a statement noting that much suffering had to be endured "to expose 'Forward Atlanta' to the eyes of the world as a city barbaric in nature. A city that has refused to concern itself realistically about the health and care of

38.2 percent of its population. . . . In order for Atlanta to progress forward, it must realize that the day has long past when the rights of a Negro citizen are what the nearest white man say they are." The SCLC called for the immediate desegregation of Grady and the city's private hospitals. Complaints about Grady's segregation went to the Hospital Authority, the aldermanic board, the Fulton County Commission, and the mayor.[92]

In November 1963, the U.S. Fourth Circuit Court of Appeals in a North Carolina case (*Simkins v. Moses H. Cone Memorial Hospital*) issued its judgment that a hospital that secured any Hill-Burton funds had to admit all races. "Separate but equal" could no longer apply to either black patients or doctors. Up to this point, federal money like Hill-Burton funds had been used for racially segregated wards or hospitals. This decision was an important breakthrough and ended the "separate but equal" facade under which federally funded hospitals operated. The *Atlanta Inquirer* noted what "separate but equal" had really indicated and expressed the hope that this court ruling would change the situation. "It is widely known that the 'separate but equal' practice right here in Atlanta has often meant that Negro patients would be housed in the hallways while there was plenty of available room space on the 'white side' [of the hospital]." The editorial went on to say that "there have been cases where Negroes have been allowed to die rather than even give them emergency treatment at federally subsidized 'lily white' hospitals."[93]

The Summit Leadership Conference entered the fray in the fall of 1963 with its "Action for Democracy" statement. Reiterating some earlier demands of the civil rights groups, Summit called for black representation on the Fulton-DeKalb Hospital Authority, the immediate integration of hospital staffs and services, the provision of more facilities for black inpatient psychiatric care, and, within Grady's training program for doctors, the elimination of the notion "that there is a difference in people because of color. 'You are training physicians to make a distinction between the races.' "[94]

In spite of the protests, the picketing, the court case, and planned further demonstrations, Atlanta's white medical establishment remained resistant. While the Fulton County commissioners appointed the Hospital Authority's first black, C. R. Yates, in 1964, in an automobile accident case that occurred during the same year, medical treatment was delayed for thirty to forty-five minutes "while the admissions personnel quibbled about [the victim's] racial background" in order to put her into the racially correct emergency ward at Grady. And although Grady officially desegregated its clinics and ambulance services soon after this incident, other facets of the hospital were still segregated, as were nearby public hospitals in DeKalb and other counties. By June 1964, Grady nursing classes had been integrated, but conditions at the hospital were still unequal. For example, there was a shortage of supplies for blacks, but not for whites; and the children's area on the black side of the hospital was overcrowded, while the one on the white side had empty beds.[95]

As of 1965, Grady's wards and nursing school dormitories still were segregated, but now they had to comply with a February 1965 federal court order to desegregate. The court gave the Hospital Authority thirty days to submit a timetable for accomplishing integration. This court order, issued four years after the Atlanta case began, prompted Grady to prepare a desegregation plan. After delays, and a court order to desegregate wards and patients by 1 July 1965, the hospital finally moved to desegregate all its facilities on 1 June. This change resulted from the court ruling plus the need to conform to Title VI of the 1964 Civil Rights Act (which prohibited both discrimination in any federally funded enterprises, including hospitals, and the provision of funds to segregated hospitals) in order to secure Medicare funds. But it took legal action to bring about this shift; nonetheless, the hospital did begin to comply. According to J. W. Pinkston, Grady's superintendent, "All phases of the hospital are on a nonracial basis, effective today [1 June]. This includes staff and physicians. We are now grouping patients strictly on their medical needs. All outpatients are together, all inpatients, all heart patients, etc." The segregated wards and services were eliminated. According to Dr. Yancey, medical care for black patients improved after integration. "It improved because people felt better. The acceptance of the individual as a first-rate human being took a definite step up. . . . Medical care all over improved with recognition of [black] nurses as full first-rate nurses, . . . residents being trained to treat everybody as a first-class human being, the attendants, medical staff, faculty, making rounds on everybody, instead of in separate groups, all that was very helpful." It also meant that black physicians were getting better training.[96]

Legacies of Segregation

Yet remnants of segregation were immediately obvious in July 1965, sometimes hampering the effectiveness of Grady's medical care. Although patients were now in integrated wards, "the former Negro wards are staffed by Negro nurses and former white wards are staffed by white nurses." Black doctors on the staff were still not fully utilized. Also, on entering the hospital, black patients were "designated on records by the code letter 'C.' The letter 'C' stands for colored." The superintendent's response to complaints about the still-segregated nursing staff was that the whites would resign if they were reassigned out of the formerly white-only wards.[97]

Other hospitals in the Atlanta area and the Fulton and DeKalb medical societies did not agree to comply with the Civil Rights Act until June 1966, soon after Department of Health, Education, and Welfare officials announced that they could withdraw federal funds from noncomplying hospitals. However, a review of Atlanta hospitals that was undertaken by HEW, the Public Health Service, and the Office of Equal Health Opportunity (OEHO) and was completed in August 1966 noted that the majority of hospitals serving Atlanta remained white. The report did state that change was taking place, although whites were reluctant: "The granting of staff privileges by hospitals to Negro physicians at other than traditionally Negro hospitals proceeds slowly." For example, Crawford Long Hospital, which had barred black doctors, finally accepted three on its staff in July 1966. Previously, Atlanta hospitals had been using various tactics to delay compliance with Title VI—tactics like requiring applicants for the hospital staff to supply a letter of recommendation from a current (i.e., white) staff member. Discussions between the OEHO and hospital officials in spring 1966 brought an end to these tactics. Some hospitals only admitted their first black patients in 1966, but once they had done so, there was neither discrimination in facility use nor segregation within the hospital.[98]

Numerous other problems remained, of course. The poor sanitation and other city services for low-income black neighborhoods was still a serious health-related issue. One 1966 report stated that residents in these areas "receive poor health care because of insufficient funds for transportation, a great dislike for the attitude of personnel, and necessity of allocating almost an entire day for each visit." As of 1966, metro Atlanta still had a shortage of black doctors—there were 53 black physicians and 1,200 white. A 1967 report on Grady for the Community Relations Commission noted numerous concerns that should have been resolved by that time. Segregated ambulance services continued to some degree: "one attendant observed that often Negro companies across town are called for Negro patients when white companies are closer," and in another such incident, a white ambulance had reportedly picked up a white man and left a black man who was injured much more seriously. The document also cited the harassment of blacks eating in the formerly white-only Grady cafeteria, and a black nurse reported "that since the nursing schools have integrated, recruitment at Negro high schools in the state has stopped." Also, a 1967 HEW report on Grady practices stated that "the services of non-white physicians, even though members of the visiting staff, were not utilized the same as the white physicians." The hospital agreed to correct this problem and allow "each non-white doctor [to] perform in the desired area in which they indicated a preference." And a study of one of Atlanta's Model Cities neighborhoods in the early 1970s revealed a high death rate; "a shortage of public health services, neighborhood doctors and dentists[; and] the absence of drugstores"—a legacy of earlier, race-based policies.[99]

Although black health care improved over the years as the result of many factors, ranging from medical advances, to black doctors' access to advanced training, to 1960s Medicaid funding, to a larger black middle class, substandard segregated facilities and the long neglect of black needs surely took their toll. In terms of cause and effect, health is so complicated an issue that it is impossible to rate the factors affecting it. Undoubtedly, the fact that by 1978 black interns and residents at Grady numbered fifty-two did some good for the health of the black community in the city. Yet continued higher rates of mortality and of many diseases among black Atlantans in comparison to whites indicates the role of poverty, unemployment, poor nutrition, lifestyle, a lack of health insurance, and other variables as well.[100]

A few points, however can be stated with confidence. Atlanta's health care system did have a negative effect not only on the poor but also on the black middle class, whose communities had inadequate hospital space and access to doctors. Furthermore, those black Atlantans who wanted to become doctors, nurses, or medical technicians encountered a hostile environment in the city. The development of a dual medical system was wasteful in terms of the limited funds available. The construction of Spalding Pavilion would have been unnecessary if more hospital space had been available to nonindigent blacks. Once other hospitals desegregated, HEW tried to reverse the usual pattern of sending black patients to Spalding and whites elsewhere: black doctors were encouraged to send their black patients to formerly white hospitals and white doctors to admit their white clientele to Spalding. Black doctors complied; whites did not. As a result, Spalding received fewer and fewer patients over the years, lost increasing amounts of money, and in 1988 was finally closed for private patients. It was used for Grady's patient overflow when the hospital was refurbished; later it became a children's hospital.[101]

By 1988, Spalding's losses due to underuse were approximately $200,000 per month. It was simply a relic of earlier days. Fulton County Commission chairman Michael Lomax stated "that a small hospital built during segregation for black patients had never been a superior facility. It was an inferior, segregated facility. The fact is, no one can afford to pay for the center [Spalding], which, as far as I'm concerned, is a vestige of segrega-tion." Dr. Yancey felt that while Spalding was constructed well and at first had good equipment, it was underfunded "for continued growth and de-velopment as time went along, partly due to the opening up of white hospitals to black patients, which reduced Spalding's income."[102]

Grady, too, reflected the problems of a segregated past. The 1980s–1990s remodeling of the hospital, which had been rebuilt between 1954 and 1958, was delayed because the Fulton County Commission refused to provide the funding until complaints about racism—"that black patients are mistreated, that doctors who use historically black Hughes Spalding Medical Center were ignored in the renovation plans"—were resolved. Furthermore, the remodeling was partly necessitated by the hospital's segregated design—dual emergency rooms, dual wards, and dual facilities overall (except for the operating rooms, but including the postoperative recovery rooms), which wasted space and money. Lomax commented that the segregated set-up "hampered an efficient modern operation." Dr. Yan-cey stated that the segregated design, with two hospital wings that were mirror images of each other, "was the cause for the renovation. The build-ing of the building as a segregated one did, no doubt, cause a greater expense, and it interferes somewhat now, but that was minimized by plan-ning, by doing something with these various rooms." However, having white and black emergency rooms at Grady, he stated, was an expensive duplication that harmed patients. The inefficient bed utilization based on race also caused problems for patients. Furthermore, not only did the floor plan clearly recall segregation, but some black sections of the hospital also indicated earlier decades' prevailing attitude toward black patients and visitors: whites entered the building through a front entrance, while blacks entered through the back into a smaller lobby.[103]

The city emerged into a new era of unified health care after the 1960s. One indication of the change is that Emory University's medical school now shares Grady with the Morehouse School of Medicine, established in 1975. The new medical school and its work at Grady is designed to in-crease the number of Atlanta's and Grady's black doctors. In many ways, the impact of the policies of the segregation years lingered on.[104]

D. The Shaping of Atlanta's Police and Fire Services

The evolution of Atlanta's police and fire departments in the twentieth century and the problems evident by the 1970s and 1980s also reveal the role of race in the shaping of these city services.

Atlanta's police department was one that historically had very little positive contact with the black community. As early as 1867, and well into the twentieth century, black leaders had asked the city government to appoint black police. No blacks were hired for many decades, though, and there were constant complaints from Atlanta's blacks about police brutality and the neglect of crime in their neighborhoods. Both neglect and brutality on the part of policemen were particularly evident during the 1906 riot. In another situation in 1911, as historian John Dittmer writes, "White Atlantans ignored 'Jack the Ripper' murders of black women until their terrified maids refused to come to work. Only then did city officials press police to find the murderer." While white police did patrol black neighborhoods, they did not display much concern about black-on-black crime. Rather, they mainly enforced an unofficial curfew in these areas. Herbert Jenkins, Atlanta's police chief from 1947 to 1972, acknowledged that the white police "didn't want to spend a lot of time" in black neighborhoods; "they'd rather go patrol" in white areas. And when they were in the black parts of the city, "they had no enthusiasm for what they were doing."[105]

Except for two black matrons and a black probation officer hired in the early 1920s, the police department made no effort to deal with black demands. By the 1930s, after increasing reports of police brutality and neglect of black neighborhoods, these long-smoldering issues flamed into a major effort to convince the mayor and council to hire black police. The Atlanta branch of the NAACP, the Georgia Commission on Interracial Cooperation, the Atlanta Negro Chamber of Commerce, the Atlanta Urban League, the Neighborhood Union, and other groups urged the city to develop a new policy to deal with the employment issue and related concerns. These organizations suggested that hiring black police, among other matters, would help avert racial friction and reduce black community resentment toward the police.[106] The white community's handling of this issue was to have the opposite effect over the years, and during the 1970s and 1980s it would lead to a much-divided department and city.

Hiring Black Police

Mayor James L. Key and the police committee of the council remained opposed to putting blacks on the police force during the 1930s, even though other southern cities such as Louisville, Knoxville, and Tampa had done so successfully. Yet at least Mayor Key realized that changes would soon come. He told Herbert Jenkins, who was then his aide, that the appointment of blacks to the police force would eventually happen and that Jenkins should therefore be prepared and should begin studying the situation in other cities.[107]

The idea of black police seemed more palatable to white politicians by the mid-1940s, given the growing importance of the black vote. Earlier, Mayor Hartsfield had remained deaf to black demands. He often refused to meet with black leaders on the issue. And on one occasion, as the Reverend William Holmes Borders states, "I remember very distinctly that I, along with Warren Cochrane, John Wesley Dobbs, A. T. Walden, C. A. Scott, and M. L. King Sr., going to Mayor Hartsfield and asking him for black police. And he told us, without the slightest blinking of an eye, that we'd get black police in Atlanta about as soon as we'd get deacons in the First Baptist Church, white." Yet Hartsfield was a smart politician and left the door open in case something changed that would affect him politically. When political changes did occur, Hartsfield was willing to respond affirmatively to this request and to bring the city council into line on the issue.[108]

The All Citizens Registration Committee's efforts to register blacks to vote was crucial in the change of opinion. So was a protest march to secure black police in early 1946 and the continued pressure from other black community organizations and leaders. For example, in 1947, C. L. Harper and H. S. Murphy, respectively the chair and secretary of the black Georgia Teachers and Education Association, wrote the mayor and council a letter explaining why they believed that black police should be hired. "Most people are convinced that the use of Negro policemen in areas occupied by colored people will unquestionably serve to reduce crime in Atlanta as it has done in many southern cities." An accompanying petition stated that "the experience of residents of those areas [black neighborhoods] has been such that there has developed a *fear of* rather than a *respect for* police authority, a situation that has become so acute that in many situations residents fear calling in the police authority, lest the immediate situation be aggravated by their presence." Along with the letter and petition, they sent a list of southern cities that had already hired black policemen.[109]

A subsequent letter to the council police committee in 1947 came from the Citizens Committee, which included Reverend Martin Luther King Sr., Morehouse College president Benjamin E. Mays, C. L. Harper, and other black leaders. This committee provided several reasons why black police should be hired. Noting the high crime rate in black areas, the committee cited the "inadequate police protection" in these sections of

Atlanta's first eight black police standing outside Butler Street YMCA, which served as a segregated black police station, 1948. Left to right: Johnnie Jones, Willard Strickland, John Sanders, Willie Elkins, Robert McKibbons, Henry Hooks, Claude Dixon, and Ernest Lyons. (Courtesy of Atlanta History Center)

the city as one factor behind the high crime level. "We believe that by appointing . . . a reasonable number of Negro policemen, say twenty-five, [you] would help reduce crime in the city of Atlanta. We know that there is no magic in Negro policemen and that . . . other factors [e.g., lack of parks and playgrounds, poverty, inadequate schools] must be cleared out before the crime rate is normal among Negroes. But we place as Number 1 among our reasons the conviction that Negro policemen will help reduce the crime rate." The committee also noted the success other southern cities, including Savannah, had had with black police; described the morale-building benefits that such a new hiring policy would have for the black community; and described how "it will generate good will between the races and foster interracial harmony." Claiming that hiring black police was "the democratic thing to do," because blacks constituted one-third of the city's population, and that Atlanta should be a pacesetter for the South, the committee urged that its request be granted "not next year, but this year." There were other reasons, as well, for black leaders to demand a new hiring policy. The hiring of black police would mean the creation of new jobs that had previously been unattainable. And the presence of black police was also seen as a form of protection for black citizens, a way of ending (or at least decreasing) police brutality and harassment. With Hartsfield's backing, a resolution to hire black police was brought before the council and its police committee in December 1947. After much debate, and with the approval of Police Chief Jenkins, the council supported the measure and the mayor approved it.[110] Finally, in March 1948, after a series of exams, background investigations, and interviews, eight blacks joined the force. Although the move was initially hailed as a racial breakthrough, there were many problems with how the black policemen were treated. These problems and further hiring concerns caused more resentment and led to years of racial friction.

"Anything But to Give You the Proper Respect"

The initial eight officers were tightly constrained in their enforcement powers. They could not arrest whites; they could only hold the white offender until the white police arrived to make the official arrest. They had a separate watch—that is, they went on patrol at a different time than whites. They could only patrol in black areas of the city, had to operate out of their own segregated station house (set up at the black Butler Street YMCA), and could not wear their uniforms home. Police Chief Jenkins claimed that these restrictions were designed to protect the black police from harassment by the white public and police, and there is some validity to this reasoning. Black leaders had expressed concern about possible harassment from white police, and this danger led to their acquiescence about the separate precinct. However, another explanation comes from Harold Fleming, who attended the council hearings on behalf of the Southern Regional Council when the issue of hiring black police was discussed. Fleming stated that one of the arguments against hiring black police was that they would harass white women and, since they could legally carry guns, would cause other problems. As a result, Fleming noted, "The argument was to greatly limit the powers and the entitlements of Black officers." He concluded that "the whole thing was just resistance to Blacks being in any kind of authority with respect to White people." Whatever the motivation, the black policemen and the black community alike deeply resented the limitations imposed on the black police.[111]

Many white policemen were, as expected, a problem. Klan elements among the police and the officers' general anger over the hiring of blacks, led to incidents that indicated a great deal of animosity. While not all white police were hostile—in fact, some tried to help their black colleagues—there were many instances of friction. On one occasion, when a black policeman arrested a white, the police wagon refused to come and pick the individual up, and the black police officer was reprimanded for exceeding his authority. And Billy McKinney, one of the early black officers, reported that when a black was arrested and the wagon was called, "They might pull up on the other side of the street, and if you had an unruly prisoner, they might just sit there and not help you get him in the wagon. They'd do almost anything to irritate you and show disdain for you." At times white patrolmen tried to run down their black colleagues as they crossed the street. They also tried to frame them by claiming that the black policemen were drunk or by putting something in their lockers that would get them into trouble. In court, where the blacks could not wear their uniforms, some white policemen would sit in back laughing at them. The court cases that involved the black police were called only after the white police cases were finished. And according to O. R. McKibbons, one of the initial eight blacks, "For years after getting on the force, there were superior officers who would still . . . address you as 'boy' or 'John' or what have you." In other words, McKibbons continued, they would say "anything but to give you the proper respect as 'Officer.'" Chief Jenkins did respond to some of the complaints; for example, he either transferred those white policemen who could not accept black police or had them in for a talk and told them to stop harassing the black police. Nonetheless, the problems continued.[112]

Such inequities and insults might be expected initially, as racial adjustments were made. But they lasted over a number of years and had serious effects on the department's development and functioning. McKinney recalled, "Pretty soon there was frustration on the part of black police, that they couldn't lock up white people, that they couldn't get promoted, that everything was done on a token basis." Changes in the system were eventually made, but they came slowly and with great reluctance on the part of the city's white leaders. "Maybe it was best it took place in steps," McKinney said, "but for the people involved, you felt discriminated against." He also commented that "every step of the way there was a fight. There was never anything being given without a fight for it." Changes that did take place during the next few years included moving the black precinct from the YMCA to the basement of the regular police station on Decatur Street in 1950; allowing black police to wear their uniforms home and to court; and permitting some of them to patrol in police cars rather than on foot. But any significant hiring of more blacks and the promotion of those already on the force was stalled for years. At first Chief Jenkins made no effort to hire any more blacks or promote any of the first eight. He felt that once blacks were on the force, the job was completed. Concerned that the police department would become all-black, he moved very slowly. He also commented, "We weren't committed to promote them. We never agreed to promote them. They weren't considered." Over the years, black leaders pressured the city to hire more black officers and to promote them. This policy was eventually accepted, but for a long time it was only a minimal effort.[113]

Change under Mayor Allen

As late as 1959, there were only forty blacks on a police force of 650 (6.1 percent). Two blacks had been promoted to detective in 1955. White police officers' brutality and insulting behavior toward black Atlantans remained an issue in the early 1960s. After Ivan Allen was elected mayor in 1961, with substantial black support, the Atlanta Negro Voters League strongly urged Jenkins to eliminate police brutality, which occurred with even "a simple traffic violation, a routine inquiry or an ordinary arrest." They also wanted him to remove all restrictions from black policemen, to increase their numbers, and to promote more of them. While Jenkins agreed to respond to the police brutality issue, he asserted that there were "no plans for up-grading Negro patrolmen" or for hiring more. However, when Allen assumed office in 1962, he and Jenkins eliminated an earlier restriction on black police that had been a sore point for many years: black officers could now arrest whites.[114]

In 1962, Mayor Allen broke another color line by hiring Atlanta's first black firemen, who received training and joined the force in 1963. This step had not been taken earlier because firemen lived together in the firehouse; for this reason, maintaining segregation posed more difficulties for the fire department than it had for the police force. Nonetheless, after years of pressure from the black community, and after other southern cities such as Charleston had opened up their fire departments, Atlanta's white leaders finally agreed to this change. After their first month on the job, the initial sixteen black firemen were assigned to a newly built and segregated firehouse, Station 16. This fire station had been designed and built especially to maintain a segregated force, with partitioned rooms that would keep blacks and whites separated. The problems of the black firemen and the black community regarding firefighting services were similar to those regarding police services and inspired comparable resentments. For example, the black neighborhoods on Atlanta's west side were not sufficiently

Atlanta's first black firemen, 1963. Front row, left to right: Marvin Reed, James Maddox, Robert Ware, Quinton Redding, William Callier, Emmitt Smith, Johnny Belcher, and Harvey Bowens (with Lieutenant Dillashaw and Captain Gossett, company officers); back row, left to right: Frank Bolden, Milton Harp, Ralph Lester, William Hamer, Elbert Morrow, Harold Rosemond, Theodore Ector, and Marion Jordan Jr. (with Lieutenant Sheffield and Captain Block, commanding officers). (Courtesy of Atlanta Fire Department and Atlanta History Center)

protected, because there were no firehouses in this area. Station 16 was the first one placed in a predominantly black neighborhood except for a station in the city's oldest black section, near the downtown area. This new station meant a quicker response time for fires on the black west side. Black firemen complained that the whites on the force resented them and at times worked against them. James Maddox, one of the original black firemen, commented, "White companies would just quit fighting fires when we got there and let us do it all. They made it as tough as they could." According to Maddox, the white firemen from other stations were convinced that the blacks would fail to do the job and felt that the best way to get rid of them was not to help them, to let them do it all themselves. William Hamer, another of the initial black firemen, said that the whites "wanted to see what we could do—if we could measure up." Another problem was that the companies in black neighborhoods received the oldest equipment. And, of course, hiring and promotion soon became issues of contention.[115]

During Mayor Allen's two terms, police and fire services improved for the black community, as did the hiring of black patrolmen and firefighters, but problems continued as well. According to reports on police department discrimination sent to the Reverend Samuel Williams, cochair of the Atlanta Summit Leadership Conference, black complaints about the police department in the mid-1960s included the following: black police worked longer hours than whites; there were separate dressing rooms for white and black officers; blacks were unable to get positions in certain departments, such as the traffic division; black officers were not assigned to the office where prisoners were booked, and as a result, when blacks came to bail people out, they were "not treated courteously." The black police wanted "to be transferred to all divisions of the department according to qualifications or preferences rather than race. And once transferred [they wanted to] work under whoever commands that division": at first black superior officers supervised only black policemen, and blacks were promoted only to jobs designated as black positions. This situation guaranteed that "promotional vacancies are filled according to race. . . . There are Negro quotas that are not exceeded, no matter how qualified Negroes are to advance on the force." Moreover, there were few black detectives and no black female police officers; a separate black watch still existed; blacks were allowed to patrol only in black neighborhoods; blacks arrested by black policemen went to a segregated courtroom; and there was no merit system for promotions. Promotion results for detective, for example, were listed by race. One report noted, "The Negroes who pass are pre-picked and know that they will pass before the test [an oral interview] is taken." But few blacks were so chosen. Finally, there were continued complaints about inadequate police protection in black areas and police brutality. As a result of these factors, according to the reports, "Negro morale [in the department] is at rock bottom." "Atlanta is a disappointment," the *Atlanta Inquirer* concluded as a result of these revelations, "for once you go beyond its facade, the interior leaves much to be desired."[116]

For the fire department, there were similar complaints about discrimination in hiring, promotions, assignments, segregated working conditions, and neglect of the city's black areas. For example, the black firemen charged in 1969 that unequal hiring practices and unfair promotion tests were used in order to keep the department's leadership white. Firefighter William Hamer remembered the harsh reality: "They weren't going to promote blacks until we forced them to. We knew that and they knew it." As for neglect of black neighborhoods, the Atlanta Community Improvement Program reported in 1967 that "the fire protection services as provided are not equitable in *outlying residential areas* in which Negroes live as compared with services provided in *outlying residential areas* as a whole."[117]

While some issues had been resolved in the police department by the end of the 1960s, change came slowly. Late in 1965, black police began to receive transfers to other departmental divisions, such as traffic, and to other watches. By 1966, a black sergeant had been given an administrative position over black and white officers. By 1969, there were one black captain and six black lieutenants. Spurred by the Civil Rights Act of 1964 and the establishment of the Equal Employment Opportunity Commission, affirmative action demands grew. By 1968, there were 130 blacks on a police force of 970 (13.4 percent), and in 1969 there were 180 black firemen (but no black officers) in a department of 959 (19.7 percent). Despite this progress, blacks were still sorely underrepresented in these departments. As of 1969, Atlanta's black population was about 48 percent. The inadequate and slow minority hiring by these two city services was indicative of a larger problem involving a generally poor record of black hiring in all city departments. In 1970, the Community Relations Commission called for an effective affirmative action program for Atlanta.[118]

Hiring and Promotion

Blacks remained underrepresented in the police and fire departments and among its officers in the early 1970s. And up to that time, efforts to deal with such issues as segregated sleeping quarters and locker rooms for black firemen had been resisted, but were resolved during this period through the Community Relations Commission's intervention. However, the end result of the resistance and continued racism in the fire department, according to the *Atlanta Inquirer*, were that "some Black firemen are said to be quitting because of injustices including the apparent unwillingness to promote Black firemen." Given the long history of discrimination, hostility, neglect, and slow-paced integration within these two city services, the stage was clearly set for the promotion and hiring racial battles of the 1970s and 1980s—battles that further divided the city and its departments. In both cases, complaints about discriminatory behavior in hiring and promotions continued. In 1973, the Afro-American Patrolmen's League (AAPL), which had been formed in 1969 after the mainly white Fraternal Order of Police removed black policeman DeWitt Smith from its ranks for publicly complaining about white police beatings of black prisoners, joined other black officers and applicants to file federal lawsuits charging discrimination in hiring, promotion, and other policies. The following year, a group of black firemen did the same. For example, the black police complained of the "lack of assignment of blacks 'to integrated patrol car teams'" and alleged that the written test for hiring was discriminatory and that the criteria for promotion were too subjective. These lawsuits and the attendant racial splits in the two departments resulted in years of sporadic hiring and promotion freezes and conflict over the criteria for employment and advancement.[119]

The election of Maynard Jackson in 1973 presented an opportunity for a black mayor to use the powers of his office to redress black grievances. Jackson was a strong advocate of affirmative action, and the police department was one of his special concerns. Efforts to deal with police issues led to a long battle with John Inman, the white police chief who had been appointed in 1972 during the administration of the previous mayor, Sam Massell, for an eight-year term. Massell was initially considered an ally of the black community, and he had increased black hirings and promotions. But Inman turned out to be more resistant to black demands, opposed the city personnel board's recommendations to hire a certain number of black police, demoted some black officers who complained of police department racism and discrimination, and replaced the force's highest-ranking black, Assistant Police Chief J. H. Amos. Although the black community protested against Inman's actions, Massell could do little. Mayors could nominate department directors, but they could not hire or dismiss them. Police chiefs were officially appointed by the board of aldermen and could be fired only with its approval by a two-thirds vote. The disagreements under Inman's administration also involved hiring and promotions, particularly black demands for a city residency requirement for employment and charges of police officers' excessive use of force against blacks. The Afro-American Patrolmen's League (AAPL) supported the residency requirement and wanted some action against police brutality. The AAPL was opposed by the white Fraternal Order of Police (FOP) and by Inman. The FOP saw the residency requirement as a tactic to decrease the number of white police, because many of them lived in Atlanta's suburbs.[120]

By the early 1970s, there were four central problems, all of them tied to the racial factor: first, the long-standing hiring and promotion issue; second, Inman's poor response to demands for affirmative action in the police department; third, increasing accusations of police brutality; and fourth, the disagreements that had emerged between the AAPL and FOP. All four

Protest march against Police Chief John Inman, 1974 (Courtesy of Atlanta History Center)

issues split the police department along racial lines. Mayor Jackson, after much legal wrangling, eventually handled Inman by using the powers of the new city charter to create a public safety department and a public safety commissioner, under which the police and fire bureaus (as well as corrections and civil defense) would be subordinate. In 1974 Jackson brought in A. Reginald Eaves as the new public safety commissioner and thereby effectively ended Inman's control. As the first black in charge of these bureaus, Eaves became part of the solution but part of the problem as well, because he was a strong advocate of hiring more blacks in the police and fire bureaus. According to Jackson, many Atlanta residents saw the hiring of Eaves and the easing out of Inman strictly in racial terms. Therefore, attention remained fixed on this factor.[121]

Rather than solving the problems, Eaves's appointment and tenure resulted in further controversy, except for the police brutality issue. Use of excessive police force in black neighborhoods was largely eliminated. However, other issues remained. Hiring freezes continued on and off as the groups contended over employment criteria. Promotions also remained a contentious issue in both the police and fire departments. Promotion criteria in the police department included a written exam; evaluations of officers by their supervisors, who sent their reports to the chief; and an oral interview. The police chief (who, like the supervisors, had a great deal of discretion in this area) then made his recommendations to the police committee of the board of aldermen. Thus, the system that existed for promotions involved subjective criteria and could easily be manipulated by personal and racial considerations. Eaves tried to create a formal merit promotion system, and at the same time he tried to bring in more black officers. The same was true for the fire department. Eaves argued that "any service operation should reflect the racial composition of the city it serves." By 1975, a formal promotion system based on merit—a first for these departments—had been installed. With the merit process, promotion in the police bureau, for example, was based on a written test for each rank (worth 50 percent), an evaluation of the officer's record (20 percent) and performance (20 percent) on the force, and an oral interview (10 percent). However, the fairness of the promotion exam itself became a source of conflict in both departments, as did the racial makeup of those hired and promoted. Eaves also implemented a residency requirement for hiring, which had been passed by the city council in 1976. The Fulton County Superior Court and the Georgia Supreme Court declared the residency requirement for new hiring in the police and fire departments illegal in 1977, but it reappeared later in the decade as a qualification for promotion to high-level police positions. Whites now claimed reverse discrimination in a city increasingly under black control. The FOP battles with AAPL and the racial split in the fire bureau divided the forces so thoroughly that worker's demands were not being met. The racial struggles over hiring, promotions, exams, and police use of force in the black community had consumed all the time and energy of the various support groups. The AAPL and the black firefighters' organization (Brothers and Sisters Combined) refused to work with either the FOP or the mainly white International Association of Firefighters on raise issues until critical racial concerns had been settled.[122]

By 1976, in his two years as commissioner, Eaves had presided over significant racial change, even as the court battles continued. In the police department, 87 percent of those who quit the force between 1974 and 1976 were white and 74 percent of those brought on the force were black. In police ranks, blacks had increased their representation as well. Under Inman, for example, two out of eight majors were black; under Eaves, five out of ten were black. As a result of these racial changes, federal district court judge Charles A. Moye barred further hiring and promotions based on racial considerations. Suits, countersuits, freezes, and the U.S. Justice Department's 1975 entry into the dispute created a chaotic situation. The federal district court began to supervise all hiring criteria. Another issue entered the controversy when it was revealed in 1977 that some black officers had been allowed to cheat on a 1975 promotion exam by seeing the exam beforehand. This was not solely a race-based situation: in fact, the case was first brought to the public's attention by black police officers who had not been involved in any cheating. Nonetheless, because all those accused of cheating were black, many viewed the exam scandal as a problem caused by the department's process of racial change. The FOP then brought suit to cancel these promotions. Although it was never proved "that Eaves authorized the cheating, ... he knew about it in time to stop it and didn't." As a result, Eaves resigned in 1978 under pressure from Mayor Jackson and was replaced by Lee Brown.[123]

In a system that had favored whites for many decades, it was inevitable that as blacks secured more political power in the city, an effort would be made to correct discriminatory hiring and promotion policies. The only way to secure a racially representative proportion of the police and fire departments, one that would reflect the city's racial makeup, was to have racial goals and make a special effort to recruit and promote blacks. But it was also inevitable that many whites would object to this tactic and look on it not as the result of past discrimination but a clear sign of present or "reverse" discrimination, as they called it.

By 1978, a serious personnel shortage had developed in the police department as many officers (mainly white) left the force and hiring remained irregular. Police officials admitted that as a result, "services are suffering" in numerous ways; for example, response time to calls was slower than it had been. And as a result, the bureau was relying more and more on overtime by those already on the force. The cost of overtime in 1978 was approximately $25,000 per week. A comprehensive agreement was finally reached in 1979 that was supposed to create an equitable hiring and promotion system (and exam) and deal with past inequities. For example, acknowledging previous discrimination in police hiring and promotion, the city agreed to hire and provide back pay to both black and white applicants who had been rejected due to discriminatory policies if they still desired employment and met present standards. In addition, the city agreed "to promote a number of officers on an approximately 50–50 black-white basis." There was to be no residency requirement for hiring. Even with this settlement, however, disagreements continued, mainly in relation to promotion exams.[124]

A similar personnel shortage was evident in the fire department. Blacks, represented by Brothers and Sisters Combined, challenged discriminatory hiring and promotion policies that favored whites, and whites, under the leadership of the International Association of Firefighters, leveled charges of reverse discrimination and complained of favoritism toward blacks. As in the police department, the charges and countercharges in the fire department disrupted hiring. By 1978, there was a serious shortage of personnel, and overtime and some temporary employees were being used to fill the gap. An agreement for the fire bureau was worked out in 1979 (shortly before the police case was settled). This accord set percentage goals for the hiring and promotion of black and white firefighters and made plans to establish objective hiring and promotion tests that would be developed by an outside company.[125]

By the late 1980s, because of the racial controversies, concern still lingered over a racial split in the bureaus, a decline in morale, and a shortage of experienced supervisory personnel. As Mayor Andrew Young stated in 1987, "There are still factions and racial tensions within our police force that impact on policing in a variety of ways." The long dispute over hiring and promotion revealed a basic problem that most cities have faced in the post–civil rights movement era. As an *Atlanta Constitution* story on fire department promotions pointed out, "The city's position underscores a modern urban dilemma, how to maintain racially balanced police and fire departments while providing a system of promotion that does not favor one race over another." A 1989 U.S. Supreme Court case involving an affirmative action program in the Birmingham, Alabama, fire department in some ways fueled the controversy. The court ruled that whites had the legal right to challenge affirmative action programs even if they had been in place for years. A related situation has developed as a consequence of Atlanta city officials' efforts to preserve a certain racial balance at each fire station, if possible, in order to maintain integrated firehouses. The result, according to one black firefighter, has been that requested transfers to another station can be rejected if they would upset the balance of white and black. Through the 1980s and into the 1990s, race-based disagreements over promotions and exams have continued, and freezes on promotions have recurred at various times in both departments.[126]

Atlanta's situation reflects what has happened in many cities in terms of police and fire service hiring and promotion.[127] The city essentially created its own future problems by, for many decades, maintaining a policy that denied police and fire service jobs to blacks, segregated them within the bureaus, promoted them insufficiently, and ignored or abused black citizens in their own neighborhoods. The historical lack of a true merit process eventually prompted the black community to try to equalize the system through affirmative action and other tactics. Those efforts in turn led to a hostile white reaction. By the 1970s and 1980s, the results of the initial race-based policies included divided and weakened departments, extra costs for the city, and decreased services to all neighborhoods and all Atlantans.

E. Seating and Service: Mass Transit and Race

The development of Atlanta's transportation services affected the African American community and therefore the city in numerous ways. From the humiliation of segregated seating to the neglect of their neighborhoods, blacks faced difficulty in using a system that cared little for their needs. Black political empowerment brought a more responsive transportation network but one that still clearly indicated the significance of both a race factor and, to a lesser extent, a class factor.

Efforts to segregate streetcars began in the 1890s, but black Atlantans ably used boycotts to resist the ordinances and court rulings. However, after the 1906 riot, segregated streetcar seating was tightly enforced and lasted into the 1950s. Blacks had to sit from the back to the front and whites from the front to the back, with whites occupying any disputed seats. While this practice caused many disputes and was a daily reminder to blacks of how degrading life in Atlanta could be, its impact was limited.[128] Far more important to the well-being of the black community was service delivery. But here, too, blacks were treated as second-class citizens.

As early as 1917, black leaders were complaining about problems with transportation services. Walter White, secretary of the NAACP's Atlanta branch, wrote in that year, "We . . . are getting photographs of crowded streetcars in certain localities where the service is inadequate and where there is a good deal of discrimination. This with other data that we are gathering will cause the streetcar company to open their eyes and if this does not, other more stringent measures will be adopted."[129] One effort to deal with the problem was the creation of the Colored Jitney Bus Association, a private black-owned bus line that operated in Atlanta's black neighborhoods from 1922 to 1925. The company had sixteen buses, operated by black drivers, that provided service using the same routes as the Georgia Power Company's streetcars. Unwilling to face competition from any source, Georgia Power (as it had done with white-owned jitneys) enlisted the help of the police and city council to drive the black firm out of business. Realizing that the black bus line was making inroads into their territory, Georgia Power used the police to harass and ticket the company. The Atlanta city council finally forced the end of the Colored Jitney company by stating that only vehicles with seventeen or more seats could operate in the city; the company's buses had fewer than sixteen seats.[130]

In keeping with the black community's usual response to official neglect, it tried to solve its own problems through organizational or entrepreneurial efforts. With the demise of the Colored Jitney Bus Association in 1925, the black-owned Atlanta Coach Lines tried to secure city council permission to operate a bus line, but the council refused its request because a white firm had a monopoly on bus service. In the 1940s, a black-owned bus line did provide service to one outlying black area not handled by the white company but this line too did not last.[131]

The failure of black companies to gain a permanent niche in the city's mass transit system led not only to a continuation of earlier service problems but also to a higher rate of accidents. C. R. Strong, a Georgia Power transportation services representative, commented in 1934 that conflicts between white and black passengers "resulted in a high number of accidents, because the conductors could not give the operators proper starting and stopping signals." The conductors' attention too often was focused on the racial disputes over seating.[132] The Georgia Commission on Interracial Cooperation and affiliated organizations tried to secure an improvement of service and work out an easing of the seating disputes but ultimately failed to achieve either goal.[133]

In 1945, the Southern Regional Council reported that "no outlying Negro sections are served by trackless trolleys and buses, nor are there any of these sections served by feeder bus lines. These services are made available to many, although not all, outlying white sections of the city." Georgia Power, for example, "refused service to the colored people in the new Dixie Hills and Pine Acres section, where at present a private Negro bus line is in operation. The company said the Negro population of this area did not warrant its extension of services." People traveling into the city's business area from this section had to pay double fares—first for the black-owned bus service and then for the white-owned Georgia Power line into the central business district. In one case in a westside black neighborhood just past the racially transitional Mozley Park area, a simple extension of an established route would have provided those black residents with ready transportation. But even after numerous complaints, the transit company rejected this request because its officials did not want to make it easier for blacks to travel into the west side: they were concerned with holding the racial line in various neighborhoods. It was not until the mid-1950s, after the Mozley Park area had completely undergone racial change, that transportation service was finally extended into this black neighborhood. The transit company neglected the transportation needs of this neighborhood's black residents, forcing them to walk long distances to their destinations or to transit stops and thereby making the section less attractive to black inmigration.[134] The continued neglect of black neighborhoods and abuse of black passengers not only caused blacks problems in getting to work but also isolated their communities.[135] Eventually, during the 1960s civil rights movement, it would spur demands to redress black grievances by concentrating on black needs in the design of the new rapid rail lines.

The segregated seating on bus and other transit lines was actually ended legally in 1956 after a Supreme Court desegregation decision on the issue in *Browder v. Gayle*, based on the Montgomery, Alabama, bus segregation case involving the Montgomery Improvement Association. Some cities desegregated on the basis of this ruling, but in Atlanta it took the combined efforts of the local NAACP and the ministerial association to implement the decision.[136]

Led by the Reverend William Holmes Borders, under the banner of the newly formed "Love, Law, and Liberation Movement," Atlanta's black ministers decided to bring a case to court that would result in the desegregation of the city's transit lines. Eventually working with Mayor Hartsfield, Borders and the other black ministers boarded a bus, sat where they wanted, and later, as planned, were arrested. Hartsfield was eager to eliminate any conflict over transit segregation, for as he stated, "Atlanta has an excellent record before the nation for its good race relations. We in Atlanta have felt this was a desirable thing, not only for the sake of decency but from the standpoint of business as well." Concerned about the downtown merchants, the mayor wanted the courts to declare the locally enforced transit segregation law unconstitutional. Hartsfield was motivated by the city's reputation, by business interests and, assuredly, by black votes; but in any case, his actions, along with those of the black ministers and the NAACP, which filed suit, led to a January 1959 federal district court decision that eliminated the city's transit segregation laws.[137]

Although the Atlanta Transit System officials, worried about a decline in passengers due to the controversy over segregation, and the mayor, concerned about the city's reputation and business interests, were cooperative in following the court order, the other issue of routes and service delivery was left untouched.[138] As was typical in Atlanta, change skimmed the surface to give a facade of reform while more serious racial issues remained.

A 1960 survey of black ridership on Atlanta's buses suggested that many problems remained. The city's blacks used the bus service at a greater percentage than their population size would indicate. Although they represented approximately "one-third of the population of Atlanta, [blacks] provide 59 percent of the bus patronage during the rush period." The reason given for this disproportionate use was that "no major Negro residential area [was] within close proximity to a major employment area. . . . Atlanta's Negro community must rely upon public transportation." Residential patterns hence dictated a dependence on the buses and trolleys.[139]

Given previous racial factors in transit policy and the substantial black use of the bus lines, it was inevitable that the development of rapid rail transit would involve race-related issues. In the Metropolitan Atlanta Transit Study Commission's report of 1962, revised in 1966 by the Metropolitan Atlanta Rapid Transit Authority (MARTA), the basic outline emerged of a service that included subways, at-grade lines, and elevated lines. The MARTA board was also selected; one of its members, banker L. D. Milton, was black. As the plan's concepts unfolded, it was clear that black neighborhoods had once again been neglected. The black community's response came in December 1966 from the Atlanta Summit Leadership Conference, which voted "to oppose the development of the city's proposed rapid transit system unless plans are changed to provide better access by a large segment of the Negro community." The concern was about the west leg of the planned system, which did not extend deep enough into the westside black neighborhoods. State senator Leroy Johnson, head of Summit's rapid transit committee, commented that the system "must be effected for the benefit of Negro citizens too. This committee recommended going so far as seeking funds-cutoff if Negroes are not included in on the groundwork."[140]

Rapid transit at first took on a planning process similar to that of public housing development: blacks were being planned for, not with. Unlike housing programs, however, mass transit needed voter approval (for both the design and the financing plan), and this situation allowed the black community to wield some power. In January 1967, MARTA officials contacted various black leaders to arrange a meeting to discuss the contentious issues and to note "changes and proposed changes [in the original plan] now being considered by the engineering consultants." Summit's dissatisfaction with MARTA's efforts continued to involve service to black neighborhoods. A letter from Summit leaders Jesse Hill and Reverend Samuel Williams to MARTA's chairman stated that "of the 36 miles of transit system to be opened by 1975 only 4.3 miles have been earmarked to serve the large Negro westside population, and this short transit leg . . . is totally unacceptable, inadequate and unrealistic as a westward limit." Concerns were also expressed about routes and about nondiscrimination in employment. This letter also mentioned the significant black voting population. By the mid-1960s, white politicians' interest in black areas' city service needs was on the rise; however, this concern did not yet extend to the rapid rail plans, which were seen in terms of helping downtown businesses rather than neighborhoods.[141]

Deftly playing their hand, Summit leaders warned that Atlanta's blacks would not vote for MARTA and the financing plan in November 1968 "without more clear agreement and commitments regarding employment practices at all levels, plus fair and convenient service access to the rapid transit system by the Negro community." Agreement was reached in early February 1967 on the employment issue, and discussion was to continue on routes, with black input. However, disputes surfaced again in May 1968, when public hearings were held on the transit plan.[142]

Once again, Summit found MARTA's plans "unacceptable to the Negro community. Unless certain changes are made in proposed routes and services, along with a clear understanding regarding employment and staff recruitment, we could not recommend MARTA to the Negro community. We could not recommend to Negro voters the upcoming bond or tax referendum for MARTA unless changes are made." Contending that the plans resulted in the neglect "of the Negro communities and poor white and poor Negro areas," Summit wanted a longer western line and new lines for the southern and northwestern areas. Of particular importance was their request for rail service to the isolated black community in Perry Homes on the northwest. They also asked to see a "detailed description" of the system's right-of-way plans in order to prevent the destruction of black neighborhoods. The plan was seen as one designed by whites for the downtown businesses in order to move white suburbanites to jobs and shopping.[143]

Summit urged a vote against MARTA in the 1968 referendum. Although they agreed that Atlanta needed a rapid transit system, some black community members felt the city was not ready for it, based on the city leaders' evident lack of commitment to dealing with racism in other facets of Atlanta's life—housing, jobs, schools. On the basis of problems in these areas that were never corrected, some black leaders were convinced that blacks either would not get a fair share of the transit system or, worse, would be displaced by its construction: "It will be just like urban renewal," they predicted; "it will be black removal." Although MARTA's general manager, H. L. Stuart, was agreeable to restudying certain issues, few commitments were made. Strong race- and class-based suspicions of white city officials and business leaders were factors in the MARTA referendum defeat in 1968. (White suburbanites also opposed the plan.) A survey prior to the 1968 vote noted that low-income blacks represented the city's highest percentage of undecided votes. Many felt—with good reason, given the city's history—that whites would try to trick them in some way.[144]

The referendum defeat did bring some change. There was a greater desire to listen to and meet black demands for "lower fares and better service" before the next MARTA vote. As Glenn Bennett, executive director of the Atlanta Metropolitan Planning Commission, stated in 1969, "The determination to meet the basic requirements of these groups [low-income and minority] is now more genuine and more widespread than it ever has been." Also, minority representation on MARTA's staff—specifically a community relations director, and people in important policy positions, such as the board of directors—increased by 1971 "in an effort to overcome an unfavorable image the agency has had among Atlanta's Negroes."[145] Jesse Hill, cochair of Summit and active in the criticism of MARTA, was appointed to the board in 1968.

Action Forum, a biracial group of the white business leaders and the black leadership, was formed in 1969 to bring blacks more fully into the discussion about such issues as MARTA, school desegregation, and redevelopment. The attention paid to black requests that were made in 1971 indicates a shift. Black community leaders expressed a desire for "an aggressive and productive affirmative action program in the area of policy, employment, contracting, and consumer services." They declared, "We are determined that the specific welfare of the Black community, so often and so callously neglected in the past, will receive equal or compensatory consideration and treatment in the MARTA plan and program if such a program is to exist." Then they made a number of demands, including black employment of at least 35 percent on the MARTA staff "at all levels"; an increase in black voting membership on the MARTA board; a fifteen-cent fare for ten years; rapid rail service to Perry Homes; "priority to those dependent on public transit"; "public transit service from all inner city communities to major employment centers," particularly in the suburbs ("many low-income, transit dependent communities . . . have no or very poor access to public transit, and as a result, no or poor access to jobs, hospitals, schools"); the provision of "at least 35 percent of each services and goods contracts to minority firms and consultants"; and the purchase of the independently owned Atlanta Transit System in order to provide service to areas that were not currently served and crosstown service from poor areas to job centers.[146]

MARTA's development brought out years of pent-up frustrations over black support for city services and neglect of this community. As black leaders explained, "Historically the Black Community has given full support to programs and individuals claiming to improve the quality of life in the entire Metropolitan Community, only to find that once the goals of the White community have been realized, no further consideration is given to the needs, desires and interests of the Black community." The black leadership wanted to avoid this situation by urging a written response to the issues raised and, in appropriate cases, to include the response in the MARTA referendum package. They also urged city officials to "consider rapid transit as only one component of a forward Atlanta thrust, and that other social and civil matters will be given equal attention."[147]

MARTA executives had already been moving to redress black grievances, and they made it official a few weeks later, when the MARTA board agreed to support an affirmative action plan, training programs, and minority representation in companies doing business with the Authority. On the issue of routes, Ray Blount, MARTA's chairman, noted that the construction of an east-west line (which would best serve the black community) would be given first priority. Final route plans would pay attention to the needs of those traveling from residential sections to work, hospitals, and shopping areas, and crosstown service would be improved. Also, after securing the Atlanta Transit System, improvements in bus service would be made to selected black neighborhoods as requested. The Perry Homes area would be served by a rail line (the Proctor Creek spur) as desired. The fare issue was resolved in a compromise between black city and white suburban interests—a fifteen-cent fare for seven years and a sales tax for ten. This solution provided whites with the financing method they wanted and blacks with low fares.[148]

Racial issues remained a large part of the prevote discussions among both whites and blacks. Some blacks were still concerned that MARTA would benefit whites more than blacks, no matter what the revised plans indicated; and some whites feared that MARTA was the first stage in dispersing blacks into the white suburbs and thereby causing school desegregation throughout the Atlanta metro area. Nonetheless, the 1971 MARTA referendum showed that blacks supported the measure, which passed. Atlanta blacks, who comprised 43 percent of registered voters, backed MARTA with 54.8 percent of their vote. Atlanta whites, who made up 57 percent of the city's registered voters, gave the referendum 54.7 percent of

Georgia Black Caucus meeting with MARTA board, January 1973 (Boyd Lewis Collection, Courtesy of Atlanta History Center)

their vote. Although the referendum was strongly rejected in two largely white suburban counties nearby, and although MARTA secured more no votes than yes votes in the region, it did pass in Fulton and DeKalb Counties—the two main areas for MARTA development.[149]

By 1972, MARTA had implemented its minority training, employment, and minority business programs. The initial rail lines were east-west lines, as blacks had wanted, but the Proctor Creek spur (going the full distance to Perry Homes) was still being debated in the 1990s, because MARTA officials claimed that it was not economically feasible to construct such a spur due to population loss and a lack of business development in the area. According to Leroy Johnson, head of Summit's rapid transit committee, over the years there were attempts to renege a number of times on the Proctor Creek spur as well as on the fifteen-cent fare promise. Nonetheless, racial politics required the rail spur to be built, and most of it (to Bankhead Station) was opened in 1993, although it did not extend the extra 1.5 miles to Perry Homes.[150]

Atlanta's mass transit improved considerably in the 1970s in regard to service and minority involvement. More neighborhoods were served, and blacks were now in policy-making positions. However, race-based disagreements—for example, over the selection of a MARTA board chairman—and white suburban resistance to the extension of MARTA continued into the late 1980s.[151] The role of race in mass transit development and operation remained significant. As with other services, Atlanta's transportation network indicated the long-term impact of racial factors.

In the most basic needs of Atlanta's black residents—street paving, garbage collection, park space, health facilities, police and fire department service delivery, and mass transportation—there was a consistent intertwining of race and public policy. Viewed over the course of the twentieth century, the city's physical maintenance and appearance in regard to streets, parks, and playgrounds; the health care for its inhabitants; the degree of security for its environment in terms of crime and fire; and the extent to which its citizens could move easily around the community reveals the shaping role of race. That the city did not develop with more problems related to general white neglect and hostility was due to the persistent determination of Atlanta's blacks to use political or other pressure or their own community self-help efforts to secure neighborhood services, better health care, an integrated police and fire department, and a transportation network that included black neighborhoods. White allies who understood the pernicious effects of racially exclusive policies were also important.

Nonetheless, the intersection of racial attitudes and policy forged a city clearly marked by previous and continuing racial issues. This situation was also true in regard to the school system.

CHAPTER 6

But so long as the white man purposely excludes us from the life, thought and sentiment of the South, and designedly inveigles legislation to stunt our growth, denies us the best educational advantages and refuses us the opportunity to make bread, there will be race problems and friction.—*Atlanta Independent*, 1907

Separate and Unequal: Atlanta's Public Schools to 1954

The dual school system, which had been created in the nineteenth century on a separate and unequal basis, became the prototype for all that followed in the schools during the twentieth century. Policy decisions based on racial considerations formed and subsequently shaped the system. Race was the single most important factor in determining the quality of education that Atlanta's schoolchildren received. And it was also the single most important factor in creating the problems that almost destroyed the city's educational system and thereby weakened its economic base.

Funding and Neglect

The main issue was the allocation of funds. Initially, neither black nor white schools received adequate finances to provide for a quality education, but clearly the white schools were strongly favored. Although black schools improved over the course of the twentieth century, they continued to reflect the inequality of the dual system. Problems like lack of school facilities for the black community and overcrowding in its schools emerged quickly but were never corrected, even though such issues received attention early on. For example, Atlanta superintendent of schools W. F. Slaton commented in 1900 that "four rooms were added to the Houston Negro School in August. With this exception, no additional provision has been made for the negro children in several years. The white schools are crowded, but the negro schools are doubly crowded. . . . And yet there are more than a thousand negro children unprovided for."[1] In 1903 there were twenty white schools for 14,465 students, but only five existed for 8,118 blacks. The lack of school buildings for blacks meant that many black children could not go to public school. These early trends continued: by 1913, still only a little more than 50 percent of the black children in the city were going to public school.[2]

Many whites objected to black academic education, seeing it as unnecessary within a southern caste system that regulated which jobs blacks could take. Some of this thinking was based on the idea that an academic (literary) course of study would educate blacks above their station in life and make them discontent. Yet even vocational classes at times faced opposition and had to be defended. A special plea in the 1901–3 annual report of the Atlanta Board of Education called for vocational shops in Negro schools. White schools had received the funding to equip these shops, the report noted, but black ones had not. However, "from those attending these [black] schools are coming the masses of our workmen and laborers. Our industrial conditions require that they should be capable of doing the work of their calling or trade in an efficient manner. . . . Manual training and the rudiments of the domestic arts properly taught in the negro schools would be an economical investment for the City in the consequent saving in policemen and police courts." Many whites did not recognize the need to provide an adequate public education, either academic or vocational, for this large segment of the population (39.7 percent in 1900). They preferred an unschooled and untrained black population that could more easily be kept subservient. The story of continued and long-term neglect reveals both the intentions of most whites and the aspirations of blacks.[3]

In 1900 there were 99.2 black and 56.6 white students per teacher in the Atlanta public elementary schools. By the 1934–35 school year, these schools had 82.7 black and 35.4 white pupils per teacher; and by 1949–50, the numbers were 36.2 and 22.6 for blacks and whites respectively (see Table 9). Although this table reveals that there was significant improvement over the years, it masks bigger problems. It indicates, for example, that black schools continually received less funding than whites. More funds could have enabled black schools to hire more teachers, accommodate more black children, and achieve the lower teacher-pupil ratios that white schools had. And while class size did decrease over the years, overcrowding remained: black schools had to hold double sessions throughout this twentieth-century period. Black elementary students went to school for only about three hours per day in order to accommodate double sessions, while whites had the full school day as of 1917.[4]

The Black Reaction

The black response to these inequities and the response of white allies in such organizations as the Commission on Interracial Cooperation, was a persistent effort to correct the situation and to compensate for it. Even if the state and city would not provide adequate educational facilities, blacks who could pay the tuition could attend elementary and high school classes, including industrial education courses, offered by the black colleges—Atlanta University, Spelman, Morehouse, Clark, and Morris Brown—or by other private schools. As of 1905, kindergarten classes were also available through the Gate City Free Kindergarten Association (with substantial funding from Alonzo Herndon) and the First Congregational Church. This church established a free library as well. The Neighborhood Union provided vocational classes.[5] As usual, Atlanta's black community had resources available to counter white attempts to limit black aspirations.

But the main effort was toward safeguarding the meager educational facilities they already had and pressing for more—a task that became more difficult after the white primary was established and blacks lost most of their political leverage. One of the first major issues in the twentieth century was a 1913 board of education committee plan to eliminate academic schooling for blacks in the seventh and eighth grades—the two highest public school grades available to blacks—and to substitute voca-

Table 9. Atlanta Public Elementary Schools, Students per Teacher, by Race, 1883–1950

Year	Black Students per Teacher	White Students per Teacher
1883	92.3	52.6
1895	117.6	64.6
1896	89.2	61.4
1900	99.2	56.6
1910	75.3	40.8
1914	65.8	35.0
1927–28	75.5	37.4
1934–35	82.7	35.4
1941–42	70.9	29.1
1944–45	42.8	32.5
1947–48	53.0	32.0
1948–49	40.5	22.9
1949–50	36.2	22.6

Sources: Eleventh Annual Report of the Board of Education, Atlanta, Georgia, for the year ending January 1, 1883, pp. 8–9, Atlanta Historical Society; Twenty-fourth Annual Report, 1895, pp. 15, 17; Twenty-fifth Annual Report, 1896, p. 14, Atlanta Historical Society; Twenty-ninth Annual Report, 1900, p. 32; Paul E. Peterson, *The Politics of School Reform 1870–1940* (Chicago: University of Chicago Press, 1985), p. 124 (for 1910); "Report of Hon R. J. Guinn, president, Atlanta Board of Education, December 29, 1914," Box 4, Aldine Chambers Papers, Atlanta Historical Society; "Report of the Superintendent, Atlanta Public Schools, Atlanta, Georgia 1934–35," Atlanta Public School Archives; "Report of the Superintendent, 1943–44," Atlanta Public School Archives; "A Report of Public School Facilities for Negroes in Atlanta, Georgia," 1944, Atlanta Urban League, Grace Towns Hamilton Papers, Atlanta University Center, Robert W. Woodruff Library; "Making Americans: Superintendent's Annual Report to the Board of Education, Atlanta Public Schools 1944–45," Atlanta Public School Archives; "Petition to Ira Jarrell, Superintendent, and Atlanta Board of Education, April 4, 1949," Southern Regional Council Papers, Atlanta University Center, Robert W. Woodruff Library; "An Analysis of per-Pupil School Expenditures by Race—1948–49—1949–50, Atlanta, Georgia," prepared by the Atlanta Urban League, August 15, 1950," Grace Towns Hamilton Papers, Atlanta University Center, Robert W. Woodruff Library.

Note: There are conflicting reports of some of these ratios in other sources, but all of them reveal a higher ratio for blacks than for whites.

tional training instead. Although the board of education eventually rejected this recommendation, the black community immediately sprang into action to protect its children. In a letter to the *Atlanta Constitution*, Lugenia Burns Hope, founder of the Neighborhood Union and active on its Women's Social Improvement Committee, noted that "we are sure that a loss of the seventh and eighth grades would impair the very labor efficiency at which the Board's proposal is aiming and this loss would so limit the Negroes in merely rudimentary education that they would be even less morally and economically efficient than they are now." Black leaders led by the Reverend H. H. Proctor attended a board committee meeting to ask "that the literary work in the Negro Grammar Schools be not curtailed. . . . and that the Negroes be given a Central Industrial High School in addition." It was decided that although manual training and domestic science would be added to the seventh and eighth grade work, an academic (literary) curriculum would continue as well. Blacks could support these provisions. But the committee also stated that "we need more industrially trained workers and fewer professionals among the negro population."[6]

At the same time, black leaders and organizations were requesting that the board of education and the city council improve black schools and deal with their overcrowded condition. The Neighborhood Union, for example, argued for better schools by stressing an environmental emphasis so evident in the Progressive Era. In 1913 the group suggested that improved educational facilities would "reduce crime, and . . . make of our children good citizens." Some whites, too, were interested in bettering black schools through improvements in their facilities. For example, in 1913, the board committee acknowledged the dismal condition of the existing black schools and recommended the construction of new ones: "As to the negro schools, a decent regard for the opinions of mankind demands that the present condition of these schools be remedied, if it were not necessary from the standpoint of health and safety. . . . A mere inspection of these schools by any impartial observer will amply justify our recommendation." Yet relatively little was done to substantially improve the black schools, and this situation would continue through the next five decades.[7]

In 1914, Atlanta's board of education eliminated the eighth grade due to funding problems. This left black students with seven grades, while whites, for whom high school was available, had eleven. In 1917, in a further attack on black schooling, the board had a plan to secure funds for a white junior high school by removing allocations from and thereby eliminating the seventh grade in black schools. An emergency committee of the newly formed Atlanta branch of the NAACP was set up and went before the board of education to oppose the plan. At this lively meeting, when one board member blamed the plan on the school system's lack of money, the black spokesmen said that they should get the money "from the same sources that they had gotten money" to construct the many white schools. Complaints were also registered about overcrowding in black schools, which necessitated double sessions; the lack of a high school for blacks; and the need for better vocational workshops. One white, James L. Key (then a school board member and councilman but soon to be mayor), spoke on behalf of black demands and asked that the seventh grade be left intact. The end result was that the seventh grade remained and that more vocational classes were offered. Walter White, secretary of the NAACP's Atlanta branch, asserted, "This is our first fight and our first victory and we feel that we have only begun to fight."[8]

The Atlanta NAACP soon became the major organization pushing for black school reforms and opposing the constant white efforts to weaken black education. Its members focused on achieving equality in the schools while maintaining the separate aspect of the system. The concern centered on four issues—overcrowding, lack of funds, the need for a vocational junior high school for students who would not be going on to college, and a high school (a goal first expressed in 1872). The overcrowding problem was clearly related to the privileged way in which white schools were treated. The Atlanta school board made strong efforts to eliminate double sessions for whites, but it barely considered the black situation. In 1917 the Atlanta newspapers reported that double sessions had been eliminated in the city's schools, forgetting (or not caring) that the black schools were still burdened in this way. When an NAACP committee approached the board of education to discuss the double sessions that still existed in black schools, one board member commented that he was against "giving one nickel more for the education of the Negro children as they were already getting more than they deserved." If the reaction from the board members was not this sort of outright hostility, it was a general indifference that led to few efforts to improve education for the black community. The board members' attitude was partly due to a negative white reaction to their earlier seventh-grade decision. In response to the board's inaction, the NAACP planned a large silent protest against double sessions.[9]

In 1918 and 1919, the black community flexed its muscles in one area where it could still have an impact—bond and tax referendums. Although there was a poll tax, after an NAACP registration drive the number of black registered voters jumped from 715 to 1,216 for the March 1919 vote and to 1,723 for an April referendum. Previously, in 1903 and 1910, blacks had aided the passage of bond issues that included funds for schools. Their interest in supporting these earlier bonds was based on white promises to improve black schools and provide other benefits to the black community. But white city officials had largely reneged on their school pledges, and as a result, black schools had deteriorated. The 1910 bond had not even offered much for the black schools—$38,200 out of a $600,000 bond issue—but the July 1918 and March 1919 bonds offered them nothing at all. The NAACP and others in the black community were determined not to have this happen again, and they urged the community to reject both the bonds and a 1919 property tax increase to provide more support for the schools. For example, T. K. Gibson, vice president of the NAACP's Atlanta branch, wrote an open letter in which he asked pointedly, "WHAT PROMISES HAVE BEEN MADE TO US FOR OUR SUPPORT?" Benjamin Davis, editor of the *Atlanta Independent,* also voiced his opposition to the bonds, complaining that black appeals for additional schools were met with white excuses of lack of money, while "the authorities continue to build white school houses." All the bond and tax measures failed to pass; blacks (and many whites concerned about taxes and government spending) rejected them by voting no or not voting at all. Whites, by not bothering to vote, often played the significant role in a number of bond defeats, but the perception was always that black voting power was responsible for bonds' rejection.[10]

After the March 1919 vote, the NAACP laid out its demands for better schools and other necessities, declaring, "We too believe in Bonds, but when they are issued they should carry specific and unalterable provisions for a division of the funds so that the Colored schools will be amply taken care of." Before another bond issue would be supported, the city had to provide assurances that the black community would receive something in return. Most of the demands would generally remain unfulfilled, although they stayed high on black Atlantans' list over the next fifty years. These demands included more and better schools (the condition of the schools "constitute a menace to the health and morals of our children, which in turn menaces the health and morals of the entire city"); an end to double sessions and the return of an eighth grade; equal pay for black teachers; a black high school; playgrounds, swimming pools, libraries, and better hospital facilities; and more attention to street paving, garbage collection, and sewers in black neighborhoods.[11]

Some in the white community—for example, white ministers in an interracial group called the Inter-Faith Church Committee—supported a few of the black demands, but generally the white community reacted very slowly, at first ignoring most black requests. On hearing that blacks had defeated the bond and tax measure, Mayor Key even suggested right after the March vote that the state legislature force the bond and tax passage, since "it is very clear that the white people—the vital interests of the city— voted for the increase." Although before the next vote in April, whites offered a few old school buildings to the black community, this offer was not only considered inadequate, but there was also little assurance that it would actually materialize. White leaders still went ahead with the April bond and tax increase vote, which also failed. The loss of the bond funds affected white as well as black schools. Some white schools had to resort once again to double sessions, and the black schools became even more overcrowded. (This situation was also due somewhat to the implementation in 1920 of a state compulsory attendance law that mandated school attendance by children between the ages of eight and fourteen.) White community leaders were aware that the white schools were going to be hurt by the loss of bond money. Although he generally blamed blacks for the problems, C. D. McKinney, a prominent white proponent of increased school funds, spoke at a teachers' meeting before the April bond vote and acknowledged what continued failure to adequately fund the schools would do. "We have been hindered by the negro, or at any rate, have allowed the negro to hinder our progress. But if we withhold our means and our efforts in the selfish fear that the negro will benefit, . . . at the same time we are starving the minds of all white children concerned, denying to them their heritage."[12]

Prior to the next bond vote, scheduled for 1921, whites did some rethinking. Behind the scenes, black leaders made it clear that they would not support the bond unless whites promised to provide a high school for the black community. When black leaders asked what their community would receive from a new bond, city officials publicly announced and gave assurances that the funds would be divided on the same ratio as the city's white and black population—that is, about two-thirds for whites and one-third for blacks. Also, black elementary students would be put on single sessions, and the black community would acquire its first high school, as well as more elementary schools (some newly built and others converted from existing white schools). Furthermore, an eighth grade was added to some black schools in 1920, and for the first time a black was hired as a supervisor. Blacks supported this bond, as did many whites who were concerned that their school system would decline to the level of the black schools. As a result, this bond passed.[13]

To determine what the school system needed and exactly how the bond would be spent, the board of education decided to hire outside specialists to study the system. The Strayer-Engelhardt survey, conducted in 1921–22, reported that the schools for blacks were "totally unfit for school children" and that the white schools too needed substantial improvements. Eleven percent of the white elementary schools and 66 percent of the black schools were considered unsafe for use. The black schools lacked adequate playgrounds and sufficient classroom size, equipment, auditoriums, and lunchrooms. Pointing out that "no plan for the adequate housing of colored children has ever existed in Atlanta," the report suggested the building of new schools, including a combination junior-senior high school on the west side. The construction of a high school for blacks began in 1922. However, not all of the white leaders' promises were honored. In 1923, the school board reneged on its pledge to use fully one-third of the school bond funds for black schooling. However, after a bond issue failed in 1924, funds for black schools were increased. This last controversy hardly mattered, though, given that the desire for a black high school was being fulfilled: this advance, for the time, overshadowed all else.[14]

"Our Supplies Were Secondhand"

Booker T. Washington High School, Atlanta's first black public junior-senior high school, opened on the west side in 1924. (Whites already had eight junior high and high schools by this time.) The building of this high school was surely not the end of the problems, for even this new school proved inadequate very quickly. Washington High School, which also initially included junior high school grades, was built for a student body of 1,500 but opened with 1,947 students. By 1929, 2,703 students were enrolled, and by 1934, that number had climbed to 3,600. Atlanta's black population was hungry for a high school education and came to this school from across the city. According to Flossie Jones, a teacher at Washington when it opened in September 1924, "the streets were literally covered with students . . . of all ages." Washington's students included those who had finished the elementary grades earlier—those who were twenty or twenty-one and had long desired to go to high school but could not afford the private schools. Neighboring black communities sent their children to Washington, too, since no high school existed in their areas. Living with

Booker T. Washington High School, 1935. This facility, which opened in 1924, was Atlanta's first black high school. (Courtesy of Atlanta History Center)

relatives or friends in the city gave them an Atlanta address and made them eligible for the school.[15]

Like other black schools in Atlanta, Washington was not as well equipped as the white schools and was given white hand-me-downs. Used books and furniture were sent from the white schools; labs were equipped with fewer resources than labs in white schools had; and supplies throughout the school were scarce. Washington also had no auditorium or gym, although the latter had been promised during construction. E. T. Lewis, a teacher who began working at Washington in 1929, described the situation thus:

> Our supplies were secondhand. We used books that white schools had discarded. As we added to the school, even the blackboards were blackboards that were taken out of white schools. They would do that thing this way: if we needed say . . . five . . . blackboards in five rooms at Washington High School, they would order new slate, but they would take that slate to some white school and put that new slate up, take the old slate out of that school, and bring it to Washington. . . . So we always got something that had been used, in most instances, for quite a long time.

Estelle Clemmons, who taught at Washington from 1937 to 1947, recalled that she was always short of books for her classes and that the books were hand-me-downs from white schools. She remembered one incident in which "a big truck drove up behind the main building . . . piled up with a lot of books. And because of the wind, some of the pages blew out of the books all over the campus. And I said to myself, 'This is what is being sent out here for our students to use.' And it hurt. It really did hurt."[16]

But the school still represented progress for the black community and an important addition to its educational system. It was a well-built structure. And not only was secondary education now available at a public school for the first time, but blacks graduating from Atlanta's black colleges could now find more teaching jobs in the city instead of having to look elsewhere for employment. In this way, Atlanta's black middle class was buttressed by Washington and the other high schools that followed.[17] But even this relatively meager supplement to black education drew criticism from some whites. That Washington had been built before Girls' High School (for whites) was finished was used as an issue to attack the former mayor, James Key, in his bid to return to office in 1924. Key had lost the mayoralty to Klansman Walter A. Sims in 1922, and in 1924 he faced Sims once again. In that contest, Sims used the approval and construction of Washington to suggest that Key favored blacks over whites. Although the contest featured other issues as well, this one surely contributed to Key's defeat.[18]

The establishment of Washington High School did not end the black drive to secure better schools. The fight continued relentlessly over the following decades. The inadequacies of the black schools led blacks to support a 1926 bond and contribute to its approval. But the amount promised was not forthcoming, although the black schools remained overcrowded and in disrepair. The school board planned to build thirteen new white schools but none for the black community. In allocating the bond funds, the board decided that white school needs had priority over black ones. As a result, in August 1927 a Colored Citizens Committee that included John Hope, A. T. Walden, and Benjamin Davis presented the board of education with a petition that noted the poor quality of black school buildings and the double, sometimes triple, school sessions. Complaining about the bond issue, which slighted blacks and gave them only one-tenth of the funds for their one-third of the school population, the petition requested more black schools and additions to existing black schools in order to eliminate the overcrowding. The response over the next year was that the black schools received even less of the bond funds.[19]

"Does Atlanta Know and Approve These Conditions?"

The Great Depression weakened an already deficient black school system and provided whites with some financial excuses to limit further black education. In 1932, two out of the four black night schools were eliminated, though white facilities were not touched. It was only after objections from various white and black civic groups that the board relented. Generally, the board of education tried to limit the impact of the depression on white schools by cutting funds from black ones—a continuation of existing policies. For example, the forty-four white kindergartens remained intact, although blacks had no kindergartens at all. By the 1934–35 school year, there were forty-four white elementary schools (with 25,401 students) and eleven black ones (with 13,773 students). Regardless of black school deficiencies, the next bond vote, in 1935, offered little to the black community. And what was offered before the bond's approval was again delayed or decreased afterward. Blacks were not strongly supportive of this bond issue, and they rallied against the next one, in 1938. It was not always lack of funds that prevented the building of new black schools. In 1931, the city turned down an effort by the Atlanta Committee on Women's Interracial Activities to secure approval for a new black school "because of the aversion of white people living in the neighborhood." The continued neglect of black schools is revealed in the fact that while 8 percent of white elementary school students were on double sessions in the 1934–35 school year, 89 percent of blacks were. One aspect of the neglect developed from state policies. For example, in 1933–34 the federal government provided Georgia with almost $5 million for education. Of this money, the black schools in the state received only 12.7 percent, although blacks represented slightly over 39 percent of Georgia's schoolchildren. New Deal work relief funding also favored white schools. Money spent under PWA and other programs for schools was first earmarked for whites; after their needs were satisfied, black school deficiencies were considered.[20]

Willis A. Sutton, Atlanta's white superintendent of schools during the 1930s, recognized the city's problem and urged that the black schools receive better treatment from the Atlanta Board of Education and, specifically, that the congestion at Washington High School be alleviated soon. There were certainly whites who responded to the plight of the black schools and did so either on humanitarian grounds or because of the potential impact of inadequate black schooling on the white community. But policies to substantially upgrade black schools lagged far behind any supportive rhetoric. As a 1937 state Department of Education bulletin stated, "The Negro constitutes practically one-half of the population of the state. By no principle of economics can there be permanent prosperity for the state with half of the population idle, unskilled[,] . . . ignorant. . . . Neglect of the Negro by the white man and indifference to his home life, his health, his education, his training for useful and gainful employment all have to be paid for."[21]

Another aspect of white concern that should have had more impact was the waste a dual system fostered. A 1938 report by the Atlanta and Fulton County governments noted this waste in a number of situations. Commenting on a temporarily built white junior high school in a white area that was beginning to change to black, the report considered whether this junior high school, "entirely housed in portables," should be rebuilt as a new permanent white school. Building such a school only made financial sense "if it could be turned over to negro use when it became economically undesirable to use it for white children. The state of public opinion is apparently such, however, that such transfers must wait for practically the last white family to move from the territory." The report also commented on small versus large schools, stating "that small schools are much more expensive to operate than the large schools. . . . *If all Atlanta white children could be sent to schools of over 500 the annual savings on operation, maintenance, and instruction costs alone would be approximately* $90,330." In 1936–37, nineteen out of forty-four white elementary schools and three black ones had enrollments of under five hundred. In an integrated environment, and with the many blacks and whites who lived within the same or adjoining school districts, larger schools could have been built and smaller schools consolidated or closed, thereby saving school funds.[22]

The case of Calhoun Elementary School draws the above issues together. The report considered the operation of this white school wasteful because of the school's excellent and plentiful facilities, which were underused because of a declining white population. Yet there was a "crying need for negro school accommodations in that area. Calhoun school is located in a district in which the population, save for a few houses[,] . . . is entirely negro." The report makes it clear that white students from Calhoun could easily have been transferred to other white elementary schools whose district lines overlapped with Calhoun's. The report continued, "We recognize the difficulty of establishing a negro school in an area in which there is even a meager white population. But the city of Atlanta cannot afford to continue to educate regular elementary school children in buildings as expensive and wasteful in operation as Calhoun." For the time, though, Calhoun remained a white school within a black neighborhood that needed schools, and its situation was repeated elsewhere in the city. A racially unified school system would have avoided such waste and would also have been able to make use of larger, more cost-effective school buildings. For example, to get the black elementary schools on a single-session basis would have required about one hundred more classrooms. This space was available, and had been for many years, within a number of underused white schools. In 1916 the white Ashby Street School, located in a black neighborhood, had only eighty-four students, while the black school in the area had more than seven hundred and was on double sessions.[23]

The situation for black schools did not appreciably improve, however, and there was of course no consolidation of black and white schools. In response to the bond vote of 1938, the Atlanta Civic and Political League's pamphlet "DOES ATLANTA Know and Approve These Conditions?" delineated the general neglect of black schools. The pamphlet stated, "None of the Negro schools, except Walker Street (which was formerly used as an elementary school for white children) have auditoriums or gymnasiums. . . . Practically all of the schools are without cafeterias, library space and facilities." The league called for funds to build classrooms, cafeterias, libraries, auditoriums, gyms and, in one case, more desks, the installment of a clock and bell system, and an improved lighting system. The pamphlet continued, "Within the past quarter of a century there has been very little increase in the number of class rooms added to Negro schools." The result was that about 88 percent of black elementary schoolchildren were still on double sessions, as were many in the high school.[24]

Another school bond referendum in 1940 would have provided blacks with only $100,000 out of a $1.8 million fund, further illustrating the persistent lack of white concern. The bond was defeated after efforts to increase the funds for black schools failed. Black teachers, among others, expressed their dismay with this bond issue. In 1940 a black teachers' organization called the Gate City Teachers' Association filed a petition with Superintendent Sutton that requested more classrooms and schools for black children. Complaining about double sessions, which provided only half-days for black students and thereby caused them to fall behind in their studies, the group asked for schools to be built or expanded in particular neighborhoods where the black population was increasing. Complaining that their "building program [has been] almost at a standstill since 1924," the association urged that school bonds acknowledge black needs. The Atlanta Baptist Ministers' Union, the Civic and Political League, and the

Atlanta NAACP also spoke out against the bond because of its inequitable appropriation for black schools.[25]

Most changes came with glacial slowness. The first public kindergarten program for black children was not started until 1945, by which time every white school had a kindergarten. (Kindergartens for white schools had been set up in 1899.) In 1941, Atlanta's school-aged population was 37.4 percent black and 62.6 percent white, yet 20 percent (thirteen) of the schools in the city were for blacks and 80 percent (fifty-two) for whites. The construction of some black schools had been started years before but had never been completed. The majority of black teachers, but no white teachers, taught double sessions. Double sessions also meant—as one pamphlet on Atlanta schools, written by a coalition of black organizations, noted—that "large numbers of unsupervised Negro school children are roving the streets and alleys, throughout the day." The dual system's neglect of black needs is clearly indicated by the fact that in 1941–42 the city spent under 16 percent of its annual school funds for black schools and activities.[26]

Postwar Planning

Late in 1944, after the board of education had announced its postwar school improvement plans and a bond to finance them, a study on the city's black schools was released in response by the Atlanta Urban League, which was concerned that the plans and bond allocations would maintain or increase the inequities in the dual system. The league's study revealed that while the black population of the city had increased by about 36,000 since 1922, when Washington High was being constructed, no new black schools (except for some WPA projects) had been built. The only post-1922 black school improvements were that some white schools had been converted to black use and some classrooms had been added to old schools.[27]

Although white Atlantans liked to consider themselves progressive in terms of black schools, according to the report, Atlanta ranked last among the four other southern cities studied with black populations at or over 19 percent (Houston, Dallas, Jacksonville, and Nashville) in regard to the number of black schools for their school population. Atlanta, with a 34.6 percent total black population (for 1940) and a 37.4 percent black school population (for 1941), provided fewer schools per 1,000 black schoolchildren than Dallas, which had a 19 percent total black population and an 18 percent black school population, or Jacksonville, which had a 33 percent total black population and a 28 percent black school population.

Jacksonville had twenty-six black schools for 10,046 black schoolchildren; Atlanta had just thirteen for 26,528 black students. In an earlier era, Atlanta had lagged behind other southern cities in providing public high schools for black children. Birmingham, for example, had a black high school as early as 1901. Little Rock, Dallas, Nashville, Houston, Knoxville, and other cities had black high schools by 1915; but many other southern cities, including Atlanta, waited until the mid-1920s.[28]

The report noted other problems as well. The black schools needed not only more classrooms but also more teachers. Also, except for some poorly equipped shops at Washington High School, no vocational training facilities existed for Atlanta's blacks. "Next to the inequalities created by the double sessions," the Urban League stated, "no other one factor is so responsible for the inequality of opportunity offered to Negro youth by the Atlanta school system as the lack of sufficient opportunity for trade and industrial training."[29]

The board of education's immediate response to the Urban League report was to admit that "it has not been able to furnish to the colored children of Atlanta adequate educational opportunities." Noting that conditions were not good for whites either, the board argued that blacks' educational system was better than it had been twenty years earlier. Citing recent improvements in black schools in regard to overcrowding and pupil-teacher ratios, the board asserted that black children and teachers were treated better in Atlanta than in the rest of Georgia or in other similar southern cities. This argument was certainly questionable in regard to other southern cities, and in any case it was a poor defense. Recognizing that conditions could be improved in the school system, the board supported "a continuation of the policy of gradually improving standards and narrowing as fast as practicable whatever gap might exist between facilities for white and colored."[30]

The white Atlanta newspapers urged the board to do something to correct the inequities. A 1944 *Atlanta Journal* editorial stated that "if Atlanta is duly to progress, the progress will have to be measured in terms of her entire population, not in terms of two-thirds." A year later, the newspaper still stressed, "It is generally acknowledged that the well-being of a community is dependent upon the progress of all its people. So long as a segment of the population is denied adequate educational opportunities, the entire community will suffer in juvenile delinquency, crime, poor citizenship and economic distress." But even these pleas brought few positive accomplishments: the addition of one cafeteria, a few libraries in the elementary grades, two new classrooms at Washington High School, and the black community's first two public kindergartens (one in March 1945, one in September 1945).[31]

In the immediate postwar period, the gap between white and black schools persisted. Overcrowding and lack of sufficient school buildings also continued. One way to deal with these problems was suggested by the Bond Commission and was supported in Superintendent Ira Jarrell's 1945–46 annual report. She said that the Atlanta Board of Education had agreed that high schools should become neighborhood rather than city-wide schools and should pull their students from the surrounding neighborhood even if it meant crossing county lines. "The Community Schools are its [Atlanta Board of Education] answer to the economical problem of providing the best education possible by making efficient use of the existing school plants and facilities." Of course, the board meant within racial divisions; it was not suggesting integration. But logically, the superintendent's argument implied that efficiency required a unitary school system.[32]

The new bond proposal being developed in 1944–45 was inadequate to deal with the school problems in the black community. Only 10 percent of the bond funds were to be used to improve black schools. According to the Citizens Committee on Public Education, a coalition of black civic groups formed by the Urban League and NAACP after the 1944 report, and organized in an effort to change the bond allocations and board of education plans, "The gap between the quality and quantity of education Atlanta offers to its white children and to its Negro children is not being narrowed 'as fast as practicable' by the present bond issue." The committee argued that by offering blacks so little, the bond actually widened the racial gap in schooling. Asking that the bond allocate substantially more money to blacks, the committee noted that these added funds could decrease the inequities by providing for two new black high schools (one vocational), four new black elementary schools, and eighty-six additional classrooms in existing black schools, as well as new auditoriums, gyms, cafeterias, and libraries, and better bathroom facilities. The money could come from a larger bond so that nothing would be taken away from white school improvements.[33]

Black parents also held protests and circulated petitions about the bond and planned building program. By October 1945, when they realized that the board of education was showing little inclination to substantially improve the black schools and that public pressure did not seem to be working, the black leaders discussed a new approach. Another circumstance that spurred a rethinking of tactics was that Georgia's state constitution had recently been amended to eliminate the clause that separate white and black schools be "as nearly uniform as practicable." Instead, the constitution now simply required that "an adequate education" be provided.[34]

The new approach raised the possibility of legal action to push the board of education into narrowing the racial gap. As Grace Towns Hamilton, acting executive of the Citizens Committee on Public Education, explained, it was "decided that the time has come to 'precipitate a crisis' and it was suggested that action to require the equalization of pupil-teacher ratios between the white and Negro schools might be a possibility"; this strategy would force the building of more classrooms and the hiring of more teachers. Before taking legal action, black parents petitioned the board of education and School Superintendent Ira Jarrell in December 1945 to correct the inequities voluntarily. They pointed out that black children represented over one-third of the school age population and one-third of the total of those enrolled in Atlanta's schools but had only one-sixth of the total school land and building investment. The proposed bond would reduce planned school building and land investment for blacks to even less than one-sixth. The parents requested 297 more classrooms and 235 more teachers in black schools to achieve some equality with whites.[35]

The main issue raised by the parents was the city's misuse of state school allocations. Georgia provided funds for one teacher for every forty elementary students and for every thirty-five junior high and high school students, according to the average daily attendance of the preceding year. This formula was used for both black and white schools, but the actual funds were separate. Based on the 1944–45 school year, the state allotted "627 white teachers and 358 Negro teachers to the Atlanta Public Schools." However, the city's board of education "employed for the day schools a minimum of 409 more white teachers than were allocated by the state, and 37 less Negro teachers." Because funding was separate, the board was giving money back to the state that it could be using to hire more black teachers. The petition requested that the city hire the number of black teachers funded by the state and that the money provided for black schools not "be less than the percentage the Negro population bears to the total population of Atlanta."[36]

The controversy created by the 1944 Urban League report, the pressure exerted afterward, and the growing importance of the black vote in the waning days of the white primary apparently effected some change in the bond's funding priorities. In January 1946 the board of education stated that it would redesign its postwar school plans. White groups concerned about Atlanta's schools also applied pressure by this time. Joining with the Citizens Committee on Public Education, representatives of white organizations formed the biracial Co-ordinating Committee on Public Education to urge the board of education to revise its postwar school plans. The initial bond proposal had provided $1 million to blacks and $10 million to whites. In April 1946, the board announced a new plan that offered slightly over $3 million for school improvements for blacks and about $5.5 million for whites. Supporters of the revised bond hoped that it would end double sessions and overcrowding and provide the buildings and classrooms requested in the 1944 Urban League report. Although the bond passed in August 1946, its promise was not fulfilled.[37]

As of 1948–49, according to Urban League follow-up studies and other reports, the amount authorized for white school construction was 26 percent above the bond allocation; for black schools, it was 1 percent below. Some improvements were being made for black students and teachers, but they represented less than had been promised and were not enough to correct the inequities. The bond had called for three new black elementary schools, the shift of two white elementary schools to black use, and a number of additional classrooms in black elementary schools, as well as gyms, cafeterias, library rooms, auditoriums, and a stadium. But what had been accomplished? The white Opportunity School was transferred to the black community in 1947 (and renamed C. W. Hill School), but the building did not receive any of the renovations that had been promised; the Wesley Avenue School was replaced with a new building, but it had fewer classrooms than the bond had specified; classrooms were added to some black schools, but the number of classrooms added was fewer than the bond had stipulated. No gym, auditorium, cafeteria, or stadium had been built for Washington High School, as provided for in the bond, although Howard High School (a former elementary–junior high school that had become a high school in 1946) did receive an auditorium/gym. Also, the Carver Vocational School opened in the 1947–48 school year. The low number of new classrooms meant that double sessions continued for most black elementary students, although the elimination of double sessions had been one of the bond's major goals. By August 1949, the board of education had appropriated 97.6 percent of the funds designated in the bond for white schools but only 68.6 percent of the money designated for black schools. The slowness in spending the funds for black schools continued until 1950, when the Fulton County Grand Jury forced the board of education to use those funds as allocated in the 1946 bond. Yet the school

Table 10. Atlanta Public Schools, Average per Pupil Expenditure, by Race, 1935–1948

School Year	Black	White
1935	$41.00	$119.00
1941–42	$37.80	$108.70
1943–44	$44.11	$119.61
1944–45	$47.78	$124.00
1945–46	$51.92	$128.53
1946–47	$59.88	$139.73
1947–48	$75.13	$178.69

Sources: Paul E. Peterson, *The Politics of School Reform 1870– 1940* (Chicago: University of Chicago Press, 1985), p. 174; "A Supplemental Report on Public School Facilities for Negroes, Atlanta, Georgia 1948," Atlanta Urban League, Grace Towns Hamilton Papers, Atlanta University Center, Robert W. Woodruff Library; *Atlanta Journal*, 14 December 1944; "Petition to Ira Jarrell, Superintendent, and Atlanta Board of Education," 8 April 1949, Southern Regional Council Papers, Atlanta University Center, Robert W. Woodruff Library.

superintendent still was claiming in her 1948–49 report that the "Board of Education is leaving no stone unturned to provide the educational facilities for its Negro students."[38]

The 1948 Urban League follow-up studies and other reports noted that by the 1947–48 school year, the gap between per pupil expenditures for whites and blacks had increased—that, in fact, more than twice as much was still being spent for the education of whites than for blacks from kindergarten through high school (see Table 10). Furthermore, "in 1947–48, the average white school child received his education in a school having facilities representing an investment of $383.87 per pupil" (see Table 11). For blacks the investment was $153.42 per pupil. The disparity in this case would increase by 1948–49. The figures on facilities indicate the insufficient numbers of school buildings, classrooms, auditoriums, and other school accommodations for black students. The end result was that overcrowded schools, overcrowded classrooms, and double sessions persisted. Moreover, in 1946–47, many of the available teaching jobs in black schools were not filled. The bond had failed to equalize the dual school system not so much because of a lack of total funds as because of a lack of concern among the white educational leadership. At the very least, blacks

Table 11. Atlanta Public Schools, Average per Pupil Investment in School Facilities, by Race, 1946–1949

School Year	Black	White
1946–47	$128.89	$439.27
1947–48	$153.42	$383.87
1948–49	$228.05	$570.00

Source: Atlanta Urban League, "A Report of Atlanta Public School Building Program Financed by 1946 Bond Issue," 15 August 1949, National Urban League Papers, A-104, SRO, LC.

wanted to secure control over white schools in black neighborhoods, but this change too occurred very slowly. The reports also called for equality in teacher-pupil ratios, number of school buildings, length of school day, "auditorium, gymnasiums, libraries, health rooms, cafeterias, playgrounds and other physical facilities."[39]

When the reports of unfulfilled bond promises were released, black parents petitioned the school superintendent and board of education for an end to school inequities. Citing the gap between expenditures for black and white students, the inferior black school buildings, the double (and sometimes triple) sessions that black children (especially in the elementary schools) had to endure, and the high teacher-pupil ratios in black schools (three out of five black elementary schools had extremely high teacher loads), the parents called for change. Like the 1948 Urban League study, this petition noted one issue of concern that could be dealt with quickly: the parents stated that their children in various sections of the city "are seriously handicapped by lack of public school facilities in the neighborhoods where they live. The schools located in these sections are still designated as schools for white children despite complete change in the racial composition of the neighborhoods, despite a steady decrease in the enrollment of white children and despite resulting inefficient use of the school facilities." As a result, black elementary students in these areas were forced to walk long distances outside their neighborhoods to go to overcrowded schools elsewhere. Even though the board of education acknowledged that the poor school building facilities were "a major handicap in the provision of equal educational opportunity for Negro children," relatively little was done to correct the situation, particularly in the elementary grades.[40]

By 1948–49, therefore, black children were still going to school one-half or one-third the time whites attended, and many of them had to go long distances to reach their schools, some of which had no running water or flush toilets. While blacks made up 39 percent of Atlanta's school children in 1949, they had only 24 percent of the school buildings. Yet the school board still authorized more of the 1946 bond funds than were allocated for white schools and less for black ones. Continuing to profess that it had "no policy for Negro schools separate or different from that for white schools," the board stated that it was providing sufficiently for black students and with equality to what whites received. It was evident to the black parents, though, that the board's inability to deal with the children equally or even to acknowledge that they were not doing so would mean that the unfair treatment would not only continue but would get worse. The parents already knew the outcome of such policies: "the social consequences of prevailing inequities in the Atlanta public schools have been all too evident, too long."[41]

"There Can Never Be Equality under Segregation"

In the early 1950s, on the eve of the Supreme Court's ruling in *Brown versus Board of Education of Topeka, Kansas*, there was still little indication that Atlanta's handling of the dual school system had undergone any substantial change. The black schools were better than they had been earlier in the century, but there was no area in which they were equal with white schools, and white leaders had made no concentrated attempt to correct the inequities. Black leaders now began to realize that there could be no equality for black students under a dual system, and as a result they pressed for an end to segregated schools.

In 1950, a suit was filed in U.S. district court to end segregation in Atlanta's public schools and to eliminate inequities based on race "in the opportunities, advantages and facilities provided by the Atlanta school system." The general motivation behind such a suit was clear. As black educator Benjamin Mays noted concerning progress for black schools, "The thing that lies back of the Atlanta suit is the growing conviction that there can never be equality of educational opportunities under segregation, and that the Atlanta Board will hardly spend more money on Negro schools than it spends on white schools in order to equalize the Negro schools."[42]

As a result of the suit, Atlanta newspapers responded to the inequity issue with, at times, imagined notions of the equality and progress within the dual system. The *Atlanta Journal-Constitution* editorialized that "progress in equalizing white and Negro school facilities is truly remarkable"; the paper supported the continuation of these efforts but expressed opposition to ending segregation. The *Constitution* commented that "Atlanta of all places is one where the launching of such an attack [against segregated schools] might have been least expected. The record of our City Board of Education gives proof of its honest, earnest effort to bring the Negro schools up to a high standard." Pointing to the increase in numbers of black teachers hired, the equalization of teacher pay, and the school building program made possible by the 1946 bond, the newspaper concluded that "these are a few among many evidences of a conscientious and fruitful effort to meet Atlanta's moral as well as legal responsibilities in the field of Negro education."[43]

The newspaper's arguments were only partly correct. Improvements had occurred, but the schools were far from equal. The gradualism that was supported by white Atlanta would not have removed the inequities in the near future, if ever. The 1950 threat of a desegregated unitary school system did speed up the process, however, and turned the white local and state leadership's attention to the black schools.

And some important changes did take place, most notably the election of Rufus Clement to the school board in 1953. However, given than Clement was the only black on the board, his ability to institute change was limited. In 1951, in a speech welcoming the NAACP convention to Atlanta, Mayor Hartsfield pointed to the number of black teachers hired since 1944, as well as the new school facilities provided for black children. "We are spending millions," he told the conventioneers, "in the erection of modern schools of the very highest quality."[44] In 1952–53, a new school bond issue provided for thirteen new white elementary schools and eleven new black ones, indicating an increase in funding for black schools. These new buildings—dubbed "Supreme Court schools" because they were built in response to the imminent *Brown* decision and the fear of integration—provided too little and came too late. The decisions made in the previous decades to limit educational funding for black children and to create a separate and unequal system left the black schools in such a poor state by the 1950s that it would take considerable effort to bring them up to par with white schools and merge them into a unitary system.

While many factors are involved in poor student performance, and higher expenditures do not always result in higher pupil achievement, the disparities in Atlanta were so enormous that they surely had some impact on the students. And the desire for equality and merger was not evident in the majority of the white community: as the school desegregation battles heated up immediately after 1954, white Atlanta resisted any changes. Racial attitudes continued to influence policy decisions into the period of desegregation and resegregation.

CHAPTER 7

The only "freedom-of-choice" in Atlanta's school integration plan is the freedom school officials have to keep most Negro students out of nearby-white schools.—**Julian Bond**, 1965

Desegregation and Resegregation: Atlanta Schools after 1954

Although 1954 stands as a legal turning point regarding the dual school system, little real change in school policies occurred through the 1950s and 1960s. Segregated schools continued, as did the neglect of black schoolchildren. The race-based policies that had shaped Atlanta's school system before 1954 persisted in the decades afterward into the period of resegregation. The pattern had been set many years earlier; the impact was felt into the future.

Court Cases, Petitions, and Delays

The Supreme Court's 1954 *Brown vs. Board of Education* decision met with hostility in Atlanta, as it did throughout the South. The reaction from the white community is epitomized by Mayor Hartsfield's comment that "the City of Atlanta is now engaged in defense of segregation in the public schools of Atlanta, and we expect to continue to defend that suit"; another indicative response was the board of education's plan to switch several schools from white to black in order to relieve immediate overcrowding and satisfy some black demands.[1] In June 1955, nine black parents petitioned the Atlanta Board of Education and school superintendent to end segregation in the public schools at once. Threatening to revive a 1950 antisegregation suit and backed by the NAACP, the parents expected some response. One result was the board's pressure on the parents to withdraw their petition. The issues were laid out, but there was not any move toward integration, even though the June 1955 petition was soon followed by four similar appeals. It was clear that the board was going to sit still on desegregation until the court ordered it to take action.[2]

The board did respond in various ways. The conversion of elementary schools from white to black increased, as did the planned building of black schools. A 1956 construction plan proposal was to build fifteen black and eleven white elementary schools by 1958, which would add 285 classrooms for blacks and 163 for whites. Spending would total $7,202,500 for blacks and $4,273,500 for whites. This plan represents the first time the spending proposals for black schools had exceeded those for whites.[3] Equipment and supplies to black schools were also upgraded and increased.[4] Clearly, an effort was being made to improve the black schools in order to squelch black demands for an integrated school system. This plan was also formulated on the state level. Georgia began constructing new black schools, upgrading salaries of black teachers, and "otherwise improving Negro educational standards. It hopes that this 'equalization' program will induce Negroes to accept voluntary segregation, and that it will raise their social and economic standards."[5] But it was too late for such stopgap actions. Besides, the new school construction strengthened segregation. In Atlanta, schools were built within the black community, and officials avoided building in racially transitional sections. Efforts were made to direct blacks away from white schools by providing new or upgraded schools in their communities. Sometimes a white school was located close enough to a black neighborhood that it would have been a logical one for area blacks to attend; but to prevent that, the board authorized the construction of a black school nearby to prevent demands for desegregation. This effort to prevent desegregation resulted in extra costs for the school system and relied on race rather than population and economic factors to determine school locations. Some of these schools were eventually phased out; their locations, which made little sense in the first place, made even less as integration increased.[6]

Furthermore, the Atlanta board issued a report in 1957 that indicated the gap between white and black schools. The report was authorized in 1955 to show how difficult it would be to merge the schools into a unitary system and can be viewed as a board effort to impede desegregation. What it also illustrated, however, was that any gap was the result of the long-term segregated and unequal educational system—something black Atlantans already knew and continued to complain about. The *Atlanta Daily World* commented that through this report, "the old fallacy of the 'separate but equal doctrine' in public school education was drawn into clearer focus." Although the board study was challenged by another study in 1960, the board's objective—to prevent desegregation—did not change.[7]

Since the board had not shown any desire to terminate the segregated system, in January 1958 the NAACP Legal Defense and Education Fund (LDF) brought a class action suit in federal district court against the Atlanta Board of Education and the superintendent (*Vivian Calhoun, et al., v. A. C. Latimer, et al.*). Once again, the board's immediate reaction was to strike out at the black parents involved in the suit. Any outstanding loans they had were called in for repayment; some of them lost their jobs; and in general they were subjected to economic harassment.[8] The tactics of the board appeared to be to delay action and try to satisfy black parents with upgraded segregated schools.

The suit was finally heard in June 1959 and ushered in an extended period of court actions involving desegregation. In June 1959, Judge Frank Hooper of the U.S. court overseeing Georgia's northern district stated that the Atlanta schools were segregated, and he called on the board of education to develop an integration plan by December 1959. The board filed its plan on time, and the court finally approved an amended version in January 1960. The course of action involved desegregation of one grade per year, beginning with the twelfth grade in fall 1960, under a very limited freedom-of-choice plan based on such criteria for pupil placement as availability of space and transportation; the student's educational skills, abilities, and intelligence; the effect of transferring the student on the "academic progress" of those in the student's desired school; and the student's morals, conduct, and psychological profile.[9]

State laws would not permit implementation of the plan. Any school system that accepted desegregation would be in violation of Georgia laws and would lose state funds. An outpouring of state legal actions against integrated schools began in the early 1950s in anticipation of the Supreme Court decision, and these efforts stymied any court-ordered desegregation in Atlanta. The immediate conflict between the state's intransigence and Atlanta's court-ordered changes led to a one-year delay in implementing the plan. During this year Griffin Bell, Governor Ernest Vandiver's chief of staff, asked banker John A. Sibley to head a commission on the school issue. The commission, set up by the legislature in February 1960, was to hold public hearings around the state to gauge opinion and suggest policy. The debate in Atlanta had already prompted the creation of various groups that wanted to "save the public schools." (The most notable was HOPE, or Help Our Public Education, a white group formed in 1958.) Faced with the closing of the University of Georgia as well as the public school systems in Atlanta and elsewhere in the state, the legislature relented under public pressure and warnings of economic repercussions similar to those that had occurred in Little Rock, Arkansas. In January 1961, the legislature eliminated its laws on the funding cutoff for integrated schools and accepted a local option plan which the Sibley Commission had suggested in its May 1960 report and which Hartsfield had endorsed as early as November 1958. Under this plan, local communities could decide on future actions regarding desegregation and the opening or closing of schools. The final pronouncement from the court was to begin desegregation in September 1961, starting with the eleventh and twelfth grades and then integrating downward one grade a year.[10]

A Meager Beginning

The years following the plan approval in 1960 brought into sharp focus the general gulf between white and black desires. The slowness of desegregation, the white exodus from the city, the black frustrations at white intransigence, and the school system's effort to resegregate illustrated both the strong emotions brought out by the issue of integration and the role of race in shaping the city's future school system.

The desegregation plan of one grade per year emerged as one of the problems, and blacks objected to this gradual process immediately. One could easily view this approach as a delaying tactic. It would extend the process over a number of years and would initially concentrate on the higher grades, where racial attitudes were generally set, rather than the early years, where students might be more accepting. Also, most juniors and seniors in high school would be reluctant to transfer just as they approached graduation. John Letson, who became superintendent of Atlanta's schools in July 1960, commented later, "I firmly believe that it was done on the assumption that there would be fewer black students who would want to leave their schools." If he had been involved in that decision, he said, younger students would have started the desegregation process. He viewed the twelfth-grade starting point as something that was done to impede desegregation.[11] Yet at first he did nothing to change the one-grade-a-year plan.

Other measures were also used to stall desegregation. Those students in the "desegregated" grades who wished to transfer were first assigned by race to schools, then they had to apply for transfer. Application forms were available only at city hall. The students then went through a battery of psychological and academic tests to assess their ability to function within white school settings. Rather than quickly eliminating the dual school system, board members chose a slower course, one filled with obstacles, and required that blacks initiate the application process. Given that school desegregation was to have been achieved "with all deliberate speed," as the Supreme Court stated, it could have been accomplished with school-mandated transfers beginning in the early grades or the use of nonracial school zones that contained both white and black children. That this was not done, black leaders maintained, was the fault of Letson's go-slow program. Going too slow, it was felt, gave whites the time to flee. Letson contended that speeding up the process would have resulted in more white flight.[12] It is difficult to determine whether moving slowly or quickly to integration would have changed anything in regard to white flight, but as we will see, other actions by Letson indicated that real integration was not one of his goals and caused blacks not to trust him.

The 1961 desegregation planning centered around two issues—avoiding violence and selecting black students. On the first point, the city did well. Atlanta's business elite was concerned about the city's reputation and continued ability to attract investments. Once the court made its final judgment, Hartsfield and other city leaders worked to cast Atlanta in a positive light. It was in relation to the peaceful desegregation process that Hartsfield again spoke of Atlanta as "a city too busy to hate." Although this phrase does to some extent describe the initial days of racial integration fairly well—especially when one compares Atlanta to some other southern cities—the *real* desegregation of the city's schools and most whites' unwillingness to end the dual system indicated a good deal of hate. As the

Greater Atlanta Council on Human Relations stated, "Measured in units of open schools, no bombs and no boycotts, Atlanta school desegregation is an unqualified success. Measured in units of steps toward the elimination of race as a factor in pupil placement, of efficient use of school facilities or improvement in human relations, there might be some question." For example, in 1961, while blacks made up almost 45 percent of the total number of students, they only occupied approximately 33 percent of Atlanta's school buildings.[13]

Of the 133 black students to request transfer to white schools in 1961, only ten were accepted, and nine actually went to four white schools. Whites tended to regard this small number as an indication of a new era, but many blacks viewed it with less enthusiasm. Jesse Hill expressed disappointment, saying that he expected the court to look at how the school system had dealt with the pupil-placement process. He added prophetically that "what the Atlanta board had done will eventually lead to less, instead of more, integration." John H. Calhoun complained that "the approval of 10 [transfers] doesn't scratch the surface of the problem of inequality of educational facilities and opportunities."[14]

The school board thus initiated a policy (approved by the courts) that would lead to years of stalling substantial integration. Meanwhile, blacks, concerned about the long-term overcrowding in their schools, tried to quicken the pace both by challenging the board's decisions on applicants and by appealing to the courts. In May 1961, NAACP field secretary Amos Holmes recommended that black leaders appeal any rejected transfer applicants; help the students who were chosen in preparing for the desegregation process; and, in a suggestion that indicates the related racial problems, "utilize offers of jobs for families of applicants, who meet with economic reprisals."[15]

Efforts to secure more black transfers to white schools faced a cynical circular argument. Since overcrowding diminished the quality of education, and since the black schools were terribly overcrowded, many whites felt that black students generally could not compete in white schools and that the rejection of numerous transfer applicants was therefore justified. However, policies that aimed to "broaden the curriculum" and relieve overcrowding in black schools or allow transfers into relatively empty white schools were rejected. Overcrowding therefore remained and provided white officials with an excuse for avoiding real desegregation. Although Letson acknowledged that overcrowding had an adverse effect on the caliber of education, he refused to allow sufficient numbers of black students to transfer to the underused white schools. He felt that moving some blacks from overcrowded schools to white schools would have resulted in a negative reaction from whites. However, many black students were suffering from an inadequate educational system, and quick action was needed. The token desegregation solved no problems relating to educational quality and spurred Hill to ask, "How long will Atlanta's Negro citizens permit the Board of Education to give them the runaround, while parading Atlanta before the world as fair-minded and good-hearted."[16] It was clear, as James O. Gibson, executive secretary of the NAACP's Atlanta chapter, lamented, that overcrowding at black schools "is a problem that the Board cannot handle through halfway measures intended to preserve the segregated pattern."[17] And through the next few years, the board's emphasis seemed to be on maintaining that pattern. The Atlanta desegregation process was very similar to segregation policies used in northern schools at the same time—for example, race-based school site selection, difficult transfer policies for blacks but not for whites, and the underutilization of white schools.[18]

Redress would have to be achieved through the courts, for as a report from the Greater Atlanta Council on Human Relations stated, "*Atlanta obviously assumed that school desegregation is not desirable since it took no steps to bring it about except as an alternative to the catastrophe of no schools, and since methods accepted both by the school system and the community were such as to discourage and slow down the process*" (emphasis in the original). The report further commented that the board took action on desegregation only after the federal courts forced it to do so, and that it had done so little that its actions cannot be considered "'progress' toward the goal of the placement of students according to educational needs and the utilization of facilities according to maximum efficiency."[19]

In 1962, black plaintiffs asked the court about what they considered the unfairness of the desegregation process. For example, black students had to take exhaustive tests to get into a school for which whites were not tested. Also, a dual racial system in the "desegregated" grades (grades 10–12) was still evident. The process had simply "maintained, not ended segregation." Blacks wanted the court to order the board to stop putting students and teachers into schools by race, to end its racial school zone system, and to abolish the process of maintaining both black and white schools. The evidence from the 1962 school year indicated little progress. Of 266 transfer applicants, only forty-four were approved to go to white schools. As a result, in July the black plaintiffs filed an alternative desegregation plan that would have resulted in teacher desegregation by September 1963 and the end of the dual system for students by 1965. Under that

plan, "all school zone lines were to be redrawn and students in the immediate vicinity of the schools were to be assigned without regard to race."[20]

Judge Hooper of the U.S. court's northern Georgia district refused the
request to accelerate desegregation, stating that the board was following
the agreed-upon court-ordered plan. The NAACP Legal Defense Fund
appealed to the Fifth Circuit U.S. Court of Appeals, but it was again
disappointed in June 1963. The court agreed that the Atlanta Board of
Education was following the district court plan, although it did order some
changes. The psychological, intelligence, and other various criteria for
black transfer applicants were dropped so that whites and blacks would
have the same standards for transfer to the same school. Proximity to the
school desired was the main criteria now. But students would still have to
request a transfer rather than being assigned on a nonracial basis to the
nearest school.[21]

The courts were correct that the school board was abiding by the desegregation plan—but it was clearly doing no more, although a bolder design,
even within the confines of the court's plan, could have relieved some of
the problems at the black schools. Desegregation at this point meant one
black student in a white school, and the board was providing that. However, considering just the high schools, in 1962 the black high schools were
overcrowded by 4,133 students. In contrast, the white high schools were
underused by 4,700 students. The solution was obvious, and more aggressive action in regard to grades already desegregated would have eliminated
the harmful overcrowding. It would also have made financial sense, since
fewer new classrooms would have to be built.[22] In the lower grades, which
were not yet desegregated, it would have also been economically sound.
Underused West Haven School, for example, was not open to black students, yet many walked by West Haven on their way to black schools
that were overcrowded. The same was true of Margaret Fain Elementary
School, which had 250 white students in a school that could hold 600.
Rather than move the black students from their overcrowded schools in
the area (the neighborhood was undergoing racial change), fully utilize
the building, and speed up desegregation to the lower grades, the school
board converted it to black use, and it remained racially segregated.[23]

It was clear, as the Greater Atlanta Council on Human Relations said in
1962, that "if the goal is to have as little desegregation as possible, the
measure will be different from what it will be if the goal is to bring about
an atmosphere friendly to desegregation." The council complained that
the token desegregation was not eliminating the "mounting educational
expenses of two systems" and called on the board of education to make

transfers easier, build schools "so as to provide as far as possible easy access to both white and Negro students," and allow blacks to use special facilities housed at white schools, such as the planetarium at Clark Howell School. Even the white press began to see the folly of maintaining segregation during a period of court-ordered desegregation. An article in the *Atlanta Journal* pointed out that the school system could reduce "its building needs sharply if it didn't have to contend with traditional racial patterns." Rather than the three hundred new high school classrooms that were planned, only seventeen would have to be built if the system could make use of already-constructed schools and disregard racial factors. Also, if a new school that offered easy access to both white and black students could be built, two separate schools would not be needed. The approach so far had been to convert schools from white to black use "as quickly as neighborhood changeovers permit." But as the article stated, another way to handle this situation was to grant more transfers. In 1962 the school board was developing a new bond issue that would have been largely unnecessary if racial issues had not been forcing unneeded construction.[24]

The city's black press, as well as the various civil rights and human relations organizations, kept up a steady demand to deal with the overcrowding problem by increasing the pace of desegregation through transfers of black students rather than, as the *Atlanta Inquirer* put it, by continuing this "eyedropper" approach toward racial transfers. There was no indication of any change in the school board's inaction into 1963, though, and the same newspapers and organizations continued to point out the financial folly of maintaining, for as long as legally possible, the dual system.[25]

The stalling tactics of the Atlanta school system are best illustrated by two disparate facts. First, when Atlanta is compared to a number of other southern cities in 1963 in regard to school desegregation, it comes up next to last in the total number of students desegregated: "Atlanta's present total is, among all the cities, whether starting earlier or later, the lowest, except for much smaller Greensboro."[26] Second, in the section of Atlanta that was covered by mainly white Murphy High School and Smith High School, blacks made up more than 50 percent of the population but represented only about 1 percent of these schools' students. Most black high school students went to the overcrowded black Howard High, although many of these Howard students lived within three blocks of Murphy High.[27]

The failure of Atlanta's desegregation plan by 1963 is also illustrated in the fact that blacks made up more than 50 percent of the city's elementary students but had only fifty-one schools, while whites had sixty-nine. Black teachers in the elementary grades numbered 1,134, white teachers 1,153. Whites had more schools and more teachers but fewer students—and therefore no overcrowding. About 5,400 black elementary students attended double sessions. For the older children, blacks had seven high schools with 15,252 students and 573 teachers; whites had seventeen high schools with 17,929 students and 764 teachers.[28]

Equality in education had been a long-term demand by Atlanta's civil rights organizations. During the period of intense civil rights activities in the city, schools were always on the list of crucial issues. In 1960, in its report "A Second Look," the Atlanta Committee for Cooperative Action commented on the double sessions and lack of textbooks in black schools. The "Appeal for Human Rights" also focused on the unequal school system. In 1963, the Summit Leadership Conference's "Action for Democracy" report called for total desegregation of the schools, the administration, and teaching staffs. Noting that "in Metropolitan Atlanta, according to 1960 census data, median school years completed by Negroes is only 63 percent of the white median," the report urged that conditions be improved and that the main guideline for student desegregation be "availability of space and availability of desired programs of study."[29]

SNCC was active in the city, initially through its South Atlanta Project, and responded to the school problems. In the grievance report "The City Must Provide," which was written with SNCC's help, neighborhood civic leaders complained to the mayor that "Negro children still attend overcrowded, understaffed, and poorly equipped Negro schools, some of which operate on double and triple shifts, while classrooms in white schools have empty seats. . . . Negro children must travel long distances to schools designated for Negroes, passing white schools on route which could and should accommodate Negroes. . . . Schools are still predominantly Negro and predominantly white in areas where the racial composition of the neighborhoods dictates that the schools should be integrated." The report demanded "that admission of *all* students—Negro and white— to *all* schools be automatically determined on a geographical basis." Attacking the school system, which had used delaying tactics, and critical of city officials, who had ignored this poor area, the report called for immediate and total desegregation. In 1963, only 143 black students in grades nine through twelve were in majority white schools; by 1964, as the eighth grade was added, there were only 637 black students in these schools. And this was ten years after the *Brown* decision.[30]

After the appeals court decision in June 1963, the NAACP Legal Defense Fund appealed to the U.S. Supreme Court. The U.S. Department of Justice also supported an acceleration of Atlanta's desegregation and expressed that position to the Court. In April 1964, after Supreme Court inquiries about the proximity criterion and further prodding from the plaintiffs, the board of education revised its desegregation plan to a new freedom-of-choice method for transfers or assignments. The criteria used by this new method included student or parental preference, the availability of space, and the student's proximity to the desired school. This plan was to be implemented during the 1964–65 school year for the eighth grade and for the higher grades, which had already been desegregated according to the original criteria.[31]

At this time the black plaintiffs urged the Supreme Court to order the board to do more to desegregate—for example, by creating school zones based on geography, not race, and by desegregating all grades by September 1965. The Court, which had to approve the board's amended plan, was to evaluate both that plan and the plaintiff's recommendations for further revisions. In May 1964 the Court ordered the desegregation case back to the district court in order to study the board's April proposal and appraise the whole Atlanta situation in terms of the possibility of accelerating desegregation in the city.[32]

In November 1964, the board again revised its plan, in expectation of the district court's ruling that desegregation should be quickened and in light of a recent appeals court judgment on the inadequacy of grade-a-year plans. The board agreed to desegregate two grades a year, working upward from kindergarten and the first grade using the freedom-of-choice method. The downward desegregation would stop with the eighth grade. The NAACP continued to push for school zones "drawn without regard to the racial complexion of surrounding communities and requiring children to attend designated schools within each zone." In April 1965, as expected, the district court mandated that desegregation be speeded up to two grades a year, starting in fall 1965 with kindergarten and first grade; all grades were to be desegregated through freedom of choice by fall 1968.[33] However, nothing was said about the staff and administrative desegregation that the NAACP lawyers had proposed. And for those in grossly overcrowded schools, this plan, like the first, moved too slowly and was based on vague criteria.

Recognizing the inevitable, and under pressure from the federal government as a result of the Civil Rights Act of 1964 (Title IV of that act allowed the attorney general to begin school desegregation suits on complaint from parents, and Title VI barred discrimination in any federally assisted activity) and from civil rights organizations, in July 1965 the board decided to desegregate all grades by fall 1965; many other Georgia school systems had already done so.[34] This decision was also related to an agreement between black leaders and the board of education. As part of the civic center complex construction, the black C. W. Hill Elementary School was to be razed. Blacks wanted the two-grades-a-year plan to be eliminated and all grades desegregated so that these children could use empty seats in nearby white schools until a new school could be built. Instead, the board wanted the black students to use temporary classrooms set up at the already-overcrowded and poorly suited Howard High School annex. The agreement reached in July 1965 called for use of the Howard annex in 1965–66 in return for desegregation of all grades through the use of requested transfers. Black pupils to be sent to the annex could also apply for transfers to other schools. A new C. W. Hill School was to be built by September 1966 in the black Bedford-Pine renewal area, just east of the civic center. If the school board and black leadership had not come to terms, protest would have continued against the construction of the civic center complex. To prevent this continued protest, and as a result of pressure by other forces, the board reluctantly and suddenly desegregated all grades ahead of court decrees.[35]

Resegregation Begins

It was essentially in the 1964–65 period that the school board began shifting its tactics away from desegregation, as slow as it was, to a process of resegregating the schools. In other words, once the courts ordered desegregation on a systemwide basis and at a faster pace, delaying tactics were replaced by white abandonment of schools, which was encouraged by the school board and superintendent and was also part of a general migration to the suburbs.

One notable case was that of Kirkwood Elementary School, on Atlanta's east side. As the 1964 school year began, black parents wanted to place their children in the underused white Kirkwood School. The black elementary schools in the neighborhood (Whiteford and Wesley) were very overcrowded (some black students went to classes in a nearby church because there was no room at the schools). The board refused to allow the students to transfer to Kirkwood, even though for some of them Kirkwood was closer to their homes than the black elementary school they attended. Whiteford was about 675 students above capacity; Kirkwood was 750 below. One could understand the frustration of black parents with the illogical attitude of white administrators, who permitted "the use of mobile units at Whiteford and three children sitting in one chair" and the "unnecessary economic burden of public transportation" to get to this school rather than have black children attend the nearby, below-capacity Kirkwood School. Besides stalling on Kirkwood—which, regardless of need, was still not covered under the desegregation plan until fall 1965, since it was an elementary school—the board suggested that new black schools in the area would be built to deal with increased black migration into the neighborhood.[36]

The school board and superintendent claimed that they were concerned about white flight in this area if they moved too fast toward desegregation. Letson, for example, later said that whites "would have left the neighborhood" and that he wanted "to maintain some semblance of a white school system, a white population in the school system." Yet the events indicated that the board and superintendent speeded up white flight and had little interest in stabilizing this neighborhood or the school. At its November 1964 meeting, the Greater Atlanta Council on Human Relations proposed to work in the Kirkwood community in order to stabilize it as an integrated neighborhood. The American Civil Liberties Union of Georgia reported later that "the school was centered in an area which human relations groups had hoped to stabilize, heading off resegregation." However, the school system leadership sabotaged any hope of accomplishing this feat. In November 1964, after black parents picketed Kirkwood, the board agreed to desegregate the school before the courts mandated it.[37]

Conditions in the neighborhood indicated an increasing black population and a decreasing white one, but there were still 473 white children at Kirkwood in September 1964 and 376 by the beginning of January 1965. Superintendent Letson certainly did not cause the white flight, but he encouraged it. Black students were to begin desegregating this school at the end of January 1965. Just before the arrival of the black children, Letson mailed letters to the parents of the white students at Kirkwood announcing the plan to desegregate the school and telling them when black students would arrive. The whites (students and faculty) were told that they could transfer to other schools before this happened. As the *Atlanta Inquirer* stated, Letson "gave the students and faculty the 'go ahead and get out before they come' sign by giving permission for transferral," and the newspaper urged that "a stand is going to have to be made by the parents, civic leaders and teachers against this type of so-called desegregation." By the end of January, when four hundred blacks transferred to the school, only seven white students and the white principal remained. What Letson had done was not illegal, but it clearly illustrated a method white school officials could use to "influence the exercise of choice in ways that intensify segregation." No effort was made to maintain the whites in the school. In federal court, Letson stated that the Kirkwood situation was an example of how "voluntary desegregation" led to an almost complete racial turnover. In fact, though, the Kirkwood affair was not a good argument against a quickened desegregation process but a good example of the duplicity of the school system administrators. When the 1965–66 school term started, Kirkwood was all black and overcrowded, while once again, predominantly white elementary schools located nearby had space for more students. The stalling of desegregation (in the number of black children allowed to transfer to majority white schools) continued, and a resegregation process was under way.[38]

Kirkwood was not an isolated case of resegregation; this pattern of desegregation and resegregation was evident in other Atlanta schools as well. For example, in 1964 a junior high school (Central Junior High School) was opened for blacks in the downtown area in a building that had formerly housed the white Smith-Hughes Vocational School. Black parents protested the opening of an old building, although renovated, for only one race during a time when desegregation was the professed plan. Also, the building was not supposed to be refurbished and used until unoccupied seats in other schools were utilized. Yet 1,200 black students were transferred to this school, and no whites were, although many whites lived nearby. Blacks interpreted this situation as resegregation and urged a three-day boycott of the school at the opening of the term. An angry petition to the school board strongly objected to the segregated school, and a flyer issued by the parents of children assigned to that school stated that the boycott would "show the Atlanta Board of Education that the Negro parents in Atlanta cannot and will not allow the re-segregation of their children into a TOTALLY NEGRO school without some form of active protest." According to the school system administrators, this school was set up in order to deal with overcrowded all-black schools, and "'resegregation' isn't in any way involved." But the creation of another black-only school when there were still empty seats in white schools worked to fortify, rather than dismantle, the traditional segregated system.[39]

In another case, 150 white students were allowed to transfer out of West Fulton High School in 1964 as the school began to contain a black majority. The editors of the *Atlanta Inquirer* asked why these transfers were so expeditiously accorded, given that the school was not overcrowded and many of the transferred white students lived nearby. To the newspaper, the answer seemed simple: the whites did not want to be in classes with blacks and were allowed an out. Yet, the paper continued, blacks who go to over-crowded schools with poor facilities and at distances from their homes and who travel "past better equipped more spacious 'white' schools are denied transfers."[40] This complaint was a common one. Also, blacks were allowed easy transfer to certain schools, but to others they were prevented from going in large numbers. As one black parent commented, it is hard to "understand the ease with which [black parents] can get transfers to change their children from one all-Negro school to another, but have to go to the area office . . . to get transfers to the predominantly white schools. . . . We can ask for transfers, but getting them is another thing."[41] Julian Bond commented that "the only freedom-of-choice in Atlanta's school integration plan is the freedom school officials have to keep most Negro students out of nearby-white schools." Transfer policy criteria stressed "available facilities," and this requirement became a way to prevent racial moves.[42] It seems as if some schools were earmarked for black majorities, while others were slated for a token black presence—a process that was different from the pre-1961 segregated system but came as close as possible within the court rulings.

There were also situations in which some black students, but not whites, were transferred from a desegregated public school (e.g., Center Hill Elementary School in 1965) to a nearby, overcrowded black school (Grove Park Elementary). However, many white students who lived close to Grove Park, and should have been the ones transferred, continued to go to Center Hill. Once again, a selective transfer policy that worked against desegregation was evident. As the NAACP stated, not only was the one-grade-a-year plan a slow process that limited desegregation; it was also "rigged to allow white pupils an escape from desegregated schools."[43]

White Flight and School Quality

White flight was taking place especially in those neighborhoods that, through housing and other spatial control policies, were designated to be black. Areas that were the focus of public housing construction soon became overcrowded with over-capacity, segregated black schools.[44] Housing and school policies were linked. However, if white flight was occurring, was there a chance to slow or reverse it? One good clue to understanding the dynamics of the white migration is to look at an area where an effort was made to limit it. Southwest High School illustrates well the possibilities of integration and the machinations of the school system. This school was located in Cascade Heights, an affluent area that was undergoing racial transition in the mid-1960s. Many neighborhood residents made a sincere effort to maintain an integrated community, including integrated schools. From 1967 to 1971, the Southwest Atlantans for Progress (SWAP) worked as a biracial stabilizing neighborhood association. This group allowed Cascade Heights' residents to discuss racial fears and transition, and as Xernona Clayton, secretary of SWAP, noted, its existence indicated the willingness of many whites to stay. The main issue in determining whether or not to move was the quality of the schools and the stability of academic standards. More than one community leader stressed concern about the schools as the overriding factor. This concern involved not only Southwest High but also its feeder schools, such as West Manor Elementary. At first, according to community leader Mrs. H. Y. Hutcheson, who was active in the West Manor school, there was "no evidence of lowering academic standards at West Manor." The school had 298 whites and 181 blacks at the end of the 1966–67 school year.[45] But changes came.

What finally drove the whites away, according to Clayton, was a fear of declining schools. She also maintained that while SWAP tried to handle these fears, Superintendent Letson did not share SWAP's concern. The organization tried to get Letson to provide Southwest High with some type of special program as a sign that the school system was interested in maintaining quality education in the school. Since affluent whites could move elsewhere for good schools or transfer their students out through the freedom-of-choice plan, SWAP needed to get assurances and proof that Cascade Heights' schools would remain excellent. The school system never provided that proof, Clayton noted; this point is also made in a report to the Community Relations Commission. Eliza Paschall, a white civil rights activist, commented in 1967 that "an increasing number of white children are transferring out of the schools in the Southwest area." Citing a neighborhood source, she reported that "there have been no efforts on the part of school officials to discuss the situation with parents in the area and to plan an affirmative program to make the schools of highest quality or to enlist the parents' cooperation in developing really integrated schools." Paschall suggested that the CRC had to make sure that the city gave special attention to programs and services in transitional neighborhoods and that the school board developed "a positive program to turn 'desegregated schools' into integrated schools."[46]

Others, such as Robert Tuve, chairman of a mainly white organization called Better Schools Atlanta, a group interested in improving schools in racially mixed areas, recommended "assistance in efforts toward neighborhood stabilization by providing superior facilities and instruction in border areas." Clayton contends that when SWAP approached Letson on a number of occasions, he always had an excuse for why the schools could not be so accommodated—for example, funding problems. Financial considerations were, of course, a factor. But SWAP was doing its job; the school was holding an integrated student body. According to Clayton, if the board of education or school bureaucracy had decided to focus some attention and money on this neighborhood's schools, many whites would have stayed, and blacks would have been reassured of Atlanta's interest in the education of their children. Perhaps a statement like that made by the board in 1971 under a black chairman (Benjamin Mays) was needed. This statement read, "It is the policy of this Board to make every effort to prevent the resegregation of integrated schools. Any decline in the level of services to and administrative support of integrated schools will be considered a direct violation of this policy." But that guarantee was never provided for Southwest High School. Southwest High, which had 676 whites and 420 black students in 1967 and 418 whites and 657 blacks in 1968, had in effect become resegregated by the 1969–70 school year, with 62 whites and 964 blacks. West Manor showed a sharp drop in white students during the 1967–68 school year, and by 1968–69 it had 499 black and 17 white students. Both schools indicated initial white flight but also a willingness to stay in an integrated school by a segment of the white community. It was this segment of the white population that school board policies could have influenced to remain. Other city services in the neighborhood, such as police protection and sanitation work, remained at a high level, and SWAP was effective in keeping these services at that level at least until 1970, when the area became black. (From then on, complaints were voiced about the lack of city services to deal with an increased population in the community.) Also, public housing and moderate-income multifamily housing, which neighborhood residents had opposed in 1967 and 1969, were rejected by the board of aldermen due to concern about the racial balance in the area. However, when blacks became a majority in the neighborhood, sections were rezoned from single-family to multifamily use. But the schools were another matter, and city officials had little control over what the school board or bureaucracy did.[47]

By 1967 it was clear that freedom of choice was not working and that Atlanta schools were not desegregating sufficiently but rather resegregating. Also, there was little effort to bring blacks into the high administrative school positions where decisions were made, even after the system was over 50 percent black, or to integrate the faculty of each school. The problem, besides school board tactics to avoid integration, was that the freedom-of-choice plan depended too much on individual student and parental decisions that could be blocked through bureaucratic actions. Black leaders wanted the school system to take a more positive, assertive approach by simply assigning or transferring black students and providing free busing to enable them to go to unfilled, predominantly white schools. Letson did not support this plan but instead wanted to provide temporary (mobile) classrooms at overcrowded black schools to eliminate double sessions. School construction also played a role in resegregating the system. There was still a lot of new school building in one-race areas, rather than in border or transitional neighborhoods where new schools could have had a balance of both races. Of the five new schools opened in 1967, four were 100 percent black and one was 100 percent white—a continuation of building policies begun in the period of segregation, when schools were expressly built for one race in their sections of the city.[48] Although race riots in Atlanta and elsewhere in 1966 and after increased concern in the city and spurred a desire to build more black schools to relieve overcrowding, there was little change in race-based school policies that maintained segregation.

The Atlanta newspapers agreed, as the *Journal* stated, that it was time to support administrative transfers and "abandon the notion that parental preference is adequate reason to permit an all-Negro school to be grossly overcrowded and in temporary facilities while other schools have room available." The *Journal* editorial continued that tensions exist "because of the school system's performance so far in the face of obvious inequities based obviously on race."[49] Yet there was no policy shift by school officials, in contrast to a growing sense of urgency among white city leaders, such as Mayor Allen, that they would have to deal with black discontent by beginning to upgrade black neighborhoods.

The school board and system administrators defended their policies in 1967 by noting, for example, that overcrowding in the black schools was unavoidable given the numbers of blacks entering the system in the previous five years. However, black schools had been overcrowded for many years, and white school capacity was still under-utilized. The board also claimed that the transfer policies were "not a racial matter but one based upon a sincere desire to achieve the best possible education for all." But the facts said otherwise, given the number of black schools that were still overcrowded and on double sessions and the school system's slowness in approving transfers of black students. An editorial in the *Journal* again correctly assessed the situation by commenting that "a gross inequity exists in the fact that half the Negro high schools have been on half-day sessions. This was an inequity that any responsible school official could observe— and one that could have been avoided. But some time elapsed as school officials parried complaints by saying that these half-day sessions really were better in many ways than regular sessions and that the present 'freedom of choice' plan is an equitable means of administering school enrollments." Letson admitted later that freedom of choice did serve to allow whites to avoid desegregation, but he defended his policies by claiming that a different approach would have accelerated white flight.[50]

The Failure of the Freedom-of-Choice Plan

A 1967 report by the U.S. Commission on Civil Rights affirmed the problems with the freedom-of-choice plan and demonstrated how Atlanta and other cities had used it to maintain segregation. First, school system officials could discourage transfers by stressing the racial identity of schools. Preventing teacher integration would help maintain schools as white or black no matter what the board said about supporting desegregation. "In Atlanta, only four of the fifty-nine schools 90 percent or more Negro had any white teachers by 1965." Second, if too many students selected a particular school for transfer, over what the school could handle, preference was given to students living near that school. Where students lived remained an important factor in desegregation transfers, especially when school officials used different criteria for white and black schools in deciding whether overcrowding existed. Therefore, segregation could be maintained in some cases by declaring a white school "above capacity" and allowing only those living closest to the school to attend. According to one account, white school officials removed desks from a white school in Atlanta in order to claim that it was filled to capacity and could not admit blacks. Third, freedom of choice could be used to transfer white students into a white school out of their area. "In Atlanta," the commission's report related, "the nearest high school for many elementary students attending Bolton (100 percent white), Chattahoochee (100 percent white) and Mount Vernon (92 percent white) is Archer High School (100 percent Negro). Under strict geographical zoning these three elementary schools normally would feed into Archer High School. Under Atlanta's free choice system, however, students graduating from these elementary schools attend O'Keefe High School (97 percent white)." White children could always secure transfer to a white school, regardless of distance from their homes. In other words, the choice plan so persistently maintained by the school board could easily be used to encourage school segregation.[51]

There were other problems as well. In 1967, a coalition of black organizations (including the NAACP and the SCLC) complained to the board that textbooks had been issued to classes late or not at all, and they made a number of requests, including the following: a school that was 60 percent or more black should have a black principal; a black school superintendent should be appointed, and by January 1968, a black should be put in as a first associate superintendent; blacks should be appointed, also by January 1968, to head some school departments; double sessions should be ended; and racist textbooks should be replaced. In a special meeting in September 1967, the board agreed to appoint Hilliard A. Bowen, a black area administrator, to the newly created position of assistant superintendent; it also agreed to change racist texts and set up a biracial textbook committee. On other requests the board hesitated, claiming that hiring a black principal in a school that was at least 60 percent black or stating that the next superintendent would be black or mandating that black department heads be appointed was against school policy, which required that hiring be done "without regard to race." The board did promise to try to achieve "a better white-Negro ratio in the administrative staff of each major division" and to work to end double sessions and ease transfers. But significant change still came slowly and reluctantly. For example, Bowen did not get an associate superintendent's position, as desired, and in his new job he had no influence over school curriculum, hiring, promotions, or other policy decisions. But even these mild alterations were only accomplished with pressure from the black community and concerned whites. For example, Martin Luther King Jr. threatened to lead demonstrations on the school issues unless the grievances were redressed. The black community was not satisfied with the meager board concessions, and there was a call for Letson's resignation.[52]

An October 1968 Better Schools Atlanta report echoed the dismal descriptions of black schools before desegregation and indicated that the 1960s changes were having limited effect. This predominantly white organization verified what blacks had been saying through the 1960s: "students in black schools . . . attend larger first grade classes, have fewer textbooks per student, go to school in buildings of less value per student and equipped with less valuable furniture and equipment per student, attend schools with higher pupil-teacher ratios, [and] attend schools with less site area per student." Although black children made up 60 percent of the student population in 1967, they occupied only 40 percent of the school facilities. At the beginning of the 1968 school year, 92.3 percent of all black elementary students went to all-black schools.[53]

The reaction to this report was varied. Without consulting Letson, the attorney for the board of education hired detectives to investigate members of Better Schools Atlanta. But the board also admitted that "there is no argument about the fact that little was equal about the 'separate but equal' days. Nor is there any question about the fact that Atlanta still has a backlog of building and equipment needs which fall heavily upon the Negro community." The board also pointed to the amount of money being spent on majority black schools. Black leaders again called for the superintendent to resign. The white Atlanta Education Association and the black Gate City Teachers' Association and others asked that an outside group appraise the school system.[54]

The National Education Association's Commission on Professional Rights and Responsibilities prepared a study that was issued in 1969. This analysis went through the history of Atlanta's school desegregation and praised the city's avoidance of violence but issued a biting indictment of the school system's intentions. For example, it noted that when freedom of choice was instituted, rather than simply transfer black children from their overcrowded schools to under-capacity white ones, as blacks wanted, "school authorities dealt with congestion at black schools in other ways, none of which was designed to further the course of racial integration." The report called for the elimination of the freedom-of-choice plan. Also, the report stated that although there had been vast improvements in black schools in terms of construction and pupil-teacher ratios by 1967–68, and textbook and supplies by 1968–69, it was not enough. Even spending equality would not solve the problem, because of the pervasive earlier pattern of discrimination and inequality. Black schools and students would still have a handicap related to past school board actions. But as of 1967–68, equality did not exist anyway; there were still many inequities in the system. For example, in elementary schools that were 95 percent or more white, the average number of library books per pupil was 12.1, and the average number of textbooks per pupil was 15.9. In elementary schools that were 95 percent or more black, the numbers were 10.0 and 12.3, respectively.[55]

In a further effort to achieve desegregation and a unitary system, in 1968 the district court ordered an end to the use of proximity as one of the criteria in the freedom-of-choice plan. In October of that year, the black plaintiffs asked the court for an end to freedom of choice in Atlanta and, as the U.S. Supreme Court had ruled in May 1968 in *Green v. New Kent County, Virginia*, the institution of other desegregation methods in cases where the freedom-of-choice concept was not working.[56]

The maintenance of a system that still had all-black and all-white schools in 1968–69 indicated the general failure of freedom-of-choice desegregation and the success of resegregation. Time was running out for a real integration plan as more whites left the system. Of the 124 elementary schools in the city, only twenty-five were considered desegregated according to the school superintendent (i.e., having at least 5 percent of the other race); out of twenty-seven high schools, only eleven could be called desegregated. What had happened in the 1960s was a product of white flight spurred on by a school system that supported either token desegregation or none at all. Yet by 1969, the school board prematurely claimed that it had created a unitary, nondiscriminatory system and that any remaining segregation was de facto and due to white migration to the suburbs and increasing housing segregation in Atlanta. The board's claims were based on a number of changes in school policies that did not constitute integration but did reveal the discrimination that had existed. For example, athletic equipment was now being provided to schools using nonracial criteria; school personnel were being "employed, assigned, promoted, disciplined and discharged on a non-racial, non-discriminatory basis"; both blacks and whites were attending the new area technical vocational school (the original plan had been to build a school for each race); school construction and land-buying priorities "are established on the basis of need in a non-racial, non-discriminatory manner"; school supplies, equipment, and books were being provided to schools equitably, without race as a consideration; and even "variations in the quality and wholesomeness of school lunches have been eliminated."[57]

Black leaders such as Horace Tate, a school board member from 1965 to 1969, were probably pleased with the above changes but did not perceive any overall effort to desegregate. Tate said, "Ever since I have been on the board I have not sensed a real integration policy, although I've asked for one." He continued, "Choice, proximity and space don't constitute factors for integration, but for circumnavigation of it. . . . We do not have a policy this board has approved to put white and black students in the same schools and keep them there." Tate later said that he felt that those three criteria were used to block desegregation. "If one factor didn't rule you out another one did—blacks lived too far from the school or there wasn't enough space in the white school." Frances Pauley of the Georgia Council on Human Relations agreed that "everything was done to make it [desegregation] difficult." The National Education Association's report too concurred, commenting that "the failure of the Atlanta School Board to adopt a formal policy and plan of desegregation has signaled to black communities a clear lack of board commitment to the goal of racial integration."[58]

New Plans

What the black community had wanted for some time was not freedom of choice (which school officials could limit by blocking transfers) but assignment of students according to school zones that would encourage integration. The choice plan was seen as an impediment to desegregation. Their view of the plan and what to do next is supported in studies done on this method of desegregation. In a 1967 report to the U.S. Civil Rights Commission, a research group appointed by the commission stated that "with no [officially defined school] boundaries, the initial assignment of pupils and the disposition of student transfer requests allow personal preferences, conscious or unconscious, and biases on the part of parents and school officials to influence significantly racial attendance patterns. In a freedom-of-choice system, feeder patterns are meaningless except as principals and area superintendents exercise superior judgment." The report suggested that "formal school boundaries" were needed if desegregation was to work. This proposal dovetailed with the Community Relations Commission's requests in 1968 that new schools be placed in parts of the city that "will maximize integration." This had not been done before. The construction of schools in fringe black-white areas with zones that overlapped into both neighborhoods would have provided desegregation through administrative assignments. Finally, faculty desegregation was not working. By 1968–69, 91 percent of black elementary teachers and 90 percent of black high school teachers taught in all-black or majority black schools.[59]

Other suggestions were offered as well. A 1968 report of the Atlanta and Fulton County Local Education Commission supported merging the city and county systems as a way to save money and end duplication of school services. This plan led to a new court case in 1972. Also, in December 1969 the Fifth Circuit Court of Appeals ordered a faculty integration plan that applied a racial proportional strategy. In order to mirror the entire school system's teacher population, each school was to have 57 percent black and 43 percent white teachers. This plan would be accomplished through transfers, beginning in March 1970. Although Letson presided over the transfer process, he did not support it, and at one point he resisted pressure from the federal government to increase the number of teachers transferred. Later in the 1970s, each school staff was to closely reflect whatever the system's teacher racial ratios were, but it did not have to be exact. This meant that each school had to be aware of the staffs' racial percentages so that black or white teachers could be transferred in or out. Many white teachers resigned rather than transfer, which left the school system with a 62 percent black and 38 percent white teaching staff by 1973. Of the teachers remaining in the system, according to various sources, the white and black teachers with the most experience and training were put into majority white schools.[60]

During this same period, in January 1970, the school board elected noted educator and former Morehouse College president Benjamin Mays as its first black president. Due to the *Green* case, the courts also ordered the Atlanta schools to try other methods of desegregation. In January 1970, the school board adopted the M to M Program, in which students who wished to go to a predominantly "other" race school could do so ("transferring from a school in which their race is in the majority to one in which their race is in the minority"). This new "majority to minority" or "M to M" transferal plan—which was actually a modified freedom-of-choice plan that would prevent majority white schools from becoming majority black—and new plans for zoning and pairing schools to foster integration seemed to offer some hope of achieving a somewhat desegregated system. In February 1970, the U.S. district court for Georgia's northern district ordered the Atlanta school system to offer free transportation to M to M students. Also, in an April 1971 Supreme Court case titled *Swann v. Charlotte-Mecklenburg (North Carolina)*, the Court called for the implementation of any method of pupil placement that would promote desegregation and eliminate the lingering impact of previous discrimination. The court affirmed the use of busing as a way to secure this goal. In 1971–72, during a time of court jockeying over whether Atlanta had achieved a unitary system and eliminated the dual school system and over an NAACP busing plan for the city, Atlanta school and civil rights leaders tried to work out a plan that would satisfy both the judges and the city's residents. By 1971 the school population was 72 percent black and 28 percent white, as white flight to the suburbs continued.[61]

The courtroom battles provided a further example of the stalling tactics of the 1960s. A statement by Good Government Atlanta perhaps said it best when it commented, "If one half the energy that has been devoted to opposing and protesting the recent federal court orders had been devoted to making them work and to developing support for the public schools, we would have only a small problem. . . . The anguish of recent weeks is due in part to footdragging and unwillingness to face reality during the past 12 years. It is time for all Atlantans to accept the concept of a unitary school system." The U.S. Fifth Circuit Court of Appeals echoed this theme in October 1972 when it ordered that the Atlanta schools desegregate quickly, in "the fullest cooperation with the spirit as well as the letter of this order." The statement affirmed what many Atlantans had believed for a number of years—that the school board and system had meticulously done only what the courts specifically stipulated and had made little attempt to do any more to desegregate.[62]

The appeals court order stipulated that the school system develop and implement a new desegregation plan by the end of November 1972 that would eliminate any segregation. (The court regarded schools with 10 percent or less of the other race as segregated). This judgment reversed a July 1971 federal district court ruling that prematurely affirmed that Atlanta now had a unitary rather than a dual school system and that except for large-scale busing the city "had done all it could" to eliminate the earlier school segregation. The district court had ruled out busing as a "possibly remedy" and claimed that housing patterns were the cause of any remaining school segregation. In the 1972–73 school year, 106 of 153 Atlanta public schools were "totally or virtually totally segregated." Most of these schools had never been desegregated; others had been white but were changed to black schools by the board of education in the period between 1959 and 1964, when the school system's effort to desegregate was minimal. Any new plan would have to be more extensive and drastic to achieve desegregation at this point. The court asked for "the use of pairing or grouping contiguous schools for racial purposes" and eliminating "the racial identity of twenty white schools."[63]

While the appeals court directed itself to the initial NAACP segregation case, another case was pending as well. Through a summer 1972 suit (*Armour v. Nix*), the Georgia ACLU was supporting a five-county metro-wide merger or combined operation of school systems in order to foster desegregation. This idea had been suggested as early as 1950 during discussions on the Plan of Improvement. However, many blacks opposed this plan because it would weaken their growing power in the educational system and merge the Atlanta schools with nearby county systems that were 90 percent or more white and that were having their own desegregation problems. Outside of the city—on the state level, for example—blacks clearly had less power. While the Atlanta school board had integrated years earlier, the state board had no black members. Also, the state superintendent, associate superintendent, and deputy superintendent were white. As the *Atlanta Inquirer* lamented in 1972, "Not a single department or unit head in the State Department of Education is Black."[64] Going beyond Atlanta presented difficulties. Nonetheless, a merger would have resulted in a more economical system.

Superintendent Letson set out to develop a new desegregation plan, as the court had ordered. In statements to the press between mid- and late October, Letson noted that some schools would not be included in the plan (e.g., schools already considered desegregated, and mainly black schools that had been erected after 1967, since court supervision made sure that "no segregationist policy influenced the location of schools constructed since then"). But for schools still segregated, Letson said, the plan would probably feature pairing and grouping. For example, "an elementary school . . . might have only the first three grade levels," and the one it was paired with would have the higher grades. This design would enable the schools to use larger school zones, which "would extend beyond the traditional 'neighborhood school' zone and include a higher racial mixture." Schools could also be paired in nonadjacent zones. Finally, busing would be used to transport students within these larger zones and to distant schools. The new plan, which needed court approval, would also include busing for M to M students. For any school that was maintained as segregated, exempt from the new design, the school system had to offer the court explanations to justify that school's racial composition. New and extended zone line alterations, pairing, busing, and M and M transfers would presumably provide the full desegregation plan that school officials had resisted for so long.[65]

The court orders plus the threat of the ACLU metro desegregation suit (which had now dropped its proposal for a cross-county school system merger in favor of student transfers across county lines) apparently spurred the school system to take action. Also, a federal court had ordered in a comparable Richmond, Virginia, case that county lines be crossed, through busing, to achieve desegregation. The ACLU believed that crossing county lines and bringing suburban whites into a desegregation plan was the way for the city to implement real desegregation.[66]

The tentative plans of Letson and others—such as white school board member Frank Smith, whose ideas largely paralleled Letson's—underwent revision as an effort was made to develop a final plan that would be acceptable to all. The NAACP, the LDF, the legal committee of the board of education, and a court-appointed biracial committee chaired by Lyndon Wade, executive director of the Atlanta Urban League, all worked to reach a compromise. Action Forum, the coalition of black and white leaders that included some of those already involved in this situation, was the catalyst for a compromise—bringing both sides together and pressuring them to reach an out-of-court settlement. The Forum discussions had started in mid-October at the same time that Letson was developing his own plans. The national and local NAACP and the LDF all had supported large-scale busing in the city to achieve, in each Atlanta school, a racial balance that reflected the ratios in the entire school system. However, given Atlanta's small white school population (22.6 percent or 21,683 in 1972), the resegregation that had already occurred and the resistance cross-county busing would have engendered, the local chapter of the NAACP decided in 1973 to agree to a compromise with the school board that the national leadership could not accept.[67]

The Atlanta Compromise

The NAACP chapter, under the direction of Lonnie King, came to understand that the numbers for citywide integration were no longer there and that large-scale busing might cause more whites to flee. As Benjamin Mays concluded, "Massive busing would be counter-productive at this point. We'd end up with no whites to bus." King also felt that the compromise would result in a better educational system for blacks. He said that in the early 1960s, large-scale busing and other tactics, such as pairing, "would have made a difference. But while Letson was holding everyone at bay for those 15 years, white flight was continuing . . . and therefore in 1972, when we came to a time where we wanted to try to settle this case, there was nothing here to settle. There were no white kids to bus. . . . You'd be busing children from an 87 percent black school to another 87 percent black school." King would have agreed to a busing plan if enough whites had remained in Atlanta's schools, but he decided instead to choose a solution that would "make black people accountable for their own destiny in terms of education" and allow them to determine the school curriculum, programs, and spending (in 1973, majority black elementary schools still were getting "less resources than other schools in terms of experienced teachers, teachers with higher degrees, and material goods").[68]

The Atlanta Compromise of 1973 was thus developed in order to end the suit, minimize busing, and pursue an aggressive plan to increase the number of blacks in administrative positions (in an effort to prevent the usual desegregation outcome, in which black teachers and principals were replaced by whites). This last goal would be accomplished both by creating new positions for blacks and by replacing whites as they retired from certain posts. A detailed program of administrative desegregation was developed (with U.S. district court approval and supervision) that called for a goal of 50 percent blacks on the administrative staff and the hiring of a black superintendent (to begin on 1 July 1973). Each administrative position was designated for either white or black. For example, there were to be five area superintendents—three blacks and two whites. As the compromise stated, these racial designations were included "to remedy . . . past discriminatory practices . . . [and] are for a one-time basis only." Subsequently, all administrative personnel decisions were to "be based on non-discriminatory individual qualifications without regard to race." School staffs were to be carefully desegregated, to the point "that in no case will the racial composition of a school's staff indicate that a school is intended for either black or white students." Each school was to have a black-white teacher ratio that mirrored the staff racial ratios in the entire school system. Dr. Asa Yancey, a black school board member, later commented that "if you have racial balance in administration from the superintendent at the top right on through all personnel who deal with students, then there can't be any racial discrimination against any child." Resources would flow equally to all schools. As the settlement developed in subsequent years, the superintendent's office kept records of the percent of white and black teachers at each school. Teachers would be transferred if the school was not in compliance, but they could be transferred only to schools where they would not upset the ratios.[69]

Furthermore, new magnet high and middle schools would be created "in racially unidentifiable areas that will be available to Black and White scholars city-wide." It was hoped that the magnet program would interest whites in transferring to these schools. When the plan went into effect, an expanded and more carefully planned M to M transfer program focused specifically on eleven majority white schools but included others as well. By October 1973, 2,882 blacks and twenty-five whites were in the M to M program. Pairing, transfers, closing of certain schools, rezoning, and some busing were all used to secure a unitary system objective of at least 30 percent black students in each school. The agreement called for a "commitment by the school system to achieving certain levels of racial balance in specified schools by September, 1973." Decisions were made concerning each school. For example, Sylvan Hills Elementary was 14 percent black in 1973. To increase its black enrollment, sixty-four students were transferred through M to M, and by May 1974 the school had a 30.3 percent black student population. In another case, ninety-five black children in the M to M program went to Moreland Elementary in 1974, raising the school's percentage of blacks to 30.1 percent. Schools' racial ratios continued to be monitored. Those that were not in compliance had teachers or students transferred. The plans did not always work, since whites sometimes fled. For example, Morningside Elementary School had only 1.2 percent blacks in 1972–73. It was paired with C. W. Hill Elementary, which was 100 percent black. Many whites left Morningside between June and September 1973, leaving the school 51 percent black by October 1973. Some whites stayed, though, and a number of schools achieved an integrated status for the first time as its initial black students enrolled. But many schools remained all-black. Furthermore, most Atlanta white and black students did not move out of their mainly white or black schools, since large-scale busing was not implemented. Also, the new administrative positions created in the compromise "increased Atlanta's administrative costs to well over the national average."[70]

With an integrated school staff, an increase in M to M transfers, a school board whose chairman (Benjamin Mays) was black, and, by 1974, a black majority on the board, Atlanta seemed to many of both races to have integrated its school system as much as possible given the white flight that had occurred. By 1972, black students represented 77.1 percent of the school population, and by 1973, 81.5 percent. As Mays lamented, "Atlanta may have had a chance to preserve interracial schools as recently as 10 years ago, . . . but it chose to fight integration."[71]

But the Atlanta School Compromise precipitated a bitter internal dispute within the NAACP. The local chapter thought it had the support of the national headquarters; but after initially indicating his support, Roy Wilkins, the NAACP's executive director, ordered the Atlanta chapter to reject the settlement. The LDF agreed with Wilkins. Both Wilkins and the LDF were under considerable pressure from supporters of integrated schools elsewhere in the United States to reject the compromise plan because it emphasized administrative integration over student integration (many Atlanta schools remained all-black). As LDF lawyer Howard Moore had commented earlier, the compromise represented a trading of "the constitutional rights of Negro pupils for the constitutional rights of Negro administrators." The national NAACP and the LDF affirmed their support for large-scale busing to secure equality in education, and the Atlanta chapter reaffirmed its support of the settlement. As a result, Lonnie King and the other officers and leaders of the group's Atlanta branch were suspended. The national NAACP and the ACLU continued to back a plan for large-scale busing across county lines. (Later this plan also included pairing and magnet schools.) Basically, the local chapter had agreed to a traditional Atlanta negotiated settlement that, in this case, was to address black middle-class needs over that of the general black population. The compromise provided needed and upgraded jobs for blacks within the school system and traded away any further hope of substantial busing to achieve integration for black students in poorer areas, who were still going to substandard schools. And as Wilkins said, "If you can't give black children equal education by tomorrow, then bus them to where the education is." Middle-class black parents had stated their opposition to busing and felt that their neighborhood schools provided a high-quality education.[72]

This compromise involved a number of factors: a sense by some blacks that an end to a demand for massive busing would lessen white flight (Atlanta had "one of the higher levels of white student flight of any city in the United States"); some feeling that black children did not have to go to a largely white school for a good education (this could be achieved in good majority black schools in black neighborhoods in a school system controlled by blacks); concern among the black middle class about the effects of continued school-related racial conflict on the city's economy; a desire by whites and blacks to finally move away from these school issues after years of litigation; a need to secure top school positions before a possible merger with majority white suburban school systems took place; a sense that a black-controlled school administration could produce an excellent educational system for black students; and, as later expressed by Alonzo Crim, the new black superintendent of schools, the thought that the compromise was relatively mild and easy to accomplish, compared to what other cities were still going through. The compromise provided for an increase in black decision-making power in the city, which had long been desired, and less disarray for black neighborhoods and schools, since under the other plan, black children would have faced large-scale busing.[73]

While many black leaders in the city (Andrew Young, Joseph Lowery of the SCLC, and Lonnie King) supported the compromise, it had its detractors as well. The SCLC went on record in support of maximum desegregation and against this minimum desegregation plan. Ralph Abernathy of the SCLC also opposed the settlement. White civil rights activists and those speaking for lower-class blacks rejected it. The *Atlanta Voice* saw the compromise as a beginning but noted that it had its flaws, "many of them having to do with harsh class factionalism in the Black community." The district court approved the plan in April 1973, and in May 1974 it issued a final decree accepting settlement of the initial school suit.[74]

The years of neglect and the race-based policies of segregation before

1961—when, as Lonnie King said, "the bulk of the tax dollar historically followed the white child"—and the minimal desegregation and extensive resegregation in the 1960s created a school system by the 1970s and 1980s that had a multitude of problems related to prior race-based school, hiring, service, and economic policies. Blacks now controlled it, but it was one of the eleven most segregated in the nation and the most segregated among southern cities.[75] Housing patterns, suburban migration, and spatial segregation were surely part of the reason for the failure of desegregation. Some white flight was impossible to stop, of course, but the resegregated school system was also a product of school policies intent on undermining desegregation. This process had not developed and functioned without plan. Earlier in the century, the plan had been to maintain segregation; little had changed by the 1960s. Had the provisions of the 1973 compromise been implemented earlier, coupled with efforts to place new school buildings where they would enhance integration and to increase funding and program development at schools in transitional areas, more whites, such as those in the Cascade Heights neighborhood, would have chosen to stay. White flight may not have been so extensive.

Class emerged as an issue mainly in the 1970s, when blacks began to take over the school system and the interests of middle-class and lower-class blacks diverged, as with the school compromise. It was also a factor as middle-class blacks increased their migration to the suburbs or chose to send their children to private schools, eventually resulting in a system by the 1980s that indicated the problems of both racial and class segregation.[76] Nonetheless, through the decades in all periods of the systems's history—from segregation to desegregation to resegregation—race had remained the *prime* shaping factor in the school system's development. Race was also the main element in explaining the failure to achieve metrowide school system mergers.

PART 4

The Role of Race

The problem of the twentieth century is the problem of the color line.—**W. E. B. Du Bois**, *The Souls of Black Folk*, 1903

CHAPTER 8

The racial issue absorbed everybody's time and thoughts—What

to do about it? How to handle it? Other issues were pushed

aside, or if not, affected in some way by the racial issue.

—Herbert Jenkins, *Presidents, Politics and Policing*, 1980

(on the early 1950s)

On Race and Cities

Race was a prime factor in the shaping of Atlanta's institutional and physical development. It certainly was not the only element involved, and it was not part of *every* decision, but it was a consistent and significant component in many important policy decisions both before and after black political control of the city. Its impact was wide-ranging and touched all aspects of city life—politics, housing, street and highway patterns, neighborhood formation, annexation, employment, basic city services, park and recreational space, health care, mass transit development, and schooling. One way to perceive its influence is to picture Atlanta during the nineteenth and twentieth centuries without its

African American population. The city would be a vastly different place, even in regard to its physical environment.

Therefore, Atlanta is very much the product of a past that emphasized racial issues. Policy decisions made decades ago to divide the races and maintain African Americans' status as second-class citizens had long-range and often debilitating effects on the city, although these effects were not always obvious at the time of implementation. In some cases, when blacks could command some response through bond votes (as in the 1920s), or later, when black votes were important in mayoral contests (as in the late 1940s to 1960s), white city officials would redress some black grievances. And black mayors would turn to some of these grievances as well. Race-based polices ultimately could affect the black community either positively or negatively, though the possibility of positive effects is a relatively recent development. But either way, racial considerations were significant. Class was also an element in the city's shaping, as is evident in some differences in services to poor and rich white neighborhoods. Yet since *all* black areas were neglected, it is clear that race remained a strong shaping factor into the period of black political ascendancy.

After the election of black mayors, the corrective measures that were taken—for example, changes in police hiring—still indicated the role of race in shaping the city. However, the class splits within the black community became sharper and illustrated more clearly the part class factors play in urban development. Particularly in regard to housing, employment, and schools, the black leadership responded with policies that aided the middle class and reflected that group's concerns and needs. An illustration of class factors at work is the case of Willis Mill Road. Split and closed in the 1950s as a racial barrier, the road remained closed in the late 1980s even after city officials had discussed reconnecting it. Middle- and upper-class blacks opposed its opening because they were concerned that poorer black Atlantans would then move into and travel through their neighborhood, even though, according to the *Atlanta Constitution*, such a change "would improve police and fire response times in that area." Earlier, *any* black was barred; now, as blacks inhabited the upscale area, the black poor are excluded.[1] A more recent example is the treatment of low-income black neighborhoods during the planning and construction of the Georgia Dome and 1996 Olympic sites. In the 1960s, as a stadium and civic center were built and blacks were displaced, race was a prime factor and fit into a long history of racial residential control and the maintenance of segregation. Class issues were also evident but were of less significance. In the late 1980s and early 1990s, low-income black neighborhoods again became the focus of development and displacement when the Georgia Dome and Olympic structures were planned and built. Although in some cases more was done to involve the residents in the planning and relocation process, residents retained much of the suspicion of city officials' intentions that had developed in earlier years, and for good reasons. Now that a black administration was in office, efforts toward racial segregation had ended, but black class divisions were evident, and the affected areas did not get all that was promised to them in terms of housing, improved city services, and revitalization.[2] The Olympic site development became part of a larger story in which some segments of the black community benefited more than others from black empowerment—a continuation of earlier intra-group white policy in which middle-class white areas were favored.

The black response to a city being shaped by segregation was to form their own self-help organizations, develop businesses and colleges to serve the African American community, negotiate for land and housing, fight for political inclusion, and, most important, to continually point out to white Atlantans what should have been obvious: measures that diminished black life in the city also had negative effects on whites. Black Atlanta's community development, resistance to or bypassing of white policies, and implementation of their own policies after 1973 were some of the shaping aspects of race that one could see in Atlanta.

Now, at the end of the twentieth century, even a cursory walk around Atlanta reveals the legacy of race relations for the urban environment. One can still readily see the impact of earlier racial policies in such aspects of Atlanta life as public housing placement, southside business development, traffic flows, some changing street names, school segregation, and slum development. A brief look at a few copies of the local newspapers would further reveal the racial legacy in politics, city service hiring and promotion, annexation plans, and the Minority Business Enterprise program.

Very often what seemed to many in Atlanta to be innocuous city policies in reality had some racial motivation. Shifting a highway site, tearing down a slum, even repairing a street could be part of a long-standing racial pattern to cut off black migration to an area, move blacks away from the downtown business district, or deprive black neighborhoods of services in order to spend more city dollars on whites. Many of Atlanta's problems by the 1970s and 1980s were related to these earlier policy decisions.

But was Atlanta's experience unique, or can race be used as an interpretive tool to understand the development of other cities? Do the aspects of city life determined by a community's handling of minority issues provide a model that can be used in analyzing the development of many American cities? While there has not been a great deal of study on the long-term and comprehensive impact of racial attitudes on public policy and their effect on city life, there are enough examples to suggest that both northern and southern cities experienced the shaping elements of racial factors.

In his study of post–World War II Chicago housing and ghettoization, Arnold Hirsch writes, "The most distinguishing feature of post–World War II ghetto expansion is that it was carried out with government sanction and support. . . . Government urban redevelopment and renewal policies, as well as a massive public housing program, had a direct and enormous impact on the evolution of the ghetto." He further reveals that "government powers under the guise of 'urban planning' [were used] in order to reshape the local environment and control the process of [racial] succession." Although he views the postwar housing developments as "basically economic in motivation," he details the manipulation of black residential mobility and the transition process through various government policies. Race was a consideration in all that was done.[3] In Atlanta, an officially segregated city, this process was more clearly race-based, although economic motivations were evident as well.

Through its Housing Authority, the city of Newark, New Jersey, put blacks displaced by renewal into a neighborhood that was already experiencing racial transition in order to hasten racial succession in that community and thereby provide more housing for blacks.[4] City officials apparently had determined that the area would be for black housing. This maneuver recalls Atlanta's efforts to determine which sections of the city could be used for black expansion.

One Philadelphia neighborhood underwent selective clearance that "removed every house occupied by a black household" in certain blocks; in "Baltimore county, Maryland some suburban black enclaves were zoned for nonresidential use even though adjacent white areas were zoned residential"; in Richmond, "the city's white power structure believed that planning afforded a necessary vehicle to ensure race separation and black political impotence"; in 1920, Milwaukee passed an ordinance that "zoned the entire southern half of Milwaukee's black district for commercial and light manufacturing," thereby preventing any further construction for residential purposes for two decades.[5]

Miami is another city that has used government policy to regulate black mobility. By the 1930s, the city had already indicated which areas were to be open to new black housing. County racial zoning was used up to 1946, when the Florida Supreme Court ruled against it. In Miami as in Atlanta, during the early 1950s black housing was removed, buffers were created, and zoning was manipulated to serve racial and other purposes. Public housing for blacks was carefully placed so as not to disrupt any stable white neighborhoods.[6] Segregation was strengthened not by chance but by plan.

Highways could also serve racial purposes in terms of barriers, buffers to protect white neighborhoods, and excuses to destroy black sections of a city. In Miami, the main interstate road tore through the black ghetto, displacing many of its residents in the hope (not always fulfilled) of pushing them primarily in already-designated directions. In a number of cities besides Atlanta, highways appear to have been used as racial walls. Interstates in Gary, Indiana, served as barriers between the blacks in the northern part of the city and the whites to the south. In Memphis, Tennessee, "the interstates have . . . served as boundaries to the black community" on the north side. The downtown expressway in Richmond, Virginia, planned and constructed in the 1960s, "would form a barrier" between neighborhoods becoming black and "established middle-class white neighborhoods." In Kansas City, Missouri, "three radial elements of the Interstate Highway System entering the city from the east, north, and west followed curiously winding routes, each of which eliminated a black neighborhood enclave" and pushed blacks into the main ghetto.[7] Whether all these highways were developed, as in Atlanta, with racial uses in mind requires further research on these cities, and I will leave that research to others. However, so far the evidence strongly suggests that the use of highways and roads, in addition to other policies, to separate the races is extensive throughout the United States.

City planning professor Yale Rabin, who studied more than fifty U.S. cities, towns, and counties in the period from the 1960s to the 1980s, concluded that the use of racial barriers such as highways, the displacement of blacks, the manipulation of public housing site selection, and other similar tactics have been widespread and have played a significant role in neighborhood transition and segregation patterns. He asserts, "Segregation in the 1980s is the legacy of many decades of government complicity in the process of racial isolation."[8] It is small wonder that African Americans are still the most segregated minority in the United States.

Racial policies also influenced the development of public schools throughout the nation. From Chicago to Boston to Richmond to Atlanta, and elsewhere, black children sat in schools with inferior facilities. Often these were officially segregated schools, and race-based public policies had created these situations. School segregation could also be a product of residential patterns, but these too bore the mark of public and private racial policies to control black migration in the city. While there were some variations in the desegregation process, since some cities began to desegregate earlier than Atlanta (Baltimore in 1954, Louisville in 1956), the northern and southern resistance to school integration, the manipulation of freedom-of-choice plans to limit desegregation, and the process of white flight and resegregation reveal that race played a vital role as well.[9]

There are also studies that note the purposeful neglect of black neighborhoods;[10] the inadequate mass transit, recreational facilities, and police protection; city governments' involvement in the segregation of housing; health care systems in which racism was rampant; private and public employment opportunities that were limited because of racial factors; and significant racial aspects of a city's political life. Cities as diverse in size and location as Norfolk, Richmond, Houston, Milwaukee, New York, Nashville, Detroit, Cleveland, and Daytona Beach indicated all or some of these race-based policies. Generally, Atlanta's experience resonated in a number of cities and perhaps is summed up best in historian William Chafe's comment on Greensboro, North Carolina: "The focus was upon stability, with change in race relations occurring only when concessions offered a means of restoring peace and retaining an effective image in the world."[11]

Long-term racial policies helped create the cities of today. Because of the major changes in the economy and the lack of a sustained federal commitment to solving urban problems, there is greater difficulty at the end of the twentieth century than earlier in redressing urban grievances. Black political empowerment and the election of black mayors—which, for example, previous black leaders in Atlanta thought would solve the black community's problems—is limited by a number of factors, including, for example, the legacy of racist policies, class divisions within the black community, and the continued white economic control of the city, which in Atlanta necessitated a good working relationship with a business community that rarely considered low-income black needs. While improvements were made in black neighborhoods and for the black community after the civil rights movement and after blacks gained political control, the progress was not as much as had been expected, it did not benefit all classes, and, for low-income neighborhoods, it was not sustained. Many aspects of city life were better for Atlanta's blacks by the 1980s; many were not. But all bore the imprint of the decades-old intersection of racial attitudes and policy.

Notes

Abbreviations

ABP	Atlanta Bureau of Planning Papers
AHS	Atlanta Historical Society
AUC	Atlanta University Center, Robert W. Woodruff Library
APSA	Atlanta Public School Archives
CIC	Commission on Interracial Cooperation Papers
CRC	Community Relations Commission Papers
CU	Columbia University, Butler Library, Rare Book and Manuscript Library
EUSC	Emory University, Special Collections Department, Robert W. Woodruff Library
GCHR	Georgia Council on Human Relations Papers
LC	Library of Congress
MLKC	Martin Luther King, Jr. Center for Non-Violent Social Change
MSRC	Moorland-Spingarn Research Center, Howard University
NA	National Archives
NAACP	National Association for the Advancement of Colored People Papers
NU	Neighborhood Union Papers
NUL	National Urban League Papers
SCLC	Southern Christian Leadership Conference Papers
SNCC	Student Non-Violent Coordinating Committee Papers
SRC	Southern Regional Council Papers

Chapter One

1. Atlanta Urban League statement, ca. 1948, Walden Papers, AHS.

2. Rabinowitz, *Race Relations in the Urban South*, 263; Watts, *Social Basis of City Politics*, 14, 21; Watts, "Black Political Progress in Atlanta," 272–73; Russell, *Atlanta 1847–1890*, 177–78, 181.

3. Watts, *Social Basis of City Politics*, 24, 163; Watts, "Black Political Progress in Atlanta," 271, 273; Rabinowitz, *Race Relations in the Urban South*, 265, 268–69, 311; Russell, *Atlanta 1847–1890*, 177–81, 213–14; Drago, *Black Politicians and Reconstruction in Georgia*, 81; Turner-Jones, "Political Analysis of Black Educational History," 90.

4. Rabinowitz, *Race Relations in the Urban South*, 279–83, 302, 306–9; Watts, *Social Basis of City Politics*, 53; Watts, "Black Political Progress in Atlanta," 268–69.

5. Rabinowitz, *Race Relations in the Urban South*, 294, 298, 302–3; Russell, *Atlanta 1847–1890*, 207.

6. Quoted in Rabinowitz, *Race Relations in the Urban South*, 294.

7. Ibid., 299–300, 315–17; Russell, *Atlanta 1847–1890*, 208, 210–14; Drago, *Black Politicians and Reconstruction in Georgia*, 157; Watts, *Social Basis of City Politics*, 27–29, 164; John Hammond Moore, "Negro and Prohibition in Atlanta," 56.

8. Watts, *Social Basis of City Politics*, 20–21, 23; Rabinowitz, *Race Relations in the Urban South*, 312–14, 318–19, 323–24; Russell, *Atlanta 1847–1890*, 214.

9. Russell, *Atlanta 1847–1890*, 206; Watts, *Social Basis of City Politics*, 163; Rabinowitz, *Race Relations in the Urban South*, 134.

10. Du Bois, "Some Efforts of American Negroes," 52–53; Rabinowitz, *Race Relations in the Urban South*, 140, 144, 211; Russell, *Atlanta 1847–1890*, 230; Thornberry, "Development of Black Atlanta," 166–68; Rouse, *Lugenia Burns Hope*, 64.

11. On early black neighborhoods and segregation patterns, see "Historical Trends in Negro Population Areas," ABP, AHS; Thornberry, "Development of Black Atlanta," 1, 8–9, 12–16, 20–22, 25, 30–31, 33, 37, 42–43; Porter, "Black Atlanta," 89, 92–93, 104–14; Kellogg, "Negro Urban Clusters in the Postbellum South," 315–17; Dana White, "Black Sides of Atlanta," 208–13; Russell, "Politics, Municipal Services, and the Working Class in Atlanta," 469, 475, 477–78; Rabinowitz, *Race Relations in the Urban South*, 100–103, 105–6, 108, 112–15, 124.

12. Doyle, *New Men, New Cities, New South*, 264–69; Rabinowitz, *Race Relations in the Urban South*, 63–66, 68, 81, 85–88, 90–91, 93; Russell, *Atlanta 1847–1890*, 156–58 (quote on p. 156); Hopkins, "Occupational and Geographic Mobility in Atlanta," 204–5. On black occupational mobility from 1870 to 1896, see Hopkins, "Occupational and Geographic Mobility in Atlanta," 205–7; Du Bois, "Negro in Business," 68, 71.

13. Rabinowitz, *Race Relations in the Urban South*, 67–68; Wingo, "Race Relations in Georgia," 236–37; Dittmer, *Black Georgia in the Progressive Era*, 30–33; Maclachlan, "Women's Work," 77–78, 81–82, 83, 86.

14. Rabinowitz, *Race Relations in the Urban South*, 118–20, 122–24, 134–38, 336–39, 366 (n. 76); Russell, *Atlanta 1847–1890*, 179–80, 187, 191–93, 217, 222–23, 225, 228; Du Bois, "Mortality among Negroes in Cities," 23–25; Galishoff, "Triumph and Failure," 41; Watts, "Police in Atlanta, 1890–1905," 172–73.

15. Du Bois, "Mortality among Negroes in Cities," 23; Du Bois, "Social and Physical Condition of Negroes in Cities," 11–12, 15; Rabinowitz, *Race Relations in the Urban South*, 127, 137–38, 146–49; Hopkins, "Public Health in Atlanta," 296, 300–301; and Doyle, *New Men, New Cities, New South*, 279–81, 283. Doyle argues that to some extent segregation emerged "as a means of protecting the white race from contamination" from the higher disease rates of blacks.

16. Rabinowitz, *Race Relations in the Urban South*, 127, 196.

17. Ibid., 153, 162, 164–67, 170, 175–76, 181; Russell, *Atlanta 1847–1890*, 180, 194–95, 228, 230; Doyle, *New Men, New Cities, New South*, 271–73, 278; Racine, "Atlanta's Schools," 4–5, 9–11, 33–34, 36; Wright, "Development of Public Schools for Blacks in Atlanta," 117–21, 126; Collins, "Origin of Public Secondary Education," 18; Crimmins, "Crystal Stair," 85, 121, 211, 216–17.

18. Rabinowitz, *Race Relations in the Urban South*, 169–72; Russell, *Atlanta 1847–1890*, 195, 228, 230; Doyle, *New Men, New Cities, New South*, 277–78; Peterson, *Politics of School Reform*, 29, 124.

19. Wright, "Development of Public Schools for Blacks in Atlanta," 127; Racine, "Atlanta's Schools," 39–40, 115–16; Peterson, *Politics of School Reform*, 98–100; Turner-Jones, "Political Analysis of Black Educational History," 55–58.

20. On the 1906 riot and related events, see Dittmer, *Black Georgia in the Progressive*

Era, 100–101, 124–30; Mixon, "Atlanta Riot of 1906," 485–86, 522–24, 526, 528–34, 543, 548–49, 575, 587, 591, 624–26, 642, 751, 754; Kuhn, "Atlanta Papers Kindle Racist Violence," 8–10; Crowe, "Racial Violence and Social Reform," 234–56; Godshalk, "In the Wake of Riot"; Deaton, "Atlanta during the Progressive Era," 186–202; Matthews, "Studies in Race Relations in Georgia," 169, 171, 354–56; *Atlanta Constitution*, 22, 30 November 1906; *Atlanta Journal*, 25 September 1906.

Chapter Two

1. Dittmer, *Black Georgia in the Progressive Era*, 94–96, 101–3, 110–11; Grantham, *Southern Progressivism*, 52–53, 120, 123–26, 231; McCraw, "Progressive Legacy," 194; Crowe, "Racial Violence and Social Reform," 245.

2. Matthews, "Studies in Race Relations in Georgia," 115–16, 118, 122–24; Epps, "Participation of the Negro," 38–40, 43–45.

3. Dittmer, *Black Georgia in the Progressive Era*, 20–22, 112–14; Grantham, *Southern Progressivism*, 124–26, 231; Rabinowitz, *Race Relations in the Urban South*, 315–16.

4. Bolden, "Political Structure of Charter Revision Movements," 92, 94, 140. See also Chapter 6, below.

5. L. C. Crogman to J. R. Shillady, 18 April 1919, 1-G, Box 43, branch files, NAACP, LC; Bolden, "Political Structure of Charter Revision Movements," 90–91.

6. *Atlanta Journal*, 31 May 1920; *Atlanta Daily World*, 13, 14, 15, 16, 18 March 1932; "Neighborhood Union Works to Prevent the Attempted Recall of Mayor Key," 1932, Box 3, 14-B-32, NU, AUC; Kuhn, Joye, and West, *Living Atlanta*, 322, 325–26; Sudheendran, "Community Power Structure in Atlanta," 114, 118, 121–22, 339, 341–42. In *New Deal in the Urban South*, on p. 255, Douglas Smith notes that out of 6,000 registered black voters, only about 1,000 voted in 1932. According to the *Atlanta Daily World* right before the recall vote, the correct statement is that prior to the registration drive there were 6,000 eligible blacks but only 1,000 were registered. The registration figures increased by 2,500 during the drive.

7. *Atlanta Daily World*, 21 March 1932; statement by Committee on Women's Work of Commission on Interracial Cooperation, 18 April 1934, CIC records, Box 27, Papers of John and Lugenia Burns Hope, AUC.

8. Smith, *New Deal in the Urban South*, 254; interview with Clarence Bacote, Living Atlanta Collection, AHS; statement on establishment of a citizenship school, January 1933, 1-G, Box 44, branch files, NAACP, LC; King, *Daddy King*, 99–101; Bunche, *Political Status of the Negro*, 300, 487–91; Turner-Jones, "Political Analysis of Black Educational History," 139. See also Chapter 6, below.

9. Interview with Bacote, Living Atlanta Collection, AHS; author's interview with Calhoun (a founder of the Atlanta Negro Voters League, president of the NAACP's Atlanta branch from 1956 to 1957, and a city councilman from 1974 to 1978); *Atlanta Daily World*, 2 January 1944; see also 21, 23 March 1932.

10. Interview with Bacote and Calhoun, Living Atlanta Collection, AHS; author's interview with Calhoun; Kuhn, Joye, and West, *Living Atlanta*, 341, 368, 371; Goldfield, *Black, White and Southern*, 32–33.

11. Interview with Herbert Jenkins, Living Atlanta Collection, AHS.

12. Interview with Bacote, Living Atlanta Collection, AHS; Citizens Democratic

Club of Fulton County (C. A. Scott, president) to J. Lon Duckworth, chairman and members of the Georgia Democratic Executive Committee, 21 June 1944, 2-B, Box 211, Legal File, NAACP, LC.

13. Interview with Bacote, Living Atlanta Collection, AHS; author's interview with Hamilton (Hamilton was executive director of the Atlanta Urban League from 1943 to 1960 and the first black woman elected to the state legislature, serving in the Georgia House from 1966 to 1984); Spritzer, *Belle of Ashby Street*, 71–74.

14. Interview with Bacote, Living Atlanta Collection, AHS; *Atlanta Constitution*, 5 April 1946.

15. Interview with Bacote, Living Atlanta Collection, AHS; Clarence Bacote, "The Negro Voter in Georgia Politics, Today," 1957, SRC, AUC; Frick, "Influences on Negro Political Participation," 47; *Atlanta Constitution*, 5 May 1946; letter to pastors from All Citizens Registration Committee, 21 March 1946, Jacob Henderson Voter Registration Collection, Atlanta-Fulton Public Library; *Atlanta Daily World*, 2 May 1946. See also "Portrait of a Voter Registration Campaign in Atlanta, Georgia, March 6–May 4, 1946," Box 35, Martin Luther King Jr. Papers, MLKC; letter of All Citizens Registration Committee, Box 5, Long-Rucker-Aiken Family Papers, AHS.

16. Author's interview with Cochrane (executive director of the Butler Street YMCA in the 1940s and 1950s and executive director of the Atlanta Negro Voters League); interview with Bacote, Living Atlanta Collection, AHS; Walker, "Protest and Negotiation," 45.

17. Author's interview with Cochrane; author's interview with Johnson (Johnson was youth director of the Atlanta Negro Voters League and served in the state senate in the 1960s); interview with Bacote, Living Atlanta Collection, AHS.

18. The "Charlie Brown for Mayor Organization" flyer (addressed to "Dear Fellow Voter"), August 1949, Box 9, Hartsfield Papers, EUSC.

19. Letter to "Negro Voters of the City of Atlanta," 29 August 1949, Box 9, Hartsfield Papers, EUSC.

20. *Atlanta Journal-Constitution*, 14 August 1977; Martin, *William Berry Hartsfield*, 51; a comparison of Hartsfield and Brown records, 1949, Box 10, Hartsfield Papers, EUSC.

21. *Atlanta Daily World*, 8 September 1949; Atlanta Negro Voters League to Hartsfield, 20 August 1949, Box 9, Hartsfield Papers; Atlanta Negro Voters League letter to voters, 2 September 1949; Hartsfield speech, 25 July 1949, and campaign flyers, 1949; Hartsfield to Miss Wylene Askew, 21 September 1949; Hartsfield letter to Negro Voters, 7 September 1949; James A. Young of Charles A. Rawson Associates (Hartsfield's public relations firm during the campaign) to Hartsfield, 10 September 1949, all in Box 10, Hartsfield Papers, EUSC.

22. A. T. Walden, Atlanta Negro Voters League, to Hartsfield, 13 August 1949, Box 9, Hartsfield Papers, EUSC.

23. *Atlanta Daily World*, 8, 9 September 1949; Stone, *Regime Politics*, 30. On the annexation of affluent white areas, see Chapter 3, below.

24. Floyd Hunter, *Community Power Structure*, quote on p. 138; see also pp. 127–29, on black-white contacts; author's interview with Cochrane; interview with Bacote, Living Atlanta Collection, AHS; author's interview with Young.

25. Henderson and Roberts, *Georgia Governors in an Age of Change*, 36–38, 105,

110, 146, 148, 197, 199; Harold Paulk Henderson, *Politics of Change in Georgia*, 49, 102–3, 137–51; *Atlanta Daily World*, 1, 27 January 1944. See also *Atlanta Journal*, 10 August 1942; *Atlanta Constitution*, 2 June 1946, 21 September 1950; "A Declaration of Principle," an appeal to voters of Georgia, Bacote Papers, AUC; Georgia Negro Voters League, Special Call Meeting, 5 August 1954, Bacote Papers, AUC; 1958 Annual Report, NAACP, Southeast Region, SRC, AUC.

26. *Atlanta Daily World*, 7 May 1953; Martin, *William Berry Hartsfield*, 100–101.

27. *Atlanta Constitution*, 26 February 1952; Martin, *William Berry Hartsfield*, 94–95; Brown, *Charlie Brown Remembers Atlanta*, 240–42; 1953 campaign, list of people coming in to see the mayor and what they wanted, "April 30—Mrs. Henry Eskew," Box 12, Hartsfield Papers, EUSC. See also "Ideas on the Mayoralty Campaign," 1953, Box 12, Hartsfield Papers, EUSC; *Atlanta Constitution*, 28 April 1953; *Metropolitan Herald*, 12 March 1953; Hartsfield letter to friends, 20 March 1953, Walden Papers, Atlanta Negro Voters League Box, AHS.

28. Walker, "Negro Voting in Atlanta," 382–83; *Atlanta Journal*, 14 May 1953.

29. *Courier-Journal*, 19 July 1960.

30. Stone, *Regime Politics*, 30–31; *Atlanta Journal*, 14 May 1953; *Atlanta Daily World*, 15 March, 7, 11 April, 12, 13, 14 May 1953; Legal Petition, 24 March 1953, City Executive Committee correspondence, City of Atlanta records, 24-I-2, AHS.

31. Bacote, "Negro Voter"; *Brunswick News*, 4 May 1957; *Atlanta Journal and Constitution*, 5 May 1957; "Report of the Metropolitan Voting Council on the Election Year of 1957," Box 14, Hartsfield Papers, EUSC; Martin, *William Berry Hartsfield*, 123; *Atlanta Journal*, 16 September 1957; *Tampa Sunday Tribune*, 8 December 1957.

32. Campaign Meeting Notes, 1 July 1957, Box 14, Hartsfield Papers, EUSC; *Atlanta Journal*, 23 September 1957; *Atlanta Citizen's Weekly*, 3 October 1957; Martin, *William Berry Hartsfield*, 128–29.

33. *Atlanta Journal*, 5 December 1957; *Atlanta Constitution*, 5 December 1957; Bacote, "Negro Voter"; *Tampa Sunday Tribune*, 8 December 1957; *City Builder* 22 (June 1957). See also Jennings and Zeigler, "Class, Party, and Race," 398–99.

34. *Atlanta Constitution*, 5 December 1957; Martin, *William Berry Hartsfield*, 142.

35. Bacote, "Negro Voter"; *Reporter*, July 1957. See also *Atlanta Daily World*, 21 May 1957. For Alexander's account of his campaign, see his book *Beyond the Timberline*, 173–96.

36. Hartsfield to W. G. Hastings, 14 December 1961, Box 6, Hartsfield Papers, EUSC; *Atlanta Journal-Constitution*, 11 October 1959; interview with Eliza Paschall, Living Atlanta Collection, AHS; Martin, *William Berry Hartsfield*, 68.

37. "A Second Look: The Negro Citizen in Atlanta," The Atlanta Committee for Cooperative Action, January 1960, SRC, AUC. See also Whitney Young to Norris Herndon, president of Atlanta Life Insurance Company, 6 December 1959, Box 32, Young Papers, CU; Fort, "Atlanta Sit-In Movement," 133; and Walker, "Sit-Ins in Atlanta," 65.

38. *Atlanta Daily World*, 9 March 1960; Walker, "Sit-Ins in Atlanta," 64–66; Fort, "Atlanta Sit-In Movement," 132–33, 157–58.

39. Fort, "Atlanta Sit-In Movement," 129–30; interview with Lonnie King, 1 March 1970, by Willie Harriford, MLK Oral History Collection, MLKC; *Atlanta Constitution*, 10 March 1960.

40. Walker, "Sit-Ins in Atlanta," 67–74.

41. Ibid., 68, 70–71, 75–77; Fort, "Atlanta Sit-In Movement," 135, 139; interview with Julian Bond, 1986, by Jed Dannenbaum, The Center for Contemporary Media; Raines, *My Soul Is Rested*, 87–88.

42. Walker, "Sit-Ins in Atlanta," 68, 78; Fort, "Atlanta Sit-In Movement," 139.

43. Walker, "Sit-Ins in Atlanta," 78–87; "The Atlanta Lunch Counter Desegregation Agreement of 6 March 1961," Box 51, SNCC, MLKC.

44. Walker, "Sit-Ins in Atlanta," 75–76, 87–90; author's interview with Bond; interview with Lonnie King, 29 August 1967, interview with Ivan Allen, 23 January 1968, and interview with Benjamin Brown, 16 August 1967, all by John Britton, in Civil Rights Documentation Project, MSRC.

45. Sheet with appointment times for mayoral candidates and questions to ask, and statement on mayor's race, 1961, in political file, Bacote Papers, AUC; J. H. Calhoun, chairman of Organization Committee to Atlanta Negro Voters League, August 1961, "Report on the Summary of Interviews on Candidates for September 13, 1961 Primary," Walden Papers, AHS; *Atlanta Inquirer*, 29 December 1962; Hornsby, "Negro in Atlanta Politics," 10.

46. Dennis L. Dreseng, "The Political Power Resources of Negroes in Atlanta," 1966, p. 6, unpublished paper in Williams Collection, Atlanta NAACP Box, AUC; Hornsby, "Negro in Atlanta Politics," 10–11; author's interview with Allen; *Atlanta Daily World*, 17 August 1961. See also *Atlanta Daily World*, 9 September 1961; *The Courier*, 7 October 1961.

47. Author's interview with Allen; Calhoun, "Report on the Summary of Interviews"; Mays, "My View"; *Atlanta Daily World*, 17 August 1961.

48. *Atlanta Inquirer*, 30 September 1961; Walker, "Negro Voting in Atlanta," 384; Mays, *Born to Rebel*, 285. Mays mistakenly identifies the votes as those of the 1965 election, but his vote totals are for 1961. Maddox went on to become governor in 1966.

49. Allen, *Mayor*, 53–54; "Preliminary Statistical Study of Little Rock and New Orleans Business Response Subsequent to the School Difficulties," August 1961, prepared for Ivan Allen Jr., Box 10, McGill Papers, EUSC; *Atlanta Inquirer*, 17 June 1961.

50. *Atlanta Daily World*, 6 March 1962; *Atlanta Journal*, 9 March 1962; statement on mayor's race, 1961, Bacote Papers, AUC; statement by Ivan Allen Jr. before Committee on Commerce regarding S. 1732—Bill to Eliminate Discrimination in Public Accommodations Affecting Interstate Commerce, 26 July 1963, SRC, AUC; Allen, *Mayor*, 81; author's interview with Allen. Appointments of blacks were made not only by Allen but also by the Fulton County Commission and Fulton County legislators.

51. Allen, *Mayor*, 87; Hornsby, "Negro in Atlanta Politics," 12; *Atlanta Constitution*, 6 March 1987. On Allen and neighborhoods, see Chapter 3, below.

52. *Atlanta Daily World*, 26 January 1950, 28 March 1964; Lesler, "Leroy Johnson Outslicks Mister Charlie," 36; Mullis, "Public Career of Grace Towns Hamilton," 222–24, 226–27, 235.

53. Mullis, "Public Career of Grace Towns Hamilton," 223–24; interview with Bacote, Living Atlanta Collection, AHS.

54. *Atlanta Journal*, 10 May 1962; John H. Calhoun, "A Quarter Century of Political Action in Georgia," *Atlanta Daily World*, 6 March 1963; *Atlanta Constitution*, 6 June 1963.

55. Report on voter registration meeting, 15 July 1963, by Rev. Fred C. Bennette, field director, All Citizens Registration Committee, and flyer, both in SRC, AUC.

56. Gwendolyn Isler to Mayor Allen, 14 March 1963, Box 95, SNCC, MLKC; Hornsby, "Negro in Atlanta Politics," 16. See also *Atlanta Inquirer*, 10 March 1962.

57. "Action for Democracy," 1 November 1963, Box 139, SCLC, MLKC; author's interview with Coleman (director of community services for the Atlanta Urban League in 1959 and director of the southern regional office of the National Urban League from 1962 to 1972).

58. "Action for Democracy"; Atlanta Summit Leadership Conference, "The Strategy Committee's Suggested Plan to Totally Desegregate the City of Atlanta," Box 10, SNCC, MLKC; news release titled "Atlanta 'Open City' Drive Continues," 16 January 1964, and James Forman, executive secretary of SNCC, undated letter, both in Box 49, SNCC, MLKC; Council on Human Relations of Greater Atlanta, tentative draft report, 27 March 1964, SRC, AUC; Council on Human Relations of Greater Atlanta, 18 December 1963, GCHR, AUC; memorandum, 6 January 1964, Box 10, SNCC, MLKC; Hornsby, "Negro in Atlanta Politics," 16–17.

59. Council on Human Relations of Greater Atlanta, tentative draft report; Bond, *A Time to Speak*, 76–77.

60. Muggsy Smith letter to editor, *Northside News*, 10 September 1965, Box 46, McGill Papers, EUSC; Hornsby, "Negro in Atlanta Politics," 19–20.

61. *Atlanta Constitution*, 17 March 1969. See also Chapters 3 and 4.

62. Allen, *Mayor*, 220–25; Hornsby, "Negro in Atlanta Politics," 22–25; Stone, *Regime Politics*, 78–79; author's interview with Tate; author's interview with Allen; author's interview with Johnson; *Atlanta Inquirer*, 25 October 1969.

63. Rooks, *Atlanta Elections of 1969*, 4, 6, 9–10, 12, 17, 19, 21, 34; Hornsby, "Negro in Atlanta Politics," 26.

64. Allen, *Mayor*, 222; report to the Executive Committee of the Atlanta Chamber of Commerce from the Atlanta Chamber Long Range Planning Committee, 20 September 1971, Alexander Papers (privately held); Stone, *Regime Politics*, 78.

65. Author's interview with Massell; Jones, "Black Political Empowerment in Atlanta," 100; Hornsby, "Negro in Atlanta Politics," 27–28; Stone, *Regime Politics*, 79.

66. Hornsby, "Negro in Atlanta Politics," 27–29; *Atlanta Constitution*, 17 April 1970, 8 January 1971; Jones, "Black Political Empowerment in Atlanta," 102; Stone, *Regime Politics*, 80.

67. "Citizen Attitudes toward Public Policies and Political Authorities: Their Perspectives on the Atlanta Data," Final Report of the Atlanta Urban Observatory, October 1971, Box 22, Bullard Papers, EUSC.

68. Floyd Hunter, *Community Power Succession*, 151–52, and *Community Power Structure*, 222–23.

69. "Statistical Analysis of Negro Vote in the Fifth Congressional District General Election, November 3, 1970" and "Statistical Analysis of the Black Vote in the Fifth Congressional District General Election, November 7, 1972," in Bacote Papers, AUC; Eisenstat and Barutio, "Andrew Young"; *Atlanta Journal*, 13 October 1971, 25 January 1973.

70. Leroy Johnson also ran in this election but secured only 4 percent of the black vote. See "Statistical Analysis of the Black Vote cast for Mayor in City of Atlanta

election, October 2, 1973," Bacote Papers, AUC; Whelan and McKinney, "Coalition Politics in a Southern City," 131–32.

71. Author's interview with Massell; *Northside News*, 30 September 1973; *Atlanta Daily World*, 27 September 1973; author's interview with Cochrane; *Atlanta Inquirer*, 29 September 1973.

72. "Statistical Analysis of Black Votes cast for Mayor and for President of City Council in City of Atlanta Election of October 2, 1973 and run-off election of October 16, 1973," Bacote Papers, AUC; Whelan and McKinney, "Coalition Politics in a Southern City," 136–37; on at-large versus single-district voting and their impact on blacks, see *Metropolitan Herald*, 25 July 1956, and author's interview with Alexander. For citywide elections other than mayoral elections see Jones, "Black Political Empowerment in Atlanta," 106–7. In most of these elections, blacks voted more strongly for white candidates than whites for black candidates.

73. Author's interview with Jackson, 23 November 1987.

74. Stone, *Regime Politics*, 87–88; author's interview with Jackson, 23 November 1987.

75. Author's interview with Johnson.

76. Author's interview with Sweat. Sweat had also been Ivan Allen's chief administrative officer and, for the first one-and-a-half years of his administration, did the same for Massell. In this capacity he served as the liaison between Massell and vice mayor Maynard Jackson. He also served as the first executive director of the Atlanta Regional Commission before the CAP position. He directed the CAP from 1973 to 1988.

77. *Atlanta Constitution*, 21, 25, 26, 27 September 1974, 7 October 1976; Stone, *Regime Politics*, 89–90; author's interview with Sweat.

78. *Atlanta Constitution*, 26, 27 September 1974; author's interview with Jackson, 4 January 1988. On annexation, see also Chapter 3.

79. *Atlanta Constitution*, 10 October 1974.

80. *Atlanta Journal*, 27 December 1974; *Atlanta Constitution*, 23 March, 18 December 1975; Jones, "Black Political Empowerment in Atlanta," 112.

81. *Atlanta Constitution*, 7 October 1976; Butler, "Racial Conflict and Polarization," 91, 137–38, 141, 209–10, 214, 299, 301–3, 307, 313–14; author's interview with Bond.

82. Author's interview with Sweat; *Atlanta Daily World*, 9 October 1977; Butler, "Racial Conflict and Polarization," 306, 309–15; Holmes, *Status of Black Atlantans* 1993, 5; *Atlanta Constitution*, 26 October 1981.

83. John Wesley Dobbs, speech before Georgia Voters League, 10 March 1956, Box 3, Dobbs Papers, Amistad Research Center, Tulane University.

84. *Atlanta Constitution*, 25 March 1975, 5 April 1977; Jones, "Black Political Empowerment in Atlanta," 114–15.

85. *Atlanta Constitution*, 28 August 1989; Stone, *Regime Politics*, 135–36, 144. For a good discussion on the limitations of southern black mayors and other officials, see Goldfield, *Black, White and Southern*, 191–94, 205, 229, 245–46. For discussion of black mayors' impact and problems and of race and class issues in Newark, Philadelphia, and Baltimore, see Harris, "Paradox of African-American Mayoral Leadership."

Chapter Three

1. On HOLC-FHA and banking policies in Atlanta, see "Security Area Descriptions, Atlanta, Georgia," 22 June 1938, Home Owners' Loan Corporation, Box 82, RG 195, NA; "Report of Survey, Atlanta, Georgia, for the Division of Research and Statistics, Home Owners' Loan Corporation," 25 June 1938, Box 37, RG 195, NA; Flint, "Zoning and Residential Segregation," 392–96; *City*, January–February 1971, pp. 35–37; *Atlanta Constitution*, 2, 5 May, 27 July (quote), 7 December 1988; *Atlanta Journal-Constitution*, 1, 8, 15 May, 17 July, 11 September 1988; 22 January, 25 April 1989; 15 March 1992.

2. For sources on early black neighborhoods see Chapter 1, n. 11.

3. Discussion of the segregation ordinances and racial zoning plans and their impact on the city can be found in Flint, "Zoning and Residential Segregation," 135, 276, 303, 309, 313, 320, 325–26, 334–36, 341–43, 357; Stephenson, "Segregation of the White and Negro Races in Cities," 1–4, 7–10; Dittmer, *Black Georgia in the Progressive Era*, 13–15; Roger L. Rice, "Residential Segregation by Law," 181, 193–94; West, "Black Atlanta," 34–36, appendix; "Atlanta Zoning Plan," 114–15; Dana White, "Black Sides of Atlanta," 216; Brownell, "Commercial-Civic Elite and City Planning," 357, 359, 362, 364; City of Atlanta, General Council Minutes, 20 May 1929, p. 525, 16 March 1931, p. 518, AHS; *Atlanta Journal*, 11 April 1922, 30 November 1939; *Atlanta Daily World*, 17 February 1953.

4. Preston, *Automobile Age Atlanta*, 98, 101.

5. Quoted in Thompson, Lewis, and McEntire, "Atlanta and Birmingham," 19–20.

6. Preston, *Automobile Age Atlanta*, 102–3; Flint, "Zoning and Residential Segregation," 86, 341; *Atlanta Journal*, 21 December 1928.

7. *Atlanta Daily World*, 22 October 1948; statement of Atlanta Urban League presented to Joint Congressional Committee on Housing in Atlanta, 29 October 1947, SRC, AUC.

8. The six expansion areas of the Atlanta Housing Council were not exactly the same as the Planning Commission's areas, but there was some overlap. The Planning Commission used the earlier plan as a guide (author's interview with Thompson, 17 July 1985). Thompson was industrial secretary, housing secretary, associate director, and executive director (as of 1960) of the Atlanta Urban League from 1942 into the 1960s; secretary of the Atlanta Housing Council; and assistant to HUD's regional administrator for equal opportunity in the late 1960s. He was personally involved in all housing and expansion issues in the city throughout this period. See also "Proposed Areas for Expansion of Negro Housing in Atlanta, Georgia," Atlanta Housing Council, May 1947, in author's possession; Nelson C. Jackson, southern field director, to Eugene Kinckle Jones, general secretary, National Urban League, 18 November 1946, part 1, 1-C-73, NUL, LC; *Atlanta Constitution*, 7 April 1949, 12 March 1950; *Atlanta Constitution and Journal*, 30 July 1950; R. A. Thompson to George S. Mitchell, 5 June 1947, SRC, AUC; "A Report of the Housing Activities of the Atlanta Urban League, November 28, 1951," McEwen Papers, Amistad Research Center, Tulane University; *Atlanta Daily World*, 28 October 1947, 8 January 1950, 17, 18, 24 April 1952; Thompson, Lewis, and McEntire, "Atlanta and Birmingham," 22–26.

9. *Atlanta Constitution and Journal*, 30 July 1950; Mohl, "Race and Space in the Modern City," 26–30.

10. Author's interview with Thompson, 17 July 1985; author's interview with Calhoun. In addition to his work toward the founding of the Atlanta Negro Voters League and All Citizens Registration Committee in the 1940s, Calhoun was also a real estate broker and a member of the Empire Real Estate Board, co-chair of the Georgia Voters League, president of the NAACP's Atlanta branch in the late 1950s and 1960s, a city councilman in the 1970s, and a member of the Atlanta Regional Commission.

11. Author's interviews with Thompson, 17 July 1985, 15 August 1986; author's interview with L. D. Milton. Milton was president of the black-owned Citizens Trust Bank in Atlanta from 1930 to 1971 and co-owned the Yates and Milton drugstores in Atlanta; he was also involved in the National Development Company's construction of Crestwood Forest, a black single-family housing development in the Collier Heights area.

12. The head of the WSMDC was Philip Hammer, director of the Metropolitan Planning Commission. The WSMDC developed from a 1949 mayor's biracial committee that had been formed to deal with black entry into the Mozley Park neighborhood. There was also a Northeast Biracial Committee set up in 1954 by the mayor. "Resolution of Board of Aldermen," 4 October 1954, McEwen Papers, Amistad Research Center, Tulane University; O'Connor, "Measurement and Significance of Racial Residential Barriers in Atlanta," 104.

13. In some cases the WSMDC was involved in other parts of the city. Burt Sparer (technical adviser, WSMDC) to property owners and occupants on Walthall Street between Kirkwood and Wylie Streets, 18 October 1957, Walden Papers, AHS.

14. H. W. Lochner and Company and DeLeuw, Cather and Company, *Highway and Transportation Plan for Atlanta, Georgia*, 9, 12; H. Jay Wallace, "The Story Behind the 'Lochner Plan,'" 2 April 1946, ABP.

15. "Report on the Adamsville Transition Area, 26 August 1960," ABP, AHS. See also Harold G. Dennis (president, Adamsville Civic Club) to Roger Lawson (chairman, State Highway Board), 28 February 1957, ABP; Robert C. Stuart (director, Metropolitan Planning Commission) to Robert Wilson, 31 March 1958, ABP; Philip Hammer (director, Metropolitan Planning Commission) to L. W. Verner (state highway location engineer), 4 March 1953, ABP.

16. The evidence that other parts of I-20 West were also planned, at least partly, for racial purposes comes from the following: Leon Eplan, commissioner of the department of budget and planning in the mid-1970s, stated in 1968 that "even the interstate highway system was, as in the case of I-20 West, used to form a racial wall." John H. Calhoun commented that I-20 West was developed as a racial buffer, and L. D. Milton noted that I-20 was supposed to be the racial dividing line but did not hold up. The initial planning of the highway, according to the Lochner Report of 1946, which set the initial route of this expressway, was to be north of Simpson Street to Hightower Road—an area chosen because of traffic flows and depreciated property values (and north of where the road was eventually built). Rather than conforming to the Lochner plan or to a 1952 Metropolitan Planning Commission map, the final plan for I-20 West appeared to run the road along the racial boundary (with blacks to the north and whites to the south) in various parts of the west side. However, by the time the highway was completed in the mid- to late 1960s, it no longer served as a boundary in most

sections because of rapid black migration. Leon Eplan, "Background Paper," 29 May 1968, Metropolitan Atlanta Conference on Equality of Opportunity in Housing, SRC, AUC; author's interview with Calhoun; author's interview with Milton; H. W. Lochner and Company and DeLeuw, Cather and Company, *Highway and Transportation Plan for Atlanta, Georgia*, 9, 12; *Atlanta Journal*, 16 March 1952. See also Crimmins, "West End," 46–47, which discusses both the economic aspects of the highway and the promises made to whites in the 1940s about how the highway would form a racial barrier in the West End area.

17. *Atlanta Journal*, 23 September, 14 October 1952.

18. Charles R. Allen (technical adviser to WSMDC) on behalf of WSMDC to Real Estate and Home Mortgage Brokers, 30 July 1957, Walden Papers, AHS.

19. Robert C. Stuart to E. A. Gilliam (alderman), 6 February 1957, ABP.

20. William B. Hartsfield to Clarke Donaldson, 20 March 1954, and Robert C. Stuart to W. O. Duvall, 19 March 1954, ABP.

21. G. R. Bilderback to D. C. Black Jr., 27 July 1960, and Hartsfield to Bilderback, 29 July 1960, ABP.

22. Author's interview with Thompson, 17 July 1985.

23. Author's interview with Milton; Stephen Mitchell to Robert C. Stuart, 18 February 1954, ABP; Westside Mutual Development Committee and Advisory Panel on Collier Heights, Grove Park, Center Hill, and Bolton to Collier Heights resident, 11 February 1954, 5 March 1954, Walden Papers, AHS; see also Thompson, Lewis, and McEntire, "Atlanta and Birmingham," 34; and S. B. Avery (president, Southwest Citizens Association) to real estate agents [white], 28 January 1954, ABP.

24. Westside Mutual Development Committee and Advisory Panel to Collier Heights resident, 5 March 1954, ABP.

25. Hamilton Douglas Jr., "Housing the Million," report on Atlanta Housing, 10 January 1961, Alexander Papers (privately held).

26. The maps are based on census tract figures. Since the area south of Westview Drive was part of a larger census tract, Map 3 indicates a black presence in that area in 1950 when none existed. However the tract as a whole did have a black population over 15 percent. Author's interview with Thompson, 17 July 1985; Atlanta Department of Budget and Planning, "Community Building," 10; Thompson, Lewis, and McEntire, "Atlanta and Birmingham," 21, 27–32; Adams, "Blueprint for Segregation," 76.

27. Author's interview with Thompson, 15 August 1986. For more recent controversies concerning the road, see Chapter 8.

28. The maps are based on census tracts figures. Since the Peyton Forest subdivision was only part of a larger census tract, Map 3 indicates a black presence in the subdivision section in 1960, when none existed yet. However, the tract as a whole was already indicating an increasing black population. Browning, "Atlanta Wall"; *Atlanta Journal*, 17, 19, 20 December 1962; *Atlanta Daily World*, 14 December 1962; Blumberg, "Segregated Housing, Marginal Location, and the Crisis of Confidence," 323–24; O'Connor, "Measurement and Significance of Racial Residential Barriers in Atlanta," 112. See also *Atlanta Inquirer*, 5 January 1963.

29. SNCC news release, 22 December 1962, Box 49, research department files, SNCC, MLKC; Allen, *Mayor*, 71–72.

30. Allen, *Mayor*, 71–72; author's interview with Ivan Allen.

31. Browning, "Atlanta Wall"; Council on Human Relations of Greater Atlanta, *Report,* 27 March 1967, SRC, AUC; Ivan Allen Jr. to Ralph Moore (chairman of the Committee on Appeal for Human Rights), 23 December 1962, Walden Papers, AHS; *Atlanta Constitution,* 19 December 1962; *Atlanta Journal,* 19 December 1962. See also *Atlanta Daily World,* 14, 18 December 1962.

32. Southern Regional Council, *Proposed Immediate Steps on the Immediate Problem: Housing Discrimination and Low-Cost Housing Shortages,* n.d., SRC, AUC; *Atlanta Daily World,* 23 December 1962.

33. Adams, "Blueprint for Segregation," 77. However, some restrictions on black housing still remained. See Dana White, "Black Sides of Atlanta," 221.

34. Adams, "Blueprint for Segregation," 78.

35. Author's interview with Eplan; Eplan, "Background Paper," 29 May 1968, SRC, AUC.

36. Atlanta Department of Budget and Planning, Bureau of Planning, *1980 City of Atlanta Comprehensive Development Plan,* 1:48, 54.

37. Eplan, "Background Paper," 29 May 1968, SRC, AUC.

38. Adams, "Blueprint for Segregation," 80; *Atlanta Daily World,* 12 August 1960.

39. *Atlanta Journal-Constitution,* 11 October 1959; Thompson, Lewis, and McEntire, "Atlanta and Birmingham," 29, 34; author's interview with Gladin.

40. "Atlanta's Fight against Substandard Housing—Is It Working?," *Research Atlanta Report,* October 1972, pp. 47, 53, 73.

41. The elimination of housing for blacks included destruction of alley and back-lot housing as of 1954. See Stone, *Economic Growth and Neighborhood Discontent,* 47, 62–63, 79, 97–98, 177–78; *Atlanta Journal-Constitution,* 18 May 1958; *The Renewer* (newsletter of the Citizens Committee for Urban Renewal), August 1963; "Toward Equal Opportunity in Housing in Atlanta, Georgia—A Report of the Georgia State Advisory Committee to the United States Commission on Civil Rights," May 1968, p. 7, SRC, AUC; Atlanta branch, NAACP, presentation before Advisory Committee of the United States Civil Rights Commission, 8 April 1967, SRC, AUC. As of 1968, Atlanta still had separate white and black public housing application offices and thereby discouraged integration of public housing. Therefore, the official desegregation of public housing in 1962 had little immediate effect on decreasing housing segregation in public units. Because of pressure from the federal government and black leaders, some integration was evident by the mid-1960s, but generally city housing officials tried to impede housing integration into the late 1960s. See "Action for Democracy," pamphlet with recommendation from City-Wide Leadership Conference, 19 October 1963, Box 139, SCLC, MLKC; "Toward Equal Opportunity," 8, 11, 30, 40; A. R. Hanson to Marie McGuire, 9 August 1966, Box 7, RG 196, NA; Atlanta Summit Leadership Conference, press release, 3 January 1968, Williams Collection, AUC.

42. Hartsfield did appoint a black Advisory Housing Committee in 1950 to work with the Metropolitan Planning Commission, but the MPC ignored it. John H. Calhoun to Ruby Hurley, 2 June 1952, Box 38, 2-C, branch files, 1951–1953, NAACP, LC; remarks of L. D. Reddick at the public hearings, Metropolitan Planning Commission, 26 May 1952, and L. D. Reddick to W. E. B. Du Bois, 6 October 1952, Reel 68 (microfilm), Du Bois Papers, AUC; remarks of John Wesley Dobbs at the public

hearings, Metropolitan Planning Commission, 3 June 1952, Box 3, Dobbs Papers, Amistad Research Center, Tulane University; *Atlanta Daily World*, 24 April 1952; Alexander, *Beyond the Timberline*, 162.

43. Presentation of J. H. Calhoun, representing the NAACP's Atlanta branch, before Metropolitan Planning Commission Hearings, 30 May 1952, Box 38, 2-C, branch files, 1951–1953, NAACP, LC; L. D. Reddick to Du Bois, 6 October 1952, Reel 68, Du Bois Papers; remarks of L. D. Reddick at the public hearings, Metropolitan Planning Commission, 26 May 1952, Reel 68, Du Bois Papers; C. A. Scott statement to Metropolitan Planning Commission on "Up Ahead," Mays Papers, MSRC; "Excerpts from Metropolitan Planning Commission Minutes, 1951–1952," 29 May 1952, Box 1, Mule to Marta Papers, AHS; *Atlanta Daily World*, 19, 24, 25, 26, 29 April 1952.

44. Stone, *Economic Growth and Neighborhood Discontent*, 67–71; Stone, *Regime Politics*, 40–41; Hartsfield quote in *Atlanta Constitution*, 21 February 1960; *Atlanta Daily World*, 15 May 1960, 19 July, 8, 10 August 1961; author's interview with Alexander; Locality Committees Resolution, "The Slum Clearance and Urban Renewal Program of the City of Atlanta and Its Impact on Minority Citizens," March 1958, 3-A, branch files, NAACP, LC. (Alexander was chairman of the Housing Resources Committee from 1966 to 1969, the Citizens Advisory Committee on Urban Renewal in the late 1950s and the 1960s, and the Long-Range Planning Committee of the chamber of commerce in the 1970s.)

45. Malcolm D. Jones to Hartsfield, 6 May 1960, ABP; Thomas M. Parham to Mayor William B. Hartsfield, 11 May 1960, ABP.

46. Turner, "Changing Residential Patterns in Southwest Atlanta," 37–38. In 1961, a one-time exception to the policy of not building public housing on renewal land came after the devastating Egleston rejection, when land had to be found quickly for displaced citizens who were to be put into the Egleston site housing. A project for elderly blacks (Antoine Graves Homes) was built in the Butler Street renewal area near Grady Homes, adjacent to the CBD on the south, and an addition was made to the Perry Homes project in the northwest. This action was taken because of the dire need for housing and the opposition of white neighborhoods to locating any black projects in their areas. But it did raise the question of whether, once the "no project on renewal land" policy was broken, it could happen again. See Stone, *Economic Growth and Neighborhood Discontent*, 75–76; *Atlanta Daily World*, 23 June 1961; *Atlanta Constitution*, 14, 22 June 1961.

47. Floyd Hunter, *Community Power Succession*, 6, 26; author's interview with Calhoun; author's interview with Thompson, 17 July 1985; *Atlanta Daily World*, 4 June 1958; Interview with C. C. Hart and Phoebe Hart, Living Atlanta Collection, AHS; Georgia Institute of Technology College of Architecture, "Sweet Auburn," 6.

48. Author's interview with Eplan; author's interview with Flanagan; Stone, *Economic Growth and Neighborhood Discontent*, 99; Stone, *Regime Politics*, 60–61. Eplan, a city planner and, under Mayor Jackson, the commissioner of budget and planning, did the feasibility study on the stadium. Flanagan was executive secretary of the NAACP's Atlanta branch in 1967–68, field services director from 1968 to 1978, and president of the NAACP Georgia Conference of Branches from 1978 to 1984.

49. A neighborhood protest organization in Bedford-Pine called U-Rescue (Urban Renewal Emergency, Stop, Consider, Understand, Evaluate) emerged in December

1965 to fight renewal and maintain the area's residential character. The leadership of U-Rescue was largely black (although it also included some neighborhood white merchants). Stone, *Economic Growth and Neighborhood Discontent*, 94–101, 106–13, 177–78.

50. Atlanta branch, NAACP, presentation before the Advisory Committee of the U.S. Civil Rights Commission, 8 April 1967, SRC, AUC; final report, City of Atlanta, Georgia, "Equal Opportunity in Housing," Atlanta Community Improvement Program, 1966–67, Box 1, City of Atlanta Reports, AHS. See also *Atlanta Inquirer*, 10 August 1963.

51. Atlanta branch, NAACP, presentation before the Advisory Committee of the U.S. Civil Rights Commission, 8 April 1967, SRC, AUC; Stone, *Economic Growth and Neighborhood Discontent*, 143.

52. Flanagan to John M. Flanigen (chairman, zoning committee), 3 November 1967, Alexander Papers (privately held). More information on this topic can be found in author's interview with Coleman; *Atlanta Daily World*, 25 March 1962.

53. "Toward Equal Opportunity," May 1968, 8; Spector, "Municipal and County Zoning," 7; *Atlanta Constitution*, 8 April 1967.

54. *Atlanta Constitution*, 8 April 1967; "Toward Equal Opportunity in Housing in Atlanta, Georgia—A Report to the Georgia State Advisory Committee to the United States Commission on Civil Rights," First Draft, 13 October 1967, p. 26, SRC, AUC; CRC, "Dilemmas of the City," September 1967, Box 17, Series 4, Paschall Papers, EUSC. See also Taeuber, "Residential Segregation in the Atlanta Metropolitan Area," 158–60.

55. Hirsch, *Making the Second Ghetto*, 265–66, 268; "Toward Equal Opportunity," May 1968, 13.

56. Stone, *Economic Growth and Neighborhood Discontent*, 63–65, 68, 85–87, 142–43; *Atlanta Constitution*, 14 December 1957; Alexander, *Beyond the Timberline*, 205; author's interview with Jones. Jones was the first director of the Department of Urban Renewal in the late 1950s and later became executive director of the Housing Resources Committee and the city's housing coordinator.

57. Housing Resources Committee, Minutes, 31 May 1967, in Alexander Papers (privately held); "Toward Equal Opportunity," May 1968, 48; *Atlanta Constitution*, 13 November 1958, 8 April 1967; *Atlanta Journal-Constitution*, 27 August 1967. The desire for public housing in fringe areas was similar to the wishes of those who supported school integration and wanted schools placed in racial fringe areas. See Chapter 7.

58. *Atlanta Constitution*, 5, 15 August 1967; Stone, *Economic Growth and Neighborhood Discontent*, 144–45; *Atlanta Journal-Constitution*, 27 August 1967.

59. *Weekly Star*, 14 September, 16 November 1967; Housing Resources Committee, Minutes, 2 August 1968, in Alexander Papers; *Atlanta Constitution*, 21 April 1967; Council on Human Relations of Greater Atlanta to members of Board of Atlanta Housing Authority, 20 September 1966, SRC, AUC; Atlanta branch, NAACP, "Citywide Housing Conference," 11 February 1967, CRC, Williams Collection, AUC; Spector, "Municipal and County Zoning," 7.

60. Edward H. Baxter (regional administrator of HUD) to Ivan Allen Jr., 5 May 1967, SRC, AUC; Stone, *Economic Growth and Neighborhood Discontent*, 143–47;

Atlanta Constitution, 1 February 1970; *Atlanta Journal*, 20 November 1963. See Chapter 7 for more on Southwest Atlantans for Progress.

61. *Atlanta Constitution*, 13 December 1968; Spector, "Municipal and County Zoning," 54; Stone, *Economic Growth and Neighborhood Discontent*, 146–48.

62. Resolution of Atlanta Chamber of Commerce, 10 April 1968, in Alexander Papers; Stone, *Economic Growth and Neighborhood Discontent*, 146–50; Housing Resources Committee minutes, 12 December 1968, in Alexander Papers; *Atlanta Constitution*, 1 December 1967.

63. Stone, *Economic Growth and Neighborhood Discontent*, 147; *Atlanta Journal*, 19 April 1972; *Atlanta Constitution*, 20 April 1972; *Atlanta Inquirer*, 29 April 1972.

64. Malcolm D. Jones (Housing Coordinator) to Frank Carter, 16 August 1968, Alexander Papers; Abbott, *New Urban America*, 193–94.

65. Greater Atlanta Council on Human Relations, "Reports," 19 March 1959, SRC, AUC.

66. "Techwood Neighborhood," Report 1: Social Base Map Survey of Atlanta, Georgia, WPA of Georgia, 1939, pp. 7–8, Palmer Papers, EUSC; H. A. Gray (director of housing, PWA) to K. S. McAllister (housing manager, Federal Emergency Administration of Public Works, Housing Division), 19 January 1937; and McAllister to Gray, 22 January 1937, Box 32, folder H-1101–4, Records of the Public Housing Administration, RG 196, NA; Leopold Hass and D. L. Stokes to Col. H. B. Hackett (general manager, Public Works Emergency Housing Corporation), 21 March 1934, Box 23, folder H-1100, Federal Program Project files, RG 196, NA; "Memorandum and Report on Techwood and University Housing Projects, Atlanta, Georgia, January 9, 1934," by N. Max Dunning, assistant director of planning, Box 23, folder H-1100, Federal Program Project files, RG 196, NA.

67. Thompson, Lewis, and McEntire, "Atlanta and Birmingham," 21, 27–32; *West End Eagle*, 8 April 1949; Greater Atlanta Council on Human Relations, "Report," 19 March 1959, SRC, AUC; Francis X. Serviettes (acting commissioner, PHA) to A. R. Hanson (director, Atlanta Regional Office, PHA), 22 October 1965, Box 7, folder labeled "Atlanta Regional Office, Atlanta, 1965," Commissioner of Public Housing Correspondence, RG 196, NA; *Atlanta Daily World*, 18 September 1952.

68. Housing Resources Committee memo, "Report on Vacant Land in Atlanta," 9 August 1967, SRC, AUC.

69. Atlanta branch NAACP, "Citywide Housing Conference," 11 February 1967, Williams Collection, AUC; Atlanta Chamber of Commerce, Board of Directors, 13 September 1967, Hamilton Papers, AUC; Allen, *Mayor*, 71.

70. Malcolm D. Jones to Mayor and Board of Aldermen, "Year End Review of Urban Renewal," 1959, Department of Urban Renewal, Atlanta (mimeo), in Palmer Papers, EUSC.

71. Hamilton Douglas Jr., "Housing the Million," report on Atlanta Housing (prepared for a group of Atlanta business leaders), 10 January 1961, Alexander Papers.

72. Atlanta Bureau of Planning, "The Story of Negro Housing in Atlanta," 1965, ABP; Spector, "Municipal and County Zoning," 5–6; *Atlanta Journal-Constitution*, 18 May 1958; *Atlanta Daily World*, 1 February 1970; See also Ordway, "Study of Select Political and Socio-Economic Factors," 34, 37, 329, 354–55, 360–61.

73. Spector, "Municipal and County Zoning," 5, 54; *Atlanta Constitution*, 8 September 1971.

74. "Back to the City: Housing Options for Central Atlanta," Full Technical Report, Central Area Housing Strategy Study, June 1974 (study director, Richard C. D. Fleming of Central Atlanta Progress; Project Coordinator, Frank Keller of Atlanta Department of Planning); Stone, *Regime Politics*, 71–73, 86, 110–11, 120–22, 143; author's interview with Eplan; *Atlanta Constitution*, 10 February 1987, 29 September 1988, 30 May, 28 August 1989, 3 January 1991. See also Chapter 5.

75. "Housing and Negroes in Atlanta, Georgia," Hearings testimony before U.S. Commission on Civil Rights held in Atlanta, 10 April 1959, SRC report, 24 June 1959; Adams, "Blueprint for Segregation" 74; Hein, "Image of 'A City Too Busy to Hate,'" 219; James W. Harris, "This Is Our Home: It is Not for Sale" (senior's thesis, Princeton University, 1971), p. 35, SRC, AUC; Bullard and Thomas, "Atlanta," 78.

76. Final Report, City of Atlanta, Georgia, "Equal Opportunity in Housing," Appendix I-1, Box 1, City of Atlanta Reports, AHS; "Toward Equal Opportunity," May 1968, 4; "The Growth and Extent of Segregation in Housing in the City of Atlanta," n.d., in Bacote Papers, AUC; *Atlanta Journal-Constitution*, 27 August 1967.

77. "Toward Equal Opportunity," May 1968, 10; C. R. Yates to Fulton County Grand Jury, 15 April 1960, in Young Papers, CU; final report, City of Atlanta, Georgia, "Equal Opportunity in Housing," 19, Box 1, City of Atlanta Reports, AHS; "Public Housing Strategy Report, Special Task Force on Public Housing," 25 March 1975, Mays Papers, MSRC; Council on Human Relations of Greater Atlanta to members of the Board of Atlanta Housing Authority, 20 September 1966, Box 7, folder labeled "Housing Assistance Regional Directors, Atlanta 1966," Commissioner of Public Housing Correspondence, RG 196, NA; "Equal Opportunity in Housing-Community Improvement Program, City of Atlanta, Supplementary Report on Negro Housing Needs and Resources," November 1967, City of Atlanta Reports, AHS.

78. Atlanta Negro Voters League statement, 10 December 1959, Walden Papers, AHS.

79. *Atlanta Constitution*, 19 October 1981, 29 October 1983, 27 December 1987; Preston, *Automobile Age Atlanta*, 157–58.

80. Bradley R. Rice, "Battle of Buckhead," 6–9; Stone, *Economic Growth and Neighborhood Discontent*, 34.

81. Hartsfield to influential men in Buckhead and Druid Hills, 7 January 1943, Box 29, Hartsfield Papers, EUSC; Stone, *Regime Politics*, 27, 30.

82. Bradley R. Rice, "Battle of Buckhead," 9–16, 19–20; *Atlanta Constitution*, 17, 18 September 1949; *City Builder* 16 (2 April 1951); Martin, *William Berry Hartsfield*, 85–86. A Fulton County police force, separate from Atlanta's, was reestablished in 1975 during the city's police cheating scandal. See Chapter 5, below.

83. *The Herald*, 26 October 1950; Bradley R. Rice, "Battle of Buckhead," 15. Fulton County schools in the annexed section became part of the Atlanta system beginning in September 1951.

84. Hefner, "Black Employment in a Southern 'Progressive' City," 13; Atlanta Negro Voters League minutes, General Committee Meeting, 1 February 1951, Box 11, Long-Rucker-Aiken Family Papers, AHS; Abbott, *New Urban America*, 175.

85. Hartsfield to Pollard Turman, 22 February 1965, with copies to Robert Woodruff,

James Robinson, Mills B. Lane, Ivan Allen Jr., Jack Tarver, Opie Shelton, and John Sibley, Box 7, Hartsfield Papers, EUSC.

86. *Atlanta Journal*, 12 May 1966; flyer (on reasons to oppose Sandy Springs's annexation), 7 March 1966, Box 29, Hartsfield Papers, EUSC; "Save Sandy Springs" booklet, Spring 1966, Box 29, Hartsfield Papers, EUSC; *Atlanta Constitution*, 4 February 1964, 4 April, 9 May 1966.

87. Hartsfield to Pat Healey (National League of Cities), 10 May 1966, Box 31, Hartsfield Papers, EUSC; *Atlanta Journal*, 12 May 1966; *Atlanta Constitution*, 12 May 1966.

88. Hartsfield to Pat Healey, 10 May 1966, Box 31, Hartsfield Papers, EUSC; author's interview with Johnson.

89. Hefner, "Black Employment in a Southern 'Progressive' City," 10, 13; Hartsfield to Collier B. Gladin (Atlanta planning director), 7 November 1969, and Hartsfield to Earl Patton, 19 December 1969, Box 29, Hartsfield Papers, EUSC; *Atlanta Journal*, 22 January 1968, 21 October 1971; *Atlanta Constitution*, 14 August 1969; *Atlanta Daily World*, 5 October 1967, 23 October 1969; *Atlanta Voice*, 6 February 1971; Spector, "Municipal and County Zoning," 55; Paul Anthony (Southern Regional Council) to William Howland, office of the mayor, 17 January 1968, SRC, AUC.

90. Sharron L. Hiemstra, "Significance of Elections for Pluralist-Elitist Theory: Atlanta's 1969 Mayoral Election," May 1970, p. 91, in Box 15, Bullard Papers, EUSC; Hornsby, "Negro in Atlanta Politics," 29–30; Jones, "Black Political Empowerment in Atlanta," 102; address by Sam Massell to Rotary Club of Atlanta, 27 December 1971, "Program for Progress," Box 46, Mays Papers, MSRC; author's interview with Massell.

91. Address by Massell, 27 December 1971, Mays Papers, MSRC; *Atlanta Constitution*, 28 September 1969.

92. Hornsby, "Negro in Atlanta Politics," 29–30; Jones, "Black Political Empowerment in Atlanta," 102; Lawrence Moore, "Annexation Atlanta," 40–43.

93. *Atlanta Journal*, 20 October 1975; "Georgia Legislative Review: 1976," Southern Center for Studies in Public Policy, Clark College; *Atlanta Journal and Constitution*, 30 March 1985; Eisinger, *Politics of Displacement*, 138–39, 141–42.

94. *Atlanta Journal*, 20 October 1975.

95. Author's interview with Jackson, 4 January 1988; *Atlanta Journal-Constitution*, 8 May 1983.

Chapter Four

1. Meier and Lewis, "History of the Negro Upper Class in Atlanta," 6–7; Porter, "Black Atlanta," 43; Matthews, "Studies in Race Relations in Georgia," 279; Atlanta Department of Budget and Planning, "Community Building," 26–28. On Herndon and his company see Alexa Henderson, *Atlanta Life Insurance Company*. For a comment on the impact of the black colleges, see the Q. V. Williamson quote in *Atlanta Journal-Constitution*, 8 December 1979.

2. Gatewood, *Aristocrats of Color*, 291–92; King, *Daddy King*, 107, 110.

3. Porter, "Black Atlanta," 118, 126, 130, 322; Dittmer, *Black Georgia in the Progressive Era*, 30–32, 37–38, 126; Fennell, "Demographic Study of Black Businesses," 5–6, 8–9, 13, 16, 40, 43; Tera Hunter, "Household Workers in the Making."

4. Dittmer, *Black Georgia in the Progressive Era*, 30–34; Wingo, "Race Relations in Georgia," 236–37.

5. Sudheendran, "Community Power," 54 (on the percentage of unskilled among all black workers); Tera Hunter, "Household Workers in the Making," 268.

6. Dittmer, *Black Georgia in the Progressive Era*, 188–90; Matthews, "Studies in Race Relations in Georgia," 250, 253, 257, 354; Neverdon-Morton, *Afro-American Women of the South*, 140.

7. Smith, *New Deal in the Urban South*, 13; Kuhn, Joye, and West, *Living Atlanta*, 89–93, 95; Anderson, *Education of Blacks in the South*, 233–34; Matthews, "Studies in Race Relations in Georgia," 364–65; Sudheendran, "Community Power Structure in Atlanta," 280–82; Maclachlan, "Women's Work," 259.

8. Reginald A. Johnson to Ira De A. Reid (director, department of Industrial Investigations, National Urban League), 15 June 1932, 4-D-27, NUL, LC; Report of Executive Secretary to Annual Meeting, Georgia Committee on Interracial Cooperation, 14 January 1931, Box 144, CIC, AUC; Smith, *New Deal in the Urban South*, 27–28; Kuhn, Joye, and West, *Living Atlanta*, 202, 204–5.

9. Smith, *New Deal in the Urban South*, 28, 189; Kuhn, Joye, and West, *Living Atlanta*, 204–5; Minutes—Annual Meeting of Georgia Committee on Interracial Cooperation, 14 January 1931, Box 144, CIC, AUC. The Klan was also active during the 1930s, trying to prevent union activity among blacks as well as whites.

10. "Thirteen Displaced Negro Workers," prepared for the Atlanta Urban League by the students of the Atlanta School of Social Work, 1933, 4-D-27, NUL, LC; "Georgia, December 16, 1936—A Report on the Availability of the Services of the U.S. Employment Service to Negro Applicants in Georgia," Box 1385, Lawrence A. Oxley files, RG 183, NA. See also Gaston, "History of the Negro Wage Earner in Georgia," 287–88.

11. Fulton-DeKalb Committee, Commission on Interracial Cooperation, 12 May 1939, Box 154, CIC, AUC; Works Progress Administration of Georgia, "Occupational Characteristics of White Collar and Skilled Workers of Atlanta, Georgia, 1937," p. 95.

12. Comments of Lucy Mason of Textile Workers Committee of CIO, Fulton-DeKalb Committee, Commission on Interracial Cooperation, Box 154, CIC, AUC; interview with Arthur Raper, Living Atlanta Collection, AHS; The Urban League Mirror (Atlanta Urban League), vol. 1, 20 January 1935, "Thirteenth Annual Report," 1934, Box 5, 14-C-4, NU, AUC.

13. "Twelfth Annual Report of the Atlanta Urban League, 1933," Box A38, NUL-SRO, LC; S. W. Walker, chairman, Emergency Advisory Council of Atlanta, to Mrs. John Hope, 5 October 1933, Papers of John and Lugenia Burns Hope, AUC; Smith, *New Deal in the Urban South*, 243.

14. James C. McMorries, executive secretary, Atlanta Urban League, to T. Arnold Hill, 1938; Robert A. Thompson Jr. to Lawrence A. Oxley, 13 August 1938; Oxley to Frank W. Persons, U.S. Employment Service, 18 August 1938; Oxley to Robert Thompson, 22 August 1938; Oxley to Mr. Burr (memorandum), 14 September 1938, all in Box 1385, Lawrence A. Oxley files, RG 183, NA.

15. Sudheendran, "Community Power," 55 (on percentage of unskilled among all black workers); Smith, *New Deal in the Urban South*, 20; "Negro Families in Need,"

report by students of Atlanta School of Social Work, Research Department, 1933, commissioned by Neighborhood Union, Box 3, 14-B-33, NU, AUC.

16. Blackwelder, "Quiet Suffering," 112–13, 116–19, 122.

17. Ibid., 121, 123, n. 11; "Summary of Research Projects of the Research Department of the Atlanta School of Social Work, 1931–1933," Box 3, 14-B-33, NU, AUC; Report of the Secretary of the Georgia Committee on Race Relations to the Annual Meeting, 15 March 1933, Box 144, CIC, AUC; interview with Nell Blackshear, Living Atlanta Collection, AHS; Smith, *New Deal in the Urban South*, 37–38; "Twelfth Annual Report of the Atlanta Urban League, 1933," Box A38, NUL-SRO, LC; Schulman, *From Cotton Belt to Sunbelt*, 201–2.

18. Interview with Augusta Dunbar, Living Atlanta Collection, AHS; Smith, *New Deal in the Urban South*, 232–34 (Hartsfield quote is on p. 232); Gaston, "History of the Negro Wage Earner in Georgia," 392–93; "Significant Activities and Accomplishments of the Atlanta Urban League, 1939," 5-C-8, NUL, LC.

19. "Study of the Unemployment Situation in Georgia, particular consideration given to Fulton and DeKalb Counties by Committee on Unemployment and Racial Attitudes for Fulton-DeKalb Committee on Interracial Cooperation, 1939," Box 154, CIC, AUC; Clark Foreman to Will W. Alexander, 21 September 1934, Box 30, CIC, AUC; Ellis, " 'Uncle Sam Is My Shepherd,' " 52–53; James C. McMorries, executive secretary, Atlanta Urban League, to C. F. Palmer, chairman, Atlanta Housing Authority, 26 June 1939, Records of the Public Housing Administration, Records of Intergroup Relations branch, Box 3, RG 196, NA; "Significant Activities and Accomplishments of the Atlanta Urban League, 1939," 5-C-8, NUL, LC.

20. "The West Side Unemployment Relief Committee, Annual Report," 1 February 1931–1 March 1932, Box 3, 14-B-32, NU, AUC; Smith, *New Deal in the Urban South*, 239, 240, 243; Gaston, "History of the Negro Wage Earner in Georgia," 303–5, 374; Rouse, *Lugenia Burns Hope*, 51, 86–87.

21. "Study of the Unemployment Situation in Georgia"; "Summary—Re-Survey of Atlanta, Georgia, by the Division of Research and Statistics, Field Report dated June 25, 1938," Box 37, HOLC city survey files, RG 195, NA; "Georgia, December 16, 1936—A Report on the Availability of the Services of the U.S. Employment Service to Negro Applicants in Georgia," Box 1385, Lawrence A. Oxley files, RG 183, NA; Smith, *New Deal in the Urban South*, 96.

22. James M. Boston to Roosevelt, 13 August 1938, Box 1385, Lawrence A. Oxley files, RG 183, NA.

23. Smith, *New Deal in the Urban South*, 138, 241–42; "Twelfth Annual Report of the Atlanta Urban League, 1933," Box A38, NUL-SRO, LC; National Youth Administration of Georgia, "Occupational Outlook for Georgia Youth," July 1939, vol. 5, part 3: "Occupations for Negroes in Atlanta"; Sudheendran, "Community Power," 56 (on percentage of unskilled black workers among all black workers); Fleming, "Atlanta, the Depression, and the New Deal," 327–28.

24. B. F. Ashe to Edward A. Collier (assistant director, information service, War Manpower Commission), 27 March 1943, on "Negro Employment Region VII," Box 63, McGill Papers, EUSC; Andrew F. Brimmer and Ray Marshall, *Public Policy and Promotion of Minority Economic Development, City of Atlanta and Fulton County,*

Georgia, Part 2: *Discrimination in the Atlanta Marketplace, Historical and Contemporary Evidence*, prepared for the City of Atlanta, 29 June 1990, pp. 30–31.

25. *The Georgia Observer*, September–October 1942; Mullis, "Public Career of Grace Towns Hamilton," 150–51.

26. *The Georgia Observer*, September–October 1942; Mullis, "Public Career of Grace Towns Hamilton," 151.

27. *Atlanta Daily World*, 15 December 1943; Mullis, "Public Career of Grace Towns Hamilton," 152–53.

28. Haas, "Southern Metropolis," 174–75; "Inter-Office Communication," R. A. Thompson Jr. to G. T. Hamilton, executive secretary, Atlanta Urban League, 15 November 1946, Box A77, NUL-SRO, LC; "Report of Conferences with Officials of Southern Bell Telephone, A.T. & T. and Western Electric Companies," 1946, Box A77, NUL-SRO, LC; R. A. Thompson to Hal Dumas, 19 January 1948, and Dumas to Thompson, 26 January 1948, Box A92, NUL-SRO, LC; "Labor Market Report, ES-219, Atlanta, Georgia, June 1949," Records of the Bureau of Employment Security, Box 72, RG 183, NA.

29. Harold Martin, *Atlanta Constitution*, 21 November 1946. On training facilities see R. A. Thompson to Lester Granger, executive director, National Urban League, 21 April 1953, 1-D-79, NUL, LC.

30. *Northside News*, 5 September 1956 (reprinted from *Fortune*, September 1956); McGill to Ruby Robinson, 17 April 1956, Box 6, McGill Papers, EUSC; Brimmer and Marshall, *Public Policy*, 2:37–38.

31. McGill to Robinson, 17 April 1956.

32. Atlanta Urban League, "Recommendations for Consideration on Employment, General Citizen Committee on Employment and Economic Opportunity," 1959, Box A193, NUL-SRO, LC; Subcommittee on Municipal Employment to Hartsfield, n.d.; "Report of Meeting with Personnel Director, City of Atlanta, June 1959 with Steering Committee" (included Jacob Henderson, Jesse Hill, and Carl Holman); "Report of Committee on Municipal Employment," 29 October 1959, all in Box 17, Paschall Papers, Series 4, EUSC; General Citizens Committee on Employment and Economic Opportunity, Atlanta to Hartsfield, 27 May 1959, 1-A-7, NUL, LC; *Business Week*, 20 April 1963. Hiring problems for blacks desiring jobs in city government also affected service delivery. See Chapter 5 on the police and fire departments.

33. Hubert M. Jackson (racial relations officer, Atlanta Field Office) to Philip G. Sadler, special assistant to the commissioner (racial relations), Public Housing Authority, "Progress Report on Discrimination against Negro Painters, GA-6-8, Atlanta," 27 September 1954; H. A. Sayles to Richard Nixon, chairman, the President's Committee on Government Contracts, 7 May 1956; H. A. Sayles to Hubert M. Jackson, 7 May 1956, "To the Commissioner, May 17, 1956"; Hubert M. Jackson to Philip G. Sadler, 14 July 1956, all in Box 3, Records of Public Housing Authority, RG 196, NA.

34. "The Role of the Unions," Atlanta Committee for Cooperative Action, n.d. [early 1960s], Box 17, Paschall Papers, Series 4, EUSC; "The Negro and Employment Opportunities in the South—Atlanta," a report based on a survey by the Greater Atlanta Council on Human Relations and the Atlanta Council for Cooperative Action, 1962, SRC, AUC; Hefner, "Black Employment in a Southern 'Progressive' City," 232.

35. "The Role of the Unions"; "The Negro and Employment Opportunities in the South."

36. "A Second Look: The Negro Citizen in Atlanta," Atlanta Committee for Cooperative Action, January 1960, SRC, AUC; *Atlanta Daily World*, 9 March 1960; Atlanta Committee for Cooperative Action, news release, 14 February 1960, SRC, AUC; *Atlanta Daily World*, 9 March 1960; see also 16 August 1961.

37. Vivian Henderson, "The Economic Status of Negroes in the Nation and in the South," SRC publication no. 3: "Toward Regional Realism," Box 48, McGill Papers, EUSC; "The Economic Impact of Racial Unrest," GCHR, AUC. See also Chapter 2.

38. *Atlanta Inquirer*, 4 March 1961; Clarence Coleman (assistant director, southern field division, National Urban League) to M. T. Puryear (director, southern field division), 27 September 1961, Box A207, NUL-SRO, LC.

39. *Atlanta Inquirer*, 23 April 1961; Greater Atlanta Council on Human Relations, minutes, 11 October 1961, Box 1, McGill Papers, EUSC; Arthur A. Chapin to E. T. Kehrer, southern area director, AFL-CIO civil rights department, 29 August 1966, GCHR, AUC.

40. "Public Employment" (part of same report on unions cited in note 34), Atlanta Committee for Cooperative Action, n.d. [early 1960s], Box 17, Paschall Papers, Series 4, EUSC. The Adams quote is located in the same report in the section on "Professional—Social Workers"; "The Negro and Employment Opportunities in the South"; *Atlanta Daily World*, 16 August 1961; Hefner, "Black Employment in a Southern 'Progressive' City," 227–28.

41. Vivian Henderson, "Economic Status of Negroes in the Nation and in the South"; General Citizens Committee on Employment and Economic Opportunity, "Report on Professional Schools, Curriculum and Courses of Instruction," n.d. [late 1950s], Box 17, Paschall Papers, EUSC.

42. *Atlanta Inquirer*, 24 December 1966; Hefner, "Black Employment in a Southern 'Progressive' City," 150–51; Georgia Council on Human Relations Newsletter, Occasional Special Paper no. 1, State of Georgia Boards and Commissions: "Minority and Female Representation," 1973, GCHR, AUC; *Christian Science Monitor*, 29 January 1969; *Atlanta Journal*, 22 April 1964.

43. *Atlanta Inquirer*, 29 December 1962; Greater Atlanta Council on Human Relations, topics submitted for discussion with Mayor Allen, 31 May 1962, SRC, AUC.

44. Report—"Negro Ministers Organize for Big Push in Employment," 1962; news release from Negro Ministers of Atlanta, 1963; "Operation Breadbasket Report," 22 January 1968; news release from SCLC, 24 February 1964, all in Box 172, SCLC, MLKC; *Atlanta Inquirer*, 9, 23 November 1963; SCLC Newsletter, vol. 1, September 1963, Box 122, SCLC, MLKC; *The Student Voice*, 21 November 1963, Box 49, SNCC, MLKC; "A Report of Activities in Operation Breadbasket Department to Dr. Martin Luther King, Jr. from Rev. Fred C. Bennette, Jr.," 19 July 1965, Box 33, Martin Luther King Jr. Papers, MLKC.

45. "The City Must Provide, South Atlanta: The Forgotten Community," 1963, Box 95, SNCC, MLKC; author's interview with Coleman; "Report from South East Atlanta, from Debbie Amis, October 1963 to SNCC," Box 95, SNCC, MLKC.

46. "Action for Democracy," 1 November 1963, Box 139, SCLC, MLKC; Summit

Leadership Conference, meeting with the Family and Children's Services, 19 November 1963, A215, NUL-SRO, LC.

47. *Atlanta Daily World*, 17 February 1965; clippings file, 22 July 1965, Williams Collection, Atlanta-Fulton Public Library; *Atlanta Journal*, 22 April 1964.

48. Schulman, *From Cotton Belt to Sunbelt*, 178–79, 202–3; author's interview with Hollowell. (Hollowell was regional director of EEOC as of 1966. As a lawyer, he was involved in a number of civil rights cases.)

49. Greater Atlanta Council on Human Relations Newsletter, February 1964.

50. *Atlanta Journal*, 22 April 1964; *Atlanta Constitution*, 11 May 1967, 17 March 1969; *Atlanta Inquirer*, 15 November 1969; Ivan Allen to Rev. Samuel Williams, Jesse Hill, Q. V. Williamson, and Leroy Johnson, 21 November 1967, Williams Collection, AUC.

51. Hefner, "Black Employment in a Southern 'Progressive' City," 60–63, 167, 193, 213, 287; "Black Employment in Atlanta: Special Implication for Federally-Involved Construction," statement of James A. Hefner, chairman of the Department of Business and Economics, Clark College, before the Office of Federal Contract Compliance, U.S. Department of Labor, 2 April 1971, SRC, AUC.

52. "Report—Atlanta Public School System," 1963, Box 10, SNCC, MLKC; Georgia Council on Human Relations Newsletter, "Program Highlights," February 1963, Bacote Papers, AUC; Vivian Henderson, "Economic Status of Negroes in the Nation and in the South"; statement of C. R. Yates to Fulton County Grand Jury, 15 April 1960, Box 32, Young Papers, CU; Hefner, "Black Employment in a Southern 'Progressive' City," 239, 241–42.

53. "Community Action in Atlanta—First Annual Report of Economic Opportunity Atlanta, Inc., December 31, 1965"; Hefner, "Black Employment in a Southern 'Progressive' City," 243–50, 277–81.

54. Community Relations Commission, "Report to the People," Williams Collection, AUC; *Atlanta Inquirer*, 15 November 1969; Hefner, "Black Employment in a Southern 'Progressive' City," 264, 288–89.

55. *Atlanta Constitution*, 22 June 1967; "Proposal to EEOC for Employment Program," 1967, Williams Collection, AUC; Research Atlanta, "Which Way Atlanta?," 1973, pp. 44, 46; Research Atlanta, "Decade of Decision," 1981, pp. 88, 90–91; Hefner, "Black Employment in a Southern 'Progressive' City," 222–25, 361; Bederman, "Black Residential Neighborhoods and Job Opportunity Centers," 325–26.

56. Atlanta Community Relations Commission, "Minority Hiring and Promotion Practices, City of Atlanta," report submitted by Rev. Samuel Williams to Rev. J. D. Grier, chairman, Atlanta personnel board, 31 July 1970, Williams Collection, AUC; Jones, "Black Political Empowerment in Atlanta," 100; "Special Report—Racial Conditions in the Atlanta Water Department," City of Atlanta, Community Relations Commission, 11 August 1971, Vertical Files, Community Relations Commission, AUC; *Atlanta Constitution*, 17 March 1970.

57. Jones, "Black Political Empowerment in Atlanta," 100–101; SRC news release, 28 June 1971, SRC, AUC; *Atlanta Journal*, 27 January 1971; *Atlanta Inquirer*, 19 August 1972; "Atlanta Plan" (news release), 28 June 1971, SRC, AUC. See also *Atlanta Constitution*, 16, 19 July 1970.

58. Eisinger, *Politics of Displacement*, 161–63; Eisinger, "Black Employment in Municipal Jobs," 385.

59. Eisinger, *Politics of Displacement*, 161–62; Stone, *Regime Politics*, 87. On the police and fire departments and how hiring affected service delivery, see Chapter 5, below.

60. Eisinger, *Politics of Displacement*, 163–65; "1970 Program Plan, Community Relations Commission," Williams Collection, AUC; Stone, *Regime Politics*, 136, 144–47, 166; Goldfield, "Black Political Power and Public Policy," 168.

61. Research Atlanta, "The Impact of Local Government Programs to Encourage Minority Business Development," 1986; Stone, *Regime Politics*, 146–47, 166; Brimmer and Marshall, *Public Policy*, Part 2, pp. 48, 50–52, 60–62, 67–69, 72–77, 80–85, 96, 100–101, 104, 107–9, 115–16, Part 3: *Discrimination and Economic Development, Effects on Minority and Female Business Enterprises*, 158.

62. Author's interview with Jackson, 23 November 1987; *Atlanta Journal-Constitution*, 18 February 1979; Research Atlanta, "Decade of Decision," 23–24; Lawson, *Running for Freedom*, 168; Bullard and Thomas, "Atlanta," 90–91.

63. "Atlanta Region Area Development Profile" (prepared by Atlanta Regional Commission Staff), May 1983, Box 1, Central Atlanta Progress Papers, AHS; Reed, "Critique of Neo-Progressivism," 12–13.

64. "Atlanta Region Area Development Profile"; Research Atlanta, "Decade of Decision," 79, 88; Research Atlanta, "Which Way Atlanta?," 43–44, 46; *Atlanta Constitution*, 19 October 1981; Orfield and Ashkinaze, *Closing Door*, 60–66; Bederman, "Black Residential Neighborhoods and Job Opportunity Centers," 202, 219, 222–23, 225–27, 230, 242, 284–85, 313–15, 324–25, 328.

65. Orfield and Ashkinaze, *Closing Door*, 52, 56; *Atlanta Constitution*, 28 December 1987.

66. Orfield and Ashkinaze, *Closing Door*, 192, 203–4.

Chapter Five

1. Boyer, *Urban Masses and Moral Order*, 221–22, 235–36, 242–43, 248–49; Williams, "New York City's Public Baths," 49–50; Bauman, "Disinfecting the Industrial City," 126–27.

2. Grantham, *Southern Progressivism*, xx, 126–27, 223, 235–36, 238; Deaton, "Atlanta during the Progressive Era," 176, 200, 202, 208, 210, 215; Matthews, "Studies in Race Relations in Georgia," 169; Dittmer, *Black Georgia in the Progressive Era*, 110–11, 116, 122; Ellis, "A Crusade against 'Wretched Attitudes,'" 21–22, 24–27; Sosna, *In Search of the Silent South*, 16, 18–19, 22, 24–27, 30, 38.

3. Grantham, *Southern Progressivism*, 231; Dittmer, *Black Georgia in the Progressive Era*, 95, 110–11, 116, 122; Crowe, "Racial Violence and Social Reform," 234–35; Kousser, *Shaping of Southern Politics*, 228–29.

4. Galishoff, "Germs Know No Color Line," 23–27, 34–37, 40–41; *The Courier*, 15 July 1961; Sarah Ginsberg, Atlanta School of Social Work, speech to Atlanta Committee on Women's Interracial Activities, 21 April 1931, Box 18, CIC, AUC; Ellis, "A Crusade against 'Wretched Attitudes,'" 24–25.

5. Matthews, "Studies in Race Relations in Georgia," 260–63, 266, 268; Rouse, *Lugenia Burns Hope*, 68; Neighborhood Union, "Report 1933," Records of the Neighborhood Union, Papers of John and Lugenia Burns Hope, AUC; Pamphlet, Neighbor-

hood Union, n.d., Box 1, 14-A-1, NU, AUC; "Report on Neighborhood Union," n.d., Box 1, 14-A-1, NU, AUC; Dittmer, *Black Georgia in the Progressive Era*, 63–65; Shivery, "Neighborhood Union," 149–50; Atlanta branch, NAACP, open letter to Atlanta city officials and to city, 3 April 1919, 1-G, Box 43, branch files, NAACP, LC; pamphlet, Atlanta Civic and Political League, 12 August 1938, Box 159, CIC, AUC; "Justice in Race Relations," CIC Pamphlet, n.d., Box 12, Rainey Papers, EUSC; Ellis, "A Crusade against 'Wretched Attitudes,'" 24.

6. *Atlanta Constitution*, 13 December 1911.

7. Ginsberg speech to Atlanta Committee on Women's Interracial Activities, 21 April 1931, Box 18, CIC, AUC; minutes, annual meeting, Fulton-DeKalb Interracial Committee, 5 December 1939, Box 153, CIC, AUC; *Atlanta Constitution*, 13 April 1938; Ellis, "A Crusade against 'Wretched Attitudes,'" 24–26.

8. "DOES ATLANTA Know and Approve These Conditions?," pamphlet by Atlanta Civic and Political League, 2 August 1938, 4-D-27, NUL, LC.

9. All Citizens' Registration Committee flyers, n.d., SRC, AUC, and Hamilton Papers, AUC; *Atlanta Journal*, 9 December 1949.

10. "A Report on Parks and Recreational Facilities for Negroes in Atlanta, Georgia, January 1954," Atlanta Urban League, Hamilton Papers, AUC; pamphlet—annual meeting, Atlanta Negro Voters League, 18 February 1954—"Report of Committee on Objectives," 13 February 1954, vertical files, Atlanta Negro Voters League, AUC; *Atlanta Journal*, 25 April 1956; Jennings, *Community Influentials*, 121; *Atlanta Inquirer*, 7 July 1962, 10 April 1965; Community Relations Commission, summary of meeting on housing, 19 July 1967, SRC, AUC. See also press release of NAACP, 11 January 1924, 1-G, Box 43, branch files, NAACP, LC.

11. Bayor, "A City Too Busy to Hate."

12. "Report of Program—Atlanta Urban League, 1957–1958," and "Case Work on the Community Level," May 1958, Box 48, McGill Papers, EUSC; Atlanta Negro Voters League, "Revised Preliminary Report of Committee on Objectives, 13 February 1954," Walden Papers, AHS; *Atlanta Daily World*, 9 March 1965, 1 February 1970; Education Committee Minutes, Charter Commission, 2 November 1971, Bacote Papers, AUC; Community Relations Commission, Edgewood-Kirkwood Neighborhood Hearing, 14 March 1967, Box 17, Paschall Papers, EUSC. See Chapter 7 for more information on Southwest Atlantans for Progress.

13. Judy Walborn, "The South Atlanta Project—SNCC, 1963," Box 95, SNCC, MLKC; "Report from South East Atlanta, from Debbie Amis, October 1963 to SNCC," Box 95, SNCC, MLKC; "A Proposal for a Voter Education Project, Southeast Atlanta," September 1963, SRC, AUC; "The City Must Provide, South Atlanta: The Forgotten Community," 1963, Box 95, SNCC, MLKC; press release from South Atlanta Civic Council, 1963, Box 95, SNCC, MLKC.

14. Press release from South Atlanta Civic Council, 1963, Box 95, SNCC, MLKC; "Report from South East Atlanta, from Debbie Amis, October 1963 to SNCC," Box 95, SNCC, MLKC.

15. Report on SNCC, 1966, Box 95, SNCC, MLKC; Council on Human Relations of Greater Atlanta, tentative draft report, 27 March 1964, SRC, AUC; Human Relations Council of Greater Atlanta, report, 18 December 1963, GCHR, AUC; Atlanta

Summit Leadership Conference, Workshop Report, 19 October 1963, Box 15, Paschall Papers, EUSC; "Action for Democracy," 1 November 1963, Box 139, SCLC, MLKC.

16. Council on Human Relations of Greater Atlanta, 8 January 1964, GCHR, AUC; Paschall, *It Must Have Rained*, 151; Atlanta Summit Leadership Conference to Ivan Allen, 10 May 1967, CRC, Williams Collection, AUC.

17. Stone, *Economic Growth and Neighborhood Discontent*, 117–19.

18. "To Mayor, Board of Aldermen, members of CACUR from people of Mechanicsville, Summerhill, South Atlanta, Peoplestown and Vine City," 7 October 1965, and "The Vine City Story," Box 26, Paschall Papers, EUSC; Stone, *Economic Growth and Neighborhood Discontent*, 119–24; Stone, *Regime Politics*, 69.

19. Stone, *Economic Growth and Neighborhood Discontent*, 124–26; *Atlanta Constitution*, 8 September 1966.

20. Stone, *Economic Growth and Neighborhood Discontent*, 126.

21. Ibid., 126–27; Stone, *Regime Politics*, 70–71; "Atlanta, A Special Report," 1966, Box 95, SNCC, MLKC; Carson, *In Struggle*, 191–94, 196–201, 225–26, 238–41.

22. Letter to Mayor Allen, 9 September 1966, SRC, AUC.

23. Paschall, *It Must Have Rained*, 158–59; Council on Human Relations of Greater Atlanta, news release, 8 September 1966, SRC, AUC.

24. *Christian Science Monitor*, 20 December 1966; final report, Atlanta Community Improvement Program, "Equal Opportunity in Housing," 1966–1967, Box 1, City of Atlanta Reports, AHS; Community Council of the Atlanta Area, Research Center, "Social Blight and Neighborhood Renewal."

25. Resolution submitted by Aldermen Williamson, Cook, Cotsakis, Freeman, Leftwich, and Summers, 1 August 1966, CRC, Williams Collection, AUC; "A Citizens' Agenda, First Quarterly Program Report, Community Relations Commission," May 1967, CRC, Williams Collection, AUC; Paschall, *It Must Have Rained*, 164–65.

26. Stone, *Economic Growth and Neighborhood Discontent*, 92, 127–32, 139–40, 234 (n. 4); Stone, *Regime Politics*, 71–73.

27. *Atlanta Constitution*, 22 June 1967; "Statement of Leroy R. Johnson, State Senator, before the Fulton County Grand Jury," 25 July 1967, McEwen Papers, Amistad Research Center, Tulane University.

28. "A Citizens' Agenda, First Quarterly Program Report, Community Relations Commission," May 1967; CRC to Mayor and Board of Aldermen, 28 June 1967; Community Relations Commission, minutes of meeting in Dixie Hills Area, 19 June 1967, all in CRC, Williams Collection, AUC; "City of Atlanta, Summary Plan for Improvement of Disadvantaged Areas for Summer 1968," Box 13, Paschall Papers, EUSC; *Atlanta Daily World*, 29 July 1967; *Atlanta Constitution*, 11 August 1967; Stone, *Economic Growth and Neighborhood Discontent*, 144–45. On service delivery and public housing, see also Chapter 3, above.

29. Atlanta Commission on Crime and Juvenile Delinquency, "Opportunity for Urban Excellence"; *Atlanta Constitution*, 3 December 1939; National Municipal League Consultant Service, "Governments of Atlanta and Fulton County, Georgia," 134, 137; Allen, *Mayor*, 177–78; minutes of meeting of the Citizens Crime Commission of Atlanta, 27 May 1959, McEwen Papers, Amistad Research Center, Tulane University.

30. "Opportunity for Urban Excellence."

31. Stone, *Regime Politics*, 67–68, 71–72; Dare, "Involvement of the Poor in Atlanta," 114–15, 117, 127; "Application to the Department of Housing and Urban Development for a Grant to Plan a Comprehensive City Demonstration Program," 10 March 1967, Department of Housing and Urban Development, Model Cities Reports, 1966–1973, Box 57, RG 207, NA.

32. "Atlanta's Approach: People Investment," Annual Report for 1970, CRC, Williams Collection, AUC.

33. "Recommendations to the Mayor of the City of Atlanta and the Mayor's Committee on Housing Resources," SRC, AUC.

34. Stone, *Economic Growth and Neighborhood Discontent*, 128–30, 132–37, 139; Stone, *Regime Politics*, 72. On some Model City improvements see *Atlanta Inquirer*, 5 August 1972.

35. Author's interviews with Eplan and Young; Abbott, *New Urban America*, 151; *Atlanta Journal-Constitution*, 21 June 1970; Goldfield, "Black Political Power and Public Policy," 166–67.

36. *Atlanta Journal*, 1 November 1974.

37. *Atlanta Journal-Constitution*, 16 August 1987; Stone, *Regime Politics*, 110–11, 120–22, 143. See also *Atlanta Constitution*, 28 August 1989.

38. D'Avino, "Atlanta Municipal Parks," 56–57, 72–75, 77, 80–81, 95–96, 131, 181; Rabinowitz, *Race Relations in the Urban South*, 189–90.

39. D'Avino, "Atlanta Municipal Parks," 80–81, 141, 143, 148, 161–62, 170–71, 187–88; "Report from Negro Anti-Tuberculosis Association," 20 April 1916, Box 3, Atlanta Lung Association Collection, AHS.

40. D'Avino, "Atlanta Municipal Parks," 144–46, 162.

41. Ibid., 96, 146–47; Neighborhood Union pamphlet, n.d., Box 1, 14-A-1, NU, AUC; minutes of the Negro Anti-Tuberculosis Association, 14 November 1916 and 27 July 1917, and "Report from Negro Anti-Tuberculosis Association," 20 April 1916, all in Box 3, Atlanta Lung Association Collection, AHS; Atlanta branch, NAACP, open letter to city officials and to city, 3 April 1919, 1-G, Box 43, branch files, NAACP, LC; "A Survey of the Opinions of a Hundred Heads of Families Respecting Washington Park made jointly by Neighborhood Union and Atlanta School of Social Work, December 1924," Box 2, CIC, AUC.

42. D'Avino, "Atlanta Municipal Parks," 163–65; Matthews, "Studies in Race Relations in Georgia," 343; "General Information" on recreational facilities, 1932–34, Records of the Public Housing Administration, folder H-432, Limited Dividend Applications, RG 196, NA; Smith, *New Deal in the Urban South*, 237; annual meeting, Fulton-DeKalb Interracial Committee, 5 December 1939, Box 153, CIC, AUC.

43. "Summary of the finding concerning Negro life taken from a study of Atlanta made by the Senior and Young Peoples' Departments, St. Mark's Methodist Church, Atlanta, Georgia, January 1940—edited by Fulton-DeKalb Interracial Committee," Box 163, CIC, AUC; meeting of Emergency Committee, Fulton-DeKalb Committee, 10 July 1940, Box 155, CIC, AUC.

44. Municipal Housing Authority, report on "Spotting Areas of Recreational Needs, 1940–1941," ABP.

45. *Atlanta Journal*, 17 April 1945; 1937 Directory and Souvenir Program of the

National Negro Business League Convention, AHS; "DOES ATLANTA Know and Approve These Conditions?," pamphlet by Atlanta Civic and Political League, 2 August 1938, 4-D-27, NUL, LC.

46. *Atlanta Journal*, 13 August 1946; *Atlanta Daily World*, 22 August 1952, 19 June 1958; "A Report on Parks and Recreational Facilities for Negroes in Atlanta, Georgia, January 1954," Atlanta Urban League, Hamilton Papers, AUC; *Atlanta Constitution*, 22 April 1954; Atlanta branch, NAACP, Parks and Recreation Committee report, June 1956, Williams Collection, AUC; *Atlanta Journal-Constitution*, 11 October 1959.

47. "A Second Look: The Negro Citizen in Atlanta," Atlanta Committee for Cooperative Action, January 1960, SRC, AUC.

48. Robert C. Stuart to Hartsfield, 7 August 1953, 25 March 1954, ABP.

49. *Atlanta Constitution*, 18 May, 22, 25 August 1961; *Atlanta Inquirer*, 13, 20 May 1961; Mrs. Azalee Hester (president, Blandtown Civic League), Mr. Will Ferguson (president, Carey Park Civic League), Rev. J. L. Bates (president, Perry Homes Tenants Association), Mr. L. H. Coppedge, Mr. Otelus Shellman (president, Scottscrossing Civic League), to Hartsfield, 13 March 1961, Walden Papers, AHS; "The City Must Provide, South Atlanta: The Forgotten Community," 1963, Box 95, SNCC, MLKC; "Report from South East Atlanta, from Debbie Amis, October 1963 to SNCC," Box 95, SNCC, MLKC.

50. "Planning Department to Parks Committee, *Additional Park Land Survey*," Box 21, Paschall Papers, EUSC. See also Chapter 3.

51. *Atlanta Inquirer*, 23 May, 8 August 1964.

52. Ibid., 6, 20 June, 4, 11, 18 July, 8, 29 August 1964; Stone, *Regime Politics*, 65. See also Chapter 3, above.

53. *Atlanta Inquirer*, 18 July 1964; final report, Atlanta Community Improvement Program, "Equal Opportunity in Housing," 1966–67, Box 1, City of Atlanta Reports, AHS.

54. Allen, *Mayor*, 69–70; *New York Times*, 5 August 1962; McGill, "Atlanta"; Martin, *William Berry Hartsfield*, 181.

55. *Atlanta Inquirer*, 12 June 1965; *Atlanta Journal*, 3 May 1967; *Atlanta Constitution*, 14 February 1968, 29 July 1970, 27 October 1975.

56. Quoted in Blalock, "Social, Political and Economic Aspects of Race Relations," 31–33.

57. Shivery, "Neighborhood Union," 150–53, 159; Rouse, *Lugenia Burns Hope*, 68, 71–72; Beardsley, *History of Neglect*, 105, 106, 108; "Bulletin of the National League on Urban Conditions among Negroes: Work of the Affiliated Organizations, June 1915," William Matthews Family Papers, Atlanta-Fulton Public Library.

58. Matthews, "Studies in Race Relations in Georgia," 345; Dittmer, *Black Georgia in the Progressive Era*, 206; Jesse O. Thomas (southern field director, National Urban League) to A. T. Walden, W. J. Faulkner, W. A. Bell, L. D. Milton, C. L. Harper, 12 January 1929, 5-C-8, NUL, NA.

59. Galishoff, "Germs Know No Color Line," 25–26, 37.

60. Ibid., 26, 29–30, 34, 36–37.

61. Ibid., 28; "City Tuberculosis Program for Negroes," 1914, by Rosa Lowe (secretary of Anti-Tuberculosis Association), Box 3, Atlanta Lung Association Papers, AHS.

62. Fields, "Study of the Health Education Program," 13–14; Porter, "Black At-

lanta," 82–84; interview with Ruby Baker (pseudonym), Living Atlanta Collection, AHS; Beardsley, *History of Neglect*, 132, 136.

63. Beardsley, *History of Neglect*, 80, 82; interview with Homer Nash, 1979, Living Atlanta Collection, AHS.

64. Atlanta branch, NAACP, open letter to Atlanta city officials and to city, 3 April 1919, 1-G, Box 43, branch files, NAACP, LC; author's interview with Yancey.

65. Interviews with Nash and Baker, Living Atlanta Collection, AHS.

66. Grady Hospital explained its segregated ambulance service this way: it often used vehicles at local funeral homes for supplementary ambulances, and since the funeral homes were segregated, the race of the victim had to be determined before an ambulance was called. Author's interview with Paschall; Greater Atlanta Council on Human Relations, minutes of meeting on 24 September 1961, SRC, AUC.

67. "History," Box 7, Grady Memorial Hospital Collection, AHS. On the treatment of black interns and residents in general, see Beardsley, *History of Neglect*, 79.

68. "Statistical Report of Department of Public Health, City of Atlanta, Georgia 1939," Box 156, CIC, AUC; data gathered for Conference on Health-Hospitalization-Sanitation, Fulton-DeKalb CIC, 2 December 1938, Box 154, CIC, AUC. See also Galishoff, "Germs Know No Color Line," 23.

69. Conference on Health-Hospitalization-Sanitation, Fulton-DeKalb CIC, 2 December 1938, Box 154, CIC, AUC; Grady Hospital, 1932, 1937, 1938, and 1939 Annual Reports, Grady Memorial Hospital Collection, AHS; "A Report on Hospital Care of the Negro Population of Atlanta, Georgia, 1947," p. 54, Atlanta Urban League, McEwen Papers, Amistad Research Center, Tulane University.

70. See, for example, Georgia Committee on Interracial Cooperation, minutes, 15 January 1930, Box 144, CIC, AUC; Atlanta Committee on Women's Interracial Activities, Board of Directors, minutes, 11 December 1930, Box 146, CIC, AUC; Executive Committee meetings, Fulton-DeKalb Committee, 27 February and 22 September 1939, Box 156, CIC, AUC.

71. Petition to Mayor and General Council of Atlanta, 23 May 1932, Records of the Neighborhood Union, Papers of John and Lugenia Burns Hope, AUC; *Atlanta Constitution*, 16 April 1937. See also Beardsley, *History of Neglect*, 41.

72. Beardsley, *History of Neglect*, 157–59, 161–63, 165–67, 169–71.

73. Mullis, "Public Career of Grace Towns Hamilton," 126–27.

74. *Atlanta Constitution*, 12 August 1941; Jesse Daniel Ames to W. J. Trent Jr. (racial relations officer, Federal Works Agency), 28 October 1941, Box 156, CIC, AUC; Beardsley, *History of Neglect*, 178, 184.

75. "A Report on Hospital Care . . . 1947," pp. 11, 21–22, 39, 43–44, Atlanta Urban League, McEwen Papers. A U.S. Department of Public Health formula that considers just population rather than population and need (based on birth and death rates) indicates that in 1947 blacks needed 248 more hospital beds and whites 143. Data gathered for conference on Health-Hospitalization-Sanitation, Fulton-DeKalb CIC, Box 154, CIC, AUC.

76. "Report on Hospital Care . . . 1947," 9, 39.

77. Ibid., 12, 14, 18, 42, 54–55; G. T. Hamilton, executive director, Atlanta Urban League, to Members of the Board of the Atlanta Urban League, 21 July 1948, A-92,

NUL-SRO, LC. Atlanta's black death rate was lower than that of Savannah, Little Rock, and Nashville.

78. Second Annual Report, Fulton-DeKalb Hospital Authority, 1947, Box 2, Grady Memorial Hospital Collection, AHS; Mrs. Harry M. Gershon to Mrs. Charles Liebman, 26 May 1948, Hamilton Papers, AUC.

79. *Atlanta Journal*, 27, 29 June 1948, 23 June 1952; Mullis, "Public Career of Grace Towns Hamilton," 131–32, 136; Grace Towns Hamilton to the Advisory Committee on Hospital Care for Negroes in Atlanta, 11 April 1949, Hamilton Papers, AUC; Hughes Spalding to Grace Towns Hamilton, Clayton Yates, E. M. Martin, J. B. Whittaker, and Robert Clayton, 15 April 1950, Hamilton Papers, AUC.

80. *Atlanta Inquirer*, 21 August 1960; Mullis, "Public Career of Grace Towns Hamilton," 135–38; Grace Towns Hamilton to Hughes Spalding, 9 July 1953, Hamilton Papers, AUC; Grace Towns Hamilton to Advisory Board of Trustees, Spalding Pavilion–Grady Hospital, 5 November 1959, McEwen Papers.

81. Dr. Asa G. Yancey to Dr. Ira A. Ferguson (chief of surgery, Grady Hospital), 9 August 1955, Hamilton Papers, AUC.

82. *Atlanta Daily World*, 17, 18 February 1954; R. A. Billings (chairman, Citizens Committee) to Hughes Spalding (chairman, Fulton-DeKalb Hospital Authority), 12 December 1955, and Hughes Spalding to R. A. Billings, 13 December 1955, McEwen Papers.

83. Grace Towns Hamilton to Advisory Board of Trustees, Spalding Pavilion–Grady Hospital, 5 November 1959, McEwen Papers; *Atlanta Inquirer*, 21 August 1960; Mullis, "Public Career of Grace Towns Hamilton," 138.

84. Grace Towns Hamilton to Advisory Board of Trustees, Spalding Pavilion–Grady Hospital, 5 November 1959, McEwen Papers; Hughes Spalding to American Medical Association Council, Conference Committee, Graduate Training, 18 June 1957, Hamilton Papers, AUC; Dr. Asa G. Yancey to Dr. Ira A. Ferguson, 31 August 1957, Hamilton Papers, AUC; Hughes Spalding to Dr. Ira A. Ferguson and Dr. Asa G. Yancey, 10 December 1957, Hamilton Papers, AUC. Dr. Asa G. Yancey to Fred Cannon (chairman, advisory board, Spalding Pavilion), April 1959, McEwen Papers; "Resolution to Fulton-DeKalb Hospital Authority, from Advisory Board of Trustees, Spalding Pavilion, April 29, 1959," McEwen Papers; "Hughes Spalding Pavilion Training Program in Surgery, June 2, 1959," McEwen Papers; *Atlanta Inquirer*, 21 August 1960. Yancey had been chief of surgery at the VA hospital in Tuskegee, Alabama.

85. Grace Towns Hamilton to Advisory Board of Trustees, Spalding Pavilion–Grady Hospital, 5 November 1959, McEwen Papers; Boisfeuillet Jones (vice president and administrator of health services, Emory University) to Grace Towns Hamilton, 16 September 1959, McEwen Papers; *Atlanta Constitution*, 20 August 1960.

86. Minutes of Meeting of Advisory Board of Trustees of the Hughes Spalding Pavilion, 17 November 1959, McEwen Papers; Grace Towns Hamilton to Advisory Board of Trustees, Spalding Pavilion–Grady Hospital, 5 November 1959, McEwen Papers.

87. Annual Report, Georgia State Conference of NAACP Branches, 1960, NAACP Correspondence, Williams Collection, AUC; *Atlanta Daily World*, 14 August 1960; *Atlanta Constitution*, 11, 17, 20 August 1960; Advisory Board of Trustees of Spalding, report, 11 April 1961, Hamilton Papers, AUC.

88. "A Second Look: The Negro Citizen in Atlanta," the Atlanta Committee for Cooperative Action, January 1960, SRC, AUC; Greater Atlanta Council on Human Relations, Newsletter, February 1962; SNCC, news release, 4 February 1962, Box 49, SNCC, MLKC; Atlanta branch, NAACP, "Request for Action to End Segregation Practices at Grady Memorial Hospital," 2 October 1961, Box 22, Paschall Papers, EUSC; letter from Greater Atlanta Council on Human Relations, 18 October 1961, SRC, AUC; Mrs. Clifton Hoffman, chairman, to members of Greater Atlanta Council on Human Relations, February 1962, SRC, AUC; "The City Must Provide, South Atlanta: The Forgotten Community," 1963, Box 95, SNCC, and press release from South Atlanta Civic Council, 1963, Box 95, SNCC, MLKC. There is some discrepancy on the exact number of beds for black patients at Grady, but regardless, they outnumbered those for whites.

89. *Atlanta Daily World*, 8, 9 August 1961; Greater Atlanta Council on Human Relations, fact sheet [on hospitals], 15 March 1962, SRC, AUC; Greater Atlanta Council on Human Relations, Newsletter, February 1962. Since there was inconsistency on the number of beds for black patients in Atlanta hospitals, I used the higher number, thereby perhaps overestimating the percentage of hospital beds for blacks. *Atlanta Constitution*, 24 October 1952. In 1952 the Fulton County Medical Society agreed to allow black physicians to attend the organization's scientific sessions and be considered scientific members, but they had no voting rights and were not full members of the group.

90. Paschall, *It Must Have Rained*, 37–38.

91. SNCC news release, 1962, Box 25, Paschall Papers, EUSC; *Atlanta Daily World*, 8 March 1962.

92. *Atlanta Daily World*, 3, 4 February, 6, 9 March 1962; Roy C. Bell and J. A. Middleton, statement on Grady and health care, 1962, Box 51, SCLC, MLKC.

93. Beardsley, *History of Neglect*, 264–65; *Atlanta Inquirer*, 9 November 1963.

94. "Atlanta Summit Meeting with Fulton-DeKalb Hospital Authority, Grady Hospital Board Room, Tuesday, November 26, 1963," A-215, NUL-SRO, LC.

95. Council on Human Relations of Greater Atlanta, Newsletter, April 1964; *Atlanta Journal-Constitution*, 16 February 1964; *Atlanta Inquirer*, 13 June 1964.

96. *Atlanta Constitution*, 25 February 1965; *Atlanta Daily World*, 26 February 1965, 10 June 1966; *Atlanta Inquirer*, 5 June 1965; author's interview with Yancey.

97. *Atlanta Inquirer*, 10 July 1965.

98. *Atlanta Daily World*, 10, 15 June 1966; "Report on Civil Rights Compliance, Atlanta, Georgia Hospitals," August 1966, NAACP correspondence, Williams Collection, AUC.

99. "Community Improvement Program, Social Blight and Social Resources Study, Interim Report Number 1, Social Blight and its Causes (with special reference to the blighted areas surrounding Atlanta Stadium), Community Council of the Atlanta Area, Inc., Research Center," February 1966, Box 13, Paschall Papers, EUSC; Council on Human Relations, Newsletter, September 1966; Community Relations Commission, report by J. Otis Cochran on tour of Grady Hospital, 19 April 1967, Williams Collection, AUC; Department of HEW, "Report of Walter F. Wrenn, Jr., Regional Program Director, Region IV, September 26, 1967 on complaints about Grady Hospi-

tal and Emory University Medical and Dental Schools," Box 20, Paschall Papers, EUSC; "Urban Framework Plan," Box 1, Bullard Papers, AHS.

100. Asa G. Yancey to Grace Towns Hamilton, 4 February 1980, Hamilton Papers, AUC; Holmes, *Status of Black Atlantans 1993*, 69–80, 84.

101. Newsletter of Council on Human Relations of Greater Atlanta, Inc., November–December 1966; *Atlanta Constitution*, 2 September 1988.

102. *Atlanta Constitution*, 2, 4 September 1988; author's interview with Yancey. See also *Atlanta Constitution*, 12 April 1988.

103. *Atlanta Constitution*, 18 September 1987, 21 April, 13 May 1988; author's interview with Yancey; Dusenberry, "History of Grady Memorial Hospital." Yancey went on to become medical director of Grady and associate dean of the Emory University Medical School.

104. Yancey, "Grady Memorial Hospital Centennial"; *Atlanta Journal-Constitution*, 24 May 1992.

105. Rabinowitz, *Race Relations in the Urban South*, 41; Dittmer, *Black Georgia in the Progressive Era*, 138; interview with B. B. Beamon, 29 May 1979, Living Atlanta Collection, AHS; Steve Grable, "Atlanta Police and Race Relations, 1920–1947: A Synopsis Prepared for Living Atlanta," January 1979, Living Atlanta Collection, AHS; interview with Herbert Jenkins, Living Atlanta Collection, AHS. See also press release, 1931, Box 13, CIC, AUC; *Atlanta Daily World*, 11 April 1932; "Police Brutality in Atlanta, 1933," Box 5, CIC, AUC; Mathias and Anderson, *Horse to Helicopter*.

106. "Atlanta Police and Race Relations"; *Atlanta Daily World*, 14 March, 1 July, 21 October 1933; *Atlanta Constitution*, 5 October 1933; Jessie Daniel Ames to Rev. John Moore Walker, 10 October 1933, Box 163, CIC, AUC; NAACP minutes, 1 January 1934, Box 7, 14-C-8, NU, AUC; minutes of Neighborhood Union, 9 May 1934, 14-B-34, NU, AUC; 1937 pamphlet, "Wanted Negro Police for Negro Districts in Atlanta," 1-G, Box 44, branch files, NAACP, LC.

107. Author's interview with Jenkins.

108. Interview with William Holmes Borders, 29 November 1978, Living Atlanta Collection, AHS; interview with Jenkins, Living Atlanta Collection, AHS; author's interview with Cochrane.

109. H. S. Murphy and C. L. Harper to Mayor and Members of Council, 15 July 1947, Box 4, Mays Papers, MSRC; interview with Jenkins, Living Atlanta Collection, AHS.

110. "Statement Presented to the Police Committee of Atlanta, July 16, 1947 by The Citizens Committee," Box 4, Mays Papers, MSRC; interview with B. B. Beamon, 29 May 1979, Living Atlanta Collection, AHS; Jenkins, *Forty Years on the Force*, 45–46.

111. *Atlanta Constitution*, 21 October 1985; author's interview with Jenkins; interview with Warren Cochrane, 15 November 1978, Living Atlanta Collection, AHS; interview with Harold Fleming, 21 June 1986, by Kathleen Dowdey, The Center for Contemporary Media, Atlanta; Jenkins, *Forty Years on the Force*, 46, 48.

112. *Atlanta Constitution*, 21 October 1985; author's interviews with Hooks, McKinney, and Jenkins; interview with O. R. McKibbons, Living Atlanta Collection, AHS; interview with Warren Cochrane, Living Atlanta Collection, AHS. Hooks and McKibbons were two of the original eight black officers; McKinney was the ninth black

hired as a policemen. He joined the force in June 1948, replacing one of the initial eight who had resigned within the few two months.

113. *Atlanta Constitution*, 21 October 1985; author's interviews with McKinney, Jenkins, and Hooks; *Atlanta Daily World*, 4 January 1950; statement of C. R. Yates to Fulton County Grand Jury, 15 April 1960, Box 32, Young Papers, CU; A. T. Walden and Warren Cochrane to Mayor William Hartsfield, 25 July 1955, Walden Papers, AHS.

114. *Atlanta Constitution*, 21 October 1985; Atlanta Negro Voters League, "Summary of Committee Conference with Police Chief Herbert Jenkins, 9 January 1962," Bacote Papers, AUC; *Atlanta Daily World*, 30, 31 January 1962, 2 March 1962; *Atlanta Inquirer*, 27 April 1963.

115. General Citizens Committee on Employment and Economic Opportunity, Atlanta to William B. Hartsfield, 27 May 1959, 1-A-7, NUL, LC; statement of C. R. Yates to Fulton County Grand Jury, Young Papers, CU; *Atlanta Inquirer*, 15 September 1962; *Atlanta Daily World*, 4 January 1950, 24 August 1951, 14 May 1963; Stone, *Regime Politics*, 33–34; author's interviews with Hamer and Maddox; *Atlanta Journal and Constitution*, 15 June 1985. Hamer eventually went on to become fire chief in 1985.

116. "Comments," 1 November 1965, Box 3, Martin Luther King Jr. Papers, MLKC; *Atlanta Inquirer*, 9, 23 October 1965; *Atlanta Daily World*, 25 November 1965.

117. "Report on the Grievances of Black Firemen to the Board of Fire Masters, City of Atlanta by the Community Relations Commission, December 29, 1969," Williams Collection, AUC; *Atlanta Constitution*, 9 August, 16 September 1969; *Atlanta Journal*, 29 October 1969; *Atlanta Voice*, 2 November 1969; author's interview with Hamer; final report, Atlanta Community Improvement Program, "Equal Opportunity in Housing," 1966–1967, Box 1, City of Atlanta Reports, AHS.

118. *Atlanta Daily World*, 28 December 1965; Rosenzweig, "Issue of Employing Black Policemen in Atlanta," 88; *Atlanta Constitution*, 4 June 1968, 17 March 1969; *Atlanta Journal*, 29 October 1969; Atlanta Community Relations Commission, "Minority Hiring and Promotion Practices, City of Atlanta," 31 July 1970, Williams Collection, AUC.

119. *Atlanta Inquirer*, 17 June, 16 September 1972; P. O. Williams, chief of Atlanta Fire Department, to Board of Fire Masters, 26 January 1970, Williams Collection, AUC; *Atlanta Constitution*, 7 May 1970, 27 April 1973; Jonathan Rice, "Organized Labor Activity in the Atlanta Police Department," 10, 29, in Box 17, Jenkins Papers, AHS.

120. *Atlanta Constitution*, 22, 30 June 1973, 17 November 1979, 19 June 1987; Moss, "Black Political Ascendancy in Urban Centers," 21, 24, 25 in Box 11, Jenkins Papers, AHS; Jonathan Rice, "Organized Labor Activity," 23, 26, 28.

121. Jones, "Black Political Empowerment in Atlanta," 109; Moss, "Black Political Ascendancy," 21–22, 29; Stone, *Regime Politics*, 88; *Atlanta Constitution*, 12 March 1978, 19 June 1987; author's interview with Jackson, 4 January 1988. Inman's title was now director of the bureau of police services, but he had no power nor important duties once Eaves was appointed.

122. *Atlanta Constitution*, 1 May, 2 December 1975, 8, 16 June 1976, 2 June 1977, 11 April, 9 August 1979, 19 June 1987; author's interviews with McKinney, Hamer, and

Maddox; Levi, "Conflict and Collusion," 177–78; Jonathan Rice, "Organized Labor Activity," 16–17, 25, 32–34, 36–37, 49–50; *Atlanta Daily World*, 8 April 1975.

123. Jonathan Rice, "Organized Labor Activity," 37–38, 46–50; *Atlanta Constitution*, 11, 17 September 1974, 2 December 1975, 13 March, 16 June, 8 September 1976, 20 October 1977, 12 March, 21 July 1978, 19 June, 16 October 1987.

124. Jonathan Rice, "Organized Labor Activity," 51–54, 57–58; *Atlanta Constitution*, 1 September 1978, 6 November 1979.

125. *Atlanta Daily World*, 8 April 1975; *Atlanta Constitution*, 2 December 1975, 7 September, 10 November 1978, 8, 9 October 1979.

126. Author's interview with Maddox; *Atlanta Constitution*, 24 April, 14 May 1986, 19 June, 30 September 1987, 1 March, 2 July 1989, 29 March, 5 October 1990, 20 October 1992, 15 July 1993; *Atlanta Journal and Constitution*, 8 December 1988, 2 July, 23 September 1989.

127. *Atlanta Constitution*, 14 May 1986; *Atlanta Journal and Constitution*, 2 July 1989, 11 September 1992.

128. Matthews, "Studies in Race Relations in Georgia," 128–30; Meier and Rudwick, "Boycott Movement against Jim Crow Streetcars"; interviews with Ruby Baker, Arthur Raper, and Roy Dunn, all in Living Atlanta Collection, AHS; Kuhn, Joye, and West, *Living Atlanta*, 77, 79–80, 82; *Atlanta Independent*, 23 May 1907.

129. Walter White (secretary, Atlanta branch, NAACP) to Roy Nash, 19 March 1917, 1-G, Box 43, branch files, NAACP, LC.

130. Transportation-Segregation Study, 15 August 1945, SRC, AUC.

131. Porter, "Black Atlanta," 67–68; "Racial Separation in Transportation in Atlanta, Georgia, 1945—An Action Memorandum Prepared by the Southern Regional Council," SRC, AUC.

132. Discussion with C. R. Strong, 1934, Box 34, Mule to Marta Papers, AHS.

133. Georgia Committee on Race Relations report, Box 153, CIC, AUC; report of special committee to deal with transportation problem in Atlanta, 3 November 1942, Box 155, CIC, AUC; report of committee on equity before the law, subcommittee of Georgia Interracial Commission, 1942, Box 12, Rainey Papers, EUSC.

134. "Racial Separation in Transportation in Atlanta, Georgia, 1945—An Action Memorandum Prepared by the Southern Regional Council," SRC, AUC; "Racial Separation in Transportation, Atlanta, Georgia—Situations Upon Which Recommendations and Action Programs May Be Based," report by SRC for Segregation Study Commission, 3 November 1945, SRC, AUC; Special Committee Representing the Westside Committee for the Improvement of Transit Service to Mayor and City Council, 31 October 1953, Dixie Hills Box, Walden Papers, AHS; Thompson, Lewis, and McEntire, "Atlanta and Birmingham," 33.

135. On abuse of black passengers see, for example, *Atlanta Daily World*, 20 January 1944; "Racial Separation in Transportation, Atlanta, Georgia—Situations," SRC, AUC.

136. Barnes, *Journey from Jim Crow*, 120–21, 124–25.

137. Directors' meeting, 25 July 1956, Minute Books, 1954–56, Atlanta Transit Authority Collection, AHS; minutes of NAACP Strategy Committee meeting, 21, 24, 26 November 1956, NAACP Correspondence, Williams Collection, AUC; memo from Rev. William Holmes Borders, chairman, and Rev. H. I. Bearden, vice chairman, The

Love, Law and Liberation Movement, 1957, SCLC Box, Williams Collection, AUC; A. T. Walden to Atlanta Transit System, attention Robert L. Sommerville, president, 8 January 1957, Box 35, Mule to Marta Papers, AHS; *Atlanta Daily World*, 9, 10, 11 January 1957; "From Henry Taylor's Scrapbooks," Box 116, Mule to Marta Papers, AHS; Martin, *William Berry Hartsfield*, 118–19.

138. The Atlanta Transit Company bought the system in 1950 from Georgia Power. In 1954 the transit company changed its name to the Atlanta Transit System. Atlanta Transit System, directors' meeting minutes, 26 June, 27 November 1957, Minute Books, 1957–59, Atlanta Transit Authority Collection, AHS.

139. Tilman C. Cothran and John D. Reid, "Survey of Negro Bus Patronage in Atlanta, Georgia," 1960, pp. 5, 8, 10, 19, 24, 2-B-12, NUL, LC. See also Chapter 4.

140. *Atlanta Journal*, 11 December 1966; *Atlanta Daily World*, 18 December 1966.

141. King Elliott, public information director, MARTA, to Jesse Hill, 4 January 1967; King Elliott to Samuel Williams, 4 January 1967; Jesse Hill Jr. and Rev. Samuel W. Williams, cochairs, Atlanta Summit Leadership Conference, to Richard H. Rich, chairman, MARTA, 4 January 1967, Box 116, Mule to Marta Papers, AHS.

142. *Atlanta Inquirer*, 7 January 1967; *Atlanta Daily World*, 3 February 1967; Richard Rich to Samuel Williams, 13 January 1967, Box 116, Mule to Marta Papers, AHS.

143. Atlanta Summit Leadership Conference, news conference, 9 May 1968; Atlanta Summit Leadership Conference meeting, 14 May 1968; Atlanta Summit Leadership Conference, presentation at MARTA hearing, 16 May 1968, all in Box 116, Mule to Marta Papers, AHS; Stone, *Regime Politics*, 74, 100.

144. Metropolitan Atlanta Summit Leadership Congress, press release, 10 October 1968; memorandum to Richard H. Rich, Rawson Haverty, L. D. Milton, John C. Slaton, MARTA staff, from H. L. Stuart, MARTA general manager, 15 May 1968, Box 116, Mule to Marta Papers, AHS; "Survey of Voters on the Rapid Transit Issue [for Fulton and DeKalb Counties]," 1968, Box 45, Mule to Marta Papers, AHS; Stone, *Regime Politics*, 99.

145. Memorandum to Atlanta Region Metropolitan Planning Commission from Glenn E. Bennett, executive director, on "Early Acquisition of Atlanta Transit System by MARTA," 7 August 1969, Box 1, Mule to Marta Papers, AHS; Albert J. Bows Jr., president, Atlanta Chamber of Commerce, to Richard H. Rich, 14 November 1968, Box 50, Mule to Marta Papers, AHS; *Atlanta Journal*, 10 November 1970; Stone, *Regime Politics*, 99.

146. Stone, *Regime Politics*, 97; Maynard Jackson and Leroy Johnson, representatives of the Atlanta Coalition on Current Community Affairs, to members, board of directors, Metropolitan Atlanta Rapid Transit Authority, 1 July 1971, Box 68, Mule to Marta Papers, AHS.

147. Maynard Jackson and Leroy Johnson, representatives of the Atlanta Coalition on Current Community Affairs, to members, board of directors, Metropolitan Atlanta Rapid Transit Authority, 1 July 1971, Box 68, Mule to Marta Papers, AHS.

148. H. L. Stuart to Charles S. Stinson, 4 June 1971; "Minutes of Meeting of MARTA Directors with the Atlanta Coalition on Current Community Affairs," 2 July 1971, both in Box 116, Mule to Marta Papers, AHS; Roy Blount, chairman, MARTA, to Atlanta Coalition on Current Community Affairs, Coalition of Civic Organizations, Citizens'

Transportation Advisory Committee of the Atlanta Area Transportation Study, Citizens for Sensible Rapid Transit, 22 July 1971, Box 50, Mule to Marta Papers, AHS; Stone, *Regime Politics*, 100.

149. Stone, *Regime Politics*, 100; MARTA vote in Atlanta, 9 November 1971, Bacote Papers, AUC. See also *Atlanta Daily World*, 14 November 1971.

150. Roy Blount to editor, *Atlanta Constitution*, 4 May 1972, Box 116, Mule to Marta Papers, AHS; *Atlanta Journal and Constitution*, 27 July, 9 August 1986, 29 September 1988; author's interview with Johnson; Stone, *Regime Politics*, 168; *Atlanta Constitution*, 23 September 1986, 12 May, 25 September 1992, 19 January 1993.

151. *Atlanta Constitution*, 24 April, 27 July 1986, 9 December 1988.

Chapter Six

1. W. F. Slaton, Superintendent, "Twenty-Ninth Annual Report of the Board of Education for the Year Ending December 31, 1900," APSA. See also "Organization of Atlanta Public Schools, 1908–1909," APSA.

2. Baker, *Following the Color Line*, 54; Dittmer, *Black Georgia in the Progressive Era*, 146–47.

3. Matthews, "Studies in Race Relations in Georgia," 288, 292; "Thirtieth Report of the Board of Education, January 1901 to June 30, 1903," APSA; *Atlanta Constitution*, 24 November 1906.

4. Kuhn, Joye, and West, *Living Atlanta*, 131.

5. Matthews, "Studies in Race Relations in Georgia," 303–4; Du Bois, "The Negro Artisan," 34, 47, 56, 76; Collins, "Origin of Public Secondary Education," 18–20; Dittmer, *Black Georgia in the Progressive Era*, 63–64; Rouse, *Lugenia Burns Hope*, 29, 69; Gatewood, *Aristocrats of Color*, 290.

6. Mrs. L. B. Hope, chairman, Women's Social Improvement Committee, to editor, *Atlanta Constitution*, 3 December 1913, Box 1, 14-B-11 and -12 and -13, NU, AUC; "Plan for the Improvement of the Schools, November 22, 1913—majority report of committee appointed to submit a plan for the improvement of the city's public schools," APSA; John Hope to Chapin Brinsmade, 11 December 1913, 2-L, Box 14, Addendum, NAACP, LC; Shivery, "Neighborhood Union," 152–53.

7. Neighborhood Union, Women's Social Improvement Committee, petition to Atlanta Board of Education, 19 August 1913, Box 1, 14-B-11 and -12 and -13, NU, AUC; "Plan for the Improvement of the Schools, November 22, 1913," APSA. See also "Thirty-First Report of the Board of Education, Atlanta, Georgia, January 1912," APSA; report of Hon. R. J. Guinn, president, Atlanta Board of Education, 29 December 1914, Box 4, Chambers Papers, AHS; Turner-Jones, "Political Analysis of Black Educational History," 114–16.

8. Walter White (secretary, Atlanta Branch, NAACP) to Roy Nash (secretary, NAACP), 3 March 1917, 1-G, Box 43, branch files, NAACP, LC; Turner-Jones, "Political Analysis of Black Educational History," 147–48; Collins, "Origin of Public Secondary Education," 23; Newman, "History of the Atlanta Public School Teachers' Association," 46–47.

9. Letter from Atlanta NAACP to members, 1917; Walter White to James W. John-

son (field secretary, NAACP), 27 September 1917, both in 1-G, Box 43, branch files, NAACP, LC; Walter White, *Man Called White*, 32–33; Collins, "Origin of Public Secondary Education," 23–27.

10. Dittmer, *Black Georgia in the Progressive Era*, 147–48, 206; West, "Black Atlanta," 12–17; Collins, "Origin of Public Secondary Education," 30, 35–36; Galishoff, "Germs Know No Color Line," 38; Newman, "History of the Atlanta Public School Teachers' Association," 47–48; Davis quote from Turner-Jones, "Political Analysis of Black Educational History," 154; T. K. Gibson, open letter, 26 February 1919, 1-G, Box 43, branch files, NAACP, LC; Sudheendran, "Community Power Structure in Atlanta," 209–12, 214–15, 219–20, 226, 228, 232.

11. Atlanta branch, NAACP, open letter to Atlanta city officials and to city, 3 April 1919, 1-G, Box 43, branch files, NAACP, LC.

12. *Atlanta Constitution*, 8, 9 March 1919; "Press Release of NAACP," 11 January 1924, 1-G, Box 43, branch files, NAACP, LC; Newman, "History of the Atlanta Public School Teachers' Association," 49–50; West, "Black Atlanta," 18–20; Collins, "Origin of Public Secondary Education," 39–40.

13. Racine, "Atlanta's Schools," 185–86; Henry Reid Hunter, "Development of the Public Secondary Schools," 51; West, "Black Atlanta," 22–24; Newman, "History of the Atlanta Public School Teachers' Association," 62–63; Collins, "Origin of Public Secondary Education," 41–43; Turner-Jones, "Political Analysis of Black Educational History," 163–64.

14. This study was done under the auspices of the Division of Field Studies, Teachers College, Columbia University. Strayer was director and Engelhardt assistant director. "Report of the Survey of the Public School System of Atlanta, Georgia (school year 1921–22), made by Division of Field Studies, Institute of Educational Research, Teachers College, Columbia University," George Strayer and N. L. Engelhardt, vols. 1 and 2, pp. 58, 127, 130, 142, 144, 158, 247, in APSA; "Press Release of NAACP," 11 January 1924, 1-G, Box 43, branch files, NAACP, LC; Newman, "History of the Atlanta Public School Teachers' Association," 64; Turner-Jones, "Political Analysis of Black Educational History," 171; Collins, "Origin of Public Secondary Education," 44.

15. To relieve some of the overcrowding at Washington, David T. Howard Elementary School was switched to a combined elementary–junior high school in 1929, and in 1946 it became the city's second black high school. Only two black high schools existed until 1951. Henry Reid Hunter, "Development of the Public Secondary Schools," 54–56; interview with Flossie Jones, Living Atlanta Collection, AHS; "Report of the Superintendent, Atlanta Public Schools, Atlanta, Georgia, 1934–1935," APSA.

16. Interviews with Flossie Jones, E. T. Lewis, and Estelle Clemmons, Living Atlanta Collection, AHS.

17. Interview with E. T. Lewis, Living Atlanta Collection, AHS.

18. Collins, "Origin of Public Secondary Education," 61–63; Kuhn, Joye, and West, *Living Atlanta*, 324.

19. Turner-Jones, "Political Analysis of Black Educational History," 176–81; petition filed before Board of Education, *Atlanta Independent*, 11 August 1927.

20. Half of the black night schools had already been closed in 1927 to provide extra funds for white schoolchildren. Turner-Jones, "Political Analysis of Black Educational

History," 181–83, 187–92; *Atlanta Daily World*, 11, 13 April 1932; Atlanta Committee on Women's Interracial Activities, 23 April 1931, Box 146, CIC, AUC; Newman, "History of the Atlanta Public School Teachers' Association," 158–59; "Report of the Superintendent, Atlanta Public Schools, Atlanta, Georgia 1934–1935," APSA; W. E. B. Du Bois to Arthur Raper, 1 March 1937, Reel 48, Du Bois Papers (microfilm), AUC; Smith, *New Deal in the Urban South*, 236.

21. "Report of the Superintendent, Atlanta Public Schools, Atlanta, Georgia, 1934–1935," APSA; "Report of the Superintendent, Atlanta Public Schools, Atlanta, Georgia, 1935–1936," APSA; Willis A. Sutton to W. E. B. Du Bois, Reel 35, Du Bois Papers (microfilm), AUC; "Georgia Program for the Improvement of Instruction," State Department of Education Bulletin, May 1937, Box 121, CIC, AUC.

22. National Municipal League Consultant Service, "Governments of Atlanta and Fulton County, Georgia," 5 February 1938, 1:90, 2:333.

23. Ibid., 2:335–36, 340; minutes of the Negro Anti-Tuberculosis Association, 17 October 1916, Box 3, Atlanta Lung Association Collection, AHS.

24. "DOES ATLANTA Know and Approve These Conditions?," pamphlet by Atlanta Civic and Political League, 2 August 1938, 4-D-27, NUL, LC; Turner-Jones, "Political Analysis of Black Educational History," 193.

25. *Georgia Observer*, Box 12, CIC, AUC; Gate City Teachers' Association to Willis A. Sutton, 1 April 1940, Box 155, CIC, AUC; *Atlanta Daily World*, 14 August 1940; Turner-Jones, "Political Analysis of Black Educational History," 194.

26. "Making Americans: Superintendent's Annual Report to the Board of Education, Atlanta Public Schools, 1944–1945," APSA; "A Report of Public School Facilities for Negroes in Atlanta, Georgia," Atlanta Urban League, 1944, Hamilton Papers, AUC; "The Negro School Child in Atlanta," Citizens Committee on Public Education, APSA.

27. "A Report of Public School Facilities for Negroes in Atlanta, Georgia," Atlanta Urban League, 1944, Hamilton Papers, AUC.

28. Ibid. See also *Atlanta Daily World*, 8 December 1944; Anderson, *Education of Blacks in the South*, 198, 200–201, 203–4.

29. "A Report of Public School Facilities for Negroes in Atlanta, Georgia," Atlanta Urban League, 1944, Hamilton Papers, AUC.

30. Press release, Atlanta Board of Education, 30 January 1945, 2-B, Box 137, legal file, NAACP, LC.

31. *Atlanta Journal*, 14 December 1944, 13 December 1945; "Developments since June 1945," 15 October 1945, 2-B, Box 137, legal file, NAACP, LC.

32. "Making Americans, Superintendent's Annual Report to the Board of Education, Atlanta Public Schools, Atlanta, Georgia, 1945–46," APSA.

33. "Report from the Atlanta Citizens Committee on Public Education," Hamilton Papers, AUC; The Citizens Committee on Public Education, E. M. Martin, chairman, to Atlanta Board of Education, 13 March 1945, 2-B, Box 137, legal file, NAACP, LC; *Atlanta Daily World*, 4 September 1946. See also "Is There a 'Ceiling' in Education," pamphlet by the Citizens Committee on Public Education, Box 18, Rainey Papers, EUSC; Atlanta Urban League Annual Report, 1946.

34. Grace Towns Hamilton to Thurgood Marshall, 17 October 1945, 2-B, Box 137, legal file, NAACP, LC.

35. Ibid., 30 October 1945; *Atlanta Journal*, 13 December 1945; petition to Ira Jarrell, superintendent of Atlanta schools, and board of education, 11 December 1945, 2-B, Box 137, legal file, NAACP, LC.

36. Petition to Ira Jarrell, superintendent of Atlanta schools, and board of education, 11 December 1945, 2-B, Box 137, legal file, NAACP, LC; *Atlanta Daily World*, 16 December 1945.

37. "A Summary of the Work of the Citizens Committee on Public Education Organized by the Atlanta Urban League, 1944 to 1946," Hamilton Papers, AUC; "Notes on the Atlanta and Fulton County Bond Election, held 14 August 1946," SRC, AUC.

38. "A Supplemental Report on Public School Facilities for Negroes, Atlanta, Georgia, 1948," Atlanta Urban League, Hamilton Papers, AUC; "Progress Report—Negro Schools, 1944–1948, Atlanta Public Schools," Box 54, McGill Papers, EUSC; "A Report of Atlanta Public School Building Program Financed by 1946 Bond Issue," Atlanta Urban League, 15 August 1949, and "Correction," 19 August 1949, A-104, NUL-SRO, LC; "Authorized Construction Costs of Atlanta School Plant Development" (projects planned in bond program 1946), 30 November 1948, Hamilton Papers, AUC; "A Report to the People, Superintendent's Annual Report to the Board of Education, Atlanta Public Schools, Atlanta, Georgia, 1948–49," APSA; Atlanta Urban League to Nelson C. Jackson, 3 February 1950, A-115, NUL-SRO, LC; Mullis, "Public Career of Grace Towns Hamilton," 117.

39. "A Report of Atlanta Public School Building Program Financed by 1946 Bond Issue," Atlanta Urban League, 15 August 1949, A-104, NUL-SRO, LC; "A Supplemental Report on Public School Facilities for Negroes, Atlanta, Georgia 1948," Atlanta Urban League, Hamilton Papers, AUC; Atlanta Urban League Report on Atlanta Educational System, 1948, Walden Papers, AHS; petition to Ira Jarrell, superintendent, and Atlanta Board of Education, 8 April 1949, SRC, AUC.

40. Petition to Ira Jarrell, superintendent, and Atlanta Board of Education, 14 September 1948, Hamilton Papers, AUC; petition to Ira Jarrell, superintendent, and Atlanta Board of Education, 8 April 1949, SRC, AUC; Atlanta Parents Council for Better Public Schools to the Superintendent and Board of Education of Atlanta, Georgia, 3 December 1948, A-92, NUL-SRO, LC.

41. Atlanta Parents Council for Better Public Schools to Superintendent and Board of Education of Atlanta, Georgia, 3 December 1948; Citizens Committee for Educational Opportunity, 1 February 1949, Hamilton Papers, AUC; "Answer to Petition Submitted to Miss Ira Jarrell, Superintendent and the Atlanta Board of Education at the Regular Board Meeting, September 14, 1948," 16 October 1948, Hamilton Papers, AUC; "Facts, Progress, Educational and Plant Facilities of the Negro Schools in the City of Atlanta by Superintendent of Schools and Atlanta Board of Education," 1948–49, APSA.

42. Benjamin E. Mays to editor, *Atlanta Daily World*, 1950; *Atlanta Journal*, 19 September 1950; *Atlanta Constitution*, 20, 23 September 1950. See also *Atlanta Daily World*, 20 September 1950.

43. *Atlanta Journal-Constitution*, 24 September 1950; *Atlanta Constitution*, 20 September 1950. See also *Atlanta Journal*, 20 September 1950.

44. *Atlanta Constitution*, 14 May 1953; William Hartsfield to NAACP convention, 1951, Box 34, Hartsfield Papers, EUSC.

Chapter Seven

1. *Atlanta Constitution*, 18 May 1954. See also *Atlanta Journal*, 15 November 1958, on Hartsfield and the Supreme Court decision.

2. Huie, "Factors Influencing the Desegregation Process," 25–28, 62, 75–78; *Atlanta Constitution*, 4 June 1955; Atlanta branch NAACP to Atlanta Board of Education and Ira Jarrell, attached to Board of Education minutes from 14 November 1955, exhibit D, Desegregation Folder, 1955–1959, APSA; Atlanta Council on Human Relations, Report of Council Activities, 1958–59, by Whitney M. Young Jr., executive secretary, 30 June 1959, SRC, AUC.

3. Huie, "Factors Influencing the Desegregation Process," 18–19; "In the United States District Court for the Northern District of Georgia, Atlanta Division, *Emma Armour, et al. Plaintiffs v. Jack P. Nix, et al. Defendants*—Civil Action File No. 16708, Plaintiffs Proposed Findings of Fact," 7 November 1977, APSA (p. 118 lists black schools built in 1957–62 period); *Atlanta Constitution*, 6, 13 August 1957; "Proposed School Construction Program for the Atlanta Board of Education, July 1956," APSA.

4. Author's interview with Tate. Tate is a black leader who was on the school board from 1965 to 1969 and was executive secretary of the black Georgia Teachers and Education Association from 1961 to 1970. This group merged with the white Georgia Education Association in 1970. Tate later became executive secretary of the merged organization.

5. Huie, "Factors Influencing the Desegregation Process," 104–5; author's interview with Pauley; *New York Times* article reprinted in *Atlanta Constitution*, 13 March 1956. Pauley was executive director of the Georgia Council on Human Relations.

6. Author's interviews with Tate and Coleman; *Atlanta Constitution*, 16 June 1967; *Atlanta Journal-Constitution*, 28 January 1973.

7. *Atlanta Journal-Constitution*, 18 August 1957; *Atlanta Daily World*, 14 August 1957; McGrath, "Great Expectations," 81–82, 167–69.

8. The name of this suit was later changed to *Calhoun v. Cook*. Latimer was president of the Atlanta Board of Education. Statement of Donald L. Hollowell at symposium titled "Memory, History, Media: The Desegregation of Atlanta," 11 October 1986, at MLKC. See The Center for Contemporary Media tapes. Hollowell was the chief counsel for the plaintiffs in the desegregation case.

9. Huie, "Factors Influencing the Desegregation Process," 39–47, 78–85. The text of the board plan appears in Huie's appendix.

10. Ibid., 75, 105–23; "The Economic Effect of School Closing," speech by Jim Montgomery, business editor, *Atlanta Constitution*, 19 January 1959, SRC, AUC; letter to Georgia legislators from HOPE, 21 January 1960, SRC, AUC; *Atlanta Constitution*, 15 November 1958; *Atlanta Journal*, 15 January 1959; Annual Report, Southeast Region, NAACP, 1958, SRC, AUC; Bartley, *Rise of Massive Resistance*, 332–33; *Atlanta Journal-Constitution*, 6 August 1977.

11. Author's interview with Letson. For confirmation of Letson's statement regarding

the reason for top-down desegregation, see Greater Atlanta Council on Human Relations, Report of the Council Committee on School Desegregation, 1962, SRC, AUC. See also *Fred S. Calhoun, et al., petitioners, v. A. C. Latimer, et al.*, no. 623, in the Supreme Court of the United States, October Term, 1963, Brief for the United States as amicus curiae, March 1964, pp. 23–24, APSA.

12. Author's interviews with Letson and Tate.

13. Greater Atlanta Council on Human Relations, Report of the Council Committee on School Desegregation, 1962, Box 2, Series 1, Paschall Papers, EUSC; *Calhoun v. Latimer*, "Plaintiffs' Proposed Findings of Fact and Conditions of Law," 1961, APSA.

14. *Atlanta Constitution*, 1961 clippings. See also *Atlanta Constitution*, 19 May 1961. Four of the nine black students lived nearer to the white school than to the black school they had attended (Greater Atlanta Council on Human Relations, Report of the Council Committee on School Desegregation, 1962, SRC, AUC).

15. "Reports on Atlanta School Desegregation, Recommendations by Amos O. Holmes, Georgia Field Secretary, NAACP, May 19, 1961," Williams Collection, AUC.

16. *Atlanta Inquirer*, 28 October 1961; author's interview with Letson.

17. *Atlanta Inquirer*, 5 May 1962.

18. Maslow and Cohen, "School Segregation, Northern Style," 6–7.

19. Greater Atlanta Council on Human Relations, Report of the Council Committee on School Desegregation, 1962, SRC, AUC.

20. *Calhoun v. Latimer*, no. 623, 8–10, APSA; Huie, "Factors Influencing the Desegregation Process," 49–50; Research Atlanta, "School Desegregation in Metro Atlanta, 1954–1973," 1973, p. 14; National Education Association Commission on Professional Rights and Responsibilities, "Central Issues Influencing School-Community Relations in Atlanta, Georgia: A Special Study," 1969, APSA.

21. Huie, "Factors Influencing the Desegregation Process," 49, 86–87; *Calhoun v. Latimer*, no. 623, 13, APSA; "Central Issues."

22. Greater Atlanta Council on Human Relations, April 1962 newsletter, Box 13, SNCC, MLKC. See also "Special Report—Enrollment—Capacity of Public Schools in C Areas—Atlanta," 1960, SRC, AUC.

23. *Atlanta Daily World*, 26 January, 11, 13 February 1962; C. Clayton Powell, Atlanta Negro Voters League, Atlanta Board of Education Minutes, 12 February 1962, APSA.

24. Greater Atlanta Council on Human Relations, April 1962 newsletter, Box 13, SNCC, MLKC; *Atlanta Journal*, 13 February 1962; Greater Atlanta Council on Human Relations, Report of the Council Committee on School Desegregation, Box 10, Series 1, Paschall Papers, EUSC.

25. *Atlanta Inquirer*, 17 February 1962. See also *Atlanta Daily World*, 11 July 1962; *Atlanta Inquirer*, 2 February 1963.

26. List of Southern Cities and Desegregation (list includes Charlotte, Chattanooga, Dallas, Greensboro, Houston, Knoxville, Memphis, Nashville, New Orleans, Norfolk, Richmond, and Atlanta), Box 117, Series 4, Paschall Papers, EUSC.

27. *Atlanta Inquirer*, 2 February 1963.

28. "Report—Atlanta Public School System," 1963, Box 10, James Forman Files, SNCC, MLKC.

29. The Atlanta Committee for Cooperative Action, "A Second Look: The Negro

Citizen in Atlanta," January 1960, SRC, AUC; *Atlanta Daily World*, 9 March 1960; "Action for Democracy," 1 November 1963, Box 139, SCLC, MLKC.

30. "The City Must Provide, South Atlanta: The Forgotten Community," 1963, Box 95, SNCC, MLKC; Research Atlanta, "School Desegregation," 15–16. See also "Report from South East Atlanta, from Debbie Amis, October 1963 to SNCC," Box 95, SNCC, MLKC. See Chapter 5 for more information on SNCC and South Atlanta.

31. Huie, "Factors Influencing the Desegregation Process," 53–54, 86–88; "Central Issues." See also *Atlanta Constitution*, 13 July 1965.

32. Huie, "Factors Influencing the Desegregation Process," 53–55, 88–89; *Atlanta Journal*, 28 April 1964.

33. Huie, "Factors Influencing the Desegregation Process," 55–61, 90–92; "Central Issues"; Research Atlanta, "School Desegregation," 5; *Atlanta Journal*, 16 February 1965; *Atlanta Constitution*, 17 February 1965; *Atlanta Daily World*, 17 February, 2 April 1965. See also *Atlanta Constitution*, 20 April 1965; Atlanta Board of Education minutes, 29 July 1965, APSA.

34. The state board of education and local school boards had to affirm compliance with the Civil Rights Act of 1964 in order to secure federal funds. The state board voted to eliminate segregation as a school policy in Georgia in 1965. *Atlanta Constitution*, 21 January 1965; "'Where the Pavement Ends': A Study of Planned School Integration in Five Negro Neighborhoods in Atlanta, Georgia, July 1965," a study by Atlanta University School of Social Work in cooperation with Georgia Council on Human Relations, Northside Atlanta Chapter, GCHR, AUC; *Atlanta Constitution*, 7 July 1965; Huie, "Factors Influencing the Desegregation Process," 92. See also Georgia Council on Human Relations, statement to Georgia Board of Education—from Compliance to Cooperation, 20 January 1965, SRC, AUC.

35. *Atlanta Journal*, 13 April, 6 July 1965; *Atlanta Inquirer*, 10 July 1965; *Atlanta Daily World*, 17, 18 April, 8 July 1965; *Atlanta Constitution*, 7, 8 July 1965; Board of Education, minutes of special meeting, 6 July 1965, APSA. See also Stone, *Economic Growth and Neighborhood Discontent*, 102–6.

36. *Atlanta Inquirer*, 5 September, 9, 17 October 1964.

37. Author's interview with Letson; annual meeting of the Council on Human Relations of Greater Atlanta, 30 November 1964, GCHR, AUC; "Civil Liberties" (newsletter of ACLU of Georgia), March 1970, SRC, AUC; *Atlanta Daily World*, 26 January 1965.

38. *Atlanta Daily World*, 26 January, 16 February, 19 September 1965; *Atlanta Constitution*, 26 January, 15, 16 February 1965; *Atlanta Inquirer*, 30 January, 1 February 1965; "Racial Isolation in the Public Schools—A Report of the U.S. Commission on Civil Rights, 1967," vol. 1, p. 66, APSA.

39. *Atlanta Journal*, 1 September 1964; *Atlanta Inquirer*, 13 June, 11 July, 5 September 1964; flyer and 1964 petition by "Negro parents in Atlanta," Box 13, Series 4, Paschall Papers, EUSC.

40. *Atlanta Inquirer*, 26 September 1964.

41. *Atlanta Daily World*, 15 September 1965; *Atlanta Inquirer*, 4 September 1965; Parents of C. L. Harper High School Students to Atlanta Board of Education, 4 August 1966, CRC, Williams Collection, AUC.

42. *Atlanta Inquirer,* 16 May 1964.

43. Ibid., 25 September 1965; *Atlanta Daily World,* 16 February, 9 March 1965; *Atlanta Journal,* 16 February 1965.

44. *Atlanta Daily World,* 9 March, 15 September 1965.

45. Author's interview with Clayton; *Weekly Star* (newspaper of southwest area), 6 April 1967; Mrs. Eliza K. Paschall to Mrs. Frances Pauley, executive director of Georgia Council on Human Relations, 5 July 1967, GCHR, AUC; "Racial Composition of Schools, 1958–1972," APSA.

46. Author's interview with Clayton; Eliza K. Paschall to members of Community Relations Commission executive committee, 9 June 1967, CRC, Williams Collection, AUC.

47. *Atlanta Journal,* 29 March 1969, 1 December 1970; author's interviews with Clayton and Letson; "Policy on Support of Integrated Schools," 1971, APSA; "Racial Composition of Schools, 1958–1972," APSA; *Atlanta Daily World,* 1 February 1970; Stone, *Economic Growth and Neighborhood Discontent,* 144–45.

48. *Atlanta Inquirer,* 30 July, 5 September 1966, 28 January 1967; *Atlanta Constitution,* 3, 4 October 1967; *Atlanta Journal,* 26 September, 3 October 1967; "Racial Isolation in the Public Schools," 63–64; "Central Issues," 19; "*Armour v. Nix,* Findings of Fact," 3; CRC, "Report of Racial Distribution in Atlanta Schools, 1966, 1967, 1968," CRC, Williams Collection, AUC.

49. *Atlanta Journal,* 3 October 1967. See also *Atlanta Constitution,* 4 October 1967.

50. *Atlanta Journal,* 26 September 1967; minutes of Atlanta Board of Education meeting, 9 October 1967, APSA; author's interview with Letson. On school administrators' defense of double sessions as beneficial, see also "Central Issues."

51. "Racial Isolation in the Public Schools," 63–64, 66–69; "*Armour v. Nix,* Findings of Fact," 19; *Calhoun v. Latimer,* 35–37, APSA. See also *Atlanta Inquirer,* 22 May 1965, 30 July 1966.

52. "Proposals by a Coalition of Major Atlanta Negro Organizations," CRC, Williams Collection, AUC; *Atlanta Daily World,* 22 September 1967; minutes of Atlanta Board of Education, special meeting, 25 September 1967, APSA; *Atlanta Constitution,* 25, 26 September, 3 October 1967; *Atlanta Journal,* 26 September 1967; "Central Issues," 23–24.

53. Better Schools Atlanta, "Student Achievement in Atlanta Public Schools," 1968, APSA; "Central Issues," 24. See also *Atlanta Daily World,* 19 October 1968.

54. "Central Issues," 8; Board of Education response to Better Schools Atlanta report, 1968, APSA; *Atlanta Constitution,* 5 September 1969.

55. "Central Issues," 12–13, 19, 25–26, 31–32, 36, 49–50; *Atlanta Constitution,* 6 September 1969.

56. "Central Issues," 34.

57. Ibid., 35; "Policies, Accomplishments, Purposes and Intention in Eliminating the Dual School System in Atlanta—A Statement by the Atlanta Board of Education," minutes of Atlanta Board of Education meeting, 11 August 1969, APSA.

58. *Atlanta Constitution,* 7 July 1969; author's interviews with Tate and Pauley; *Atlanta Constitution,* 6 September 1969. See also *Atlanta Journal,* 25 January 1973, on Lonnie King's views.

59. "Central Issues," 36–37; "A Report to the People," 1968, CRC, Williams Collection, AUC; *Atlanta Journal*, 16 February 1965.

60. "District Reorganization for Better Schools in Atlanta and Fulton County," Report of the Local Education Commission of Atlanta and Fulton County, Georgia, January 1968, APSA; memo from Superintendent Letson to all school personnel, 6 January 1970, APSA; Fleishman, "Real against the Ideal," 137; "Desegregation—Dr. Crim's Notebook, December 1973," APSA; author's interview with Letson; *Atlanta Constitution*, 16 December 1969; *Atlanta Journal*, 25 July 1975; author's interviews with Tate and Holmes. Holmes is a black teacher who started in Atlanta's schools in 1950 and later became the first black coordinator for the Georgia Department of Education.

61. As soon as a school shifted by even one student from majority white to majority black, other black students could not transfer there anymore. Research Atlanta, "School Desegregation," 6–8, 19–20; Good Government Atlanta, *On Issues Affecting the Atlanta Public Schools*, APSA; *Atlanta Daily World*, 3 February 1970; minutes from informal board of education meeting, 9 January 1970, APSA; *Atlanta Constitution*, 1 October 1987. See also Taeuber, "Residential Segregation in the Atlanta Metropolitan Area," 161–62; Orfield and Ashkinaze, *Closing Door*, 50–51.

62. Good Government Atlanta, *On Issues Affecting the Atlanta Public Schools*, APSA; Research Atlanta, "School Desegregation," 8–9.

63. Court order in *Vivian Calhoun, et al., v. Ed. S. Cook, et al.*, Bacote Papers, AUC; *Atlanta Journal*, 7, 10, 18 October 1972; *Atlanta Constitution*, 10, 13, October 1972; U.S. District Court, Northern District of Georgia, Atlanta Division, *Vivian Calhoun, et al. v. Ed. S. Cook, et al.*, 28 July 1971, APSA.

64. The ACLU case was *Emma Armour, et al., v. Jack P. Nix, et al.*; League of Women Voters of Atlanta and Fulton County, "Consolidation of the Atlanta and Fulton County School Districts," 1971, Bacote Papers, AUC; *Atlanta Inquirer*, 23 September 1972; Research Atlanta, "School Desegregation," 9, 21.

65. *Atlanta Constitution*, 18, 26 October 1972; *Atlanta Journal*, 31 October 1972.

66. The *Armour v. Nix* case was finally settled in 1980 when the Supreme Court ruled against the ACLU and metro desegregation. *Atlanta Constitution*, 11 April, 2 December 1972; *Atlanta Journal*, 11 April, 13 October 1972, 21 July 1975.

67. Fleishman, "Real against the Ideal"; *Atlanta Journal*, 31 October 1972.

68. Interview with Lonnie King by Jed Dannenbaum, 12 October 1986, The Center for Contemporary Media (I participated in this interview and was allowed to submit questions to King); Southern Center for Studies in Public Policy, "Consensus Politics in Atlanta," 101; *New York Times*, 25 April 1973.

69. "Plan of Proposed Settlement as Devised and Agreed upon between Plaintiffs and Defendants," in *Calhoun v. Cook*, February 1973, APSA; "Desegregation—Dr. Crim's Notebook," December 1973, APSA; Fleishman, "Real against the Ideal," 143; McGrath, "Great Expectations," 345–46.

70. Some exceptions to the 30 percent rule were made in cases where schools were racially stable and had a black student population of 20 percent or higher. "Proposed Voluntary Transfer Program for 1974–75 School Year Submitted by Community Affairs Division," 21 June 1974, APSA; "Desegregation—Dr. Crim's Notebook," APSA;

Atlanta Board of Education, minutes of special meeting, 27 March 1973, APSA; "Plan of Proposed Settlement As Devised," February 1973, APSA; "Majority to Minority News—Atlanta Public Schools," May 1974, APSA; "The Majority to Minority Transfer Plan of the Atlanta Public Schools" (booklet), APSA.

71. *Atlanta Inquirer*, 23 September 1972.

72. *New York Times*, 25 April 1973; Fleishman, "Real against the Ideal," 144, 163–66; *Atlanta Journal-Constitution*, 28 January 1973; *Atlanta Constitution*, 25 October 1973.

73. *Atlanta Journal-Constitution*, 28 January 1973; "Report on the Forums Concerning the Federal Role in School Finance, March 1973," APSA; *Atlanta Voice*, 10 November 1973; *New York Times*, 25 April 1973; author's interview with Crim.

74. *New York Times*, 25 April 1973; Fleishman, "Real against the Ideal," 170; *Atlanta Voice*, 10 November 1973.

75. *Atlanta Journal-Constitution*, 28 January 1973; *Atlanta Constitution*, 22 July 1987; Orfield and Ashkinaze, *Closing Door*, 111.

76. *Atlanta Journal-Constitution*, 28 January 1973; Orfield and Ashkinaze, *Closing Door*, 110–11, 113–16, 121, 124–27. For information on school segregation-resegregation patterns in the suburbs, see *Atlanta Constitution*, 18 June 1983, 1 October 1987, 13, 24 October, 5 December 1989, 6 August 1990, 25 February, 8 October 1991, 1 April 1992; *Atlanta Journal-Constitution*, 6 October 1991.

Chapter Eight

1. *Atlanta Constitution*, 6 July 1988.

2. *Atlanta Journal-Constitution*, 17 March, 11 August 1991, 27 December 1992, 7 March 1993; *Atlanta Constitution*, 29 September 1988, 25, 30 October, 13 December 1990, 19 March, 13 April 1991, 14 August 1992, 15 February, 7 June, 16 October 1993; *New York Times*, 7 April 1991.

3. Hirsch, *Making the Second Ghetto*, 9–10, 36, 133, 136, 153, 168, 225, 254, 274.

4. Kaplan, *Urban Renewal Politics*, 89, 157–58, 187.

5. Rabin, "Roots of Segregation in the Eighties," 216–17; Silver, *Twentieth-Century Richmond*, 13; Trotter, *Black Milwaukee*, 71.

6. Mohl, "Race and Space in the Modern City," 26–27, 30, 32–33, 35–36.

7. Ibid., 38–40; Flowerdew, "Spatial Patterns of Residential Segregation," 106; Silver, *Twentieth-Century Richmond*, 287; Rabin, "Roots of Segregation in the Eighties," 215–16.

8. Rabin, "Roots of Segregation in the Eighties," 211–13, 218, 222–23.

9. Peterson, *Politics of School Reform*, 111–15; Chafe, *Civilities and Civil Rights*, 222–23, 234–35; Formisano, *Boston against Busing*, 29, 36–37, 40; Pratt, *Color of Their Skin*, 15–16; Bullock, *History of Negro Education in the South*, 178–83, 242–44, 246, 248.

10. For other factors as to why, for example, streets were not paved in black areas (one reason provided was the white perception that blacks did not pay their fair share of taxes and therefore did not deserve services), see James W. Button's study of six Florida communities: *Blacks and Social Change*, 152–54. This issue did not appear to play a role in Atlanta.

11. Lewis, *In Their Own Interests*, 80, 83; Silver, *Twentieth-Century Richmond*, 33, 108–9, 125–27; Platt, *City Building in the New South*, 200–201, 203; Trotter, *Black*

Milwaukee, 180, 200–201, 212–13, 235–36; Connolly, *A Ghetto Grows in Brooklyn*, 115–16; Doyle, *New Men, New Cities, New South*, 283, 285–86; McBride, *Integrating the City of Medicine*, 20, 32, 64, 74, 83–84, 99, 117, 119–21, 137–41, 181–82, 194–95; Sugrue, "Structures of Urban Poverty," 99, 106–11, 113–14; Kusmer, *A Ghetto Takes Shape*, 58, 60–61, 66–68, 76, 79, 176–78, 180–84, 266–68; Button, *Blacks and Social Change*, 85–87, 89–91, 93–95, 117, 124–25, 152–54, 156, 160, 162–63. This situation has been observed in other cities as well, including Shreveport, Louisiana; Las Vegas, Nevada; and Kansas City, Missouri. Rabin, "Roots of Segregation in the Eighties," 219–21, 224; Chafe, *Civilities and Civil Rights*, 349.

Bibliography

Manuscripts and Archival Collections

Alexander, Cecil. Papers. Privately held.

Atlanta Bureau of Planning. Papers. Atlanta Historical Society, Atlanta.

Atlanta Lung Association Collection. Atlanta Historical Society, Atlanta.

Atlanta Public School Archives. Atlanta.

Atlanta Transit Authority Collection. Atlanta Historical Society, Atlanta.

Bacote, Clarence. Papers. Atlanta University Center, Robert W. Woodruff Library, Atlanta.

Bullard, Helen. Papers. Atlanta Historical Society and Emory University, Special Collections Department, Robert W. Woodruff Library, Atlanta.

Central Atlanta Progress. Papers. Atlanta Historical Society, Atlanta.

Chambers, Aldine. Papers. Atlanta Historical Society, Atlanta.

City of Atlanta. Records. Atlanta Historical Society, Atlanta.

Commission on Interracial Cooperation. Papers. Atlanta University Center, Robert W. Woodruff Library, Atlanta.

Dobbs, John Wesley. Papers. Amistad Research Center, Tulane University, New Orleans.

Du Bois, W. E. B. Papers (microfilm edition). Atlanta University Center, Robert W. Woodruff Library, Atlanta.

Georgia Council on Human Relations. Papers. Atlanta University Center, Robert W. Woodruff Library, Atlanta.

Grady Memorial Hospital Collection. Atlanta Historical Society, Atlanta.

Hamilton, Grace Towns. Papers. Used at Atlanta University Center, now at Atlanta Historical Society.

Hartsfield, William B. Papers. Emory University, Special Collections Department, Robert W. Woodruff Library, Atlanta.

Henderson, Jacob. Voter Registration Collection. Atlanta-Fulton Public Library.

Hope, John, and Lugenia Burns Hope. Papers. Atlanta University Center, Robert W. Woodruff Library, Atlanta.

Jenkins, Herbert. Papers. Atlanta Historical Society, Atlanta.

King, Martin Luther, Jr. Papers. Martin Luther King, Jr. Center for Non-Violent Social Change, Atlanta.

Long-Rucker-Aiken Family. Papers. Atlanta Historical Society, Atlanta.

McEwen, Homer C. Papers. Amistad Research Center, Tulane University, New Orleans.

McGill, Ralph. Papers. Emory University, Special Collections Department, Robert W. Woodruff Library, Atlanta.

William Matthews Family. Papers. Atlanta-Fulton Public Library.

Mays, Benjamin. Papers. Moorland-Spingarn Research Center, Howard University, Washington, D.C.

Mule to Marta. Papers. Atlanta Historical Society, Atlanta.

NAACP. Papers. Library of Congress, Washington, D.C.

National Urban League. Papers. Library of Congress, Washington, D.C.

Neighborhood Union. Papers. Atlanta University Center, Woodruff Library, Atlanta.

Palmer, Charles. Papers. Emory University, Special Collections Department, Robert W. Woodruff Library, Atlanta.

Paschall, Eliza. Papers. Emory University, Special Collections Department, Robert W. Woodruff Library, Atlanta.

Rainey, Glenn W. Papers. Emory University, Special Collections Department, Robert W. Woodruff Library, Atlanta.

Southern Christian Leadership Conference. Papers. Martin Luther King, Jr. Center for Non-Violent Social Change, Atlanta.

Southern Regional Council. Papers. Atlanta University Center, Robert W. Woodruff Library, Atlanta.

Student Non-Violent Coordinating Committee. Papers. Martin Luther King, Jr. Center for Non-Violent Social Change, Atlanta.

U.S. Bureau of Employment Security. Lawrence A. Oxley Files. RG 183. National Archives, Washington, D.C.

U.S. Department of Housing and Urban Development. Model Cities Reports. RG 207. National Archives, Washington, D.C.

U.S. Federal Home Loan Bank System. Home Owners Loan Corporation. RG 195. National Archives, Washington, D.C.

U.S. Public Housing Administration. RG 196. National Archives, Washington, D.C.

Vertical Files (Atlanta Negro Voters League, Community Relations Commission). Atlanta University Center, Robert W. Woodruff Library, Atlanta.

Walden, A. T. Papers. Atlanta Historical Society, Atlanta.

Samuel W. Williams Collection. Atlanta University Center, Robert W. Woodruff Library, Atlanta, and Williams clipping file, Atlanta-Fulton Public Library.

Young, Whitney. Papers. Rare Book and Manuscript Library, Butler Library, Columbia University, New York.

Interviews by Author

Alexander, Cecil. 17 December 1984.

Allen, Ivan. 29 July 1985.

Bond, Julian. 21 October 1986.

Borders, William Holmes. 18 July 1985.

Calhoun, John H. 7 August 1985.

Clayton, Xernona. 20 February 1986.

Cochrane, Warren. 10 October 1985.

Coleman, Clarence. 6 May 1986.

Crim, Alonzo. 8 July 1987.

Eplan, Leon. 15 October 1985.

Flanagan, Robert B. 3 December 1985.

Gladin, Collier. 15 July 1986.

Hamer, William. 27 July 1987.

Hamilton, Grace Towns. 19 August 1985.

Hollowell, Donald. 17 September 1986.
Holmes, Isabella. 11 July 1986.
Hooks, Henry. 10 November 1987.
Jackson, Maynard. 23 November 1987; 4 January 1988.
Jenkins, Herbert. 15 October 1987.
Johnson, Leroy. 11 February 1986.
Jones, Malcolm. 27 April 1988.
Letson, John. 17 February 1987.
McKinney, James E. "Billy." 20 October 1987.
Maddox, James. 5 November 1987.
Massell, Sam. 26 July 1985.
Milton, L. D. 18 September 1985.
Paschall, Eliza. 6 June 1988.
Pauley, Frances. 6 June 1988.
Scott, C. A. 18 November 1985.
Sweat, Dan. 21 January 1988.
Tate, Horace. 21 July 1987.
Thompson, Robert A. 17 July 1985; 15 August 1986.
Yancey, Asa. 2 October 1987.
Young, Andrew. 13 February 1986.

Other Interviews

The Center for Contemporary Media, Oral History Transcripts and Tapes, Atlanta.
Civil Rights Documentation Project. Moorland-Spingarn Research Center, Howard University, Washington, D.C.
Living Atlanta Collection. Atlanta Historical Society, Atlanta.
Martin Luther King, Jr. Oral History Collection. Martin Luther King, Jr. Center for Non-Violent Social Change, Atlanta.

Documents and Reports

Atlanta Commission on Crime and Juvenile Delinquency. "Opportunity for Urban Excellence." Report, February 1966. Atlanta Historical Society, Atlanta.
Atlanta Department of Budget and Planning. "Community Building: The History of Atlanta University Neighborhoods." Prepared by Mildred Warner. December 1978. Georgia Institute of Technology library, Atlanta.
Atlanta Department of Budget and Planning, Bureau of Planning. *1980 City of Atlanta Comprehensive Development Plan*, vol. 1. August 1979.
Atlanta Housing Council. "Proposed Areas for Expansion of Negro Housing in Atlanta, Georgia." May 1947. In author's possession.
Brimmer, Andrew F., and Ray Marshall. *Public Policy and Promotion of Minority Economic Development, City of Atlanta and Fulton County, Georgia*. Parts 1–8. Prepared for City of Atlanta, Georgia, 29 June 1990. Georgia Institute of Technology library, Atlanta.

Central Area Housing Strategy Study. "Back to the City: Housing Options for Central Atlanta." Full technical report, June 1974.

City of Atlanta. General Council Minutes, Atlanta Historical Society, Atlanta.

City of Atlanta Reports. Atlanta Historical Society, Atlanta.

Community Council of the Atlanta Area, Research Center. "Social Blight and Neighborhood Renewal." Community Improvement Program Study on Social Blight and Social Resources, June 1967.

Du Bois, W. E. B., ed. Atlanta University Publications: "Mortality among Negroes in Cities" (no. 1), 1896; "Social and Physical Condition of Negroes in Cities" (no. 2), 1897; "Some Efforts of American Negroes for Their Own Social Betterment" (no. 3), 1898; "The Negro in Business" (no. 4), 1899; "The Negro Artisan," (no. 7), 1902. Reprint, New York: Octagon Books, 1968.

Economic Opportunity Atlanta, Inc. "Community Action in Atlanta." First Annual Report, 31 December 1965.

Eisenstat, Stuart E., and Barutio, William H. "Andrew Young: The Path to History." Voter Education Project: An Analysis, April 1973.

Georgia Institute of Technology College of Architecture. "Sweet Auburn: A Comprehensive Urban Design Plan for Auburn Avenue, Atlanta, Georgia, prepared for the City of Atlanta, December 1975."

Levi, Margaret Anne. "Conflict and Collusion: Police Collective Bargaining." Technical Report #07-74, Operations Research Center, Cambridge, Mass., September 1974.

H. V. Lochner and Company, and DeLeuw, Cather and Company. *Highway and Transportation Plan for Atlanta, Georgia, 1946*. Prepared for the State Highway Department of Georgia and the Public Roads Administration, Federal Works Agency. Chicago: January 1946.

Maslow, Will, and Cohen, Richard. "School Segregation, Northern Style." Public Affairs pamphlet no. 316, 1961.

Metropolitan Planning Commission. "Up Ahead: A Regional Land Use Plan for Metropolitan Atlanta." 1952.

National Municipal League Consultant Service. "The Governments of Atlanta and Fulton County, Georgia, A Report of a Complete Administrative and Financial Survey of the Several Departments and Activities of the City of Atlanta and Fulton County, February 5, 1938." 2 vols.

National Youth Administration of Georgia. "Occupational Outlook for Georgia Youth," vol. 5: Atlanta, Georgia, part 3: "Occupations for Negroes in Atlanta." July 1939.

Southern Center for Studies in Public Policy. "Consensus Politics in Atlanta: School Board Decision-Making, 1974–1978." Clark College, 1979, and Georgia Legislative Review, 1976.

Spector, Samuel Ira. "Municipal and County Zoning in a Changing Urban Environment." Research paper 53, Bureau of Business and Economic Research, Georgia State University, June 1970.

U.S. Bureau of the Census. *Eighth* (1860); *Ninth* (1870); *Tenth* (1880); *Eleventh* (1890); *Twelfth* (1900); *Thirteenth* (1910); *Fourteenth* (1920); *Fifteenth* (1930); *Six-

teenth (1940); *Seventeenth* (1950); *Eighteenth* (1960); *Nineteenth* (1970); *Twentieth* (1980).

Works Progress Administration of Georgia. "Occupational Characteristics of White Collar and Skilled Workers of Atlanta, Georgia, 1937."

Newspapers and Periodicals

Atlanta Constitution
Atlanta Daily World
Atlanta Inquirer
Atlanta Independent
Atlanta Journal
Atlanta Voice
City Builder (Bulletin of the Atlanta Chamber of Commerce)
New York Times
The Renewer (Newsletter of the Citizens Committee for Urban Renewal)
Clipping File, Samuel W. Williams Collection, Atlanta-Fulton Public Library

Memoirs and Other Accounts by Contemporaries

Alexander, T. M., Sr. *Beyond the Timberline: The Trials and Triumphs of a Black Entrepreneur.* Edgewood, Md.: M. E. Duncan and Co., 1992.

Allen, Ivan, Jr., with Paul Hemphill. *Mayor: Notes on the Sixties.* New York: Simon and Schuster, 1971.

Bond, Julian. *A Time to Speak, a Time to Act: The Movement in Politics.* New York: Simon and Schuster, 1972.

Brown, Charlie. *Charlie Brown Remembers Atlanta: Memoirs of a Public Man as Told to James C. Bryant.* Columbia, S.C.: R. L. Bryan Co., 1982.

Jenkins, Herbert. *Forty Years on the Force, 1932–1972.* Center for Research in Social Change, Emory University. Decatur, Ga.: National Graphics, 1973.

Jenkins, Herbert, in association with James Jenkins. *Presidents, Politics and Policing.* Atlanta: Center for Research in Social Change, Emory University, 1980.

King, Martin Luther, Sr., with Clayton Riley. *Daddy King: An Autobiography.* New York: William Morrow and Company, 1980.

McGill, Ralph. "Atlanta: Some Pros and Cons of Culture in the South, as It Was." *Show* 3, no. 6 (June 1963).

Mays, Benjamin. *Born to Rebel: An Autobiography.* Athens: University of Georgia Press, 1987.

———. "My View." *The Courier*, 7 October 1961.

Paschall, Eliza. *It Must Have Rained.* Atlanta: Center for Research in Social Change, Emory University, 1975.

White, Walter. *A Man Called White.* New York: Viking Press, 1948.

Yancey, Asa, Sr. "Grady Memorial Hospital Centennial, History and Development 1892–1992." *Journal of the Medical Association of Georgia* (November 1992): 621–31.

Books, Articles, Dissertations, and Other Papers

Abbott, Carl. *The New Urban America: Growth and Politics in Sunbelt Cities*. Chapel Hill: University of North Carolina Press, 1981.

Adams, Samuel. "Blueprint for Segregation: A Survey of Atlanta Housing." *New South* 22 (Spring 1967): 73–84.

Anderson, James D. *The Education of Blacks in the South, 1860–1935*. Chapel Hill: University of North Carolina Press, 1988.

"The Atlanta Zoning Plan." *Survey* 48 (22 April 1922): 114–15.

Baker, Ray. *Following the Color Line*. 1908. New York: Harper and Row, 1964.

Barnes, Catherine A. *Journey from Jim Crow: The Desegregation of Southern Transit*. New York: Columbia University Press, 1983.

Bartley, Numan V. *The Rise of Massive Resistance*. Baton Rouge: Louisiana State University Press, 1969.

Bauman, John F. "Disinfecting the Industrial City: The Philadelphia Housing Commission and Scientific Efficiency 1909–1916." In *The Age of Urban Reform*, edited by Michael Ebner and Eugene Tobin, pp. 117–30. Port Washington, N.Y.: Kennikat Press, 1977.

Bayor, Ronald H. "A City Too Busy to Hate: Atlanta's Business Community and Civil Rights." In *Business and Its Environment*, edited by Harold Issadore Sharlin, pp. 145–59. Westport, Conn.: Greenwood Press, 1983.

Beardsley, Edward H. *A History of Neglect: Health Care for Blacks and Mill Workers in the Twentieth-Century South*. Knoxville: University of Tennessee Press, 1987.

Bederman, Sanford Harold. "Black Residential Neighborhoods and Job Opportunity Centers in Atlanta, Georgia." Ph.D. diss., University of Minnesota, 1973.

Blackwelder, Julia Kirk. "Quiet Suffering: Atlanta Women in the 1930s." *Georgia Historical Quarterly* 61 (Summer 1977): 112–24.

Blalock, Jesse William. "Social, Political and Economic Aspects of Race Relations in Atlanta from 1890 to 1908." Master's thesis, Atlanta University, 1969.

Blumberg, Leonard. "Segregated Housing, Marginal Location, and the Crisis of Confidence." *Phylon* 25 (Winter 1964): 321–30.

Bolden, Willie Miller. "The Political Structure of Charter Revision Movements in Atlanta during the Progressive Era." Ph.D. diss., Emory University, 1978.

Boyer, Paul. *Urban Masses and Moral Order in America, 1820–1920*. Cambridge: Harvard University Press, 1978.

Brownell, Blaine A. "The Commercial-Civic Elite and City Planning in Atlanta, Memphis, and New Orleans in the 1920s." *Journal of Southern History* 41 (August 1975): 339–68.

Browning, Joan. "The Atlanta Wall." *The Southern Patriot* (published by Southern Conference Educational Fund), January 1963.

Bullard, Robert D., and E. Kiki Thomas. "Atlanta: Mecca of the Southeast." In *In Search of the New South: The Black Urban Experience in the 1970s and 1980s*, edited by Robert D. Bullard, pp. 77–97. Tuscaloosa: University of Alabama Press, 1989.

Bullock, Henry Allen. *A History of Negro Education in the South: From 1619 to the Present*. Cambridge: Harvard University Press, 1967.

Bunche, Ralph J. *The Political Status of the Negro in the Age of FDR*. Chicago: University of Chicago Press, 1973.

Butler, Jacob E., Jr. "Racial Conflict and Polarization as a Constraint on Black Mayoral Leadership in Urban Policy: An Analysis of Public Finance and Urban Development in Atlanta during the Mayoral Tenure of Maynard H. Jackson, 1973–1977." Ph.D. diss., Atlanta University, 1989.

Button, James W. *Blacks and Social Change: Impact of the Civil Rights Movement in Southern Communities*. Princeton: Princeton University Press, 1989.

Carson, Clayborne. *In Struggle: SNCC and the Black Awakening of the 1960s*. Cambridge: Harvard University Press, 1981.

Chafe, William H. *Civilities and Civil Rights: Greensboro, North Carolina, and the Black Struggle for Freedom*. New York: Oxford University Press, 1980.

Collins, Linda Gail Housch. "The Origin of Public Secondary Education for Blacks in Atlanta, Georgia, 1917 to 1927." Master's thesis, Atlanta University, 1979.

Connolly, Harold X. *A Ghetto Grows in Brooklyn*. New York: New York University Press, 1977.

Crimmins, Timothy. "The Crystal Stair: A Study of the Effects of Class, Race, and Ethnicity on Secondary Education in Atlanta, 1872–1925." Ph.D. diss., Emory University, 1972.

———. "West End: Metamorphosis from Suburban Town to Intown Neighborhood." *Atlanta Historical Journal* 26 (Summer/Fall 1982): 33–50.

Crowe, Charles. "Racial Violence and Social Reform: Origins of the Atlanta Riot of 1906." *Journal of Negro History* 53 (April 1968): 234–56.

Dare, Robert. "Involvement of the Poor in Atlanta." *Phylon* 31 (Summer 1970).

D'Avino, Gail. "Atlanta Municipal Parks, 1882–1917: Urban Reform, Urban Boosterism in a New South City." Ph.D. diss., Emory University, 1988.

Deaton, Thomas M. "Atlanta during the Progressive Era." Ph.D. diss., University of Georgia, 1969.

Dittmer, John. *Black Georgia in the Progressive Era, 1900–1920*. Urbana: University of Illinois Press, 1977.

Doyle, Don H. *New Men, New Cities, New South: Atlanta, Nashville, Charleston, Mobile, 1860–1910*. Chapel Hill: University of North Carolina Press, 1990.

Drago, Edmond L. *Black Politicians and Reconstruction in Georgia: A Splendid Failure*. Baton Rouge: Louisiana State University Press, 1982.

Du Bois, W. E. B. *The Souls of Black Folk*. 1903. Reprint, New York: Dover Publications, 1994.

Dusenberry, Jean Lee. "The History of Grady Memorial Hospital." Research paper for History 8123, Georgia Institute of Technology, Fall 1993.

Eisinger, Peter K. "Black Employment in Municipal Jobs: The Impact of Black Political Power." *American Political Science Review* 76 (1982): 380–92.

———. *The Politics of Displacement: Racial and Ethnic Transition in Three American Cities*. New York: Academic Press, 1980.

Ellis, Ann Wells. "A Crusade against 'Wretched Attitudes': The Commission on Interracial Cooperation's Activities in Atlanta." *Atlanta Historical Journal* 23 (Spring 1979): 21–44.

——. "'Uncle Sam Is My Shepherd': The Commission on Interracial Cooperation and the New Deal in Georgia." *Atlanta History Journal* 30 (Spring 1986): 47–64.

Epps, Edgar G. "The Participation of the Negro in the Municipal Politics of the City of Atlanta, 1867–1908." Master's thesis, Atlanta University, 1955.

Fennell, Dwight. "A Demographic Study of Black Businesses 1905–1908, with Respect to the Race Riot of 1906." Master's thesis, Atlanta University, 1977.

Fields, Dorothy Anne. "A Study of the Health Education Program of the Atlanta Tuberculosis Association for Negroes in Atlanta, Georgia." Master's thesis, Atlanta University School of Social Work, 1942.

Fleishman, Joel L. "The Real against the Ideal—Making the Solution Fit the Problem: The Atlanta Public School Agreement of 1973." In *Roundtable Justice: Case Studies in Conflict Resolution*, edited by Robert B. Goldmann, pp. 129–80. Boulder, Colo.: Westview Press, 1980.

Fleming, Douglas. "Atlanta, the Depression, and the New Deal." Ph.D. diss., Emory University, 1984.

Flint, Barbara J. "Zoning and Residential Segregation: A Social and Physical History, 1910–1940." Ph.D. diss., University of Chicago, 1977.

Flowerdew, Robin. "Spatial Patterns of Residential Segregation in a Southern City." *Journal of American Studies* 13 (April 1979): 93–107.

Formisano, Ronald P. *Boston against Busing: Race, Class, and Ethnicity in the 1960s and 1970s.* Chapel Hill: University of North Carolina Press, 1991.

Fort, Vincent. "The Atlanta Sit-In Movement, 1960–1961: An Oral Study." In *Atlanta, Georgia, 1960–1961: Sit-Ins and Student Activism*, edited by David Garrow, pp. 113–82. New York: Carlson Publishing Co., 1989.

Frick, Mary Louise. "Influences on Negro Political Participation in Atlanta, Georgia." Master's thesis, Georgia State University, 1967.

Galishoff, Stuart. "Germs Know No Color Line: Black Health and Public Policy in Atlanta, 1900–1918." *Journal of the History of Medicine and Allied Sciences* 40 (1985): 22–41.

——. "Triumph and Failure: The American Response to the Urban Water Supply Problem, 1860–1923." In *Pollution and Reform in American Cities, 1870–1930*, edited by Martin V. Melosi, pp. 35–57. Austin: University of Texas Press, 1980.

Gaston, Edward, Jr. "A History of the Negro Wage Earner in Georgia 1890–1940." Ph.D. diss., Emory University, 1957.

Gatewood, Willard B. *Aristocrats of Color: The Black Elite, 1880–1920.* Bloomington: Indiana University Press, 1990.

Godshalk, David. "In the Wake of Riot: Atlanta's Struggle for Order, 1899–1919." Ph.D. diss., Yale University, 1992.

Goldfield, David R. *Black, White and Southern: Race Relations and Southern Culture 1940 to the Present.* Baton Rouge: Louisiana State University Press, 1990.

——. "Black Political Power and Public Policy in the Urban South." In *Urban Policy in Twentieth-Century America*, edited by Arnold R. Hirsch and Raymond A. Mohl. New Brunswick, N.J.: Rutgers University Press, 1993.

Grantham, Dewey. *Southern Progressivism: The Reconciliation of Progress and Tradition.* Knoxville: University of Tennessee Press, 1983.

Haas, Edward. "The Southern Metropolis, 1940–1976." In *The City in Southern His-*

tory: The Growth of Urban Civilization in the South, edited by Blaine A. Brownell and David R. Goldfield, pp. 159–91. Port Washington, N.Y.: Kennikat Press, 1977.

Harris, Kirk Edward. "The Paradox of African-American Mayoral Leadership and the Persistence of Poverty in the African-American Community." Ph.D. diss., Cornell University, 1992.

Hefner, James A. "Black Employment in a Southern 'Progressive' City: The Atlanta Experience." Ph.D. diss., University of Colorado, 1971.

Hein, Virginia H. "The Image of 'A City Too Busy to Hate': Atlanta in the 1960s." *Phylon* 33 (Fall 1972): 205–21.

Henderson, Alexa. *Atlanta Life Insurance Company, Guardian of Black Economic Dignity.* Tuscaloosa: University of Alabama Press, 1990.

Henderson, Harold Paulk. *The Politics of Change in Georgia: A Political Biography of Ellis Arnall.* Athens: University of Georgia Press, 1991.

Henderson, Harold P., and Gary L. Roberts, eds. *Georgia Governors in an Age of Change: From Ellis Arnall to George Busbee.* Athens: University of Georgia Press, 1988.

Hirsch, Arnold R. *Making the Second Ghetto: Race and Housing in Chicago, 1940–1960.* Cambridge: Cambridge University Press, 1983.

Holmes, Bob, ed. *The Status of Black Atlantans 1993.* Atlanta: Southern Center for Studies in Public Policy, Clark Atlanta University, 1993.

Hopkins, Richard J. "Occupational and Geographic Mobility in Atlanta, 1870–1896." *Journal of Southern History* 34 (February–November 1968): 200–213.

———. "Public Health in Atlanta: The Formative Years, 1865–1879." *Georgia Historical Quarterly* 53 (September 1969): 287–304.

Hornsby, Alton, Jr. "The Negro in Atlanta Politics, 1961–1973." *Atlanta Historical Bulletin* 21 (Spring 1977): 7–33.

Huie, H. Mark. "Factors Influencing the Desegregation Process in the Atlanta School System, 1954–1967." Ph.D. diss., University of Georgia, 1967.

Hunter, Floyd. *Community Power Structure: A Study of Decision Makers.* Chapel Hill: University of North Carolina Press, 1953.

———. *Community Power Succession: Atlanta's Policy-Makers Revisited.* Chapel Hill: University of North Carolina Press, 1980.

Hunter, Henry Reid. "The Development of the Public Secondary Schools of Atlanta, Georgia, 1845–1937." Ph.D. diss., George Peabody College for Teachers, 1937. Reprinted by the Office of School System Historian, Atlanta Public Schools, 1974.

Hunter, Tera. "Household Workers in the Making: Afro-American Women in Atlanta and the New South, 1861 to 1920." Ph.D. diss., Yale University, 1990.

Jennings, M. Kent, and Harmon Zeigler. "Class, Party, and Race in Four Types of Elections: The Case of Atlanta." *Journal of Politics* 28 (May 1966): 391–407.

Jennings, M. Kent. *Community Influentials: The Elites of Atlanta.* London: The Free Press of Glencoe, 1964.

Jones, Mack H. "Black Political Empowerment in Atlanta: Myth and Reality." *Annals of the American Academy of Political and Social Science* 439 (September 1978): 90–117.

Kaplan, Harold. *Urban Renewal Politics: Slum Clearance in Newark.* New York: Columbia University Press, 1963.

Kellogg, John. "Negro Urban Clusters in the Postbellum South." *The Geographical Review* 67 (July 1977): 310–21.

Kousser, J. Morgan. *The Shaping of Southern Politics: Suffrage Restriction and the Establishment of the One-Party South, 1880–1910.* New Haven: Yale University Press, 1974.

Kuhn, Clifford. "Atlanta Papers Kindle Racist Violence." *The Great Speckled Bird* (28 August 1975): 8–10.

Kuhn, Clifford M., Harlon E. Joye, and E. Bernard West. *Living Atlanta: An Oral History of the City, 1914–1948.* Atlanta and Athens: Atlanta Historical Society and University of Georgia Press, 1990.

Kusmer, Kenneth L. *A Ghetto Takes Shape: Black Cleveland, 1870–1930.* Urbana: University of Illinois Press, 1976.

Lawson, Steven F. *Running for Freedom: Civil Rights and Black Politics in America since 1941.* New York: McGraw-Hill, 1991.

Lesler, Stephen. "Leroy Johnson Outslicks Mister Charlie." *New York Times Magazine,* 8 November 1970.

Levi, Margaret Anne. "Conflict and Collusion: Police Collective Bargaining." Technical Report #07-74. Cambridge: Operations Research Center, MIT, September 1974.

Lewis, Earl. *In Their Own Interests: Race, Class and Power in Twentieth-Century Norfolk, Virginia.* Berkeley: University of California Press, 1991.

McBride, David. *Integrating the City of Medicine: Blacks in Philadelphia Health Care, 1910–1965.* Philadelphia: Temple University Press, 1989.

McCraw, Thomas K. "The Progressive Legacy." In *The Progressive Era,* edited by Louis Gould, pp. 181–201. Syracuse: Syracuse University Press, 1974.

McGrath, Susan. "Great Expectations: The History of School Desegregation in Atlanta and Boston, 1954–1990." Ph.D. diss., Emory University, 1992.

Maclachlan, Gretchen. "Women's Work: Atlanta's Industrialization and Urbanization, 1879–1929." Ph.D. diss., Emory University, 1992.

Martin, Harold. *William Berry Hartsfield: Mayor of Atlanta.* Athens: University of Georgia Press, 1978.

Mathias, William J., and Stuart Anderson. *Horse to Helicopter: First Century of the Atlanta Police Department.* Atlanta: Georgia State University, 1973.

Matthews, John M. "Studies in Race Relations in Georgia, 1890–1930." Ph.D. diss., Duke University, 1970.

Meier, August, and Elliott Rudwick. "The Boycott Movement against Jim Crow Streetcars in the South, 1900–1906." *Journal of American History* 55 (March 1969): 756–75.

Meier, August, and David Lewis. "History of the Negro Upper Class in Atlanta, Georgia, 1890–1958." In *Atlanta, Georgia, 1960–1961: Sit-Ins and Student Activism,* edited by David Garrow, pp. 3–16. New York: Carlson Publishing Co., 1989.

Mixon, Gregory. "The Atlanta Riot of 1906." Ph.D. diss., University of Cincinnati, 1989.

Mohl, Raymond A. "Race and Space in the Modern City: Interstate 95 and the Black Community in Miami." Paper presented at the Organization of American Historians meeting, Reno, Nev., March 1988.

Moore, John Hammond. "The Negro and Prohibition in Atlanta, 1885–1887." *South Atlantic Quarterly* 69 (Winter 1970): 38–57.

Moore, Lawrence. "Annexation Atlanta—1972: A Look at the Political Process." Master's thesis, Georgia State University, 1972.

Moss, Larry E. "Black Political Ascendancy in Urban Centers and Black Control of the Local Police Function: An Exploratory Analysis." San Francisco: R & E Research Associates, 1977.

Mullis, Sharon Mitchell. "The Public Career of Grace Towns Hamilton: A Citizen Too Busy To Hate." Ph.D. diss., Emory University, 1976.

Neverdon-Morton, Cynthia. *Afro-American Women of the South and the Advancement of the Race, 1895–1925*. Knoxville: University of Tennessee Press, 1989.

Newman, Joseph W. "A History of the Atlanta Public School Teachers' Association, Local 89 of the American Federation of Teachers, 1919–1956." Ph.D. diss., Georgia State University, 1978.

O'Connor, Michael J. "The Measurement and Significance of Racial Residential Barriers in Atlanta, 1890–1970." Ph.D. diss., University of Georgia, 1977.

Ordway, O. Nicholas. "A Study of Select Political and Socio-Economic Factors Influencing Zoning Decisions in the City of Atlanta during the Period December 22, 1954, to December 22, 1975." Ph.D. diss., Georgia State University, 1978.

Orfield, Gary, and Carole Ashkinaze. *The Closing Door: Conservative Policy and Black Opportunity*. Chicago: University of Chicago Press, 1991.

Peterson, Paul E. *The Politics of School Reform, 1870–1940*. Chicago: University of Chicago Press, 1985.

Platt, Harold L. *City Building in the New South: The Growth of Public Services in Houston, Texas, 1830–1915*. Philadelphia: Temple University Press, 1983.

Porter, Michael L. "Black Atlanta: An Interdisciplinary Study of Blacks on the East Side of Atlanta, 1890–1930." Ph.D. diss., Emory University, 1974.

Pratt, Robert A. *The Color of Their Skin: Education and Race in Richmond, Virginia, 1954–1989*. Charlottesville: University Press of Virginia, 1992.

Preston, Howard L. *Automobile Age Atlanta: The Making of a Southern Metropolis, 1900–1935*. Athens: University of Georgia Press, 1979.

Rabin, Yale. "The Roots of Segregation in the Eighties: The Role of Local Government Actions." In *Divided Neighborhoods: Changing Patterns of Racial Segregation*, edited by Gary Tobin, pp. 208–26. Newberry Park, Ca.: Sage Publications, 1987.

Rabinowitz, Howard N. *Race Relations in the Urban South, 1865–1890*. New York: Oxford University Press, 1978.

Racine, Philip. "Atlanta's Schools: A History of the Public School System, 1869–1955." Ph.D. diss., Emory University, 1969.

Raines, Howell. *My Soul Is Rested*. New York: Penguin Books, 1977.

Reed, Adolph, Jr. "A Critique of Neo-Progressivism in Theorizing about Local Development Policy: A Case from Atlanta." Paper presented to American Political Science Association meeting, Washington, D.C., 28–31 August 1986.

Rice, Bradley R. "The Battle of Buckhead: The Plan of Improvement and Atlanta's Last Big Annexation." *Atlanta Historical Journal* 25 (Winter 1981): 5–22.

Rice, Jonathan. "Organized Labor Activity in the Atlanta Police Department: A Study of Racial and Labor Conflict." Senior thesis, Emory University, 1980.

Rice, Roger L. "Residential Segregation by Law, 1910–1917." *Journal of Southern History* 34 (May 1968): 179–99.

Rooks, Charles S. *The Atlanta Elections of 1969*. Atlanta: Voter Education Project, 1970.

Rosenzweig, Charles L. "The Issue of Employing Black Policemen in Atlanta." Master's thesis, Emory University, 1980.

Rouse, Jacqueline Anne. *Lugenia Burns Hope: Black Southern Reformer*. Athens: University of Georgia Press, 1989.

Russell, James Michael. *Atlanta 1847–1890: City Building in the Old South and the New*. Baton Rouge: Louisiana State University Press, 1988.

——. "Politics, Municipal Services, and the Working Class in Atlanta, 1865–1890." *Georgia Historical Quarterly* 66 (Winter 1982): 467–91.

Schulman, Bruce J. *From Cotton Belt to Sunbelt: Federal Policy, Economic Development and the Transformation of the South, 1938–1980*. Durham: Duke University Press, 1994.

Shivery, Louie Davis. "The Neighborhood Union." *Phylon* 3 (1942): 149–62.

Silver, Christopher. *Twentieth-Century Richmond: Planning, Politics and Race*. Knoxville: University of Tennessee Press, 1984.

Smith, Douglas. *The New Deal in the Urban South*. Baton Rouge: Louisiana State University Press, 1988.

Sosna, Morton. *In Search of the Silent South: Southern Liberals and the Race Issue*. New York: Columbia University Press, 1977.

Spritzer, Lorraine Nelson. *The Belle of Ashby Street: Helen Douglas Mankin and Georgia Politics*. Athens: University of Georgia Press, 1982.

Stephenson, Gilbert T. "The Segregation of the White and Negro Races in Cities." *South Atlantic Quarterly* 13 (January 1914): 1–18.

Stone, Clarence N. *Economic Growth and Neighborhood Discontent*. Chapel Hill: University of North Carolina Press, 1976.

——. *Regime Politics: Governing Atlanta, 1946–1988*. Lawrence: University Press of Kansas, 1989.

Sudheendran, Kesavan. "Community Power Structure in Atlanta: A Study in Decision Making, 1920–1939." Ph.D. diss., Georgia State University, 1982.

Sugrue, Thomas J. "The Structures of Urban Poverty: The Reorganization of Space and Work in Three Periods of American History." In *The "Underclass" Debate: Views from History*, edited by Michael Katz, pp. 85–117. Princeton: Princeton University Press, 1993.

Taeuber, Karl E. "Residential Segregation in the Atlanta Metropolitan Area." In *Urban Atlanta: Redefining the Role of the City*, edited by Andrew Marshall Hamer, pp. 155–66. Research Monograph No. 84. Atlanta: Georgia State University, 1980.

Thompson, Robert A., Hylan Lewis, and David McEntire. "Atlanta and Birmingham: A Comparative Study in Negro Housing." In *Studies in Housing and Minority Groups*, edited by Nathan Glazer and David McEntire, pp. 13–83. Berkeley: University of California Press, 1960.

Thornberry, Jerry. "The Development of Black Atlanta, 1865–1885." Ph.D. diss., University of Maryland, 1977.

Trotter, Joe William, Jr. *Black Milwaukee: The Making of an Industrial Proletariat, 1915–1945.* Urbana: University of Illinois Press, 1985.

Turner, Claudia M. "Changing Residential Patterns in Southwest Atlanta from 1960 to 1970." Master's thesis, Atlanta University, 1970.

Turner-Jones, Marcia. "A Political Analysis of Black Educational History: Atlanta, 1865–1943." Ph.D. diss., University of Chicago, 1982.

Walker, Jack L. "Negro Voting in Atlanta: 1953–1961." *Phylon* 24 (Winter 1963): 379–87.

———. "Protest and Negotiation: A Case Study of Negro Leadership in Atlanta, Georgia." In *Atlanta, Georgia, 1960–1961: Sit-Ins and Student Activism*, edited by David Garrow, pp. 31–58. New York: Carlson Publishing Co., 1989.

———. "Sit-Ins in Atlanta: A Study in the Negro Revolt." In *Atlanta, Georgia, 1960–1961: Sit-Ins and Student Activism*, edited by David Garrow, pp. 59–94. New York: Carlson Publishing Co., 1989.

Watts, Eugene J. "Black Political Progress in Atlanta: 1868–1895." *Journal of Negro History* 59 (July 1974): 268–86.

———. "The Police in Atlanta, 1890–1905." *Journal of Southern History* 39 (February–November 1973): 165–82.

———. *The Social Basis of City Politics: Atlanta, 1865–1903.* Westport, Conn.: Greenwood Press, 1978.

West, E. Bernard. "Black Atlanta—Struggle for Development, 1915–1925." M.A. thesis, Atlanta University, 1976.

Whelan, Robert K., and Michael W. McKinney. "Coalition Politics in a Southern City: An Analysis of the 1973 Atlanta Mayoralty Election." *Georgia Political Science Association Journal* 3 (Fall 1975): 123–46.

White, Dana F. "The Black Sides of Atlanta: A Geography of Expansion and Containment, 1970–1870." *Atlanta Historical Journal* 26 (Summer/Fall 1982): 199–225.

Williams, Marilyn Thornton. "New York City's Public Baths: A Case Study in Urban Progressive Reform." *Journal of Urban History* 7 (November 1980): 49–81.

Wingo, Horace C. "Race Relations in Georgia, 1872–1908." Ph.D. diss., University of Georgia, 1969.

Wright, C. T. "The Development of Public Schools for Blacks in Atlanta, 1872–1900." *Atlanta Historical Bulletin* 21 (Spring 1977): 115–28.

Index

Abernathy, Ralph, xv, 45, 115–16, 250
Abram, Morris, 60
"Action for Democracy," 40, 41, 116, 137, 169, 230
Action Forum, 193, 247
Adams, Frankie, 114
Adams, Samuel, 68
Adamsville, 61, 62–63
Adamsville Civic Club, 64
Affirmative action, 44, 49, 94, 121, 122, 124, 125, 182, 183, 187, 193, 194, 236
Afro-American Patrolmen's League (AAPL), 182–83, 185
Aldermen. See Board of aldermen
Alexander, Cecil, 44, 273 (n. 44)
Alexander, T. M., 31, 71
All-Citizens Committee for Better City Planning, 67
All Citizens Registration Committee, 23, 24, 39, 134, 150, 175, 270 (n. 10)
Allen, Ivan, 268 (n. 76); and 1961 mayoral race, 35–37; as mayor during the civil rights movement, 37–38, 39, 40, 41–42; reelection and second term, 42; and Massell's term as mayor, 43, 44, 46; as mediator between white business leaders and black community, 50; and Peyton Road "Wall," 66, 67; and urban renewal controversies, 74, 75, 76, 78; and housing for blacks, 78, 79, 81, 83, 138, 142; support for proposed annexations, 87, 88–89; and city jobs for blacks, 114, 116, 117, 118; and city services for blacks, 138–43; and parks, 153; and desegregation of Atlanta's police and fire services, 179, 181; and school desegregation, 238
American Civil Liberties Union, 233, 245, 246, 249
American Fascist Association (Black Shirts), 98, 99
Amos, J. H., 183
Amos, Miles G., 29
Annexation, 27, 29, 45, 50, 54, 85–91
Anti-Defamation League, 140
"Appeal for Human Rights," 33, 39, 40, 112, 165, 230
Armour v. Nix, 245
Arnall, Ellis, 23, 27
Arrington, Marvin, 121
Ashe, B. F., 106
AT&T, 108
Atlanta and Fulton County Local Education Commission, 243
Atlanta Anti-Tuberculosis Association, 154, 155
Atlanta Board of Education: and vocational education for blacks, 107, 119, 198, 199–201; proposes elimination of blacks' highest grade, 201–2; and double sessions in black schools, 202; use of 1921 and 1926 school bond funds, 205, 207; and Great Depression, 208; and post–World War II school conditions, 211, 213, 214, 215; use of 1946 school bond funds, 215–16, 217, 218; and 1950 suit against segregated schools, 218, 219, 222; responses to *Brown* and other pressure toward desegregation, 222, 223, 226–49 passim
Atlanta Bureau of Planning, 61, 82
Atlanta Business League, 71
Atlanta Chamber of Commerce, 35, 41, 44, 59, 79, 87, 96, 273 (n. 44); "Forward Atlanta," 96, 168
Atlanta City Council, 189, 201
Atlanta Civic and Political League, 20, 23, 133, 134, 150, 159, 210–11
Atlanta Civic League, 12, 131
Atlanta Coach Lines, 189
Atlanta Colored Committee on Unemployment Relief, 104

Atlanta Commission on Crime and Juvenile Delinquency, 143–44

Atlanta Committee for Cooperative Action (ACCA), 32, 33, 34, 39, 112, 135, 165, 230; "Second Look," 32, 112, 135, 165, 230

Atlanta Committee on Women's Interracial Activities, 159, 208

Atlanta Community Improvement Program, 141, 182

Atlanta Comprehensive Plan, 68

Atlanta Compromise of 1973, 247–51

Atlanta Concentrated Employment Program, 119

Atlanta Constitution, 12, 50, 51, 109, 110, 120, 134, 138, 155, 159, 187, 201, 256. See also *Atlanta Journal*; *Atlanta Journal-Constitution*

Atlanta Daily World, 19, 20, 26, 27, 33, 36, 48, 71, 72, 135, 223, 263 (n. 6)

Atlanta Department of Budget and Planning, 68

Atlanta Department of Urban Renewal, 73, 274 (n. 56)

Atlanta Economic Development Corporation, 85

Atlanta Education Association, 241

Atlanta Fulton Bag and Cotton Mill, 8

Atlanta–Fulton County Planning Board, 69, 87

Atlanta–Fulton County Recreation Authority, 153

Atlanta–Fulton County Stadium, 139, 140, 153, 256, 273 (n. 48)

Atlanta Georgian, 12

Atlanta Housing Authority, 70, 76, 79

Atlanta Housing Council, 59, 71, 269 (n. 8)

Atlanta Independent, 154, 203

Atlanta Inquirer, 114, 152, 153, 164, 169, 181, 182, 229, 233, 234, 246

Atlanta Journal, 12, 21, 51, 87, 88, 90, 91, 145, 149, 213, 229, 238–39. See also *Atlanta Constitution*; *Atlanta Journal-Constitution*

Atlanta Journal-Constitution, 91, 147, 219. See also *Atlanta Constitution*; *Atlanta Journal*

Atlanta Labor Advisory Committee, 107

Atlanta Life Insurance Company, 24, 32, 69, 74, 94, 109, 124, 277 (n. 1)

Atlanta Negro Chamber of Commerce, 100, 174

Atlanta Negro Voters League, 25, 26, 28, 36, 67, 85, 115, 134, 135, 179, 264 (nn. 16, 17), 270 (n. 10)

Atlanta News, 12

Atlanta Parks Department, 153

Atlanta Personnel Department, 44, 118, 121; director, 110, 113, 122

Atlanta Plumbers and Pipefitters Union, 120

Atlanta Project (formerly South Atlanta Project), 136, 137, 139, 166, 230. *See also* Student Non-violent Coordinating Committee (SNCC)

Atlanta Regional Commission, 270 (n. 10)

Atlanta School of Social Work, 98, 99, 100, 101, 106, 114

Atlanta State Savings Bank, 94

Atlanta Transit System, 190, 193, 194, 294 (n. 138)

Atlanta University, 5, 10, 19, 59, 71, 94, 109, 113, 114, 199

Atlanta University Center, 109, 113, 114

Atlanta Urban League, 3, 28, 93, 112–13, 116, 134, 246, 267 (n. 57), 269 (n. 8); and black voter registration, 23; efforts to find development property for blacks, 59; efforts to provide training and employment opportunities for blacks from the 1920s through the 1940s, 97–108 passim; and displacement of black employees, 98, 99; and the New Deal, 102, 104; puts pressure on mayor regarding city jobs for blacks, 117; and blacks' self-help efforts, 133; efforts to obtain improved and desegregated city services, 135, 148, 150, 154, 159, 160, 161, 162, 163, 174; 1944 education report and subsequent efforts to improve Atlanta's black schools, 211, 213, 214, 215, 216, 217

Atlanta Voice, 250

Atlanta Weekly Defiance, 5

Atlantic Steel Company, 110

Auburn Avenue, 41, 71, 72, 74, 75, 94, 110, 134

Bacote, Clarence, 19, 20, 21, 23, 24, 25–26

Bagley Park, 58

Baker, Ruby, 156, 157

Bankhead Courts, 146

Bedford-Pine, 75, 139, 152, 232, 273 (n. 49)

Bell, Griffin, 224

Bell, Roy C., 166, 168

Bell, William Jr., 107

Bell Aircraft, 107

Bennett, Glenn, 193

Better Schools Atlanta, 236, 240, 241

Birmingham, Ala., 27, 31–32, 82, 162, 187, 212

Black Shirts (American Fascist Association), 98, 99

Bloc voting, 26, 29, 30, 31, 42

Blount, Ray, 194

Board of aldermen, 21, 40, 41, 63, 110; and 1957 election, 31; black representation on, 42, 43, 44, 45; replaced with a city council, 48; and zoning/urban renewal issues, 66, 73, 78, 79, 82, 237; and efforts to end discrimination in city jobs, 113, 120, 121, 122; its professed willingness to "standardize the services" throughout Atlanta, 141–42, 143; and parks for blacks, 150, 152; and complaints about Grady Hospital's segregation, 169; and police force, 183, 185

Board of Zoning Appeals, 65

Bond, Julian, xv, 33, 34, 38, 41, 51, 137, 235

Bond issues, 17, 20, 37, 134, 141, 150, 152, 153, 155, 192; and education, 202–5,

207, 208, 210–11, 213, 214, 215, 216, 217, 218, 219, 229

Booker T. Washington High School, 107, 205, 206–7, 208, 211, 212, 213, 215, 296 (n. 15)

Booker T. Washington Park, 148, 150

Borders, Reverend William Holmes, 24, 33, 35, 175, 190

Boulder Park, annexation of, 88

Bowen, Hilliard A., 240

Bridges, Dan, 21

Brockey, Harold, 50

Brothers and Sisters Combined, 185, 186

Browder v. Gayle, 190

Brown, Ben, 91

Brown, Benjamin, 35

Brown, Charlie, 25, 26, 28–29, 36

Brown v. Board of Education, 218, 219, 222, 230

Buckhead, annexation of, 86

Bullard, Helen, 28

Butler Street YMCA, 6, 28, 177, 264 (n. 16)

Buttermilk Bottom, 75

Calhoun, John H., 24, 39, 71–72, 226, 270 (nn. 10, 16)

Calhoun Elementary School, 209–10

Calhoun v. Latimer, 223

Camp, Thomas, 21

Carey, Dan, 148

Carmichael, Stokely, 139, 142

Carver Homes, 150

Carver Vocational School, 119, 215

Cascade Heights, 66, 68, 236, 251

Cemeteries, 7, 67, 69

Center Hill, 63, 64; school, 235

Central Atlanta Progress (CAP), 49, 50, 268 (n. 76)

Central business district (CBD), 55, 70, 72–75, 83, 84, 85, 189

Central Relief Committee, 102

Chapin, Arthur, 113

Chapman v. King, 23

Chicago, xv, 53, 77, 78, 84, 258, 259

Downtown Atlanta, 8, 12, 34, 43, 50, 54, 70, 71, 91, 94, 110, 125, 180, 190, 192; removal of blacks from, 72, 73, 85; boycotts and picketing in, 112, 115, 135; and Underground Atlanta, 147. *See also* Central business district

Druid Hills, annexation of, 86

Du Bois, W. E. B., xv, 8

Dunbar, Augusta, 102, 103

Eastside Atlanta, 7, 232; black neighborhoods and expansion in, 54, 68; roads as racial barriers in, 55; white and transitional neighborhoods in, 60, 86; loss of black neighborhoods to urban renewal in, 69, 72, 74, 75; proposed construction of public housing units in, 72, 73, 79; run-down neighborhoods in, 139; lack of parks and recreational facilities in, 150, 152. *See also* Bedford-Pine

Eaves, A. Reginald, 184, 185, 186, 292 (n. 121)

Economic Opportunity Act, 119

Economic Opportunity Atlanta Inc., 119, 144, 145

Economy, 4, 38, 49, 93–125 passim; relationship between economic policies and racial policies, 8, 85, 89, 91, 146, 246; economic reform, 16, 20; negative economic results of racial violence, 30, 34, 37, 82, 130, 224, 250; economic factors in highway planning and urban renewal, 61, 70, 74, 77; blacks' economic power, 69; relationship between educational system and economy, 197, 198, 209, 213

Edgewood Avenue, 8

Education, 4–5, 8, 9, 10–11, 20, 25, 28, 117, 119; missionary-run schools, 10; desegregation of public schools, 10, 31, 34, 39, 40, 75, 82, 135, 138, 152, 221–51 passim; white children considered the first priority, 10, 197–220 passim; private, 11, 199, 205, 251; curriculum issues, 11, 201, 226, 240, 247;

students-per-teacher ratio, 11, 199, 240, 241; white opposition to integrated schools, 30, 219; construction of new schools, 36, 201, 202, 205–15 passim, 219, 222–23, 229, 238, 241, 242, 243; overcrowded schools, 78, 84, 136–45 passim, 198, 199, 201, 202, 204, 207, 213–17, 222, 226–41 passim; county schools, 87, 243, 245, 246; lack of educational equality hinders blacks' employment opportunities, 120, 123, 124–25, 145; health care in, 154, 160; double sessions, 144, 199, 202, 203, 204, 208, 210, 211, 213, 215, 216, 230; school equipment and supplies, 205, 206–7, 222, 240, 241, 242; night schools, 208, 296 (n. 20); freedom-of-choice plan, 223, 231, 234–44; school zones, 225, 227–28, 231, 239, 243, 244, 246; racial ratios in desegregated schools, 240, 244, 247, 248, 249

—elementary schools, 10–11, 199, 204, 205, 208, 209, 210, 213, 214, 215, 217, 219, 222, 229–30, 232, 233, 234, 239–47

—high and junior high schools, black, 10, 17, 199, 202–16 passim, 225–34 passim, 239, 242, 243, 296 (n. 15); Washington High School opens in 1924, 205. *See also* Booker T. Washington High School

—higher education for blacks, 7, 54, 78, 94, 105, 109, 113, 114, 115, 118, 132, 199, 207, 277 (n. 1), 162; nursing schools, 158, 161, 164. *See also* Atlanta University; Clark College; Emory University; Morehouse College; Morris Brown College; Spelman College

—teachers, black, 8, 11, 101, 199, 207, 210–17 passim, 219, 247; teacher segregation/desegregation, 11, 227, 239, 243, 244, 248–49; paid less than white teachers, 11, 203, 222; numbers, 230

—vocational/industrial training, 11, 107, 111, 118–19, 120, 198, 199, 201, 202, 213,

215, 242. *See also* Negro Vocational School
—*See also* Atlanta Board of Education
Egleston Hospital, 72–73, 76, 273 (n. 46)
Emory University Medical School, 155–56, 162, 163, 164, 165, 168, 173
Empire Real Estate Board, 64, 65, 71, 151, 270 (n. 10)
Employment. *See* Jobs
Eplan, Leon, 68, 83, 270 (n. 16), 273 (n. 48)
Equal Employment Opportunities Act, 122
Equal Employment Opportunity Commission (EEOC), 117–18, 122, 182, 282 (n. 48)

Family and Children's Services, 117
Farris, Milton, 51–52
Federal Emergency Relief Administration (FERA), 102, 103, 159
Ferguson, Ira A., 164
Finch, William, 4
Finley Ordinance, 123
Fire protection, 9, 87, 147, 195, 196; black demands for black firemen on the city's west side, 26, 28, 36, 37, 41, 110, 112, 115; blacks allowed to serve as firemen, 135, 179–87; insufficient in black areas, 130, 141
Flanagan, Robert, 76, 273 (n. 48)
Fleming, Harold, 177
Florida Supreme Court, 258
"Forward Atlanta," 96, 168
Foundation for the Advancement of Medical and Nursing Education, 164
Fowler, Wyche, 51
Fraternal Order of Police (FOP), 182–83, 185, 186
Free Employment Bureau and Opportunity Training School, 97
Fulton County, 25, 26, 51–52, 172, 266 (n. 50); registration of black voters in, 23, 24, 39; bond commission, 37; representation in state legislature, 38; and black housing, 58, 82; and post-war road construction plans, 61, 68; and annexation/consolidation, 88, 89, 90; and jobs for blacks, 103, 114; movement of middle-class blacks into, 125; and parks for blacks, 150, 153; health care and blacks in, 161, 168, 169, 171; and MARTA, 195; schools in, 209, 243, 276 (n. 83); separate police force, 276 (n. 82)
Fulton County Commission, 169, 172, 173, 266 (n. 50)
Fulton County Grand Jury, 150, 215
Fulton County Medical Society, 171, 290 (n. 89)
Fulton County Superior Court, 67, 185
Fulton-DeKalb Hospital Authority, 160, 162, 163, 164, 168, 169, 170

Gate City Teachers Association, 210, 241
Gautreaux, Dorothy: legal case, 77
Geer, Peter Zack, 39
General Citizens Committee on Employment and Economic Opportunity, 116
Georgia, 131, 156
Georgia Baptist Hospital, 72, 97
Georgia Board of Education, 107, 301 (n. 34), 303 (n. 60)
Georgia Council on Human Relations, 242
Georgia Department of Education, 208–9
Georgia Dome, 256–57
Georgia Education Association, 299 (n. 4)
Georgia League of Negro Women Voters, 20
Georgia legislature, 23, 36, 38–39, 45, 86–91 passim, 137, 143, 204, 264 (n. 13)
Georgia Power Company, 189, 294 (n. 138)
Georgia Real Estate, Loan and Trust Company, 8
Georgia State Employment Service, 100, 104, 113

for white and black, 76, 272 (n. 41), 273 (n. 45), 274 (n. 57); construction of, 104, 110, 111, 113

Housing and Community Development Act, 146, 147

Housing Resources Committee, 79, 81, 273 (n. 44), 274 (n. 56)

Houston Street, 55

Howard High School (formerly Howard Elementary School), 215, 229, 232, 296 (n. 15)

Howell, Clark, 16

Hughes Spalding Pavilion, 163, 164, 165, 166, 168, 172, 173

I-20, 61, 74, 270 (n. 16)

I-75/85, 74

Industrial areas, 7, 54, 55, 62, 69, 81, 83, 91, 135. *See also* Jobs: industrial

Inman, John, 45, 183–84, 185, 292 (n. 121)

Interdenominational Theological Center, 94

Inter-Faith Church Committee, 204

International Brickmasons Union, 105

Isler, Gwendolyn, 39

Jackson, Maynard, 43, 121, 268 (n. 76), 273 (n. 48); 1973 mayoral election and first administration, 47–52; 1977 reelection, 51–52; and low-income black interests, 52; policies regarding black displacement and urban renewal, 83; and annexation, 91; affirmative action efforts during first mayoral term, 122, 123, 124; and public housing, 146–47; and parks, 153; and police and fire departments, 183, 184, 186

Jarrell, Ira, 213, 214

Jenkins, Herbert, 21, 174–75, 177, 178–79

Jobs, 27, 32, 34, 93–125 passim, 198, 250; local and state patronage jobs, 5; domestic and personal service, 8, 94, 96, 100, 101, 104, 107, 108, 148, 198, 201; replacement of blacks with

whites, 8, 96, 97, 98, 99, 100, 102, 104; skilled labor, 8, 96, 104, 105, 106, 107, 108, 110, 113, 122; unskilled or semi-skilled labor, 8, 94, 96, 100, 103, 104, 105, 106, 107, 108, 113, 114, 124; occupational mobility, 8, 96, 262 (n. 12); in city government, 36, 37, 39, 45; distance of black public housing from, 84, 91, 145; white-collar, 96, 105, 106, 113, 118, 119, 121, 124, 125; and construction of public housing, 104, 110, 111; industrial, 100, 103, 104, 105, 106, 108, 111, 112, 114, 118; job training, 124, 125, 144; and Underground Atlanta, 147; police force and, 177, 181, 187

Joel Chandler Harris Homes, 65, 80, 81

Johnson, Albert, 142

Johnson, Leroy, 32, 38, 39, 42–43, 49, 88, 191, 195, 264 (n. 17), 267–68 (n. 70)

Johnson, Reginald A., 98

Jones, Malcolm, 73, 81, 274 (n. 56)

Julius Rosenwald Fund, 105

Key, James L., 17, 19, 21, 174, 202, 204, 207

King, Lonnie, 33, 34–35, 247, 249, 250, 251

King, Martin Luther Sr., 19–20, 35, 43, 94, 163, 175

King, Martin Luther Jr., xv, 27, 34, 139, 240

Kirkwood Elementary School, 232–34

Ku Klux Klan, 17, 27, 36, 177, 207, 278 (n. 9)

LeCraw, Roy, 20, 21

Legal Defense and Education Fund (LDF) of the NAACP, 223, 228, 230–31, 246, 247, 249

Letson, John, 225, 226, 233–43 passim, 246, 247

Lindsay, Archie, 30, 31

Little Rock, Ark., 27, 30, 37, 82, 224, 288–89 (n. 77)

Local 102 of the Brotherhood of

83, 88, 90–91, 121, 122, 125, 143, 146, 153; political mobilization of black community by SNCC, 136, 137; white politicians' growing attention to blacks, 175, 190, 192, 195. *See also* Voters, black; Voters, white

Population and population movement, 6–7, 19; migration of rural blacks to Atlanta, 4; movement of whites and middle-class blacks to the suburbs, 79, 125, 225, 232, 233, 235, 237, 239, 242, 244, 247, 249, 250, 251; percentage of blacks in, 83, 87, 88, 90, 100, 108, 166, 168–69, 176, 182, 191, 233

Poverty, 45, 46, 50, 80, 83, 119, 123, 125, 143, 147; linked to crime and disease, 140, 144, 172, 176; and lack of city services, 141, 144, 154, 158; black poor, 9, 52, 69, 70, 89, 136, 145, 158, 192; white poor, 9, 16, 20, 129, 131, 192

President's Committee on Equal Employment Opportunity, 111

President's Committee on Fair Employment Practices, 107

President's Council of Economic Advisors, 114

Proctor, Reverend H. H., 201

Proctor Creek, 65, 152; spur line, 194, 195

Progressive Era, 130, 131, 132, 133, 135, 140, 141, 146, 149, 201

Prohibition, 6, 16, 17

Public Health Service, 171

Public Works Administration, 103–4

Public Works Emergency Housing Corporation, 80

Railroad lines, 3, 7, 54, 58, 69

Ramspeck, Robert, 21

Reconstruction, 4

Recreation. *See* Parks and other recreational facilities

Reddick, L. D., 71

Republicans, 4, 10, 25, 28

Residential and zoning patterns, 4, 6–7, 53–83 passim, 138, 235, 237, 245, 251;

restriction of black housing to certain sections of the city, 54, 58–67 passim, 71–85 passim. *See also* Urban renewal and displacement

Richmond, Va., xv, 53, 162, 246, 258, 259, 260

Rich's Department Store, 34, 50, 115

St. Louis, 84

Sanders, Carl, 39, 51

Sandy Springs, annexation of, 87–88

Sanitation services, 9, 87, 130, 132, 133, 141, 143, 146, 153, 154, 155, 171, 237; sewer lines, 9, 65, 133, 134, 135, 143, 145, 154, 155, 203; water supplies, 9, 132, 134, 135, 143, 155, 218; sanitation workers, 45, 52, 97, 116

Savannah, 176, 288–89 (n. 77)

Sayles, H. A., 110–11

Scott, C. A., 33, 72, 163, 175

Scripto, 110

"Second Look," 32, 112, 135, 165, 230

Self-help among blacks, 6, 104, 132–34, 138, 148, 154, 159, 196, 199, 257

"Separate but equal" concept, 148, 160, 169, 223, 241

September 1906 riot, 11–12

Sibley, John A., 224

Simkins v. Moses H. Cone Memorial Hospital, 169

Sims, Walter, 17, 207

Slaton, W. F., 198

Smith, DeWitt (black policeman), 182–83

Smith, Hoke, 16

Smith, M. M. "Muggsy" 36, 42

Smith-Hughes Vocational School, 119, 234

Smith v. Allwright, 21

Social Security, 100, 160

South Atlanta Civic Council, 137

South Atlanta Project (later Atlanta Project), 136, 137, 139, 166, 230

Southern Bakery Company, 115

Southern Bell, 108, 110, 113

Southern Christian Leadership Conference (SCLC), 36, 40, 43, 45, 115, 168, 169, 240, 250. *See also* Summit Leadership Conference

Southern Regional Council, 67–68, 119, 140, 146, 177, 189

Southside Atlanta, 7; black neighborhoods and expansion in, 54, 59, 88; white and transitional neighborhoods in, 68; loss of black neighborhoods to urban renewal in, 69, 73, 74; public housing units in, 70, 77, 78–79; relatively sparse development in, 85, 257; and Massell's annexation plans, 90; black leaders from, 116; neighborhoods in need of improved city services, 135, 136, 137, 138, 139, 151; SNCC and, 136, 137, 138, 144–45, 151, 166; lack of parks and recreational facilities in, 146, 150, 151; lack of health clinics in, 166; public transportation into, 192. *See also* Carver Homes; South Atlanta Project; Summerhill area

Southwest Atlantans for Progress (SWAP), 135, 236–37

Southwest High School, 235, 236, 237

Spalding, Hughes, 162

Spelman College, 94, 155, 158, 199

Station 16 (firehouse of Atlanta's first black firemen), 179, 180

Strayer-Engelhardt survey, 205

Street maintenance and improvements, 5, 9, 17, 25, 45, 46, 65, 89, 130–46 passim, 203

Strong, C. R., 189

Stuart, H. L., 193

Stuart, Robert C., 63

Student-Adult Liaison Committee, 33

Student Non-violent Coordinating Committee (SNCC): and 1961 mayoral contest, 36; and Summit Leadership Conference, 40; and Peyton Road "Wall," 66–67; efforts to secure equal job opportunities for blacks, 115, 116, 117; black voter registration drive, 136; demands that city leaders improve services in black neighborhoods, 137, 138, 139–40, 141, 143, 151; and February 1966 rent strike, 139–40; blamed for riots, 139–40, 141; and health care for blacks, 165, 166, 168; and schools, 230. *See also* South Atlanta Project; Summit Leadership Conference

Suburbs, 59; and decline of downtown Atlanta, 85; white, 8, 85, 87, 88, 89, 90, 92, 183, 192, 193, 194, 195, 232, 242, 244, 246, 250, 251; jobs in, 120, 124, 125

Summerhill area, 139, 144, 146

Summit Leadership Conference, 137–38; creation and initial agenda, 40–41; leaders' support for Massell, 43; statements against employment discrimination, 116, 117, 118; efforts toward obtaining improved services in black neighborhoods, 137–38, 141, 142, 143; and summer 1968 riots, 143; and health care for blacks, 169; and black policemen, 181; and MARTA, 191, 192, 193, 195; and schools, 230

Sunbelt prosperity, xv, 117

"Supreme Court schools," 219

Sutton, Willis A., 208, 210

Swann v. Charlotte-Mecklenburg (North Carolina), 244

Sweat, Dan, 49, 51, 268 (n. 76)

Talmadge, Eugene, 23, 27

Tate, Horace, 43, 242

Taxes, 17, 86, 87, 89, 91, 202, 251; poll tax, 4, 16, 20, 27; municipal taxes, 4; sales tax, 194; property tax, 203, 204

Techwood, 80, 104

Temporary Committee for the Elimination of Discrimination in Employment, 114–15

Temporary Coordinating Committee on Housing, 59

Thirty percent rule, 248–49, 303 (n. 70)

Thomas, Jesse, 154

Thompson, Robert, 24, 59, 108, 269 (n. 8)

Time, 23

recreational facilities in, 148, 150; new
black health center in, 160; public
transportation into, 189, 191, 192. *See
also* Adamsville; Cascade Heights;
Collier Heights; Mozley Park; Peyton
Road "Wall"; Vine City; West Side
Mutual Development Committee
(WSMDC)
West Side Mutual Development Com-
mittee (WSMDC), 60, 62, 64–65, 68,
151, 270 (nn. 12, 13)
West Side Unemployment Relief Com-
mittee, 104
Wexler, Kenneth, 77
White, Walter, xv, 188, 202
White flight, 80, 225, 233, 235, 237, 239,
242, 244, 247, 249, 250, 251
Whiteford Elementary School, 232–33
Wilkins, Roy, 249, 250
Williams, Samuel, 43, 181, 191
Williamson, Q. V., 42, 113, 134, 277 (n. 1)

Willis Mill Road, 66, 68, 256
Women's Civic Club, 20
Woodruff, Robert, 38
Works Progress Administration (WPA),
100, 102, 103, 159, 160, 211
World War I, 156
World War II, 20, 58, 59, 86, 106, 160,
258
Wright, Louis T., 156

Yancey, Asa, 157, 163, 164, 168, 170, 173,
248
Yates, C. R., 169
Young, Andrew, xv, 27, 46, 52, 83, 147,
187, 250

Zoning. *See* Residential and zoning
patterns; Urban renewal and displacement
Zoning Board, 65